BERIA

BERIA

STALIN'S FIRST LIEUTENANT

AMY KNIGHT

PRINCETON UNIVERSITY PRESS

PRINCETON, NEW JERSEY

Library of Congress Cataloging-in-Publication Data

Knight, Amy W., 1946–
Beria, Stalin's first lieutenant / Amy Knight.
p. cm.
Includes bibliographical references and index.
ISBN 0-691-03257-2
ISBN 0-691-01093-5 (pbk.)
1. Beria, L. P. (Lavrenti≥Pavlovich), 1989-1953.
2. Politicians—Soviet Union—Biography.   3. Internal security—
Soviet Union.   4. Georgia (Republic)—Politics and government.
5. Soviet Union—Politics and government—1936-1953. I. Title.
DK268.B384K58   1993   947.084'2'092—dc20   93-3937   CIP

10 9 8 7 6

To Malcolm

CONTENTS

LIST OF ILLUSTRATIONS

ACKNOWLEDGMENTS

M Y FIRST debt of gratitude goes to my friend and colleague Ihor Gawdiak, who gave me the idea for this book. I am also deeply indebted to Vladimir Babishvili, who not only translated several long articles from the Georgian language, but also paved the way for my trip to Tbilisi by putting me in contact with his friends there. Professor Vakhtang Chichinadze and his wife Lena, Levan Dalakishvili, Akakii Surchava, Professor Avtandil Menteshashvili, Levan Toidze and many other Georgians went out of their way to help me with my research. Special thanks go to Iia Kavkasidze and the other wonderful women at the State Public Library in Tbilisi, who were so warmly hospitable.

I am grateful to a number of scholars who have helped me by reading and commenting on the manuscript and sharing source materials and information with me: Robert Tucker, Stephen Jones, Robert Slusser, Graeme Gill, Barbara Chotiner, Eugene Huskey, Shimon Redlich, and William Taubman. I also want to thank Kevin Windle, who kindly sent me drafts of his own research on Beria and alerted me to sources, Werner Hahn, Robert Conquest, Ronald Suny, George Leggett, J. Arch Getty, Peter Lerner, Stephen Rapp, Thane Gustafson, and Peter Reddaway for their help.

My colleagues at the Library of Congress have been especially helpful to me: Albert Graham and Irene Steckler have generously given time and effort to my research needs, here and in Moscow; Harry Leich, Grant Harris, and Ken Nyrady have located sources for me on countless occasions. I also am grateful to Glen Curtis for translating materials from Georgian, and to Boris Boguslavsky, Eric Johnson, and Maya Keech.

Research for this book would not have been possible without a grant from the National Council for Soviet and East European Research in Washington, which enabled me to pursue my study of Beria for a full year in 1989–90 and to travel both to Ann Arbor, Michigan, and to the Hoover Library in Stanford, California. The National Council also provided me with the means to hire an excellent research assistant, Gail Albergo, whose efficient and dedicated work helped me immeasurably. I want to thank Robert Randolph of the National Council and Harley Balzer of Georgetown University for their kind help during this year and Joe Proctor and Richard Granson for their assistance during the book's final stages. Two short-term travel grants from the International Research and Exchanges Board made it possible for me to travel to the former Soviet Union in October 1990 and again in August 1992 to conduct research in libraries and archives.

Thanks are also due to the staff at various archives that I have visited during the course of my research: the Hoover Institution, the National Archives in Washington, the Central State Archives and the former Party Archives in Tbilisi, and the Russian Center for the Storage and Study of Documents of Recent History, the Center for the Storage of Contemporary Documentation, and the Central State Archives in Moscow. I appreciate being allowed to cite unpublished materials from these archives. I am especially grateful for the kind assistance of Ludmilla Gorskaia, Sergei Mironenko, Sofia Somonova, and Vladimir Ashiani during my archival research in Moscow. I also want to thank Vittoria German for her warm support of my efforts there and Oleg Khlevniuk, for sharing his insights with me.

I am indebted to Elizo Kviatashvili, for kindly allowing me to cite parts of the memoirs of her father, Nicholas Merab Kviatashvili.

My editor at Princeton University Press, Lauren Osborne, deserves much credit for her encouragement of this project from its early stages and for her efficient and thorough editing. I also wish to thank my production editor, Molan Chun Goldstein, and Alan Greenberg, who prepared the index.

Lastly, I owe much to my family: my daughters Molly, Diana, and Alexandra; Ricarda, who has come to be part of our family; and my husband, Malcolm, to whom this book is dedicated. He generously took the time to go over the manuscript carefully, helping me with his keen judgment and clarity of expression to make significant improvements.

Georgia, 1991

(Courtesy of Library of Congress)

Legend:

- —— Republic boundary
- —··— Autonomous republic (ASSR) boundary
- — — — Autonomous oblast (AO) boundary
- ⊛ Republic capital
- ◉ Autonomous republic (ASSR) center
- ⊕ Autonomous oblast (AO) center
- +—+—+ Railroad
- —— Road

*Area with no oblast-level administrative divisions, where rayons are under direct republic jurisdiction.

0   25   50   75 Kilometers

0   25   50   75 Miles

801962 (R00088) 12-91

CHRONOLOGY OF BERIA'S LIFE

29 March 1899	Born in village of Merkheuli, Sukhumi District of Georgia.
1915	Enrolls in Baku Polytechnic for Mechanical Construction.
March 1917	Joins Bolshevik wing of Russian Social Democratic Labor Party.
June 1917–January 1918	Serves in Russian Army at the front.
1919	Graduates from Polytechnic; works for Musavat government in Baku.
1920	Conducts underground work for Bolsheviks; enrolls in new Baku Polytechnical Institute.
February 1921	Joins Azerbaidzhan Cheka.
Autumn 1921	Marries Nino Gegechkori.
November 1922	Moves to Georgian Cheka, Tbilisi, as a deputy chairman.
1924	Son, Sergo, born.
1926	Becomes Chairman of Georgian GPU (successor to Cheka).
April 1931	Takes over as Chairman of Transcaucasian GPU.
October 1931	Appointed First Secretary of Georgian Communist Party.
October 1932	Appointed First Secretary of Transcaucasian Regional Party Committee.
January 1934	Acquires Georgian Party leadership.
August 1938	Moves to Moscow, as First Deputy Chief of NKVD.
November 1938	Appointed Chief of NKVD.
March 1939	Elected Candidate Member of Politburo.
January 1941	Achieves rank of General Commissar of State Security; Appointed Deputy Chairman of *Sovnarkom*.
June 1941	Becomes a member of GKO.
May 1944	Promoted to a deputy chairman of GKO.
July 1945	Achieves rank of Marshal of the Soviet Union.
mid-1945	Takes charge of atomic bomb project.

January 1946	Relinquishes post as head of NKVD; remains a deputy chairman of *Sovnarkom*.
March 1946	Achieves full Politburo membership.
29 March 1949	Awarded Order of Lenin.
March 1953	Becomes Chief of MVD; First Deputy Chairman of Council of Ministers.
26 June 1953	Arrested.
23 December 1953	Shot.

ABBREVIATIONS

CC	Central Committee
CHEKA	Extraordinary Commission for Combating Counter-revolution and Sabotage
CPSU	Communist Party of the Soviet Union
GKO	State Defense Committee
GPU	State Political Administration
GUGB	Main Administration of State Security
JAC	Jewish Antifascist Committee
MGB	Ministry of State Security
MVD	Ministry of Internal Affairs
NKID	People's Commissariat of Foreign Affairs
NKVD	People's Commissariat of Internal Affairs
OGPU	Unified State Political Administration
OSS	Office of Strategic Services
RSDRP	Russian Social Democratic Labor Party
SED	Communist Party of East Germany
SMERSH	Death to Spies (Soviet Military Counterintelligence)
SOE	Secret Operations Executive
Sovnarkom	Council of People's Commissars
Stavka	General Headquarters of the Soviet High Command
TsKK	Central Control Commission
Zakkraikom	Transcaucasian Regional Party Committee
ZSFSR	Transcaucasian Federated Soviet Socialist Republic

BERIA

INTRODUCTION

> The facts of history are indeed facts about individuals, but not
> about actions of individuals performed in isolation. . . . They
> are facts about the relations of individuals to one another
> in society and about the social forces which produce
> from the actions of individuals results often at
> variance with, and sometimes opposite to, the
> results which they themselves intended.
> *(E. H. Carr,* What Is History?*)*

A S LAVRENTII Beria stood over Joseph Stalin's deathbed in early March 1953, witnesses observed that he could barely contain his pleasure in watching the leader edge toward his final moments of life. The two men had been through a great deal together since they had first met in the 1920s. Indeed Beria, who oversaw the Soviet police apparatus and had been a key member of Stalin's government for years, was at Stalin's side during some of the most dramatic crises of his leadership. But around 1950 their relationship, while outwardly still close, had taken a bizarre turn. Stalin had come to distrust Beria and was plotting to get rid of him. Beria knew this, so it was not without reason that he welcomed Stalin's death.

But Stalin's death provided only a temporary reprieve for Beria. Three months later he was arrested by his Kremlin colleagues in a dramatic coup led by Nikita Khrushchev. In an effort to justify their coup, Beria's opponents denounced him as a spy and a traitor. Following—or perhaps even before—a closed trial in December 1953, Beria was executed and his name officially expunged from public memory. As a symbol of his "nonpersonhood," the editors of the *Great Soviet Encyclopedia* sent out a discreet notice to all their subscribers recommending that they cut out "with a small knife or razor blade" the entry on Beria. They provided as a replacement text an entry on the Bering Sea. For the next thirty years no Soviet history, no textbook, no officially sanctioned memoirs mentioned Beria's name, except for the occasional reference to him as a criminal or evildoer. Those who lived through the Stalin era did not forget Beria, however. Associated as he was with the dreaded police and labeled a traitor by his Kremlin opponents, he came to symbolize all that was evil in this period, haunting the public imagination to this day.[1] Whereas some might still view Stalin with ambivalence, giving him grudging credit for his leadership abilities, the general reaction to Beria is fear and loathing.

That Beria was a villian who committed terrible acts there can be no doubt, but the myths and legends about him have obscured the complexities of his career and detracted from the important role that he played in Soviet domestic and foreign policy from the prewar years onward. The conventional image of Beria as just another of Stalin's ruthless policemen has prevented historians from recognizing that, however evil he was, Beria was a highly intelligent and efficient administrator whose influence on Soviet policy was pervasive. Moreover, the fact that he became a forceful proponent of liberal reforms after Stalin's death has not been fully understood.

This study, based on a reassessment of old sources and on new materials that have emerged as a result of *glasnost'*, does not serve in any sense to "rehabilitate" Beria. But it does challenge some basic assumptions, both about Beria and about the Stalinist system in general. One of these assumptions concerns the extent to which Stalin himself dominated political events. Most historians have viewed Stalin as an absolute dictator, whose powers, after the mid-1930s at least, knew no bounds. Although they have disagreed about the reasons for his rise to power and debated the relative strengths and weaknesses of the Stalinist system, few have doubted that he was firmly at the helm in his position as Soviet leader. His subordinates have generally been dismissed as pawns or vassals, who acted as "little dictators" in their own realms but always bowed to their leader's will.[2] Given the prevalence of this view of Stalin's leadership, it is not surprising that scholars have focused their attention almost exclusively on Stalin, treating the members of his inner circle as peripheral characters. They have combed Stalin's past for details that might shed light on his personality and analyzed his motivations from all perspectives, but they have shown little interest in the character or motives of other members of the leadership. Only Khrushchev has been deemed worthy of serious biographical treatment, because he managed to achieve the top leadership post after Stalin died.

In view of Stalin's impact on history, this preoccupation with his personality may be justified. But no dictator's power is truly absolute, in the sense that it always depends on the loyalty of those directly below him. Thus the motivations of Stalin's subordinates and the dynamics of his relationship with them should also be a concern for historians. However powerful he might have appeared to others, Stalin never felt secure with the members of his inner circle. Indeed, his biographers have argued that his insecurity, stemming as it did from deep psychological imbalances, went far beyond the bounds of rationality and developed, as he grew older, into an intense paranoia.[3] He became deeply suspicious, so obsessed with the possiblity of betrayal from any quarter that he trusted no one. This is why he could never tolerate the idea of an heir apparent and continually intrigued against his subordinates with the aim of pitting one against the other, isolating them, and warding off any possible collective initiative on their part by having them report to him personally.

Stalin's strategy of "divide and rule" was successful, particularly because he could use the threat of physical annihilation as the ultimate deterrent against disloyalty on the part of his lieutenants. With the latter aware that the slightest sign of disobedience could bring death, Stalin never had to face overt opposition to his rule.[4] But his paranoia inevitably detracted from his effectiveness as a leader and, more important, it made him vulnerable to psychological manipulation. Fortunately for Stalin, he managed for the most part to surround himself with maleable bureaucrats who lacked the imagination or insight to penetrate his mind, but Beria was an exception.

Born in 1899, twenty years after Stalin, Beria was not part of Stalin's generation of revolutionaries who had fought against the Tsar. He did not join the Bolshevik party until 1917. But he was, like Stalin, a Georgian and he shared with his mentor an ability to employ the most extreme measures of repression against his countrymen. During the 1920s and 1930s, as police chief and later party chief of Georgia and Transcaucasia, Beria had won Stalin's confidence by his ruthless enforcement of Soviet domination and by his ambitious efforts to further Stalin's personality cult. Unlike most other leaders of national republics, he managed to survive the 1936–38 purges, though he did come dangerously close to arrest. By the time he moved to Moscow in 1938 to head the dreaded Soviet political police, the NKVD, Beria already had the blood of thousands of his fellow Georgians on his hands. Although a relative latecomer to Stalin's entourage, Beria soon insinuated himself into Stalin's inner circle, rising to become the second most powerful person in the Kremlin for the next decade and a half.

As NKVD chief, Beria was responsible for intelligence, counterintelligence, and domestic security during the pre-World War II and war years. He also commanded the vast slave labor network, the GULAG, which furnished a significant portion of the manpower for the Soviet economy. During the war he oversaw the enormous task of evacuating defense industries to the East as the Germans advanced, and in 1945 Stalin placed him in charge of the Soviet atomic bomb project. Although Beria relinquished formal control over the police and security apparatus to trusted subordinates in 1946, he retained oversight for this sphere in his position as a full Politburo member and a deputy chairman of the Council of Ministers. This gave him an advantage over his Kremlin colleagues in the power struggles that characterized Kremlin politics and became increasingly bitter as Stalin's physical and mental health declined in the postwar years.

Beria was by all accounts an astute politician who made good use of the extensive political networks he had established in Transcaucasia and in the security police by cultivating a group of supporters who owed their allegiance to him. Indeed his career is a testimony to the importance of patronage, particularly that based on regional loyalties, in the Stalinist system. But his unique sway over Stalin also contributed to his power. Although his relations with Stalin were not always smooth, even in the early days, Beria was able to weather the crises because he understood better than his comrades Stalin's peculiar psychopathology. As a fellow Georgian, he was familiar with the cultural and social world in which Stalin had grown up, the society that had instilled in him the values and orientation that remained with him for life. Georgians have always been deeply conscious of their national tradition and closely tied to their cultural and societal roots. Although Stalin eventually became thoroughly Russified on the surface and shunned his Georgian past, at a personal level he retained the influences of his Georgian heritage.

Foremost among these influences, as historian Ronald Suny has argued, was the Georgian ideal of manhood—fearless, determined, tall, physically strong, proud, and fiercely loyal to friends, family, and nation. A Georgian man should also be lavishly hospitable and able to hold his alcohol. In Georgian society honor is accorded the highest value and to fail in fulfilling the ideal of manhood is to lose one's honor and bring shame upon oneself and one's family. Stalin shared this ideal, calling himself in the bolshevik underground by the nickname "Koba," the protaganist in a famous Georgian novel who embodied all the traits of Georgian manhood.[5] Yet he failed miserably to measure up to this ideal, just as his father, Beso Dzhugashvili, had. The latter, who died in a brawl when Stalin was a boy, was a drunkard, unable to provide for his family and prone to violent beatings of both Stalin and his mother.

Stalin was deprived of a model of traditional patriarchical authority that he might have emulated, relying instead on his strong-willed mother, who assumed the dominant role even before his father's death. Short in stature, with an arm permanently weakened by an accident, and scarred by smallpox, Stalin was also disadvantaged by his physical appearance. And despite his mother's reported devotion to him, the beatings by his father in early childhood, as Stalin's biographers have hypothesized, created a deep sense of anxiety and inferiority, which further inhibited him from approaching the Georgian ideal of manhood. The abusive treatment also left Stalin with an inherent distrust of other people and a strong vindictive streak, traits that were reinforced by Georgian societal norms:

> The high value on friendship, loyalty, and trust in a fiercely competitive society increased the potential for disappointment and disillusion. Betrayal of a friend

was the worst sin. Competition leads to judging superiority and inferiority—who is stronger, drinks more, is better at toasting—and in turn creates tensions, frustrations, and mutual suspicions. Close to the reliance on trust is the omnipresent fear of betrayal. Friendship and family networks provide security and protection, resources of all kinds, but they cannot eliminate the anxiety of betrayal and loss of trust or honor.[6]

In Stalin's development, then, a complex interaction of cultural and familial experiences contributed to a deeply neurotic, paranoid personality, alienated and out of touch with normal human emotions. Beria understood these influences not only because he was Georgian, but also because he had suffered a similar upbringing. He, too, was from a poor peasant family and grew up in an impoverished rural area. He, too, lost his father at an early age and was brought up by his mother, without the role model of an adult male.

Recognizing Stalin's insatiable need for praise to compensate for his deep feelings of inferiority, Beria flattered him endlessly. He also played on Stalin's fear of betrayal by feeding his suspicions, a task he was well positioned to undertake by means of his control over the political police and the files on Stalin's colleagues and subordinates. As Robert Tucker observed: "A craving for praise was not the only need in Stalin to which Beria ministered. There was also . . . the active propensity for distrusting others, the need born of Stalin's own self-accusations to expose, accuse and punish others as enemies. From this standpoint, the function of a Beria was to supply Stalin with ever new objects of distrust and condemnation."[7]

As the only Georgian in Stalin's inner circle, Beria was in a sense Stalin's alter ego. He was a constant reminder to Stalin of his ethnic origins, speaking to him in Georgian in front of the others and often addressing him as "Koba." Yet Stalin had intensely ambivalent feelings about Georgia, which is not surprising given his unfortunate childhood, and he gradually tried to sever himself from his Georgian self. Ironically, Beria helped him to do this by serving as his accomplice in two acts that symbolized a repudiation of his heritage. The first was in 1935, when Beria published his notorious book, *On the History of Bolshevik Organizations in Transcaucasia*, the purpose of which was to give Stalin a leading role in the revolutionary movement in the Caucasus by falsifying the historical facts and thereby denigrating the role of other revolutionary figures. It is not clear whether Stalin had the idea of writing the book, but in endorsing it wholeheartedly and going along with the unfounded glorification of his role at the expense of the truth, he denied any allegiance to Georgian history or respect for the past. Then, in 1937, Stalin failed to attend his mother's funeral in Georgia. Beria, who was party chief there at the time, acted as his surrogate, making the arrangements and presiding over the ceremony. Whatever the reasons for Stalin's absence, it was not only a terrible insult to the memory of his dead mother but also a shocking breech of cultural and societal tradition in a country where veneration of the dead is accorded the highest importance.[8]

Beria was, then, not simply a sycophant who gained Stalin's favor by insidious means. He actively encouraged Stalin's neuroses and his sense of self-alienation, "stirred him up" as no one else could do. Stalin depended emotionally on Beria, who was at his side constantly from the early 1940s onward. Beria acted as the unofficial toastmaster at Stalin's endless dinners, which all members of his inner circle were required to attend, forcing the guests to consume large quantities of alcohol and making crude, scatological jokes. Aside from his daughter, Stalin was not close to members of his family and he hated to be alone, so he insisted that his subordinates keep him company during all his waking hours. They even went with him on vacations.

The lack of distinction between their public and private lives doubtless strengthened the sense of emotional dependency that existed between Stalin and the members of his circle, as did their isolation from the outside world. Stalin and his entourage were so out of touch with the rest of the country, so involved in their own group dynamics and court intrigues, that what happened "below" seemed almost irrelevant to them. Milovan Djilas, a Yugoslav Communist who spent considerable time with Stalin's inner circle after the war, aptly portrayed this atmosphere in a description of a dinner scene at Stalin's villa in 1949. The guests, all members of the leadership and including Beria, were playing a game at the table. Each of them had to guess what the temperature was outside and then drink one glass of vodka for every degree by which his estimate was off the mark. "This apportioning of the number of vodka glasses according to the temperature reading," writes Djilas, "suddenly brought to my mind the confinement, the inanity and senselessness of the life these Soviet leaders were living, gathered about their superannuated chief even as they played a role that was decisive for the human race."[9] Isolated, caught up in themselves, and blighted by a kind of group neurosis, Stalin and his lieutenants made their decisions with little or no regard for the Soviet people. Indeed, what bound them together was their contempt for human individuality and their ability to inflict terrible cruelty on their people with no remorse.

However strong was Beria's emotional hold on Stalin, he was playing a dangerous game. It was inevitable, given Stalin's paranoia, that he would eventually begin to distrust Beria. And he had good reason. Beria was becoming increasingly contemptuous of him behind his back. By this time, however, Stalin's suspiciousness and fear of death had overcome him to such a degree that he could no longer manipulate men and events to suit his purposes. Or perhaps he was still able to manipulate, but his purposes had become vague. Although he continued to instill fear in his subordinates, including Beria, and to command their outward obedience, there was more than a little covert resistance and by the early 1950s the intense battle for the succession had begun to take on a life of its own.

The chief contenders were Beria and Khrushchev, then a powerful Central Committee secretary. Once Stalin died, Beria was free to act and he immediately took formal control of the vast police apparatus, a move that was seen as threatening by his colleagues, especially Khrushchev. This has generally been cited as the reason for the opposition to Beria and his subsequent arrest. But as this study shows, Beria's reform program aroused equal concern. Beria embarked on a series of initiatives aimed at reversing many of Stalin's policies. The changes he advocated were so bold and far-reaching that, while greeted with relief by the public, they alarmed his colleagues. Ironically, it was Khrushchev, acclaimed later as a courageous de-Stalinizer, who was chiefly responsible for putting a halt to Beria's reforms by leading the plot against him. As this biography suggests, Beria's program aimed at undermining the Stalinist system and therefore might have led to its demise. Khrushchev's policies, while reformist, in fact perpetuated Stalinism. Though Khrushchev eliminated the role of police terror, many would argue that the system remained essentially totalitarian.

The present study, then, might be considered a revisionist history because, in examining the career of one political figure, it questions some common assumptions about Stalinism. The approach to this biography is a dual one. The narrative describes the rise of Beria in the political and social climate of the Stalin era, chronicling his successes and failures and assessing his influence in terms of the dynamics of the Soviet system. At the same time, the study considers Beria's career at a more personal level, examining his motivations and his relationship with Stalin and other colleagues. Soviet political figures have by tradition revealed little about their private lives, and Beria was no exception. Even if all the archives were opened and his personal papers were made available, it is doubtful that diaries or letters recording intimate feelings would surface. Like Stalin, Beria had little in the way of a private life, especially after he came to the Kremlin in 1938. His marriage to the beautiful Nino Gegechkori had become a meaningless formality. He was apparently fond of his only son, Sergo, who often accompanied him on trips, and there was the diversion provided by his notorious sexual attacks on young women and girls. But his wife and others who knew him have claimed that he spent most of his time working or with Stalin. And one of his closest associates for many years, Vladimir Merkulov, observed that Beria never once spoke to him about personal matters. Only in Beria's letters to his mentor, the famous Bolshevik Sergo Ordzhonikidze, does one detect a hint of personal emotion.

The seeming absence of a human dimension in Beria's personality should not prevent us from attempting to discern the causes behind his actions. He did not exist as an abstraction, but as a human being whose behavior was motivated by specific personality traits. During the course of his career, for example, Beria committed atrocious crimes; he was directly responsible for the death and suffering of thousands. Was he driven purely by rational, cynical self-interest? Or did he have some of Stalin's psychopathological tendencies? It is the aim of this biography to relate these individual factors to the broader historical forces that shaped Beria's career, with the more general purpose of offering new insights on Stalinist-type dictatorships.

With the onset of *glasnost*, Beria became the object of renewed historical interest in Russia and in Georgia. Valuable archival materials, documents, and memoirs have appeared in the press, shedding new light on Beria's career. In mid-1990, an unprecedented interview with Beria's eighty-six-year-old widow appeared in a Georgian paper, and a transcript of the dramatic July 1953 Central Committee Plenum, which was called by Khrushchev to discuss the reasons for Beria's arrest, was published for the first time in early 1991. More recently, Beria's son, Sergo, emerged from obscurity to give a series of interviews in a Kiev newspaper. But the release of archival materials has been highly selective, and the revelations about Beria that have appeared over the past few years have continued to yield diverging accounts of certain episodes in his life. Fortunately, in 1992 the Russians opened their archives to scholars, enabling this author to see numerous hitherto secret documents, which have added much to the picture of Beria and his career. It must be pointed out, however, that the archives have yet to be fully exploited and that important questions remain unanswered. This study appears at the beginning of a new phase of historiography of the Stalin period, which should, if archival access continues, yield many exciting revelations and generate new interpretations of Stalinist history. The story of Beria's political career, then, must be considered an ongoing one.

Chapter One

EARLY LIFE AND CAREER

> Ah here, o mother, is thy task. Thy sacred duty to thy land:
> endow thy sons with spirits strong, with strength of heart
> and honor bright. Inspire them with fraternal love,
> to strive for freedom and for right.
> *(Ilia Chavchavadze, "To a Georgian Mother")*

Georgian Heritage

IT IS ONE of Soviet history's great ironies that Stalin and Beria, two of its most notorious political villains, were both born and raised in Georgia, a country renowned for the beauty and charm of its people, as well as for its rich cultural history. For centuries Georgians have enjoyed a reputation for bravery, loyalty, and high-spiritedness, and visitors to Georgia have consistently praised them for their generous hospitality, enhanced by the salubrious climate and lush Georgian countryside. The German Social Democrat Karl Kautsky, who visited Georgia in 1921, wrote: "Georgia lacks nothing to make her not only one of the most beautiful, but also one of the richest countries in the world."[1]

Some historians, much to the dismay of the Georgian people, have attributed the characters of Stalin and Beria to their nationality. David Lang, for example, a noted expert on Georgia, observed: "Every medal has its reverse. In many Georgians, quick wit is matched by a quick temper, and a proneness to harbour rancour. The bravery associated with heroes like Prince Bagration, an outstanding general of the Napoleonic wars, is matched by the cruelty and vindictiveness found in such individuals as Stalin and Beria."[2] Not surprisingly, most Georgians are insulted by such slurs on their nationality, particularly since they suffered tremendously at the hands of both Beria and Stalin.[3] More to the point, they would argue, is why such men came to occupy positions of power over *all* Soviet people, not just Georgians. Indeed, it was the Soviet system, created by the Russian-dominated Bolsheviks and run from Moscow, that fostered these men and enabled them to wield awesome destructive powers.

Although the evil acts of Beria cannot be blamed on his nationality, Georgian national culture had a profound and lasting influence on him. Georgia has a rich and ancient cultural heritage. Its civilization goes back more than three thousand years, and archaeologists have found evidence that man was living there more than fifty thousand years ago, in the early Paleolithic period.[4] The Georgians cannot be classified in one of the main ethnic groups of Europe or Asia. Their languages do not belong to the Indo-European, Altaic, or Finno-Ugric linguistic groups, but rather to a southern Caucasian language group known as Kartvelian, which as far back as four thousand years ago broke up into several distinct, although related, languages. The Georgian nation itself is the product of a fusion of indigenous inhabitants with immigrants who infiltrated into Caucasia from Asia Minor in remote antiquity.[5]

The history of Caucasia, which in addition to Georgia, encompasses Armenia to the south and Azerbaidzhan to the southwest, reflects an amalgam of Eastern and Western influences. Toward the west Georgia extends to the Black Sea, which linked it to the cultures of Greece and Rome. To the southwest lay the Turks, who at various times were the dominant power in Caucasia. From the east, via the Caspian Sea, came incursions by the Persians. The continued struggles between Rome-Byzantium and Persia for the possession of Caucasia were drawn out because neither empire was able to defeat the other decisively. As a result, the small Caucasian states were able to retain some political and cultural autonomy despite the persistent threats of being overcome by outside powers.[6]

Christianity was adopted in Georgia in the fourth century during the reign of Georgian King Mirian. The conversion to Christianity provided a great stimulus to literature and the arts and helped to unify the country. It also strengthened the influence of the Roman Empire at the expense of Persia, although the latter continued to have a strong impact in Eastern Georgia. By the twelfth century a distinctive Georgian culture and civilization was formed, reflecting the influence of both Byzantium and Persia. Georgian architecture and literature flourished, and several excellent higher educational institutions were founded. Throughout the next six centuries, however, Georgia fell victim to repeated invasions which wrought havoc on its economic and political life and created internal disunity. By the mid-eighteenth century, Caucasia was "a mosaic of kingdoms, khanates and principalities, nominally under either Turkish or Iranian sovereignty but actually maintaining varying degrees of precarious autonomy or independence."[7]

By this time commercial, political, and cultural ties between Georgia and Russia had begun to strengthen and in 1783, during Russia's war with Turkey, Russia and Georgia signed the Treaty of Georgievsk, placing the eastern part of Georgia (Kartli-Kakheti) under Russian protection. Despite Russia's commitment to defend Kartli-Kakheti, it rendered no assistance when the Turks invaded in 1785 and again in 1795. The Russians illegally annexed Kartli-Kakheti in 1801, subsequently moving westward and within the next decade extending their dominance over most of Georgia. By the middle of the nineteenth century, Georgia and the rest of Caucasia were integrated into the Russian administrative system and ambitious members of the nobility identified their interests with those of Russia. The internal conflicts and invasions from the outside for the most part ceased, but Russian domination brought little relief for the average Georgian peasant or worker, who continued to be oppressed by the feudal system imposed from above. Moreover, most Georgians remained determined to preserve their culture and traditions, resisting attempts by Moscow to Russianize them.

Toward the end of the nineteenth century, at the time of Beria's birth, opposition to the autocracy had begun to take hold in the Russian empire. Nationalist sentiments combined with radical socialist ideas to produce a liberation movement, led by the Marxist Social Democrats. In 1903 the Social Democrats split into two groups, the Mensheviks and the Bolsheviks. The latter group, led by Vladimir Lenin, favored a more centralized and disciplined party organization, while the Mensheviks wanted a looser, more democratic structure for the movement. In Georgia, where Social Democrats had been active since the early 1890s, the Mensheviks predominated. When Russian Tsar Nicholas II was deposed in March 1917 the Georgians threw their support behind the new democratic provisional government in Petrograd. The bolshevik coup that overthrew the provisional government in November 1917 was opposed by Georgia and its Caucasian neighbors, which refused to recognize the new regime. On 9 April 1918, the three Caucasian republics—Georgia, Armenia, and Azerbaidzhan—declared their independence from Russia and announced the creation of their own Transcaucasian Federation.

Meanwhile, as a result of the March 1918 treaty negotiated between Germany and Russia to end Russia's long war with the Central Powers, the Russian Army abandoned Transcaucasia, leaving it vulnerable to Germany's allies, the Turks, who moved across the border and took the Georgian city of Batumi. Because of disagreements among the three republics on how to deal with the advancing Turkish Army, the Transcaucasian Federation was soon dissolved and, on 26 May 1918, Georgia became an independent country for the first time in 116 years.[8]

The new parliamentary government was dominated by the Mensheviks, who had broad roots among the peasants in the countryside and also enjoyed wide support among urban workers. One of their first actions was to sign a treaty with the Turkish command at Batumi, accepting the loss of certain territories and allowing the Turks use of Georgian railways. The Menshevik Georgian government also concluded an agreement with Germany, giving it certain concessions in exchange for diplomatic recognition and protection. (The Turks continued their advance eastward, however, taking the Azerbaidzhani city of Baku in September 1918, only to retreat a month later, when the Central Powers were forced to sue for peace.)

The Georgian Mensheviks focused their efforts on enacting land reform and improving Georgia's weak economy, while the Bolsheviks worked to undermine Georgia's independent government by subversive means. Because they had so little popular appeal, however, they were not successful. Finally, in February 1921, having forcibly taken over both Azerbaidzhan and Armenia, bolshevik troops invaded Georgia, causing the menshevik government to fall. The invasion marked the end of Georgia's brief phase as an independent nation. Georgia was now "Bolshevik Georgia," where politics would henceforth be controlled by men committed to enforcing Moscow's rule, men like Lavrentii Beria.

BERIA'S EARLY YEARS

Lavrentii Pavlovich Beria was born on 29 March 1899 in the village of Merkheuli, which is in the Sukhumi district of what later became the Abkhaz Autonomous Republic, part of the Georgian Republic.[9] Georgia is divided by the Surami mountain range into western and eastern regions. The region of Abkhazia lies in the northwest corner on the Black Sea coast. Beria was a member of the Mingrelian ethnic group, a minority that lived in a low-lying densely vegetated land on the sea coast just below Abkhazia, as well as in and around the towns of Abkhazia itself. Although the Mingrelians had their own language (closely related to the Kartvelian language group, which includes Georgian), it was not written, so Georgian was used as the literary language. Their religion, which was Georgian Orthodox, also tied them to the rest of Georgia but, like other areas of Western Georgia, Mingrelia had been more heavily influenced by the Roman and Byzantine empires than Eastern Georgia.[10] Mingrelians always had a strong sense of ethnic identity and their national pride made them deeply resentful of intrusions by other peoples of Georgia, including the Abkhazians.

The Mingrelians, whose population was estimated to have reached 72,103 by the time of the 1897 Russian census, were predominantly a peasant people and Beria himself came from a poor peasant family. Mingrelian society was highly patriarchal—and still is—with the extended family household at its core. Death, which served to emphasize kinship and solidarity of lineage, was mourned intensely, according to an elaborate set of rituals and rules.[11] Agriculture, cattle breeding, and wine production were the principle occupations of the Mingrelians. As in other parts of Georgia and in Russia, peasants in Mingrelia had been serfs, bound to a small number of landlords, until they were emancipated in 1867. Mingrelian peasants had a tradition of rebelliousness. Ten years earlier, in 1857, three thousand of them had risen in revolt against the ruling landlord family there. Eventually Russian troops were sent in and thirty-eight peasant leaders were arrested and exiled.[12] The uprising became a part of Mingrelian heritage and was looked upon with pride by later generations.

Despite the favorable climate and rich natural resources, economic productivity in Mingrelia was low, particularly during the first part of the nineteenth century. Travelers to Western Georgia noted repeatedly how poor and backward the peasants were. According to one observer:

> It must be confessed that the general appearance of the Mingrelians and Gourials denotes slothfulness and slovenliness. [Given] the consequences of the exuberant fertility of the soil, and of their own low scale in the social state, which, engendering no artificial wants, they are content with merely raising so much grain as may suffice for their own consumption.[13]

Karl Kautsky was struck by the primitive methods of Georgian agriculture during his 1921 visit from Germany, noting that rotation of crops was quite unknown there and that the implements used recalled Biblical times. Although some outsiders attributed the poverty to racial and climatic factors, Kautsky contended that feudal dependence and the prevalence of short leases impeded the development of agriculture there.[14] Whatever the causes, Mingrelia was on the outer reaches of civilization, offering little to an intelligent youth with ambition.

Beria's mother, Marta Ivanovna, was born in 1872. She was a simple, deeply religious woman who attended church regularly all her life, maintaining close ties with other members of the religious community.[15] According to one S. Danilov, who knew Beria and his family in his youth, Marta Ivanovna married twice. From the first marriage, which ended with the death of her husband, she had one son; from the second, to Pavel Khukhaevich Beria, she had three more children—Lavrentii, another son, and a daughter, Anna, born a deaf-mute in 1905.[16] In a brief autobiography written in 1923 for the Communist party, Beria mentions only his sister and a niece, born around 1910 and subsequently dependent on him, so perhaps if he had brothers they were no longer living by this time.[17] In addition to his immediate family, Beria had a number of cousins on both his mother's and father's sides, most of whom lived in Abkhazia.[18] Beria's father died while Beria was still attending higher primary school (similar to a middle school) in the town of Sukhumi, not far from his native village of Merkheuli. So, like Stalin, he was the product of a matriarchical family.

According to Danilov, Beria was a mediocre student, not excelling in any subject but considered cunning and devious. After completing school in Sukhumi in 1915 Beria went to the city of Baku in Azerbaidzhan, where he enrolled in the Baku Polytechnical School for Mechanical Construction, remaining there for the next four years. Beria probably chose Baku for his studies instead of Tbilisi, which was much closer to home, because it offered the specific course he was interested in. Nonetheless, Baku was almost six hundred kilometers from home, quite a distance for a boy of only sixteen. Beria says in his autobiography that he supported himself, his mother, his sister and young niece by doing office work during school vacations. Danilov mentions that Beria also received money from a rich Sukhumi textile merchant named Erkomoshvili, who had employed Beria's mother as a domestic servant. Beria's sister Anna eventually married a Jewish engineer, Levan Ismailovich Loladze, and had a daughter, but his mother remained dependent on her son financially up to the time of his arrest.[19]

In October 1915 Beria and a group of fellow students at the polytechnical school organized an illegal Marxist study circle, which had contacts with workers' groups and which continued to exist until the revolution of March 1917. Beria, who was adept at financial matters, was treasurer of the group.[20] Socialism was a popular creed in Caucasia and a strong and militant Social Democratic organization, led by impoverished nobility who had entered the professions, had existed there since the turn of the century. With its large alien proletariat (mainly oil workers from Russia, Persia, and Armenia) Baku provided especially fertile ground for the spread of radical ideas.

ON THE SIDE OF THE BOLSHEVIKS

In March 1917, after the abdication of the Russian Tsar and the establishment of the Provisional Government, Beria joined the Bolshevik wing of the Russian Social Democratic Labor Party, the RSDRP(B), and together with four comrades established a party cell at his school.[21] For the next four tumultuous years Beria's career took a variety of turns. As he himself observed: "During the course of events that began in 1917 in Transcaucasia I was drawn into the general channel of party-soviet work that took me from place to place, from conditions where the party was legal (in 1918 in Baku) to illegal (1919 and 1920), interrupted by trips to Georgia."[22] The Mensheviks actually dominated the RSDRP in most of Transcaucasia, but Baku was an exception and the Bolsheviks had considerable strength there.[23] Beria's studies were cut short in June 1917 when he was conscripted into the army of Russia, which at the time was still in the war against Germany, and served on the Romanian front as part of a hydrotechnical unit. While at the front, Beria, who was elected chairman of the Bolshevik party committee of his detachment, spread propaganda among the troops and also served as a delegate to several regional party conferences.

Beria returned to Baku in January 1918, resuming his studies at the polytechnical school, from which he graduated in 1919 with the diploma of "architect-builder technician." At the same time he worked in the secretariat of the Baku Soviet of Workers, Soldiers, and Peasants Deputies, which was controlled precariously by the Bolsheviks.[24] The Bolsheviks faced serious challenges at this time. Though Russia had made peace with Germany in March 1918, the new government in Russia was now fighting a bitter civil war, which would continue for the next three years. And Baku, the only city in the now independent Transcaucasia that the Bolsheviks controlled, faced an advancing Turkish Army by the summer of 1918. The food situation in Baku became critical, and the population had to rely on nuts for sustenance. The Bolsheviks finally lost control of the soviet to the Socialist Revolutionaries, another radical party, and to the Armenians, who had a substantial presence in Baku. These groups welcomed the arrival of the British in mid-August for the purpose of warding off Turkish and Azerbaidzhani forces, but within less than a month the British were forced to flee. Azerbaidzhani and Turkish troops burst into the city, massacring thousands of Christian Armenians and creating panic everywhere. Beria, who witnessed all this, apparently faced little danger himself, since he was still a student and not a prominent Bolshevik. After leaving the soviet, Beria worked briefly as a clerk at a factory, the Caspian Company, but then devoted all his time to studying for his examinations.

By November 1918 Turkish troops had withdrawn from Azerbaidzhan and a new party, the Musavat, was in control, remaining in power until April 1920, when the Red (Bolshevik) Army invaded. The Musavat Party had originally been formed in 1911–12 by a group of intellectuals associated with the RSDRP. It later shifted ideologically to the Right and became the party of the rising Azerbaidzhani bourgeoisie. After a period of cooperation with the Bolsheviks in Baku, during which they supported the soviet, the Musavatists increasingly opposed bolshevik policies. By late 1917 and early 1918 they had become the Bolsheviks' most formidable rivals.[25] In the autumn of 1919 Beria was assigned by the Bolsheviks to conduct counterintelligence within the ruling Musavat government. He also led a party circle of technical workers and carried out other tasks for the underground district Bolshevik committee.[26]

Beria's brief stint as a spy within the Musavat government was to return to haunt him. Indeed, his subsequent political enemies used this against him throughout his career, charging that he had actually been a

paid agent of the Musavat intelligence service and, as such, had carried
out traitorous acts against the Bolsheviks. It was standard practice during
the Stalin era and thereafter to accuse opponents of having been spies. As
early as 1920 the issue was raised by the Central Committee of the Azerbaidzhan Bolshevik organization and, according to Beria, resolved in his
favor. Thanks to the testimony of several comrades, he was exonerated.[27]
Nonetheless the charges never died, and Beria was to be forced to defend
himself against the accusations time and again, insisting that he had only
acted on the directions of the Bolsheviks. In fact, Beria's assignment
would not have been unusual, since historical accounts of this period show
that the Bolsheviks did assign their followers to pose as Musavatists in
order to attend their meetings and gather information.[28] But his opponents
chose to disregard this and insist that Beria had been acting on his own.

Beria gave up his undercover work in March 1920, taking up a job at
the Baku Customs House until the bolshevik seizure of power in Azerbaidzhan the next month. Shortly thereafter the Caucasian Bureau
(Kavburo) of the Central Committee of the RSDRP(B) assigned Beria to
underground work in Georgia, where he gathered intelligence for the
Revolutionary Military Council of the Bolshevik's Eleventh Army, which
was planning to overthrow the menshevik government of Georgia by
means of agitation and propaganda among the peasantry and proletariat,
calling for an armed uprising. In Tbilisi Beria set up a network of spies,
established secret contacts with members of the Georgian menshevik-con-
trolled army, and ran couriers back and forth to Baku. Not surprisingly,
he was soon arrested, along with the entire Bolshevik Central Committee
in Georgia. Thanks to the efforts of the Georgian Bolshevik Georgii
Sturua, Beria was freed on the condition that he leave Georgia within
three days. But he remained, adopting the false name of Lakerbaia and
working in the Russian Embassy, recently opened in Tbilisi as a result of
the establishment of formal diplomatic relations between Georgia and
Russia in early May 1920. Beria lived in the apartment of his first cousin,
Gerasim Beria, a student in Tbilisi.[29]

After the conclusion of a diplomatic treaty with Russia, the menshevik
government freed the jailed prisoners and legalized bolshevik publications, meetings, and demonstrations.[30] When the Bolsheviks took advantage of their new freedom by working actively to overthrow the menshevik government, however, the latter began to make new arrests. In late
May, upon returning from a mission to Baku, Beria was again arrested,
along with several others, and imprisoned in the town of Kutaisi. S. M.
Kirov, who arrived in Tbilisi that month as the first Soviet Ambassador
from the bolshevik government to Georgia, sent several notes of protest
to the Georgian government, claiming that the arrests and other repressions were a violation of the diplomatic treaty between Georgia and the
Russian Republic.[31]

Kirov's protests did not prompt the Mensheviks to release the prisoners, so the latter declared a hunger strike on 4 August. The strike ended after four and a half days because, in light of menshevik promises to respond to the demands, bolshevik leaders instructed the prisoners to give up their strike.[32] A few of the prisoners, including Beria, were released soon after and sent out of Georgia in a prison convoy.

Upon his return to Baku in August 1920 Beria enrolled as an architecture student in the newly established Baku Polytechnical Institute. He had little time for studies, however, because he was assigned to the position of administrator of affairs of the Azerbaidzhan Central Committee, a post that he held until October, when he became Secretary of the Extraordinary Commission for Expropriating the Bourgeoisie and Improving the Lot of the Workers.[33] As the name suggests, this organization was charged with forcibly seizing property on behalf of the Bolsheviks—a rather unsavory business—and Beria again was doing the paper work. When the commission was abolished in February 1921 Beria took the opportunity to persuade the Central Committee to support him in his studies as an architect-builder. He received a stipend from the Baku Soviet, but after only a couple of weeks the Central Committee made him abandon his studies to work in the Azerbaidzhan political police, the infamous Cheka.[34]

Among the leading members of the Azerbaidzhan Communist Party at this time were several men who later became key members of Stalin's entourage in Moscow: Kirov, who as head of the Eleventh Army successfully fought the antibolshevik White Army in the Caucasus and later became a member of the Azerbaidzhan Central Committee and Central Committee secretary; G. N. Kaminskii, sent from Moscow in September 1920 and a month later "elected" a member of the Politburo and secretary of the Azerbaidzhan Central Committee; and G. K. (Sergo) Ordzhonikidze, who became secretary of the Kavburo in 1920 and later secretary of the Transcaucasian Regional Party Committee (*Zakkraikom*).[35] Each of these men exerted a significant influence on Beria's early political career, particularly Ordzhonikidze, who became his mentor and served as his conduit to Stalin. Both Kaminskii and Ordzhonikidze were present in 1920 when Beria defended himself successfully against charges of working for the Musavats. But Kaminskii did nothing to dispel the subsequent rumors and, in fact, may have fueled them some years later.[36]

Beria may have met Stalin, or at least heard him speak, in November 1920, when Stalin visited Baku as part of an inspection trip throughout Caucasia. On 6 November Stalin gave a report to a session of the Baku Soviet entitled "Three Years of Proletarian Dictatorship," in which he analyzed the internal and international position of the Soviet state. He later addressed a plenum of the Azerbaidzhan Central Committee, remaining in Baku for several more days.[37] Stalin at this time was pushing for Sovietization of Georgia and Armenia (which were still independent states) and urging a bolshevik invasion. His plans were strongly backed by Kirov and Ordzhonikidze and, despite Lenin's reservations, the Bolsheviks succeeded in toppling the Armenian government in November 1920 and that of Georgia in February 1921.[38] Henceforth Beria's homeland of Georgia was to be an integral part of the new Soviet state. Whatever nationalist sentiments he may have felt toward his native Georgia, his future success lay with the internationalist tenets of Marxism and the forces of Sovietization.

MOVE TO THE CHEKA

The Azerbaidzhan Cheka (Extraordinary Commission for Fighting Counterrevolution and Sabotage) was established on 29 April 1920, immediately after the Bolsheviks took power there. Although nominally independent because of Azerbaidzhan's formal status as a separate republic, the Azerbaidzhan Cheka or AzCheka, like all the other republican Chekas, was actually controlled by the all-Russian Cheka (VeCheka) in Moscow, which in turn took its orders from the Politburo of the Russian Communist Party.[39] The Bolsheviks had established the VeCheka, with the infamous Feliks Dzerzhinskii as its chief, in December 1917 to suppress widespread opposition to their regime. Although originally authorized to uncover and investigate counterrevolutionary crimes, the VeCheka acquired powers of summary justice as opposition to the Bolsheviks grew. During the so-called Red Terror, from 1918 to 1920, the VeCheka and its subsidiaries unleashed widespread violence against many elements of the Russian population, in particular the landowning class.

By 1921, partly in response to growing criticism of its ruthless and violent methods, the VeCheka began to relax its terror in Russia. But the situation was somewhat different in the newly conquered Caucasian republics, where "political banditry" and nationalist ferment continued to pose a serious threat to the Bolsheviks. The new regime there, beseiged with opposition from numerous quarters, needed a strong political police to preserve its rule and was actively recruiting politically reliable employees to its ranks. Beria himself had already had one encounter with the AzCheka in mid-1920, when he was mistakenly arrested at his home and taken in for questioning. Thanks again to his friend Georgii Sturua, Beria was called, after some hours, into the office of the AzCheka chairman, who acknowledged the mistake and ordered Beria's release.[40]

Beria was a natural candidate for work in the Cheka. Cheka officers were recruited primarily from the ranks of young party members to which Beria belonged, and his background in underground activities and counterintelligence made him well suited for police work. Evgenii Dumbadze, a Georgian of Beria's age who entered the Georgian Cheka at this time, noted that most of those who joined were "green revolutionary youth" with idealistic notions of self-sacrifice. To him the Cheka represented something great, despite its unsavory reputation: "Whatever cruelty that [the Cheka] had to carry out receded, in my youthful conception at the time, into the foggy distance, and I pictured only the difficult, dangerous obligations in the name of humanity's happiness."[41] We have no way of knowing whether Beria shared any of these lofty sentiments or what his ideals and motivations were at this point. Although he made it clear in his 1923 autobiography that his overriding goal was to complete his education, this was to be done in the context of his service for the Bolsheviks, in whose hands Beria had placed his career. Given the choice, Beria might well not have worked in the Cheka, but he was ambitious and energetic and seemed willing to do anything that was required of him by his bolshevik superiors.

Beria's immediate superior in the AzCheka was M. D. Bagirov, an Azerbaidzhani who had joined the Bolshevik party in Baku in 1917. As an assistant to a local military commissar, Bagirov had engaged in bloody punitive operations against the populace, earning a reputation for extreme ruthlessness. Later, in 1920, he served as a deputy chairman of the Military Tribunal of the Eleventh Army, where he had collaborated with the Cheka's punitive organs within the military.[42] Thus, though he was young and had only been a member of the Bolshevik party for a short time, Bagirov was well suited to administer police repression on the part of the Bolsheviks.[43]

Bagirov, who rose to become party chief in Azerbaidzhan in the 1930s, was to play an important role in Beria's political career. The two had already become acquainted when Beria was conducting intelligence work for the Eleventh Army, and their renewed association in the Cheka forged a close relationship that was to be lifelong. By all accounts the men were cut from the same cloth, sharing a willingness to carry out the bloodiest and cruelest tasks for the sake of maintaining bolshevik rule and furthering their own careers. Both men were survivors, which in the Stalinist era required exceptional cunning, shrewdness, and a complete lack of moral scruples. What was unusual about their relationship was that, amid the intrigues and perfidy that characterized Stalinist politics for the next three decades, neither man moved against the other. Early on they apparently reached some sort of mutually protective modus vivendi, whereby they were comrades-in-arms in their efforts to achieve political success at any price. It was only after Beria's arrest in 1953 that Bagirov turned against him in a futile effort to save himself.

It may have been because of Bagirov's influence that Beria received an unusually high-ranking job in the AzCheka. Within a few weeks of his arrival, he was chief of the Secret-Operative Department and a deputy chairman of the AzCheka itself. The Secret-Operative Department was central to the functioning of the AzCheka, having overall leadership of all the other departments and carrying out a wide range of tasks, including combating counterrevolutionary crimes and counterespionage.[44] Not long after he assumed his post Beria recruited a young Georgian named Vladimir Dekanozov, an employee in the Cheka's economic section, to serve as his secretary. Dekanozov, who grew up in Baku, had been a medical student at Saratov University in Russia at the time the revolution broke out. After returning to Baku in 1918, he joined the Red Army and in 1921 became an employee of the Cheka. Like Bagirov, Dekanozov was to remain closely tied to Beria for the next thirty-two years.[45]

When Beria joined the Cheka, this organization was engaged in a fierce struggle against antibolshevik groups, including Muslim nationalists, Turks, Socialist-Revolutionaries, and Mensheviks. Some regions of Azerbaidzhan were in a virtual state of anarchy. In order to strengthen their efforts, in May 1921 the Bolsheviks created a Central Extraordinary Troika for the Struggle Against Banditry, headed by Bagirov, with subsidiary troikas at the local level. The troikas, which were empowered to shoot suspects on the spot, unleashed a bloody vendetta against bolshevik opponents. As head of the Secret-Operative Department, Beria played a key role in their operations. According to a report distributed to the delegates of the Second Azerbaidzhan Congress of Soviets in the spring of 1922: "Here it is essential to note that the apparatus of the secret-operative department of the AzCheka has borne on its shoulders almost all of the weight of the technical work of the extraordinary troikas in unmasking bandits as well as in conducting investigations."[46]

Thus Beria immediately plunged into the most bloody aspects of police work. As a result of its violent methods, the AzCheka, like its Russian counterpart, came under increasing criticism. The political opponents of bolshevism raised such a hue and cry about the "unprecedented horrors and terror carried out by the Cheka in its torture chambers" that the latter was forced to defend itself publicly. The report to the Second Azerbaidjan Congress defended the actions of the AzCheka on the grounds that subversion, banditry, and armed uprisings continued to threaten the Soviet regime.

According to later Soviet sources, the AzCheka's activities were so objectionable that they even aroused the protests of Bolsheviks in Azerbaidzhan, some of whom criticized Beria personally. In the spring of 1921 M. S. Kedrov, a prominent Bolshevik and a deputy of Dzerzhinskii, arrived in the Caucasus as plenipotentiary of the VeCheka in Moscow to inspect the operations of the republican Chekas.[47] Kedrov's biographer writes:

The inspection revealed more than strange business. Beria had released down-right enemies of the Soviet regime, closing their cases, while innocent people who had been slandered were convicted. Beria was only twenty-two years old then, and Mikhail Sergeevich Kedrov at first assumed that his youth and inexperience was behind this. But when the definitely hostile direction of Beria's activities manifested itself, Kedrov suspected treachery and informed Dzerzhinskii in Moscow.[48]

Kedrov wrote a letter describing Beria's failings and recommending that he be dismissed from his Cheka post. Kedrov's eldest son reportedly carried the letter to Moscow and delivered it to Dzerzhinskii's office. But the letter, inexplicably, produced no results, and Beria remained in his post. Later, in 1939, Kedrov and his younger son Igor, who worked under Beria in the NKVD, are said to have made renewed attempts to expose Beria's treachery and both were executed.[49]

What should be added to this account, however, is that Kedrov himself was a dubious and lowly character. As a leading Chekist he had earned a reputation for extreme cruelty in 1920 when he carried out sadistic reprisals on punitive expeditions against tsarist officers. In fact, he was eventually afflicted with bouts of insanity as a result of his cruel and brutal activities.[50] Kedrov's son Igor took part in several important NKVD cases in the thirties, demonstrating extreme ruthlessness. Thus, although both Kedrovs did fall victim to Beria's vengeance, it is doubtful that their moral indignation over Beria's failure to mete out justice was the reason for their demise.[51] More than likely, Kedrov simply had a disagreement with Beria that led him to complain to Dzerzhinskii.

Nevertheless, there can be little doubt that Azerbaidzhan Central Committee secretaries Kirov and Kaminskii were both concerned about the Cheka's growing powers. Kaminskii frequently stressed the importance of maintaining party control over police activities,[52] while Kirov, in May 1922, criticized the AzCheka for organizing surveillance of party members. This prompted a letter from Beria, who went to great lengths to defend himself and the Cheka to Kirov. On 27 June the latter responded with a letter to Beria in which he said:

Always observe that workers of your organization strive to the best of their ability to be objective, and above all, that they do not interfere in the internal life of party organizations, that their work does not assume that of secret agents, spying on party workers, as was noted in circular no. 90 of the Zakavkaz Kraikom of the Russian Communist Party.[53]

The question of relations between the party and the political police was a controversial one from the very beginning of the Soviet regime. While the party was supreme, it depended heavily on the police to enforce its rule, particularly in the early years. It was not always easy for party officials to keep the police reined in and to maintain tight controls over their activities. Nonetheless, the political police were strictly forbidden from arresting or even investigating party members. If, as this episode suggests, Beria was directing his employees to spy on the party, he was clearly overstepping his bounds and may well have aroused some bad feelings against him among party leaders in Azerbaidzhan. Some months earlier Kirov had written a very positive appraisal of Beria, noting that "Comrade Beria is an energetic and good Chekist, showing an aptitude for Chekist work."[54] But after seeing the direction that Beria's "Chekist energy" was taking, Kirov evidently began to have reservations about him.

Whatever the complaints about Beria—and he does seem to have become a controversial figure by this time—he performed his job effectively. Indeed, he was credited with unmasking several anti-Soviet organizations during 1921–22, along with remnants of the former Musavat regime.[55] In September 1922 the Azerbaidzhan Council of Peoples' Commissars announced that it had awarded Beria a gold watch for his courageous leadership and his outstanding service in liquidating the Socialist Revolutionary organization in Transcaucasia. For this same achievement he received a set of Browning automatic rifles from the central political police in Moscow.[56] He also gained prestige by extending his professional activities beyond the Cheka, serving on several government and party bodies, including the Azerbaidzhan Central Committee and the Baku Soviet.

MILESTONES

Although he was devoting much time and effort to his career, Beria did manage to make changes in his personal life. In the autumn of 1921 he married Nino Teimurazovna Gegechkori, a niece of the well-known Georgian Bolshevik Aleksandr (Sasha) Alekseevich Gegechkori. Sasha Gegechkori, who had led armed peasant uprisings against the menshevik government in Georgia, had been imprisoned at Kutaisi along with Beria in the summer of 1920.[57] When Gegechkori's wife, Meri, visited him in prison she brought along fifteen-year-old Nino, who was an orphan and was living with them in Kutaisi at the time. She was very beautiful, and Beria did not forget her. A year later, after the Bolsheviks took over Georgia, Nino moved to Tbilisi with the Sasha Gegechkori family and continued her studies. Beria became a frequent visitor to the family.

Nino was still a young and lighthearted schoolgirl. She once carelessly joined other students in a demonstration against the Bolsheviks, despite the fact that she was living in the home of a prominent Bolshevik. She later recalled, in an interview given when she was already in her mid-eighties, how on that occasion she came home soaking wet because the police had sprayed the student demonstrators with water. Sasha's wife, Meri, was furious, threatening to whip Nino because she had expressed opposition to the Bolsheviks.[58]

One day Beria stopped Nino on her way to school and asked her to meet him later for a talk. Nino agreed and when they met Beria proposed marriage. Nino recalled: "We sat on a bench. Lavrentii was wearing a black topcoat and a student's service cap. He told me that for a long time he had been very taken with me . . . what is more, he said that he loved me and wanted to marry me. I was sixteen years old at the time."[59] Beria explained to Nino that the Soviet government wanted to send him to Belgium to study oil processing, but he could only go if he had a wife. He promised that he would help Nino with her studies. Nino recalled: "I thought about it and then agreed. It was better to have one's own family than to live in someone else's."[60]

The two were married quickly, without telling anyone, perhaps because they thought that Nino's relatives would object. Beria then took Nino back with him to Baku. This may be why, as Nino explained in her interview, it was later rumored that Beria had kidnapped her and forced her to marry him, a rumor that she said had no foundation whatsoever.[61] In addition to her beauty, the fact that she was a Mingrelian and came from a family with strong bolshevik credentials made her a great asset to Beria. But, as Nino observed, Beria was so taken up with his work and career that he had little time for family life. The marriage was to become mainly a meaningless formality and the source of great unhappiness for his wife.[62]

Beria's trip to Belgium never took place, probably because his Cheka duties took precedence, but he and Nino lived in Baku for only one year. By late 1922 the political situation in Azerbaidzhan had settled down somewhat. There was still serious opposition to bolshevik rule in Georgia, however, and the strong arm of the Cheka was needed more there, so Beria was transferred to Tbilisi in November. There he assumed the same post he had held in Azerbaidzhan, that of head of the Secret-Operative Department and deputy chairman of the republican Cheka.[63]

That Beria was a Georgian made him a logical candidate for a transfer to his native republic. The Bolsheviks probably wanted more Georgians to serve in the Cheka, which at the time had only a small number of native employees.[64] The policy of recruiting natives to serve in the republican party and state administration was beginning to take hold in Transcaucasia. This policy was to become part of a more general strategy called *korenizatsiia* (indigenization), officially established in April 1923 at the Twelfth Congress of the RSDRP(B). With respect to the Georgian Cheka in particular, there were obvious advantages to hiring natives, who could accomplish their tasks more effectively with knowledge of the language and culture. Also, perhaps, repression applied by natives was seen to be more palatable than repression by Russians. Beria, whose tenure in the Georgian political police was characterized by ruthless treatment of any form of political opposition, would put this assumption to a severe test.

GEORGIAN POLITICS AFTER THE BOLSHEVIK TAKEOVER

Beria's transfer to Tbilisi coincided with the culmination of a bitter struggle among Bolsheviks about the way in which social and political transformation was to be achieved in Georgia. The new bolshevik government, led by the Georgian Revkom (Revolutionary Committee), enjoyed so little support among the population that it faced the distinct prospect of insurrection and civil war. The Bolsheviks had few ties with the Georgian peasantry, which was intensely dissatisfied over land shortages and other economic troubles. The highly politicized proletariat, with its strong menshevik tradition, was equally hostile toward the new regime, as was the intelligentsia.[65] One group of Georgian Bolsheviks, led by Filipp Makharadze and Budu Mdivani and encouraged by Lenin, favored a moderate approach toward securing Soviet power. They advocated tolerance toward the menshevik opposition, greater democracy within the party, gradual land reform, and more scope for private trade. Above all, they urged that consideration be given to national sensitivities and opposed an assault on Georgian sovereignty by the Soviet government. As Makharadze observed in a report to the Central Committee of the RSDRP(B) in Moscow in late 1921:

> We must realize that the Georgian masses got accustomed to the idea of an independent Georgia. . . . We had to demonstrate that we based our position on the independence of Georgia, but in words only, while in effect we rejected it and did not have it as our objective. [This is] an intolerable situation, as it is impossible to deceive the masses in a political question of that nature, and especially the Georgian people, who in recent years had gone through the ordeals of fire and water.[66]

Another group, led by Sergo Ordzhonikidze, head of the Transcaucasian Regional Committee (*Zaikkraikom*) of the Russian Communist Party, and Stalin, People's Commissar for Nationalities for the Russian Republic, advocated a harder line. They launched a drive to unite the Transcaucasian republics economically and politically, with little concern for Georgian national sentiment. Over the opposition of many leading Georgian Bolsheviks, Ordzhonikidze and Stalin managed to impose a treaty on Georgia, uniting it with Armenia and Azerbaidzhan into a loose federation of Transcaucasian republics in March 1922. Then, step by step, they reduced the prerogatives of the separate republics.[67]

The efforts of the "centralizers," as Stalin and his supporters were called, culminated in the establishment of a single Soviet republic, the Transcaucasian Federated Soviet Socialist Republic (ZSFSR) in December 1922. Three weeks later the new federation entered the newly created Union of Soviet Socialist Republics (USSR) as a single entity, despite strenuous attempts on the part of the Makharadze-Mdivani group to have Georgia enter as a separate republic. Meanwhile Lenin, who had favored only some form of economic integration for Transcaucasia, became alarmed over the bitterness of the conflict among Georgian Bolsheviks and sent a special commission to Tbilisi in late November 1922 to investigate the matter. The commission was led by VeCheka Chief Dzerzhinskii, whose sympathies lay with Stalin and Ordzhonikidze and who consequently tried to give Lenin a favorable picture of their activities in the commission report. But Lenin realized that the tactics of the centralizers were high-handed and insensitive and demanded that abuses against the Georgians cease.[68]

Although Stalin and Ordzhonikidze made some concessions to those who supported Georgian sovereignty, Lenin's incapacitation through illness prevented him from defending the latter group. In March 1923 Lenin tried to enlist Leon Trotsky to take over the Georgian problem, but Trotsky declined to confront Stalin on the issue.[69] Georgian national rights were gradually eroded from 1922 onward. Beria's appointment to the Georgian Cheka was a part of this process in the sense that it placed him in the camp of hardliners who had contempt for specifically Georgian concerns and seemingly little personal identification with their national interests. Ironically, the most chauvinistic officials in defending Russian prerogatives against Georgians were non-Russians who had been assimilated, such as Stalin, Ordzhonikidze, and Dzerzhinskii. Stalin, for example, had visited Tbilisi in July 1921 and delivered a fiery speech against nationalist tendencies, ordering local leaders to "crush the hydra of nationalism."[70] Although Beria never proved to be the "Russian chauvinist" that these men were, in that he later demonstrated considerable flexibility on the nationality question, he now showed no hesitation in backing the hardliners.

It is not clear who initiated Beria's transfer to the Georgian Cheka, but it was probably Ordzhonikidze. Ordzhonikidze sent another Georgian to serve in the Georgian Cheka at this time, so he may have ordered Beria's transfer as well.[71] Beria had already proved himself in Azerbaidzhan to be an effective and ruthless suppressor of political opposition. So he was the ideal man to execute similar operations in Georgia, which was teeming with political dissent, particularly on the part of Georgian nationalists. From this point onward, Beria's influence grew as the political police gained an increasing role in Georgian politics. The success of his career was closely tied to the defeat of the "national communists," those who favored more independence for Georgia, and the consequent victory of the advocates of strong centralized control by Moscow.

Chapter Two

SERVICE IN THE GEORGIAN POLITICAL POLICE

> The silence of death hung over Georgia.
> *(David Sagirashvili, unpublished memoirs)*

THE GEORGIAN CHEKA

THE GEORGIAN Cheka was established in February 1921, immediately following the Soviet invasion. Given the widespread political opposition, this organization was crucial to the Bolsheviks' survival. Its first permanent chairman was O. M. (Kote) Tsintsade, a longtime Bolshevik who had served during the 1905 revolution as head of Social Democratic armed detachments that engaged in expropriation and robbery. Although ruthless, Tsintsade was a strong proponent of Georgian sovereignty and took an active role in struggling against the Stalin–Ordzhonikidze line. This is presumably why he was removed from his Cheka post before the year was out.[1] His successor, and Beria's superior until 1926, was another Georgian, E. A. Kvantaliani, who was more amenable to the policies of the centralizers.[2]

As part of a reform of the political police, the VeCheka in Moscow was abolished in February 1922 and replaced by a State Political Administration (GPU) with subordinate adminstrations in the republics. In early 1923, with the creation of the USSR, the GPU became the Unified State Political Administration (OGPU). But the police reform did not affect Transcaucasia. Here, as a consequence of continued political turbulence, Chekas were retained until July 1926.[3] When the Transcaucasian Republic, or ZSFSR, was created in December 1922, it established a Cheka, but each of the three member republics—Georgia, Armenia, and Azerbaidzhan—retained their own Chekas, subordinate to that of Transcaucasia. The headquarters of both the Transcaucasian and Georgian Chekas were located in the same building in Tbilisi.

Beria wore the standard Chekist uniform: a serge field jacket and riding breeches, tucked into leather boots.[4] Of less than medium height and a somewhat stocky build, he had a round head with a broad, prominent nose, beady eyes, and a receding hairline fringed with dark black hair. His protruding eyes, seen through the pince-nez glasses that he wore all his life, have been variously described as green, yellow, or "cold blue," but most descriptions concur that his face was unpleasant.[5]

Beria and his wife established their home in a large, third-floor apartment at no. 57 Kiacheli Street, where they remained throughout Beria's tenure in the Georgian political police. According to Nino Beria, they lived modestly: "The times were such that to live well was shameful; there was a struggle against wealth."[6] Their private life was closely meshed with Beria's career. It was the fad then for families to live communally so Beria persuaded his boss, Kvantaliani, and his family to share quarters with him and Nino. The brother of Sergo Ordzhonikidze, Papulia, also lived in the same building. These arrangements suited Beria well, since he was highly ambitious and anxious to cultivate relations with important party and government figures in Tbilisi.[7]

Like the political police in Moscow and other republics, the Georgian Cheka contained a heterogeneous racial mix, with many Jews, Latvians, and Armenians, for example. A large number of these Chekists came from the Eleventh Army, which had been disbanded in June 1921.[8] Since most of these young men were from out of town, they resided in a dormitory that was set up in an old hotel. Beria would occasionally join them there in the evenings, when they would gather to sing and dance. According to historian Antonov-Ovseenko, his participation in the merrymaking had ulterior motives:

> At first everyone trusted Lavrentii Beria completely; but upon knowing him better they were not able to be friendly with him: he was a master of intrigue and denunciation. Like no one else he was able at the right moment to unleash a nasty rumor in order to ensnare his rivals on the way to the top. Then he would persecute them one by one. In doing so the young Beria, whenever necessary, would convincingly play the role of a "good old chap," simple and jolly.[9]

The portrayal of Beria here is borne out by testimony from others who came to know him well. He was to become, by the late 1920s, a master of political intrigue and Machiavellian tactics.

Beria did not treat all his colleagues with perfidy, however, because he apparently realized early on the importance of building a loyal following. Thus he surrounded himself from the beginning with a coterie of young Chekists who were to remain allied with him for the duration of his political career. Most were Georgians: Vladimir Dekanozov, Avksentii Rapava, Lavrentii Tsanava, Aleksei Sadzhaia, Shota Tsereteli, and Nikolai Rukhadze, a latecomer to the group who joined the police in 1926 after a brief career in the Komsomol (Communist Youth League). In addition there was Vsevold Merkulov and Bogdan Kobulov, both Armenians; and Solomon Mil'shtein, a Polish Jew from Vil'no. These men comprised the core of what was later derisively described as "Beria's gang," a cohort that rose to power in Georgia, and later in Moscow, by inflicting the severest repression on the population.

It is hard to imagine bonds of friendship among men who were capable of unspeakable cruelty. According to the Communist Viktor Serge: "The only temperaments that devoted themselves willingly and tenaciously to this task of 'internal defence' were those characterized by suspicion, embitterment, harshness and sadism . . . the Chekas inevitably consisted of perverted men tending to see conspiracy everywhere and to live in the midst of perpetual conspiracy themselves."[10] The Georgian writer Geronti Kikodze portrayed Chekists in Georgia similarly: "In the Cheka the ranks of investigator, secret agent, commander and executioner were filled by men without kith or kin, who in most cases knew no trade, had no education and were skilled only in espionage and murder. Some were sadists by nature, some entered the service as insurance for themselves."[11]

Evgenii Dumbadze described one particularly unsavory Chekist named Shul'man, who was chief of the Commandant's Office (responsible for physical security of personnel, for guarding prisons, and for carrying out executions). Dumbadze states that, although Shul'man murdered with his own hands no fewer than three hundred people during Dumbadze's tenure in the Georgian Cheka, he did not give the impression of being some sort of a vampire:

> He was essentially a bureaucrat. In his personal life, as far as I know, Shul'man was an exemplary family man. But in order to create in himself the necessary bloodthirsty mood of the "commandant of death," he would narcoticize himself by every means available and bring himself to a complete state of insanity.[12]

Outwardly, most members of "Beria's gang" projected the image of rational, efficient bureaucrats, just as Beria did. Indeed some, such as the former medical student Dekanozov, and Merkulov, who had studied mathematics at St. Petersburg University, were well educated. In academic attainment they were a cut above the average Chekist, which may explain why Beria cultivated them. Merkulov, in particular, was useful to Beria because of his Russian language skills. Beria's Russian was fluent but lacking in grammatical precision, so he came to rely on Merkulov to write speeches and articles for him.[13] That some of these men—Tsanava, Rapava, and Sadzhaia—were also Mingrelians served as an additional attraction. Beria felt a strong loyalty toward Mingrelia and probably was most comfortable when surrounded by his closest countrymen.

CHEKIST TERROR IN GEORGIA

Widespread opposition to the bolshevik regime in Georgia and other parts of Transcaucasia continued to be met with fierce repression by the authorities long after the police had eased their grip in Soviet Russia. In

1922 several rebellions erupted in various parts of Georgia, with guerrilla detachments fighting against the Bolsheviks. By the time Beria took up his post in the Georgian Cheka, a bloody vendetta against "counterrevolutionary elements" had been underway for some time, and summary justice, administered by the political police, was routine. Two months earlier, for example, the Georgian Communist Party newspaper, *Zaria vostoka* [Dawn of the East], had announced that "on the orders of the Georgian Cheka Presidium" a group of twenty "political bandits," led by princes and noblemen, had been shot. Included in the announcement was a declaration of the Cheka that it would "struggle against banditry in the most merciless way and not permit groups of former princes and noblemen with their ruffians to hamper the Soviet regime's constructive work for the betterment of the workers and peasants of Georgia."[14]

No official figures on the rate of Cheka arrests or killings in Georgia are available for this period but, judging from the accounts of Dumbadze and others, executions were an everyday occurrence, and often dispatched large groups at one time.[15] Dumbadze states that the press reported executions only when it had a political motive for doing so and estimates that, in 80 percent of cases, they were not publicized.[16] Cases of anti-Soviet resistance almost always resulted in the death sentence, and reprisals were often inflicted on families of the accused, who were imprisoned or deported. The Cheka arrested some victims simply for belonging to the wrong social class.[17]

In 1923, when the "national deviationists" were defeated and lost their influence over the bolshevik leadership in Georgia, repression intensified and the police stepped up arrests. Previously the regime had adopted a more tolerant attitude toward Mensheviks, because Georgian Bolsheviks such as Makharadze and Mdivani had personal ties with them.[18] By the summer of 1923, however, the Stalin–Ordzhonikidze line had prevailed and oppositionist parties, including the Mensheviks, were ruthlessly persecuted. This forced the opposition underground, where it continued its struggle despite defections and arrests by the Cheka.[19]

In October 1923 a secret Committee for the Independence of Georgia, which united all antibolshevik parties under the guidance of the Mensheviks, decided to organize an armed uprising. The Cheka, with Beria playing a leading role, managed to penetrate the organization and carried out mass arrests of its members. But the opposition went ahead with plans for the uprising, which occurred in August 1924.[20] It seems that Beria and his superior, Kvantaliani, actually encouraged the rebellion so they would have a pretext for destroying all political opposition. One captured rebel leader, Valiko Dzhugeli, requested Cheka officials to allow him to inform his comrades that their plans had been discovered and advise them to abandon their proposed revolt, but the Cheka refused and the uprising went ahead.[21] Although the rebels managed for a few days to hold large areas of Western Georgia where menshevik influence was strong, the revolt was unsuccessful.

Beria's perfidious role in handling the uprising was played out to the fullest on 4 September, when he met with several members of the Committee for Independence who had been arrested and imprisoned by the Cheka in Tbilisi. According to one testimony, Beria made the following proposal to the prisoners, who were tied up and facing execution:

> You are defeated, but the fighting continues here and there. We will certainly be able to exterminate these detachments but it will entail shedding blood in vain. You, the committee, are able to stop these armed detachments; make a declaration urging these isolated detachments to put down their arms and on our side we will not harm them and we will stop all arrests and mass executions.[22]

The imprisoned committee members accepted the proposal on the condition that an order to stop the mass executions be given immediately. Beria responded: "If the committee agrees, at the very instant the declaration is published the government will give the order everywhere, by direct line, to stop the executions." When asked whether or not the Cheka's decision would be approved by the government, Beria said: "Whatever is decided in this office is at the same time the government's decision." In fact, the declaration did more than urge the rebels to put down their arms. It discredited the uprising by calling it "an adventure carried out by the upper classes." But the committee members, facing death themselves, signed it in order to put an end to the bloodshed.[23]

The terror did not end, however. Having extorted this damning document from the committee leaders, Cheka officials had it published immediately, both at home and in the foreign press. They then proceeded with mass arrests and executions in flagrant violation of the agreement made by Beria with rebel leaders. The Bolsheviks retaliated against their erstwhile opponents with extreme ferocity. Armed detachments, composed of army and Cheka troops, raided villages and killed entire families. In one Georgian village all families bearing one particular last name were completely annihilated, including women and small children.[24] Some estimates on the number of those arrested and executed by the Cheka ranged as high as seven thousand to ten thousand, including prominent menshevik leaders.[25]

The persecution of the rebels and their families continued for some time.[26] Tsitsna Cholokashvili, the young daughter of an opposition leader, found herself moving in and out of Cheka prisons, together with her mother and younger sister, for several years. They endured beatings, starvation, and interrogations at the hands of the Chekists. Cholokashvili described one incident at the Telavi prison during 1924, when a young Chekist was suddenly confronted with his father, who was sentenced to be executed along with a whole group in one night. When ordered to shoot his own father, the young man shot his two superiors. This led to an all-night "blood orgy" in which hundreds of prisoners were massacred. "The streets were red with blood," recalled Cholokashvili.[27]

However cruel the Chekists were in suppressing the rebels, the party leadership was firmly behind them. Mikhail Kakhiani, a member of the Georgian Central Committee, made a speech shortly after the revolt in which he congratulated the Cheka for "acting splendidly" by quelling the rising so precipitously. He also stated: "Let everyone remember that the Soviet regime deals cruelly and mercilessly with those who are considered to be organizers of the insurrection. . . . If we had not shot them we would have committed a great crime against the Georgian workers. . . . Only with the language of revolutionary, merciless power can one talk to the pitiful, cowardly Mensheviks."[28] Dumbadze relates how at this time he saw a truckload of half-naked menshevik prisoners being transported down Ol'ginskaia Street in Tbilisi on their way to be shot. Behind this gloomy procession, in a shiny, chic automobile was a small group that included Kakhiani and Beria, who were presumably going along to witness the executions.[29]

These victims would get neither a proper burial nor any of the elaborate funeral rites that Beria had no doubt experienced on countless occasions as he grew up in his native Mingrelia. Instead they would be thrown into mass graves, where no members of their families would even be able to pay their respects. One wonders how Beria, still a young man in his mid-twenties, was able to deny so totally the morals and the values of his family and culture. He apparently had been strongly influenced by the frenzied atmosphere of terror that he had been engulfed in since the early days of bolshevik rule. Lenin and the Bolsheviks had justified terror as a legitimate weapon to be used in the defense of their cause—the success of the revolution. Increasingly, the line between revolutionary justice and indiscriminate killing had become blurred and those who inflicted the terror became inured to death.

The suppression of the menshevik rising served as Beria's final initiation into the business of mass killing, and his effectiveness in dealing with the rebellion was not lost on bolshevik leaders in Georgia. Nonetheless the public outcry over the brutalities of the Cheka had unpleasant repercussions for the Soviet regime in Moscow, which set up a special Politburo commission, led by Transcaucasian Party Chief Sergo Ordzhonikidze, to investigate the causes of the revolt and the extent of the terror. In October 1924, following the issuance of the commission's report, the Georgian Cheka was purged of "unreliable elements."[30] Presumably the Moscow leadership needed to offer up some Chekists as scapegoats in

order to mollify critics. But Beria escaped blame, as did his boss, Kvantaliani. Beria may well have been protected by Ordzhonikidze, with
whom he had become personally close. When Nino Beria gave birth to a
son in 1924, he was named "Sergo" after Ordzhonikidze, who also became his godfather.[31]

The failure of the uprising and the intensified police repression that
followed decimated the Menshevik movement in Georgia to the point
where it no longer represented a political threat to the Bolsheviks. But
Beria and his fellow Chekists continued to use the menshevik danger as
an excuse for reprisals against Georgians, particularly intellectuals and
former noblemen. During 1925–26 at least five hundred socialists were
shot without trial.[32] There was also the question of continued opposition
to the Stalinist line within the Bolshevik party itself, which Beria was
following closely, filing reports that eventually reached Stalin.

Precisely when Stalin and Beria became acquainted cannot be established with certainty, but it was probably in the mid-1920s. According to
the Georgian Communist Devi Sturua, Stalin visited Tsakhaltubo in the
mountains of Western Georgia during the summer of 1924 and expressed
the desire to have a vacation house there. Beria, probably relying on
prison labor, arranged to have the house built in record time, thereby
ingratiating himself with Stalin. Henceforth he made it a point to be on
hand whenever Stalin came to the Caucasus for a vacation.[33]

One rumor that linked Stalin and Beria at this time concerned the
deaths in a March 1925 air crash of S. G. Mogilevskii, chairman of the
Transcaucasian Cheka, and two other officials. The cause of the crash
(the plane blew up in mid-air not far from Tbilisi) was never determined,
despite the fact that three separate commissions later investigated the incident. Some suspected that Beria had arranged the catastrophe on Stalin's
behalf. Antonov-Ovseenko claims that Beria had his own motives for
doing so—the fact that these officials had information on him as well as
on Stalin that could prove politically harmful.[34] Others said that Beria
wanted to get rid of Mogilevskii in order that he might step into his
post.[35]

Leon Trotsky, despite the fact that he was Stalin's archenemy, apparently did not suspect foul play. He had been in the city of Sukhumi at the
time and claimed that the three men had been on their way to see him
as emissaries from Stalin.[36] Whatever the circumstances of the crash,
Mogilevskii's death provided Beria with the opportunity for self-promo-
tion. *Zaria Vostoka* published a gushing eulogy of Mogilevskii by Beria,
who managed to say more about himself than about his deceased
comrades:

> I saw the shocking place where our comrades perished. I saw the disfigured
> remains of the man under whose leadership I worked for two years in the

Cheka. . . . I cannot believe it, I don't want to believe it. . . . I will never again hear the soft voice of Solomon Grigorevich. . . .

In keeping with the dear habit that he possessed, he embraced me with one hand around my back and, quickly walking around his office, he began to present his views on the future tasks of the Cheka in Transcaucasia. Maximum initiative in the localities, independence in the work of the individual Chekas . . . I remember his especially attentive attitude towards me and the work of the Azerbaidzhan Cheka: "We here depend on you," he told me in comradely conversations. . . . We must make an unbreakable vow—first, as under him, to continue the struggle with all sworn enemies of communism and Soviet power in the Caucasus.[37]

In describing his close relationship with Mogilevskii and the latter's high opinion of him, Beria implied that he was Mogilevskii's handpicked successor. But Beria was still only a deputy chairman of the Georgian GPU at this time and such a promotion would have meant jumping over the heads of more senior Chekists. Mogilevskii's post was filled in early 1926 by I. P. Pavlunovskii, a prominent Russian Chekist, who remained in this job until 1928.[38] Pavlunovskii's appointment did not sit well with Beria, who may have felt that, as a Georgian with five years of police experience in the Caucasus, he should have been running things. Konstantin Ordzhonikidze, the brother of Sergo, later described an incident that occurred when Stalin visited Tbilisi in June 1926. Beria and Pavlunovskii were riding with Stalin in a car that included Ordzhonikidze and others when Beria remarked sarcastically: "This is Georgia and Pavlunovskii has nothing to do here."[39]

LEADER OF THE GEORGIAN GPU

Not long after this incident Beria did achieve a promotion to the post of Chairman of the Georgian GPU, and Kvantaliani was shunted off to apparent obscurity.[40] (The designation was changed from that of Cheka in 1926, but this did not result in organizational or operational changes.) In his new post, Beria zealously defended his prerogatives against those of Pavlunovskii, whom he did his best to discredit. Merkulov later recalled that once when Beria was away in Moscow he went to seek advice from Pavlunovksii. Beria was furious when he returned and found this out.[41] Tension between Beria and Pavlunovskii did not abate until the latter returned to Moscow in 1928. Then, for some reason, Pavlunovskii decided to mend fences with Beria in late 1929, sending him a conciliatory letter in which he assured Beria that he, Beria, was not to blame for the differences between them and said that in general his memories of their work together was positive.[42]

By this time Beria's reputation had earned him, and the GPU as a whole, many enemies. At least one attempt was made on Beria's life during his tenure in the Georgian GPU, and probably more. On one occasion, he was reportedly traveling in a convoy of two or three cars along the Georgian Military Highway to Tbilisi when the convoy ran into an ambush by Georgian terrorists. Some of his fellow Chekists were killed, but Beria survived—according to one version, he opened fire on the terrorists and thus covered the remaining passengers in his car—and received an award for his bravery.[43]

Beria's promotion at the Fifth Party Congress of Georgia in 1927, which gave him a seat on the Georgian Central Committee, coincided with important personnel changes in the Georgian and Transcaucasian party apparatuses. Sergo Ordzhonikidze, who had long been the most powerful official in the Caucasus, left his post as First Secretary of the Transcaucasian party and moved to Moscow, where he became chairman of the party's Central Control Commission (TsKK), as well as head of the Workers' and Peasants' Inspectorate (RABKRIN). Ordzhonikidze's elevated status and his personal proximity to Stalin gave him considerable political influence. He was "a friend in high places" for Beria, and Beria pinned his hopes for political advancement directly on him, doing everything possible to curry his favor. Beria began to write regularly to "Dear Sergo," keeping him abreast of political developments in Transcaucasia, with the obvious intention of having his rather biased and self-serving interpretations of what transpired there passed on to Stalin. Almost childlike in his eagerness for approval and encouragement from his mentor, Beria was upset by even the slightest criticism. Once in 1928, after learning that he had displeased Sergo, he dispatched a fawning letter of apology for his "inadvertent offence" and declared his devotion to him: "Your trust in me gives me all my energy, initiative and ability to work. Without you Sergo, I would have no one. You are more than a brother or a father to me."[44]

Ordzhonikidze's friend Mamia Orakhelashvili took over his vacated Transcaucasian post in November 1926. Like Ordzhonikidze, Orakhelashvili was no moderate. A staunch adherent of Stalin's policies, he was prepared to deal harshly with the new leftist opposition that had appeared in the Communist party as a result of mounting dissatisfaction with the party's economic policies. Initially Orakhelashvili was on friendly terms with Beria because they both saw eye-to-eye. Indeed, his advocacy of hard-line policies in Transcaucasia made the political climate conducive to Beria's advancement. But by the end of the 1920s their relationship had begun to deteriorate, largely because of Beria's attempts to undermine Orakhelashvili behind his back.

The first secretary of the Georgian party, Mikhail Kakhiani, would also fall victim to Beria's machinations, but only after a long period of

close cooperation with him. Kakhiani was a staunch advocate of the Stalinist line on opposition, instigating the ouster of several prominent left-
ists from the Central Committee in 1926. The illegal activities of these
groups, which the GPU no doubt had a hand in exposing, was strongly
condemned at party meetings throughout Georgia and their members
were threatened with reprisals. Party members were still protected from
outright arrest by the GPU, but this did not prevent the GPU from conducting investigations and maintaining files on them, which proved useful
for later prosecutions.[45] The GPU, with Kakhiani's sanction, kept an even
closer eye on the intelligentsia. In early 1927 Beria signed an order dis-
banding an association of Georgian artists on the grounds that it had ties
with "national chauvinist" groups who were out of touch with the
masses. He also ordered the famous Rustaveli Theater to be kept under
close party control.[46]

By 1929, with most of the overt dissent to Stalinist policies suppressed,
Beria began to turn against his comrades in the party leadership, with
subtle, behind-the-scenes attacks. Though he was not high in the party
hierarchy, Beria, by virtue of his police post, had potentially incriminating information on numerous party leaders, which he did not hesitate to
use to influence things in his favor. Moreover, he had a direct line to the
party leadership in Moscow because of his close relationship with Sergo
Ordzhonikidze. In his letters to Ordzhonikidze Beria displayed his strategy of "rumor-mongering" to the fullest, selectively passing on information against party officials while at the same time trying to present himself
as an innocent bystander.

Transcaucasian politics at this time was dominated by bitter in-fighting
and intense personal rivalries. While to some extent the Moscow leadership remained above the fray, allowing regional officials to fight it out
among themselves, both Stalin and Ordzhonikidze followed developments there closely and sometimes intervened to ensure adherence to their
policies, as well as to enforce discipline. In September 1929 a delegation
from Ordzhonikidze's Central Control Commission, the party's disciplinary body, was sent down to Transcaucasia to investigate reports of illegalities and excesses among party and state officials. Not surprisingly, the
commission's visit created a turmoil in official circles and gave rise to a
flurry of denunciations, denials, and recriminations among local leaders,
who had grown accustomed to feathering their nests with material luxu-
ries and ignoring the law when enforcing their rule.

Azerbaidzhan was the first republic to come under the commission's
scrutiny. As a result, Azerbaidzhan Central Committee Secretary Levon
Mirzoian lost his post, along with several other officials. Reporting on
this event to Ordzhonikidze, Beria complained that everyone blamed him,
Kakhiani, and another Georgian party official, Levon Gogoberidze, for
Mirzoian's dismissal: "Mirzoian's notes took us all by surprise. I read his

explanation, where he writes that I, Levon and Misha persecuted him, collected materials against him and so on. This is not true. We all exhibited the maximum loyalty towards him personally."[47] Beria also took the opportunity to criticize Mamia Orakhelashvili, who had defended Mirzoian and other members of the Azerbaidzhan leadership: "I cannot refrain from giving you my personal opinion that Mamia in these complex circumstances has proven to be a great hindrance. In Baku [Azerbaidzhan's capital] no one pays him any attention. The whole Baku incident completely discredited him."[48]

Beria was not in a position to interfere in the commission's work by attempting to protect someone, however. So he could do little when his friend Bagirov, the republic GPU chief, was rebuked for permitting excessive violence by GPU organs and removed from his post, along with several deputies.[49] As it turned out, Bagirov was not completely dishonored. He managed to ride out the scandal by remaining in Moscow at the Party's Institute of Marxism-Leninism for the next two and a half years.[50] Nonetheless, Bagirov's troubles disquieted Beria, who was undoubtedly worried that the commission's investigation would extend to him. Thus he stressed to Ordzhonikidze that "the effort of these comrades [from the commission] to make generalizations about things in Georgia and to make analogies with Baku are wrong. In Georgia, as everywhere else, there are not a few scandals. But it is not possible to compare it to Baku."[51]

Two days later Beria wrote another lengthy letter to Sergo, reporting that the special commission had decided to investigate the Transcaucasian and the Georgian GPU: "I of course personally have nothing against such an investigation," he assured Ordzhonikidze defensively, "except that it could not reveal anything more than we ourselves have uncovered." He went on to point out that he and his colleagues had already discovered many of the irregularities and "unhealthy practices" in the various parts of their organization. But when they tried to do something about it they met with strong opposition from party officials like Mamia Orakhelashvili and Nestor Lakoba from Abkhazia. The commission was blaming Beria and his men for being too lenient with GPU officials who break the law, but the party leadership had tied their hands. "Whenever there is a crisis," Beria lamented, "everyone absolves himself of responsibility and blames it on the GPU." He went on to describe the tremendous amount of work that his organization had to do: "It is enough only to mention the struggle with anti-Soviet parties . . . in order to judge what we accomplish in our daily work. In the Trotskyite organizations alone we eliminated more than 250 people at one time last month. . . . This is not to mention the struggle with banditry, with economic crimes and so on. Of course after all this it is offensive to listen to such criticism."[52]

Beria was obviously "under the gun" and desperately anxious to get Ordzhonikidze's support. It was typical, he complained, that at the very time when there was a lot to do and the Central Control Commission delegation was here, all of his colleagues in the party had gone off on vacation. Everyone was always finding excuses to avoid responsibility, Beria went on, and there was no strong leadership in Transcaucasia— another dig at Mamia Orakhelashvili—to change things. He ended his letter with a plea:

> Dear Sergo, I have raised the question of my departure with you more than once. This is not a caprice, or something of that sort, but a serious necessity. Every "new episode" brings me new enemies. I will give as an example my speech during the discussion of the report of the commission of the TsKK [Central Control Commission]. I didn't want to hide or cover up anything. I said openly what I knew and called things by their own names. This displeased many people. I gained enemies and nonetheless the commission reproached me for not saying what I knew. I don't know how to show my sincerity. It turns out that it is bad to talk and bad not to talk. . . . Dear Sergo, if it is not possible for me to study, then at least transfer me to other work. After all, I can't argue with everyone for my lifetime—this will ruin my nerves. Allow me the possibility to work in another area, if only in the area of industry (where the basis of all our construction lies) I will prove that I can not only uncover hostile crimes and criminals, but also carry out creative work. I beg of you, help me somehow, because I feel that I cannot go on much longer.[53]

Ordzhonikidze did not yield to Beria's entreaties and secure his transfer from Georgia, but he did protect him from disciplinary measures by the Central Control Commission. Moreover, he may have passed on Beria's complaints about Mamia Orakhelashvili to Stalin, because Stalin removed him from his post as party leader of Transcaucasia, replacing him sometime in the autumn of 1929 with a party official from Belorussia, A. I. Krinitskii.

An additional impetus for Mamia Orakhelashvili's removal may have been his objections to the rapid pace of the anti-kulak and collectivization campaigns, in which Beria played an active role. These campaigns were part of Stalin's "revolution from above," a program—launched in 1928—of rapid industrialization to be financed by compulsory requisitions from the peasantry. Peasant resistance to the government policy of securing grain at low prices led the central party leadership to decide that individual peasant agriculture had to collectivized and kulaks, or wealthy peasants, eliminated in order to implement this policy. In Georgia, where the peasantry was poorer than in Russia and the average landholding smaller, the party leadership at first adopted a moderate policy toward the peasants and avoided the confiscation measures that were carried out in Russia. But the central leadership began to exert pressure on Georgian party officials to take a more aggressive posture, extending the decision-making powers of the Transcaucasian-level organs at the expense of those of the individual republics. Those who objected to the imposition of the harsh policies of the center, including Mamia Orakhelashvili, were routed out of the Georgian leadership.[54]

With the moderates silenced, the war against the peasantry in Georgia and Transcaucasia began in earnest. Following a November 1929 plenum of the *Zakkraikom*, at which the new leader, Krinitskii, ordered party officials to maximize their efforts at collectivization, extreme methods of coercion were applied. The percentage of collectivized households in Georgia increased sharply, from 3.5 percent in October 1929 to 63.7 percent by March 1930.[55] The simultaneous "campaign to eliminate the kulaks as a class" amounted to no less than a violent and indiscriminate onslaught against the peasantry. Given that the number of well-off peasant households in Georgia was insignificant, thousands of medium-income peasants had their lands and belongings confiscated and were exiled or placed in concentration camps along with actual kulaks.

Resistance on the part of the peasants—and there was a great deal—was met with brutal reprisals by the GPU, the militia, and the army. On 6 January 1930 the Zakkraikom passed a resolution "requesting the judicial-investigative, punitive organs to conduct a widespread and more decisive struggle with kulak elements and especially to strengthen repression in cases of kulak terror, of actions against kolkhozes, poor peasants, farm laborers and so on. In these cases the method of wide-spread show trials must be applied."[56]

The official line was that such harsh measures were justified by the continued presence of representatives of anti-Soviet parties and groups in Georgia who were allegedly inciting the peasants to resist collectivization and de-kulakization.[57] As GPU chief, Beria did his best to remind the Georgian people of the dangers of these counterrevolutionary groups. In late 1928, for example, he wrote an article in *Zaria vostoka* entitled "What Have the Mensheviks Come To," in which he enumerated the sins of the Mensheviks and discussed their efforts at espionage and subversion.[58]

As the war against the peasants became increasingly ferocious and peasant resistance became stronger, some party members called for a decrease in the tempo. Then on 2 March 1930, in his famous "Dizzy with Success" article, Stalin himself announced a sudden shift in policy and, blaming local Communists for their hasty and crude policies, called for a halt in the program of rapid collectivization. This article caused considerable confusion among Georgian party officials, leading to many recriminations. Beria and his boss at the Transcaucasian GPU, who was Stalin's brother-in-law Stanislav Redens, apparently decided to turn the situation to their advantage by wiring a message to the OGPU leadership in Moscow on 10 March. The note, sent without the knowledge of Transcaucasian party officials, was tendentious, blatantly attempting to put the blame for errors in the collectivization and de-kulakization campaigns on party and officials.[59]

In their note, Beria and Redens painted a grim picture of the situation in the Transcaucasian countryside, deliberately exaggerating the extent of anti-Soviet rioting and protests. Apparently they felt that the GPU had not been given enough leverage to suppress these actions because they claimed that the situation was exacerbated by the mildness of the authorities in dealing with the kulaks and other rebels:

> The initiators and direct participants in the destruction and violence have not, with few exceptions, been arrested. In some cases attempts at arrest have necessitated confronting the resistance of an entire village, as a result of which the arrests were rescinded. All of this is interpreted by the population as a sign of weakness on the part of the authorities and encourages even more brazen protests.[60]

Stressing the dangers of the situation, the authors stated: "If decisive measures are not taken, then by spring we will have serious complications, maybe resulting in armed uprisings." They went on to urge that repression in the countryside be strengthened as the only means of putting an end to the anti-Soviet and anticollectivization riots and, finally, requested that the message be shown to Stalin and Ordzhonikidze. Meanwhile the GPU continued to inflict atrocities on the peasants. At one point the GPU announced that all peasants who had fled from their villages to escape collectivization could return to their homes without reprisals. The GPU then arrested and shot those who returned.[61]

Apparently Stalin saw the Beria/Redens note and was impressed by its contents, because the Central Committee in Moscow sent instructions to the Transcaucasian leadership to give the GPU the main responsibility for fighting the kulaks, while the party organs were to remain on the sidelines. Meanwhile, Transcaucasian party leader Krinitskii had already sent a letter to Stalin protesting the contents of the Beria/Redens note and defending the party against the charges that its policies had been responsible for the increase in kulak resistance. In a subsequent message he argued that the Central Committee in Moscow did not have enough information at its disposal to place the struggle against the kulaks in the hands of the GPU.[62]

Political Maneuvers

The GPU did not in fact take over the anti-kulak struggle, but this incident did result in another shake-up in the Transcaucasian party leadership. Krinitskii was replaced by V. V. "Beso" Lominadze, a Georgian, who was highly critical of the way collectivization had taken place in the region, and Georgian party First Secretary Kakhiani was replaced by Levan Gogoberidze. Meanwhile the GPU had gained authority over the militia (a change that occurred in all areas of the Soviet Union) and was given the task of helping the party to organize armed volunteer detachments for the protection of government buildings and property.[63]

The collectivization issue serves as an example of how Beria was able to advance his own career at the expense of others. Neither Krinitskii nor Kakhiani, by all accounts, was hesitant about using force to speed up the collectivization and de-kulakization process, so it is doubtful that Beria and Redens had serious tactical disagreements with them. Rather, they simply wanted to discredit these party leaders in order to raise their own value in Stalin's eyes. Beria himself probably instigated the idea of writing the note, because Redens was reportedly a weak-willed individual. He allowed Beria to run things to such an extent that the Chekists referred jokingly to Redens as "Berens."[64]

Beria, it seems, had been moving against Kakhiani for some time. In a September 1929 letter to Ordzhonikidze he had not failed to pass on the many unpleasant rumors that were circulated about Kakhiani: "They say, for example, that for some reason the hotel in Batumi belonging to Kakhiani's father has not been nationalized (his father also has a house in Batumi and a twelve-room apartment). They are surprised that this Central Committee secretary does not cut off ties with his father, a large property owner, and even stays at his apartment and so on."[65] Kakhiani, with good cause, blamed Beria for his dismissal from the Georgian party leadership. "Misha [Kakhiani] returned from Moscow extremely unhappy," wrote Beria to his mentor. "All his displeasure rests on us. At first he would not even receive me and Redens."[66] It should be added, however, that Kakhiani had not been above making digs at Beria in the past. At the Sixth Georgian Party Congress in July 1929, Kakhiani had singled out the peasants in Beria's native region of Mingrelia as being especially troublesome and claimed that they wanted to create a "Great [independent] Mingrelia."[67]

By this time Beria had earned such notoriety for his exploits that his reputation was known even outside Georgia. Georges Agabekov, who worked in the foreign section of the Moscow OGPU during the 1920s and later defected, met Beria in 1928 when the two were requested to arrange the capture of a political oppositionist who had fled to Iran. According to Agabekov:

[Beria] had his legend among us. He had held various posts since 1922 and it was said that he had disembarrassed himself of a member of the plenipotentiary representatives of the OGPU who had run counter to him. A little before his recent trip to Moscow he had quarrelled with an OGPU delegate who was performing some special duty in his bailiwick. In spite of powerful connections in Moscow, this official was recalled and replaced by a person not merely colorless but ridiculous.[68]

It takes little imagination to figure out that the plenipotentiary in question was one of those who had perished in the 1925 plane crash, and that the OGPU delegate with whom Beria had quarreled was Pavlunovskii. His "ridiculous" replacement was Redens, who also fell victim to Beria's intrigues. Typically, Beria soon began plotting to get Redens out of the picture. One night in 1931, on Redens's birthday, Beria got him drunk and then sent him home alone, whereupon Redens created a commotion out in the street. Beria reported the incident promptly to Stalin, who decided to have Redens transferred to Belorussia. Beria then took over as head of the Transcaucasian GPU in April 1931, while simultaneously retaining his Georgian GPU post.[69] As Merkulov later observed about Beria's bosses in the Transcaucasian GPU: "Beria was able to drive them out, one after the other, until he finally got the post himself."[70]

If Beria was able to use indiscretions by his associates as a means of damaging their careers, he apparently was able to keep damage to a minimum when it came to his own family. His wife's uncle Sasha Gegechkori, People's Commissar for Agriculture in Georgia and a full member of the Georgian Central Committee, had a great weakness for women and drink. On one occasion he was seen by a police official in the Hotel Orient, where he had rented several rooms and was having a drunken orgy with some naked women. Efforts to investigate the matter were stifled on Beria's orders. Later Gegechkori, having spent millions of rubles from government coffers on himself, committed suicide rather than having to account for the money.[71] Perhaps he did not think he could count on Beria to protect him from punishment yet again.

Clearly political life in Georgia at this time was deeply absorbing, behind the scenes at least. Agabekov, who made a three-day trip with Beria from Moscow to Tbilisi, noted that they talked mainly about party politics. He was surprised that Beria had so little knowledge about national affairs: "He knew nothing about them; the petty doings in Tiflis [Tbilisi] absorbed him to the exclusion of grand politics."[72] For the time being Beria's sights were set on Georgia, but it would not be long before he would aspire to a role in "grand politics."

Indeed, Beria was already extending his influence beyond the police apparatus and into the party leadership. In November 1930 he became a member of the party bureau (the top leadership body) of the Georgian Central Committee and thus was involved directly in policy-making. By the spring of 1931 his name was mentioned in the press immediately after those of the First Secretary of the Zakkraikom and the Chairman of the Central Executive Committee. At the funeral of the prominent Bolshevik

Vano Sturua in April 1931, Beria's position in the honor guard was on a par with that of the Georgian First Secretary.[73]

Beria's political fortunes were furthered not only by Sergo Ordzhoni-kidze but also by his ability to win favor with Stalin directly, playing on his suspicious nature with stories of intrigue and disloyalty on the part of Georgian party figures. By the late 1920s Beria was visiting Stalin often, usually while the latter was taking his summer vacations at Gagra, near Sochi on the Black Sea, about forty kilometers north of the Georgian border.[74] When Beria would hear that Stalin had arrived he would make a point of vacationing there, too.[75] Although Sochi was in Russia and therefore not under the jurisdiction of the Georgian GPU, Beria report-edly took it upon himself to oversee Stalin's security, thus having an ex-cuse for frequent visits. Stalin later told his daughter Svetlana that her mother Nadezhda Alliluyeva disliked Beria so much that she protested against his frequent presence (to no avail) as early as 1929.[76] It is not clear why Stalin's wife found Beria so odious, but she apparently sensed some-thing manipulative and unpleasant in the way he related to Stalin.

During the summer of 1931 Beria "told tales" to Stalin about several party figures, including L. I. Kartvelishvili, brought in to replace Lo-minadze as first secretary of the Transcaucasian Communist Party in late 1930, and Mamia Orakhelashvili, who was still on the Transcaucasian and Georgian party bureaus despite his removal from the job as first sec-retary.[77] Beria's connivances eventually produced results. Stalin had al-ready brooked a challenge to his policies from the Transcaucasian leader-ship in 1930, when Lominadze had urged a more moderate policy toward collectivization.[78] Having ousted Lominadze in late 1930, Stalin was now wary about the Transcaucasian party officials whom he had brought in to take the place of Lominadze and his colleagues and was thus receptive to Beria's suggestions about their inadequacies. The solution, it would seem, was to place Beria in a better position to keep an eye on things for Stalin.

This did not happen right away, however. In early September 1931 Stalin met with Kartvelashvili and decided to have him take the job of Georgian first secretary, thus holding two party jobs simultaneously. Then, just a few weeks later, Stalin summoned Kartvelashvili and other Transcaucasian officials to Moscow to propose the appointment of Beria as second secretary of the Transcaucasian Central Committee and thus Kartvelishvili's deputy. According to the account of a Georgian party official who was present, Kartvelishvili objected, saying: "I will not work with that charlatan." The majority of others present also protested Beria's promotion. This now famous meeting was described by Khrush-chev in his 1956 speech to the Twentieth Party Congress. The Kartvelish-vili group reportedly went to see Ordzhonikidze in the hopes that he would do something, but to no avail.[79]

The matter was shelved for a day or two and then it was decided that Kartvelishvili would leave Transcaucasia and be replaced as head of the Zakkraikom by Mamia Orakhelashvili, with Beria as second secretary.[80] At the same time Beria was designated first secretary of the Georgian Communist Party. Two weeks before the "election" of Beria was announced publicly, the Central Committee in Moscow issued a resolution, on 31 October, criticizing Transcaucasian party leaders for "gross errors" in the process of collectivization and in economic work, as well as for exhibiting local nationalism and extending too much personal influence.[81] This announcement foreshadowed the extensive personnel changes in the party and state apparatus that Beria was to initiate after coming to power in Georgia. Having achieved his goal of taking over the party leadership, Beria would create a party organization of his own making.

Chapter 3

LEADER OF GEORGIA AND

TRANSCAUCASIA: 1931–1936

> The subject's cynical realism dissolves precisely at the
> threshold of his self-image.
> *(Ella Leffland,* The Knight, Death and the Devil*)*

Attacking the Old Guard

B ERIA'S ASCENSION to the leading party post in Georgia was a
remarkable achievement for a man only thirty-two years old, even
by the standards of the Bolshevik party, where men rose rapidly in
the hierarchy. But it reportedly caused considerable consternation at all
levels within the Georgian Communist Party. No matter how great their
devotion to the bolshevik cause, few party members could feel comfortable with the idea of a ruthless police chief as their new boss, especially
since his promotion had been achieved by underhanded attacks on colleagues. The Tbilisi party committee leadership refused to support the
October 31 resolution and sent a group from the secretariat to Moscow
in early November to appeal Beria's appointment, but to no avail. The
Georgian party bureau sent a telegram to Moscow ordering them home
and reprimanded them for their insubordination.[1] One secretary from the
Tbilisi party committee is said to have left the republic rather than work
with Beria.[2] Several heads of Central Committee departments were so
disturbed that they decided to protest by not going to work on Beria's first
day on the job. Mamia Orakhelashvili then called them all to his office
and advised them to return. Beria had been recommended by Stalin, he
said, so they had better find a common language with him.[3]

However vehement the opposition was to his appointment, Beria did
not waver in asserting strong control over the party and state. At a meeting of the Georgian party bureau in early December, Beria pushed
through a resolution carving out his areas of responsibility as first secretary. He was to supervise the Central Committee and its bureau, the GPU,
agriculture, oil refining, health resorts, and propaganda and agitation
(which included the press). The remaining areas, including the budget,
industry, and trade unions, were delegated to other CC secretaries.[4]

Portions of this chapter have appeared in *Soviet Studies* 45, no. 4 (July 1991): 749–63.

Beria's first major appearance as Georgian party chief was on 3 January 1932, when he spoke at a republican party conference on *kolkhoz* (collective farm) construction. His lengthy report was published on the front page of *Zaria vostoka*, together with a large photograph of him, perhaps the first sign of Beria's personality cult.[5] The report focused on the many failings of previous party leaders, whom he accused of disregarding principles in carrying out the collectivization of agriculture. According to Beria, these mistakes had led to a serious problem in the countryside that called for aggressive countermeasures. He stressed the need to raise class vigilance because the Mensheviks, the kulaks, and other anti-Soviet elements had developed new, more devious tactics for hindering the process of collectivization. Beria's tone was belligerent and menacing, making it clear that his reign in Georgia would not be characterized by moderation.

Beria's attacks on deposed party figures were even harsher in a speech delivered at the Eighth Congress of the Georgian Communist Party two and a half weeks later.[6] The theme of his address centered on the implementation of the October 1931 resolution of the All-Union Central Committee, which had been highly critical of economic work in Transcaucasia. In addition to repeatedly invoking the "wisdom of Comrade Stalin," Beria devoted much of his four-page speech to singling out deposed party leaders for scathing criticism. In particular, he attacked them for mistakes in implementing nationality policies and for their failure to allow the individual republics to develop economic initiative. Although some party officials had openly acknowledged their errors, others, complained Beria, had defended their positions or not been sufficiently apologetic, thus making their actions even more reprehensible.

Beria concluded his address by reiterating his familiar exhortation to raise class vigilance. He noted ominously that the GPU had uncovered several hostile organizations within various commissariats, which were deliberately doing harm to economic activity. He urged his comrades to wage a struggle against any sort of deviation from bolshevism:

> Let us once and for all root out the seeds of *atamanshchina* [individual ambition], *artel'shchina* [adherence to small production associations]. Let us smash any manifestation of anti-party groupism, put an end to efforts to destroy party discipline, in whatever form these efforts manifest themselves. Let us call to strict account all who try to degrade the organizational and ideological principles of Leninism. Every Bolshevik in Georgia must be guided by these demands in his everyday work.

Judging from Beria's statements, one of his main goals was to discredit and dismantle the entire old bolshevik stronghold in Georgia and Transcaucasia. As a relatively young outsider with little allegiance to veteran

Bolsheviks, he was in a good position to bring about the demise of the old guard on Stalin's behalf. Over the next four years most of these men were to be swept away and replaced by men of Beria's choosing, more often than not from the political police.[7]

From the onset of his Georgian party career Beria apparently had his eye on Mamia Orakhelashvili's post as party leader of Transcaucasia, which encompassed not only Georgia but also Armenia and Azerbaidzhan, and was grooming himself for the job. In early March 1932 *Zaria vostoka* published a long directive from the Georgian Central Committee, signed by Beria, on preparations for the Tenth Anniversary of the Transcaucasian Federation.[8] Stressing Stalin's role in the formation of the federation and the significance of his historic struggle against national deviationists, Beria discussed the efforts of Transcaucasian Communists to correct the grave errors of their former leaders in nationality policies. He seemed to be speaking not just for Georgians, but for all members of the Transcaucasian Federation.

As usual, Beria kept Sergo Ordzhonikidze (and through him, Stalin) up to date on events in Georgia and Transcaucasia. In late March 1932 Beria wrote him a long, detailed letter, in which he discussed various economic and administrative issues.[9] The letter provides a good insight into the concerns and preoccupations of Beria after he assumed his new post. In an effort to strengthen the kolkhoz system, he noted, the Georgian leadership had instigated a purge of kulak and other anti-Soviet elements. Beria reported that they had sent 355 kulak families into exile. Concerned about the growing numbers of peasants leaving kolkhozes, Beria went into the countryside to talk with them personally. He concluded that part of the problem was the wage leveling, which affected the more industrious workers adversely, but he added that anti-Soviet elements in the kolkhozes had also played a role.

Beria pointed out that the city of Tbilisi was in bad shape as far as its public services, amenities, and buildings were concerned. Because of a lack of funds, however, the work on improvements had been kept to a minimum. He then recounted his views on the question of redistricting in Mingrelia, recommending that one district, where people who knew only the Mingrelian language lived, be enlarged and that the Mingrelian language be introduced in the courts and schools there—quite a concession to the interests of a national minority group. Beria also reported that he had been compelled to clamp down on the officials in his apparatus, demanding that they give more time to their tasks. As a result, many officials complained that he was pushing things too fast.

One issue Beria raised, that of conflicts within the leadership of the Transcaucasian Railway, was of particular interest to Ordzhonikidze because his younger brother Papulia was a railway official and had recently been criticized in the local press. The criticism continued, with Papulia being reprimanded for unsatisfactory work in the late summer of 1932 and Beria apparently doing nothing to stop it. Soon Papulia was forced to leave his job. Beria, in another self-serving letter to Sergo, discussed his efforts to talk to Papulia and persuade him to take another post: "It may be true that he has been through some unpleasantness, but that is in the past. I spoke to him for a long time, but nothing would help: he refused every job, sulked, cursed and threatened to go on a hunger strike."[10] Finally Papulia Ordzhonikidze did agree to take another post, but it would not be long before he was hounded again; by the autumn of 1936 he was in prison.

Not surprisingly this episode created tensions between Sergo Ordzhonikidze and Beria, tensions that may have been heightened by Beria's underhanded efforts to get rid of Mamia Orakhelashvili.[11] It is not clear exactly how Beria accomplished this but, according to one source, Orakhelashvili found it so difficult to work with Beria that he actually requested a transfer to Moscow.[12] In October 1932 Orakhelashvili left his post as chief of the Transcaucasian party apparatus to become deputy director of the Institute of Marxism-Leninism in Moscow, which was a clear demotion. He was replaced by Beria, whose job as head of the Georgian Communist Party went to a former deputy in the GPU, P. I. Agniashvili. By January 1934 Beria regained the Georgian party leadership and held both posts simultaneously.[13]

These changes suggested that Beria was acting more and more boldly in his relations with Moscow. As a full member of the Politburo and, since January 1932, as USSR People's Commissar for Heavy Industry Sergo Ordzhonikidze continued to be a powerful politician, and Beria was clearly his junior in terms of political status. But their relationship was changing and although Beria continued to defer to him outwardly he was acting more independently. This cannot have pleased Sergo, who wanted to continue exercising his patronage in his native republic.

It was probably not a coincidence that Beria's promotion was accompanied by the return to Transcaucasia of his longtime ally Bagirov, whom Ordzhonikidze reportedly detested. In October 1932 Bagirov assumed the chairmanship of the Azerbaidzhan *Sovnarkom* (Council of People's Commissars), at which time he joined the Zakkraikom bureau. Just fourteen months later, in December 1933, he was "elected" to the post of first secretary of the Azerbaidzhan Communist Party.[14] Bagirov, whose improved political fortunes could be attributed directly to Beria's patronage, demonstrated his gratitude by slavish devotion to the latter for years to come. Indeed, almost every speech or article that appeared under Bagirov's name was filled with extravagant praise for Beria.[15]

Once he arrived in Moscow Mamia Orakhelashvili had the opportunity to tell his side of the story to Ordzhonikidze, depicting Beria in the worst possible light. He was joined by Abkhazian leader Nestor Lakoba, who told Ordzhonikidze that Beria had made some extremely derogatory remarks about him, including the following: "In 1924 Sergo would have shot all Georgians if it hadn't been for me." This naturally made Ordzhonikidze furious. When Beria heard what had happened, he immediately dashed off a desperate letter, dated 18 December 1932, to Ordzhonikidze, denying everything:

> Dear Sergo, how could you even for a minute allow yourself to think that I could at any time, to anyone, including N. Lakoba, say such outlandish and even counterrevolutionary things. . . . I know that there is a lot of chatter from those who leave Transcaucasia and that it is not possible to prevent such foolish talk. I know that many false rumors are circulating about me and our work in Transcaucasia, but I cannot understand what motives comrade Lakoba may have, what aims he is pursuing, when he tells you such blatant lies.
>
> Sergo, you have known me more than ten years. You know all my faults, all my abilities. I never undermined either the Central Committee or you, and I am sure that I will not do so in the future. I give all my time to work, hoping to justify the party's and the Central Committee's faith in me. I have not had a vacation in over four years, never finding the time to get away. Right now I am in Abkhazia dealing with the tobacco crop . . . I admire you too much to say those things. I ask you only one thing—don't believe anyone . . . verify all these stories so as to put an end to the incessant provocations.[16]

Whether or not Ordzhonikidze believed Beria's protestations, at least a facade of friendship between the two was maintained. In November 1934 Ordzhonikidze paid a lengthy visit to Transcaucasia, where he traveled around with Beria, and was photographed with him several times.[17] The next year Ordzhonikidze recommended that Beria and Bagirov be awarded the Order of Lenin for their leading work in oil extraction.[18] But behind the scenes their relationship was under a definite strain. In the spring of 1933, for example, Beria, who was again confronting rumors passed by his enemies that he had spied for the Musavat government, wrote to Ordzhonikidze with exasperation: "By the way, you know well that I was sent to Musavat counterintelligence by the party and that this question was settled by the Azerbaidzhan Central Committee in 1920 in the presence of you."[19] Although in general the letter was cordial, Beria seemed irritated at Ordzhonikidze for not coming to his defense.

ECONOMIC PRESSURES

One thing that emerges clearly from Beria's letters to Ordzhonikidze is the extent to which Beria, despite his preoccupation with politics, was concerned with economic problems. The autumn of 1932 was marked by a new Soviet offensive against the peasantry, with heavy obligations imposed on the kolkhozes and increased repression against kulaks. Responding to the new campaign initiated by Moscow, the Transcaucasian party press produced countless stories of kulak sabotage of the harvests and voiced shrill cries to "smash kulak resistance" and heighten vigilance against class enemies. There were numerous reports of GPU arrests for destruction of agricultural equipment, arson, and other crimes committed by those who were said to be deliberately thwarting agricultural and industrial production in the Transcaucasus and elsewhere in the Soviet Union.[20]

Undoubtedly, underlying the shrill campaign against economic sabotage and class enemies was a real concern within the Transcaucasian party leadership about the state of the economy, a concern that was reflected in Beria's speeches. As was true in most other areas of the Soviet Union, harvests in Transcaucasia had been poor during the First Five-Year Plan, and production was lagging behind in several branches of industry. Plans for building railways and electric stations also remained unfulfilled.[21] Much of the economy of Georgia, Azerbaidzhan, and Armenia was controlled centrally by Transcaucasian commissariats, and the Second Five-Year Plan treated the economy of the three republics as a unified complex. As party leader of the region, Beria was ultimately responsible for ensuring that the plans were met and so was anxious to raise economic production. Like other regional party leaders, he was under continual pressure to meet output targets, and his speeches and addresses to party conclaves in 1933 and 1934, as reported in the press, dealt primarily with this problem. He went out of his way to demonstrate to Moscow that his region was making progress. Thus, for example, in May 1933 he wrote an article, which was published in the central party organ *Pravda*, boasting of how Georgia's tea production had increased and noting that forty new tea factories were scheduled to be built in Georgia during the Second Five-Year Plan (1933–37).[22]

The oil industry in Azerbaidzhan was a top priority in the struggle to fulfill the targets of the Second Five-Year Plan, so capital investment in this area was high.[23] In August 1933 Beria made a rousing speech to the Azerbaidzhan Central Committee, noting that some progress had been made in raising oil production but that this was no reason for complacency. He outlined changes in the organization and leadership of the administrative body of the oil industry, *Azneft*, which was plagued by problems.[24] Beria made frequent trips to Baku, where the industry was centered, to consult with Bagirov and visit the oil wells. Gradually he met with success: according to official figures, oil production rose in 1933 by 25 percent over the previous year and by another 25 percent the next year.[25]

LEADER OF GEORGIA AND TRANSCAUCASIA 53

Cotton, tobacco, and wine were other products that showed significant increases in output with the new five-year plan, and work was begun on chemical, machine-tool, and automobile factories, along with a steel mill and several hydroelectric stations. "Socialist competition," whereby production units, factories, and collective farms were awarded prizes and glorified in the press for achieving the highest production levels, helped to further the campaign to increase output.[26] As a result of his efforts, Beria was able to brag about the economic successes of his region in his speech to the Seventeenth Party Congress in Moscow in early 1934. The congress was a milestone for Beria both because it was his first national-level public appearance and because he was elected to full membership on the Central Committee of the All-Union Communist Party.[27]

FURTHERING THE CULT OF STALIN

In addition to the economy, which occupied so much time, Beria was busy ingratiating himself with Stalin by actively promoting the Stalinist cult in Transcaucasia. *Zaria vostoka* was filled with paeans to the great leader who inspired the people of Transcaucasia to achieve economic success and whose wise instructions and guidance were indispensable to the functioning of the party and the government. Hardly a day passed without a front-page picture of the omnipotent Stalin, accompanied by quotations in large bold letters. In 1935 Beria opened the newly restored birthplace of Stalin at Gori, which had a large marble pavilion built over it. Somewhat later he commissioned a series of portraits of Stalin by Georgian artists.[28]

Beria also took charge of Stalin's elderly mother.[29] He arranged her move to Tbilisi sometime before 1934 and, together with his wife Nino, looked after her solicitously. In 1934 Stalin's three children came down to Tbilisi to see her. According to Svetlana Alliluyeva, they spent a week in Beria's "magnificent apartment" and his "equally sumptuous dacha" outside the city, but they only spent a half hour with their grandmother. Nino Beria accompanied them on the brief visit and, having seated herself next to Stalin's mother, spent the entire time talking to her.[30] The next year, in October 1935, Stalin himself came to Tbilisi to see his mother, escorted by Beria. Judging from a subsequent *Zaria vostoka* interview with Stalin's mother, she was on intimate terms with Beria by this time. She described the visit in this way: "Our Lavrentii came and announced that Soso [Stalin] had arrived and that he was already here and coming in. . . . The door opened and there he stood on the threshold."[31]

As mentioned above, Stalin did not attend his mother's funeral in June 1937, violating the sacrosanct Georgian rituals associated with death.

Stalin may have designated Beria as his surrogate on this occasion partly because of his official position, but also because he was by then close to the family. Indeed, Stalin's children, particularly Svetlana Alliluyeva, came to know the Berias well. Photographs of Beria and Svetlana, taken when the latter was young, convey a proprietary manner on Beria's part. In one photograph Svetlana, who appears to be about nine or ten years old, is perched uncomfortably on Beria's lap. Judging from her expression, she did not enjoy being in his possessive grasp, particularly at her age. Beria's demeanor in this photograph brings to mind the widespread stories about him seducing, or even raping, teenage girls and young women.[32] Although these stories were embellished by Beria's opponents after his demise in 1953, there is reason to believe that they had some basis, particularly insofar as they applied to Beria's conduct once he had moved to Moscow (see chapter 5). But it is doubtful that he was regularly engaging in such practices at this point in his career. For one thing, had such stories reached Stalin, he probably would not have allowed his children and mother to spend time with Beria. Nor, for that matter, would he have encouraged Beria's political advancement.

Despite his closeness to Stalin's family, Beria was still far removed from the Kremlin and his access to Stalin was limited to occasional visits. In order to achieve a promotion to Moscow and become a member of Stalin's immediate entourage, Beria had to do more to distinguish himself in the leader's eyes. As he came to know Stalin better, Beria apparently recognized his almost pathological need for self-aggrandizement, as well as his extreme jealousy of those Georgians who had been prominent revolutionaries. Seeing in this an opportunity for advancement, Beria carried his ambitious campaign to glorify Stalin to new heights: he presided over the production of a history of the Transcaucasian Social Democratic movement that altered the facts in order to give Stalin a leading role, while at the same time discrediting his former revolutionary comrades.

The idea of revising party history to glorify Stalin by no means originated with Beria. Indeed, by the time Beria took on his project the cult of Stalin in history was well under way. As Robert Tucker argues in his study of Stalin's personality cult, it all began in October 1931 with Stalin's famous letter to the journal *Proletarskaia revoliutsiia* criticizing an article written by the historian A. G. Slutskii on bolshevik relations with German Social Democrats before World War I.[33] At the time historians were still permitted to be reasonably objective, and Slutskii had allowed that Lenin in 1914 had underestimated the danger of the position taken by certain "centrists" among the German Social Democrats. Stalin assailed Slutskii in the most scathing terms for daring to throw Lenin's revolutionary wisdom into question and accused the editors of the journal of "rotten liberalism."

Tucker argues that Stalin's letter solicited a cult in party history first by the fact that, in writing it, Stalin was presenting himself as the party's number one historian. Second, in asserting that Lenin was infallible and above criticism, Stalin implied that as Lenin's successor he should be treated similarly. Finally, the letter demanded that historians evaluate the role of revolutionary figures not on the basis of documents dredged up by "archive rats" but rather on the basis of their deeds and reputations. This meant that historians should be prepared to distort the facts in order to accommodate the higher truth established by Stalin or his spokesmen. In particular, Stalin's own revolutionary past was to be rewritten to give him a role that was in keeping with his position as supreme *vozhd* (leader), which necessitated denigrating the contributions of those revolutionaries who had been more prominent than Stalin.

Stalin's letter created a turmoil within the scholarly community, prompting a rush among ambitious historians to revise party history and a flurry of recantations and confessions of heresy.[34] Not surprisingly, the impact of the letter was felt in Georgia, where Beria, with his sensitive political antennae, was quick to realize its implications. In March 1932 *Zaria vostoka* reprinted a scathing attack from *Pravda* on a Georgian party historian, the director of the Institute of Party History in Tbilisi, Tengiz Zhgenti.[35] Zhgenti, it seems, was guilty of adopting "a nationalist, nonbolshevik point of view" in assessing developments in Georgia from 1917 to 1927 and for not exposing the "bankrupt" policies of the Mensheviks. At the bottom of the reprinted review the editors of *Zaria vostoka* regretted that the Georgian press had not recognized Zhgenti's gross errors earlier. But, they noted, Transcaucasian Party First Secretary Mamia Orakhelashvili had already criticized Zhgenti, as had Georgian Party Chief Beria in his report to the Eighth Party Congress of Georgia in January 1932. They went on to report that the Georgian party leadership had dismissed Zhgenti from his post and ordered his book to be removed from circulation.[36]

The unfortunate Zhgenti was subjected to further attacks by *Zaria vostoka*, whose editors were obviously anxious to make amends for their earlier lapses. On 9 April 1932 the paper printed a lengthy article on his work, acknowledging again that, despite Beria's explicit criticisms of Zhgenti's "distortions" at the Eighth Party Congress, *Zaria vostoka* had neglected to expose him.[37] Thus again Beria was credited with having recognized Zhgenti's gross errors even before they were mentioned in *Pravda*.

Three days later one of Stalin's "Letters from the Caucasus," written in

1909, in which he "exposed" the program and tactics of the Mensheviks in Tbilisi at the time, was reprinted on the front page of *Zaria vostoka*.[38] Stalin's letter, which denounced the Mensheviks for cooperating with the bourgeoisie, was hailed as a work of extraordinary significance for the party because it revealed the essence of "menshevik liquidators" against whom the Bolsheviks had had to struggle for so many years. Beria subsequently announced that, in view of the historical significance of Stalin's letter, the Georgian Central Committee had passed a special resolution organizing a course of study of the letter for party members and designating a special day for that purpose. Moreover, the party's Institute of Marxism-Leninism was to spend the next month reviewing all historical works from the point of view of Stalin's letter.[39]

Thus began a dual strategy, orchestrated by Beria, of denouncing historians while at the same time building up a cult of Stalin in Transcaucasian history. In March 1933, at a time when Beria had already succeeded Mamia Orakhelashvili as party leader in Transcaucasia, another article lashing out against "falsifiers of party history" appeared in *Zaria vostoka*. This time the victim of criticism was an Armenian historian whose book on the revolutionary movement in Tbilisi during the prewar years had treated the Mensheviks far too favorably, thus contradicting Stalin's interpretation of events.[40] The next month the second of Stalin's "Letters from the Caucasus" was reprinted in *Zaria vostoka*.[41]

Beria may have been paving the way for his own involvement in Soviet historiography when he spoke to the Ninth Party Congress of the Georgian Communist Party in January 1934. In his discourse, he complained that, despite the resolute struggle that had been waged on the ideological front in the two years since the last Congress, there were still deficiencies in the area of party history of Georgia and Transcaucasia:

> To our shame it must be said that up to now we do not have the slightest scholarly, academically elaborated history of our party and the revolutionary movement in Georgia. The history of our party, of the whole revolutionary movement in Georgia and Transcaucasia from the first days of its awakening, are inseparably linked with the work and name of Comrade Stalin. It is not possible to introduce a single significant fact from the history of the struggle for Lenin's line which was not permeated with the ideas of Stalin.[42]

In his speech Beria took the ominous step of singling out for criticism the prominent old Bolshevik Filipp Makharadze, author of several works on the early history of social democracy in Georgia which, as Beria lamented, still served as the basis upon which the younger generation was being taught.[43] Citing passages from Makharadze's writings, Beria chided him for his failure to portray adequately Stalin's role in leading the Bolsheviks in an uncompromising struggle against Mensheviks and suggested that Makharadze correct his errors. One of Beria's deputies then criticized Beria's predecessor, Mamia Orakhelashvili, for his mistakes in writing about the Social Democratic movement.[44] Orakhelashvili was not present at the Congress to respond to the attack, but Makharadze was and he did not seem intimidated by the criticisms of Beria, who had not even been born when Makharadze was already an active Social Democrat in Georgia. He responded with a halfhearted apology to the Congress, but also defended himself by pointing out somewhat ironically that when he wrote his histories "the tremendous role played by Stalin in the revolutionary movement had not yet come to light."[45] (In other words, this was before historians had been told to embellish Stalin's role by falsifying history.)

That these attacks were either instigated or at least sanctioned by Moscow is suggested by the fact that Avel Enukidze, a prominent Georgian member of the All-Union Central Committee and secretary of the Central Executive Committee who for years had worked closely with Stalin, became the victim of a similar campaign of criticism at the national level. Enukidze's sin was that he had written memoirs about the celebrated bolshevik underground press in Baku that operated in 1901–1905, in which he had neglected Stalin's role.[46] Thus he was forced to write a humiliating recantation of his work in *Pravda* in January 1935, only to be expelled from the party at a plenum the following June.[47] Beria was deeply involved in the persecution of Enukidze. It was he who went over Enukidze's *Pravda* article, scrutinizing it carefully before it was approved for publication.[48] And after Nikolai Ezhov, then a Central Committee Secretary, gave a speech at the June plenum denouncing Enukidze, Beria rose to his feet to demand even harsher punishment.[49] Back in Tbilisi after the plenum, Beria gave a report to his party colleagues in which he denounced Enukidze in the most scathing terms: "Enukidze turned out to be a traitor to our country and is enduring a well-deserved punishment."[50] Clearly Beria was eager to demonstrate to Stalin his enthusiasm for routing out old Bolsheviks.

BERIA'S BOOK

It is possible that the idea for the book, entitled *On the History of Bolshevik Organizations in Transcaucasia*, came from Stalin, as Anatoli Rybakov postulates in his novel *Children of the Arbat*.[51] Rybakov portrays Stalin as being obsessed with having such a history written and musing for a long time over whom he can enlist to write it. He comes up with Leningrad Party Chief Sergei Kirov, who spent much of his career in the Caucasus. Stalin calls Kirov to Sochi in the summer of 1934 to persuade him to take on the project but, to Stalin's great irritation, Kirov refuses, saying "What do I know about history?" Stalin then decides to have Beria do the job.[52]

One problem with this version is that it has the authorship still undecided in the summer of 1934. Judging from an article by Beria that appeared in *Bol'shevik* in June 1934, the project was well underway by that time.[53] The authoritative tone of the article and its publication in the party's prestigious theoretical journal suggested an effort to establish Beria as a serious thinker and a political leader of more than local prominence, hence someone qualified to write an important party history. The article discussed how Transcaucasia had overcome its prerevolutionary backwardness and was making significant strides toward achieving socialism. However, Beria also devoted a few paragraphs to Stalin's participation in the revolutionary movement in Tbilisi and Baku, developing some of the points later elaborated on in his book.[54]

Whoever had the idea for the book, it is true that Beria did not actually write it. He later confessed, after his arrest in June 1953: "Several persons undertook to write the book *On the History of Bolshevik Organizations in Transcaucasia*, but no one person wrote it. [E.] Bediia and others put the book together and I gave a report on it. Then the book was published under my name as the author. I did this wrongly, but it is a fact and I acknowledge it."[55] Bediia, who was at the time editor of the Georgian paper *Komunisti* and director of the Marx-Engels Institute in Tbilisi, was shot at the end of 1937 on Beria's orders. In a recently published account of Beria's interrogation and trial, Bediia is portrayed as a martyr who worked hard on the book only to have Beria come along and claim it as his own, subsequently having Bediia murdered to cover up this forgery. In fact, a large group worked on the book, including the rector of Tbilisi University, Malakiia Toroshelidze and Beria's close ally Merkulov.[56]

After his arrest, Beria was accused of deliberately deceiving Stalin by pretending to have written the book himself. It is doubtful, however, that Beria would have tried to keep the authorship a secret from Stalin, in view of the fact that so many people were involved and that Stalin himself made corrections in the manuscript.[57] It is not at all surprising that Beria did not write the book that appeared under his name. This was a common practice among Soviet political officials and Beria clearly was too busy running the Transcaucasian Federation on behalf of Stalin and the party to have time for historical research and writing, not to mention that he would not have been capable of doing so anyway. According to Merkulov, Beria never read anything and had no education in Marxism-Leninism. "Beria didn't do a single bit of work on the book," Merkulov stated. "For that he would have to know history."[58] Nonetheless Beria claimed authorship, presenting the manuscript in the form of a two-day lecture delivered to the Tbilisi party *aktiv* on 21–22 July 1935.

The lecture was published in full in *Pravda* over a period of eight days, from 29 July through 5 August, after appearing initially in *Zaria vostoka*.[59] It was also printed simultaneously as a book, in 100,000 copies, followed by eight further editions, some of which were translated into English and other languages. In August *Zaria vostoka* issued a full page of instructions and decrees establishing the agenda for a detailed study of Beria's work.[60] The prominent historian, Stalin's official biographer Emilian Iaroslavskii, wrote a lengthy article on the book, praising it for filling a large gap in the study of bolshevism and proclaiming its importance for the teaching of bolshevik history to future generations.[61] The journal *Proletarskaia revoliutsiia* also lauded Beria's book, which it claimed had exceptional significance for the entire communist movement.[62] In short, Beria was credited with having written the most authoritative account of Stalin's revolutionary career to date. The only thing that detracted from his glory was a reprimand issued by the Politburo a few weeks later, criticizing him and the Transcaucasian Party Committee for reprinting Stalin's articles and brochures written in 1905–10 without permission.[63] Evidently this was intended as a reminder to Beria that he should not get carried away with his status as an author. Perhaps, too, it was meant to distance Stalin from the publication of the book.

The purpose of Beria's work was to present Stalin as a leading figure in the revolutionary movement in Transcaucasia and to show that he was responsible for making the region a stronghold of bolshevism. It is instructive to compare the 1935 edition with later editions, which were revised and expanded to further embellish Stalin's role, taking into account the discovery of "new evidence" and the fact that many of Stalin's revolutionary colleagues had been exposed as "enemies of the people" in 1936–38. With most of those who had taken part in the movement out of the way, Beria was free to distort the historical facts even more. The names of these "traitors" also had to be removed so as to deny their revolutionary role and their past association with Stalin. Thus, for example, the 1949 edition, which was published in English and other languages, was different from the 1935 version.[64] But even in his initial report Beria did not hesitate to grossly misrepresent the true story of the Social Democratic movement in the Transcaucasus.

The book begins by discussing the first Georgian Social Democratic group, the Mesame Dasi, founded in the early 1890s. According to Beria, Stalin joined the Mesame Dasi in 1898, "bringing a new revolutionary element into the life of the group."[65] Because the members of Mesame Dasi restricted themselves to so-called legal Marxism, and did not recognize the importance of illegal revolutionary activity among the workers,

Stalin and two others, Lado Ketskhoveli and S. Tsulukidze (both of whom died a few years later), formed a minority opposition group. According to Beria this group was the embryo of the Leninist bolshevik organization created in 1904. It waged a determined struggle against the Mesame Dasi majority, which was later to adopt the position of the Mensheviks, and succeeded, in 1898–1900, to transform the work of the Tbilisi Social Democratic group into mass agitation and propaganda.

This account sought to demonstrate that Stalin was prophetic enough to expose the seeds of menshevism in the activities of Georgian social democracy even before menshevism arose as a movement and to credit Stalin with establishing the Bolshevik movement in the Caucausus. But Beria's version did not square with other accounts. Makharadze, who had been a leading member of the Mesame Dasi and who had written several historical accounts of this period, was completely unaware of any disagreements within the group. Indeed, Beria castigates Makharadze for characterizing the Mesame Dasi as a homogenous organization that supported Lenin's revolutionary Marxism and had no revisionist tendencies.[66] No other Social Democrats in Tbilisi appeared to have been aware of Stalin's oppositional "triumvirate," although several wrote memoirs.[67] According to one former Georgian Social Democrat: "It is clear that the struggle against 'legalism' [in 1899–1900] was an outright fantasy of Beria's."[68]

In addition to making Stalin into the first Bolshevik in Transcaucasia and the leader of the struggle against legal Marxism, Beria attributed to him an incredibly active role in practical revolutionary work at the time that he was still a student. Thus Beria's book stated that in 1898 Stalin led no fewer than eight workers' circles—by the seventh edition the number was increased to eleven—and also organized a large railway strike. As the historian Bertram Wolfe observed, these were rather remarkable feats considering that Stalin was enrolled at the Tiflis seminary, where students were virtually kept under lock and key.[69] Beria's claim did not accord with earlier accounts about the same period, including one given by Stalin himself in 1926 that Beria had quoted in his June 1934 *Bol'shevik* article. Stalin had spoken of one workers' circle being assigned to him in 1898 and noted that "there in the circle of these comrades I received my first revolutionary baptism."[70] The seventh edition actually quotes Stalin's 1926 statements but with the part about "first revolutionary baptism" left out and with the additional claim that Stalin was leading radical student circles as far back as 1896.[71]

Beria relates how Stalin organized the first conference of the Social Democratic organization in Tbilisi in November 1901, at which time he was elected into the Social Democratic Committee and then was sent to the city of Batumi to set up a revolutionary organization there. Yet, a former Social Democrat claims that no one in the committee ever mentioned Stalin as a member in subsequent accounts of this conference.[72] As Beria would have it, "Before Comrade Stalin came to Batumi there was no workers' Social-Democratic organization whatsoever." Stalin, it seems, was solely responsible for establishing the Social Democratic organization in Batumi and for "rousing the proletariat of Batumi for a revolutionary struggle against autocracy and capitalism." He maintained frenetic activity for the next several months, leading large strikes and demonstrations, while at the same time "directing" [sic] the work of the Tbilisi Social Democrats.[73]

One of the book's most notorious inventions concerned the celebrated underground printing press that was set up in Baku in 1901 and eventually supplied all of Russia with key Marxist publications, including Lenin's mouthpiece, the paper *Iskra*, and his pamphlet *What Is to Be Done?* The press was begun by the Georgian revolutionary Lado Ketskhoveli, who raised money for it through loans and donations. Enukidze's book about the Baku press described how Ketskhoveli had sent him to Tbilisi several times in 1901 to see if he could obtain money from the party organization there to help support the press. On one trip he met with two comrades from the organization, one of whom was "a young party member, Comrade Stalin." They refused to come up with any money for the Baku press unless they could take over control of it, a condition that Ketskhoveli categorically refused to accept. Finally, after another trip, these same Tbilisi comrades gave Enukidze one hundred rubles and a copy of a proclamation to be printed. Enukidze did not mention Stalin's name again in connection with the press.[74]

Enukidze's version of events was unacceptable to those who sought to affirm Stalin's leading role in every aspect of Russia's revolutionary history, even after he admitted his mistakes in *Pravda* in early 1935.[75] Beria's book presented the Baku press in a completely different light, creating the impression that the initiative for the press came from Stalin and his comrade, who sent Ketskhoveli to Baku. The first edition of Beria's book claims that "the Tiflis committee supplied comrade Ketskhoveli with type and money for organizing the underground press in Baku."[76] But the seventh edition gave Stalin more credit, noting that "on the initiative of Comrade Stalin, the leading group in Tiflis supplied Comrade Ketskhoveli with type, equipment and money for this purpose."[77]

In order to establish the credibility of this story the book discounted Enukidze completely, which meant denying that he had even worked on the press. Thus the authors dredged up one Vano Bolkvadze, an obscure compositor on the press, who is quoted as saying that no one worked there except Ketskhoveli (who died in 1903), another compositor named Viktor Tsuladze, and himself.[78] Bolkvadze, however, must have fallen into disgrace because in later editions he is no longer cited and Tsuladze is called upon from obscurity to testify that only he, Ketskhoveli, and "one other compositor" [apparently Bolkvadze, now unmentionable] worked in the print shop.[79] The book then took Enukidze to task for his "gross distortions in the history of Bolshevism in Baku and Tbilisi" and for exaggerating his own importance by "ascribing to himself a role in the first illegal Baku press."[80] (In subsequent editions Enukidze was reported to have been exposed "as a mortal enemy of the people.")

The narrative continued in this vein, attributing to Stalin the control of every subsequent aspect of the revolutionary movement in Transcaucasia. It credited him, for example, with astounding productivity in journalism, noting that during 1904–1907 he "led and directed the entire Bolshevik press."[81] The first edition merely mentions some bolshevik papers that were published at this time. By the seventh edition Stalin actually had "directed the publication" of ten papers.[82]

Beria's history asserted that in 1904–1905, following the split in the Social Democratic movement, Stalin established and then headed several regional Bolshevik party committees in Georgia, giving the impression that Stalin was leading a large movement.[83] In fact the Georgian Social Democratic movement was overwhelmingly menshevik and, as one observer pointed out, Stalin had only a small following: "He succeeded in gaining only a few adherents, rarely more than ten supporters, whom he would quickly organize into groups or clusters, giving them immediately the grand title of Committee."[84] In short, Beria's book, hailed as a path-breaking work, transformed Soviet historiography into fiction.

THE AFTERMATH

In addition to attacks on Enukidze and Makharadze, the book contained diatribes against Mamia Orakhelashvili and other Bolsheviks for falsifying the history of the party in their writings. Orakhelashvili wrote a letter to Stalin defending himself against Beria's accusations and appealing for his support.[85] He enclosed the draft of a rebuttal for publication in *Pravda*. Stalin's reply was typically equivocal:

A letter to *Pravda* ought to be printed, but I don't think the text of your letter is satisfactory. In your place I would take out all its "polemical beauty," all the "excursions" into history, plus the "decisive protest," and I would say simply and briefly that such and such mistakes were made, but that Comrade Beria's criticism of these mistakes is, let's say, too harsh and is not justified by the nature of the mistakes. Or something in this vein.[86]

Orakhelashvili's letter was never published. In subsequent editions of Beria's book he was reported as having been "exposed as an enemy of the people."

Makharadze was the only "falsifier of history" not to be shot in the purges. It is surprising that Makharadze was spared because his "distortions" were even greater than those of Enukidze and Orakhelashvili. As Beria pointed out at the Ninth Congress of the Georgian Communist Party, Makharadze mentioned not a word about Stalin's leading role in his writings about the Transcaucasian revolutionary movement. And he stated explicitly that the split among the Social Democrats, which was characterized by "squabbles, polemics and inner-party strife," did great harm to the movement.[87] This was pure heresy from the Stalinist point of view, since the essence of Stalin's activities during this period was to foment discord between Bolsheviks and Mensheviks. Makharadze made some attempt to put things right with Stalin and Beria when he wrote an article in early 1936, entitled "By Way of Self-Criticism."[88] He admitted his errors and promised to continue work on a new history which he claimed to have begun but then was forced to put aside for reasons beyond his control. He never did write the book.

Makharadze, who had continued to work for a reconciliation with the Mensheviks right up to 1917, was a "collaborator" of the worst kind from Stalin's point of view. And after the revolution he urged moderation and restraint on the part of the Bolsheviks. Given all his transgressions, Makharadze should have been one of the first victims of the purges. In fact one source claims that the police, on Beria's instructions, prepared a case against Makharadze, charging him with a counterrevolutionary plot. But someone intervened to stop Beria, and the case was suddenly dropped.[89] Makharadze then received the largely ceremonial post of Chairman of the Presidium of the Georgian Supreme Soviet and died a natural death in 1941, at age seventy-three.[90]

To attempt to explain why Makharadze was spared when so many others who had done nothing to offend Stalin or Beria perished is to look for logic in the purges when there was none. Even Bediia, who was largely responsible for writing Beria's book, was later shot. But the very capriciousness of the purges, particularly as they affected those involved in Stalin's revolutionary past, sheds light on what may have been a deeper purpose of Beria's book, which underlay the more obvious motive of creating for Stalin a glorious career as a revolutionary in order to buttress his personality cult.

Much of Beria's book was devoted to justifying Stalin's ruthless treatment of the Mensheviks by showing that menshevism was antithetical to the goals of social democracy and bolshevism from its inception and that

it never enjoyed widespread support. Although Beria may not have originated the idea of revising Transcaucasian history in book form, he sensed
Stalin's burning resentment toward the Transcaucasian Menshevik
movement that overshadowed the Bolshevik organization there and his
deep and enduring distrust of Bolsheviks who sought to reconcile with the
Mensheviks. Beria was willing to betray Georgia's proud revolutionary
history and discredit his bolshevik countrymen in order to further Stalin's
leadership cult and justify Stalin's advocacy of the brutal bolshevik invasion of Georgia and the harsh policies of sovietization. The annihilation
of his fellow Bolsheviks as part of the subsequent purges in Georgia
was in some sense an inevitable outcome of the appearance of Beria's
history. Its outlandish distortions foreshadowed the "confessions" extorted under torture during the purges of Stalin's former revolutionary
comrades.

BERIA'S PERSONALITY CULT

As an acclaimed author, party chief of Georgia and Transcaucasia, and a
full member of the All-Union Central Committee, Beria now had enough
prominence to forge his own personality cult in the region he controlled.
Since he was handpicked for his post by Stalin himself and was one of the
latter's most fervent glorifiers, he could embark on such a campaign with
Stalin's blessing. Indeed, the development of Beria's personality cult was
designed to stress his association with Stalin and was carefully coordinated to parallel, on a smaller scale, Stalin's cult, which by this time had
reached outlandish proportions.

By 1936 Beria's cult was in full bloom in Transcaucasia, and of course
Georgia especially. Factories, collective farms, theaters, educational institutions, a sports stadium, one of the loveliest squares in Tbilisi, and a
district (*raion*) all bore his name.[91] His portrait was displayed everywhere, even inserted in school textbooks, accompanied by praise for his
wisdom and genius. The press was filled with reports on his activities and
his countless meetings with workers and other groups. Adoring letters to
Beria from Georgian workers and peasants flowed into the newspapers
throughout 1936, and songs and poems were dedicated to him.[92]

Beria's crony, Azerbaidzhan Party Chief Bagirov, who had eagerly
joined the chorus of those singing Beria's praises, initiated his own personality cult (again on a lesser scale) in Azerbaidzhan. His association
with Beria enhanced his political image, mirroring in many ways Beria's
association with Stalin, although of course, as was the case with all aspir-
ing regional leaders, Bagirov's first words of praise were always for
Stalin. Bagirov later followed Beria's example and "wrote" a book on the

history of bolshevik organizations in Azerbaidzhan, which he read aloud in Baku in December 1939 to commemorate Stalin's fiftieth birthday.[93] Like Beria's book, Bagirov's work was basically a treatise, filled with distortions and exaggerations, on how important Stalin was to the revolutionary movement. Unlike Beria, however, Bagirov did not gain a promotion to Moscow.

Stalin went along with Beria's self-promotional campaign, at least for a while. In February 1936 he sent his close comrade, military commander K. E. Voroshilov, to Tbilisi to celebrate the fifteenth anniversary of Soviet power in Georgia, and Voroshilov bestowed a kiss on Beria for Stalin.[94] The next month Beria led a delegation of 146 Georgian officials and cultural figures to Moscow as part of the anniversary celebration. According to one of the delegates, the actress Nato Vachnadze, Beria was terribly anxious to ensure that the Georgians made a good impression on Stalin and was very nervous during the lengthy reception in the Kremlin: "His demeanor might be compared with that of a parent sending off his child to an important examination. He couldn't sit down in one place, but kept getting up and looking over each one of us. He was very agitated."[95] Several Georgian delegates spoke, praising Beria, and when the latter stood up to greet Stalin he received a standing ovation.[96]

Beria wrote a long article for *Pravda* on Georgia's achievements during fifteen years of Soviet rule.[97] He claimed that Georgia's economic growth was remarkable, especially during the period since the early 1930s. The proportion of industrial production in the total output of Georgia's national economy had risen to 74.9 percent. In all, 117 industrial enterprises had been built or reconstructed since the Bolsheviks came to power in Georgia. He noted that in 1936 the growth of capital investments in Georgian industry was 34.8 percent, as compared to 17.7 percent in the Soviet Union as a whole. Railway, automobile, and air transport had developed rapidly and food production was making impressive gains. As of early 1936, 70 percent of the peasant farms in Georgia had been collectivized.[98]

In keeping with Georgia's prosperity and his own official stature, Beria moved his family in 1935 or 1936 from their apartment to a spacious mansion located at no. 11 Machabeli Street.[99] He also had a lovely white stucco villa built at Gagra on the Black Sea, not far from Stalin's villa. Beria's villa, which served as a vacation retreat, was surrounded by acres of vineyards and fruit trees.[100]

It is not difficult to see why Beria would have sought the outward trappings of power, success, and wealth that most tyrants and dictators seek. But the public adulation of him—which reached such grandiose proportions—requires some explanation. As was noted earlier, Stalin's personality cult fulfilled not only political but also personal needs. Stalin's insecurity and sense of inferiority created in him an almost insatiable craving for public glory. Although Beria may have had pathological tendencies, he was not driven by a similar megalomania. The fostering of his personality cult in Transcaucasia was probably motivated more by rational political concerns, just as with Bagirov. Stalin's cult had by now become an integral part of the Soviet system, accepted by all as part of the ritual of public life and serving to legitimize Stalin's rule. Second-tier leaders like Beria and Bagirov, who were all-powerful in their own domains, also required legitimizing cults around them. The problem, of course, was to maintain a proper balance and to ensure that their cults did not grow to proportions that offended Stalin. Even for someone as politically astute as Beria this presented a difficult and dangerous challenge.

1. Headquarters of Georgian Cheka-GPU-NKVD, Tbilisi, 1921–36.

2. Beria's wife, Nino.

3. The home of Lavrentii and Nino Beria in Tbilisi after 1935, no. 11
Machabeli Street.

4. Sergo Ordzhonikidze, Beria's mentor.

5. Beria and Stalin's daughter, Svetlana Alliluyeva, at Sochi, near the Black Sea, early 1930s.

6. Beria with Svetlana Alliluyeva on his lap and Stalin seated in the background. Stalin's dacha near Sochi, mid-1930s.

Chapter Four

THE PURGES IN GEORGIA

> Beria heard everything, even the whispers of love by a couple
> in bed, the leisurely conversations of his neighbors as they sat
> around their table; as for the shrieks of agony, this dictator
> of Tbilisi was so inured to them that he probably would
> have been awakened by their ceasing as a miller
> would awake when the millstone
> stops its creaking.
> *(Geronti Kikodze, 1954)*

REPRESSION INTENSIFIED

SEVERAL MONTHS before Beria's book appeared an event took place in Leningrad that was pivotal in setting the stage for the mass arrests of 1937–38: the assassination of Leningrad Party Chief Sergei Kirov on 1 December 1934. Although no documentary evidence exists as yet, most historians believe that Stalin ordered NKVD Chief Genrikh Iagoda to arrange the murder.[1] Kirov was a popular politician who had stood up to Stalin on various occasions, and Stalin apparently had concluded that Kirov's presence in the party leadership was a threat to him. Furthermore, the assassination provided Stalin with a pretext for initiating a witch hunt for possible conspirators and thus moving against real or perceived political opponents. On the very day of the murder Stalin introduced a new procedural law that enabled the judicial organs to deal swiftly with those accused of "counterrevolutionary terrorism," depriving them of any legal rights, and arrests of former party oppositionists began.

Although Stalin almost certainly masterminded the Kirov murder, it is possible that Beria was in on the plot as well. Beria had little regular contact with Kirov after the latter moved up to Leningrad in 1925, aside from an occasional meeting in Moscow or at Stalin's *dacha* (vacation home) in Gagra, and he had no direct interest in getting rid of him. But he would have been eager to assist Stalin when called upon. Two pieces of circumstantial evidence suggest Beria's involvement. First, Beria for some reason visited NKVD chief Iagoda regularly in Moscow during 1934. (On one occasion Iagoda gave Beria's son, Sergo, a new bicycle.[2]) Second, when Sergo Ordzhonikidze was visiting Transcaucasia in early November 1934, he was stricken with a strange, sudden illness that kept him away from Moscow just before the murder. Ordzhonikidze had a close relationship with Kirov and would have done all he could to protect him. He had traveled with Beria to Baku and dined at Bagirov's apartment on the evening of 6 November. Immediately afterward he began to feel poorly and by 8 November he was suffering from internal bleeding in his stomach. Ordzhonikidze meant to return to Moscow by mid-November, but Stalin sent him a telegram ordering him to follow the advice of the doctors and remain in Tbilisi until 29 November. This was right after the conclusion of a Central Committee plenum, which Kirov had attended, and less than two days before the murder. Conveniently for Stalin, Ordzhonikidze was not well enough to go to Leningrad with Stalin and other leaders to "investigate" the assassination.[3]

It is possible that Ordzhonikidze's illness, for which the doctors could find no explanation, in fact resulted from a harmful substance administered secretly at Beria's behest in order to keep him away from Kirov and prevent him from somehow interfering with the plot. Whatever the facts, and they will probably never come to light, the Kirov affair was the first in a series of sudden deaths in suspicious circumstances that somehow involved Beria. In all these cases the deaths eliminated troublesome political figures who could not easily be dealt with by straightforward arrest.

Widespread arrests were not to occur for some time, but signs of a clamp-down came in May 1935 when a check (*proverka*) of party documents was initiated in Transcaucasia as part of a nationwide campaign to update party records and screen members. Beria discussed the *proverka* in a June 1935 speech to Tbilisi party activists, noting that disorganization and poor recordkeeping had contributed to more serious problems: "The check of party documents is finally revealing the fact that, taking advantage of the disorder in party recordkeeping, alien and anti-Soviet elements have penetrated the ranks of the party by means of various forgeries."[4] The check resulted in several thousand expulsions from the party. In February 1936, after the process was completed, nearly 19 percent of party members in Transcaucasia had been expelled and some had been arrested.[5]

This was part of a process of selective repression that helped to create a suitable public climate for a larger purge. In some cases, such as that of the author of the ill-fated book on the Baku underground press, Avel Enukidze, who was placed under police surveillance in Tbilisi, bitter attacks in the press continued for months on end. Enukidze was not arrested until late 1936, but his fate was sealed and with it the fate of many other members of the bolshevik Old Guard in Georgia. Enukidze's public disgrace marked a turning point for Georgian Bolsheviks, and for all of the older Bolsheviks, who could no longer rely on their established credentials as dedicated revolutionaries to protect themselves from accusations of traitorous activities. It was only a matter of time before most of them would be drawn into a web of denunciations and fabricated conspiracies. Because he had been a full member of the Central Committee in Moscow and was a former close comrade of Stalin's, Enukidze's tragic demise attracted considerable attention. It was widely assumed that Enukidze's memoirs on the Baku press caused him to fall out of favor with Stalin, but this may have been a pretext. A stronger reason for Stalin's disfavor was that Enukidze protested the reprisals against the Old Guard and was reluctant to sign the infamous decree of 1 December 1934, which in effect legalized summary justice.[6]

Stalin had laid the groundwork by 1936 for the impending purges. The coercive arm of the party, the political police, had gained increasing authority. In July 1934 the OGPU was transformed into a Main Administration of State Security (GUGB) and integrated into a newly formed All-Union NKVD (People's Commissariat for Internal Affairs). This united the functions of the security police with those of the regular police into one powerful body, which included border and internal troops, prisons and forced labor camps (the GULAG), and a so-called Special Board, empowered to impose sentences of up to five years imprisonment by administrative order rather than judicial means.[7]

In November 1934 Sergei Goglidze, former chief of the Transcaucasian border troops and a close associate of Beria, had replaced Tite Lordkipanidze as head of the NKVD in Georgia and Transcaucasia. The latter was transferred to the Crimean NKVD. In January 1936, in a speech to NKVD border troops, Goglidze warned against complacency and reminded them that the class enemy had by no means been defeated. The next day it was announced that Goglidze had been awarded an Order of the Red Banner, along with several other NKVD officials.[8] Goglidze's loyalty was to prove crucial to Beria in the next two years.

While some members of "Beria's gang," such as Avksentii Rapava, Nikolai Rukhadze, and Bogdan Kobulov, remained in the NKVD and worked directly under Goglidze, others moved into key party and state posts in Georgia. Dekanozov became a Central Committee secretary and, later, People's Commissar for the Food Industry, joining the Georgian Party Bureau in 1935; Merkulov became a Georgian Central Committee Department chief; and former NKVD official Solomon Mil'shtein, a *raikom* (district party committee) secretary.[9] These were just a few of the many officials who were now part of Beria's patronage network.

The Deaths of Khandzhian and Lakoba

In 1936 Beria faced a potential dimunition of his authority because of the planned dissolution of the Transcaucasian Federation in connection with the drafting of a new constitution for the USSR in 1936. This meant that the top party organization of Transcaucasia, the Zakkraikom, was also to be dissolved. Indeed Beria would be left with only his Georgian party post as of early 1937, when the new constitution went into effect.[10] Beria was probably not happy with this innovation, but of course he had to go along with it. In a June 1936 *Pravda* article he greeted the dissolution of the Transcaucasian Republic as a victory for socialism and for the Leninist-Stalinist line on nationality policy.[11]

The loss of de facto control over the Azerbaidzhan party apparatus was not very serious for Beria because its chief, Bagirov, was his henchman. But Armenia was a different matter. The party leader there since 1931, A. G. Khandzhian, had his own power base and was ill-disposed toward Beria, who had unsuccessfully tried to intrigue against him. And Beria was angry at Khandzhian because Khandzhian had protected the Armenian People's Commissar of Education, Nersik Stepanian, when the latter had criticized Beria's book for its falsehoods. Khandzhian also antagonized Beria by trying to gain as much autonomy as possible for Armenia under the proposed new constitution, traveling to Moscow in late June 1936 to plead Armenia's case with Stalin.[12]

On his return from Moscow Khandzhian stopped in Tbilisi to attend a plenum of the Zakkraikom on 9 July. The plenum, presided over by Beria, criticized Khandzhian for his nationalist attitudes and his "lack of vigilance." Beria blamed him for covering up the "traitorous activities" of Stepanian and for playing into the hands of a counterrevolutionary terrorist group that had allegedly been discovered in Transcaucasia. On 11 July the Zakkraikom and the Armenian Central Committee announced that Khandzhian had committed suicide in Tbilisi immediately after the plenum. The announcement went on to condemn Khandzhian:

> Considering the act of suicide a manifestation of cowardice especially unworthy of a leader of a party organization, the Zakkraikom of the VKP(B) considers it essential to inform party members that Comrade Khandzhian committed several political errors in his work recently, demonstrating insufficient vigilance in the case of the discovery of nationalist, counterrevolutionary Trotskyite groups. Having realized his mistakes, Comrade Khandzhian could not find the courage within himself to correct them in a Bolshevik manner and committed suicide.[13]

As if to buttress this rather feeble explanation for Khandzhian's sudden death, the announcement added that he was also depressed about the fact that he was suffering from a serious form of tuberculosis. Two days later the Armenian Central Committee, in an obvious effort to stave off further criticism, issued a lengthy statement condemning Khandzhian in more explicit terms.[14] He had, it seems, deliberately ignored the advice of his party colleagues in protecting Trotskyites and had deceived the Armenian Central Committee by covering up for Stepanian. Despite the "enormous help" rendered to him by the Zakkraikom "and Comrade Beria personally" in his daily work, Khandzhian had continued to manifest a lack of vigilance. In other words Khandzhian had refused to punish Stepanian for criticizing Beria's book.

Questions soon arose about the circumstances of Khandzhian's death, particularly among Armenians abroad, who voiced skepticism about the version presented in the official Transcaucasian press.[15] Years later, in a speech to the Twenty-second CPSU Party Congress in 1961, KGB Chief Aleksandr Shelepin claimed that Beria himself had killed Khandzhian in his office.[16] Although Shelepin gave no details, other sources have cited statements by two former members of the party's Central Control Commission, who claimed they were in the room adjacent to Beria's office when they heard a shot. Upon opening the door, they saw Beria standing over Khandzhian with a pistol. Fearing for their own lives, they agreed to be silent about the incident and participated in a cover-up. Khandzhian's body was taken back to his room, where a suicide was staged.[17]

The cover-up involved those who investigated the death immediately after Khandzhian's body was discovered. A report of the investigation (now available in the Georgian state archives), stamped "top secret" and signed by the Georgian procurator, concluded that the death was a suicide.[18] According to this report, Khandzhian had gone to his room to rest after having supper in his Tbilisi apartment with colleagues. Two of these colleagues—A. S. Amatuni, who was to succeed him as first secretary in Armenia, and another official—went to an adjacent room to sleep. Two hours later, when Khandzhian's bodyguard entered Khandzhian's room to answer a telephone that had been ringing for some time (Beria was on the line), he discovered the Armenian party chief lying on the bed in a pool of blood with a revolver by his side. That no one heard a gunshot, according to the investigation report, lends credence to the hypothesis that Khandzhian was shot elsewhere and then, perhaps with the connivance of Amatuni, moved back to his apartment. With Khandzhian out of the way, Beria was in a position to launch an attack against the Armenian party apparatus. Within a short time several officials were removed from the Armenian party bureau and Central Committee.[19]

In December 1936 another prominent Transcaucasian politician, Nestor Lakoba, suffered a similar fate. Lakoba was chairman of the Central Executive Committee of Abkhazia, which was part of the Georgian Republic, and had known both Stalin and Beria for years. If the portrayal of Beria and Lakoba in the fictional novel *Sandro iz chegema* is accurate, they came to despise each other, with Stalin deliberately fueling their animosity.[20] Lakoba, it will be recalled, informed Ordzhonikidze in 1932 that Beria had been speaking badly about him, which clearly aroused Beria's ire. Another source of conflict between Beria and Lakoba was probably the longstanding animosity between Mingrelians and Abkhazians. During the Second Five-Year Plan (1933–37) Beria initiated the resettlement in Abkhazia of large numbers of Mingrelians, Armenians, and Russians. This upset many Abkhazian Communists and they protested, but to no avail.[21]

In late December 1936 Lakoba traveled to Tbilisi with his brother Mikhail, who was People's Commissar of Agriculture in Abkhazia, to visit Beria. A few days later Nestor Lakoba's sudden death from a heart attack was announced. His body was returned to Sukhumi, where an elaborate state funeral took place, attended by thousands of mourners. According to several sources, Lakoba, who was in his forties and had no history of heart disease, was in fact poisoned by Beria.[22] Although this claim cannot be verified, it does seem that Beria was making moves against Lakoba. In early 1936 he had a protégé, former Cheka/GPU official A. S. Argba, transferred to Abkhazia to become party first secretary there, an indication that he was planning some sort of purge in that republic.[23] Moreover, Lakoba was posthumously accused of counterrevolutionary crimes, just as Khandzhian had been. Lakoba, who had been in his post for more than fifteen years, was extremely popular among the Abkhazians and Beria may have thought it unwise to have him arrested. Once he was dead it was easier to discredit him.[24] Whatever the case, Beria would never have moved against Lakoba without Stalin's sanction.

PRELUDE TO THE PURGES

In addition to the violent deaths of two potential opponents of Beria, another ominous sign of repression had come in August 1936, when an article by Beria, entitled "Scatter the Ashes of the Enemies of Socialism," appeared in *Pravda*.[25] Beria described at great length how subversives were using every means at their disposal, including terror, sabotage, and espionage, to harm the Soviet state and revealed that during the check of party documents several counterrevolutionary groups had been uncovered in Tbilisi, Baku, and Erevan. He mentioned as an example of the lack of vigilance the case of former party leader Khandzhian, who as far back as 1934 had ignored evidence pointing to the activities of counterrevolutionary groups in Armenia. Toward the end of the article Beria urged party members to step up their vigilance in order to destroy the enemies of socialism:

> Every party organization must vigilantly stand guard over the purity of its ranks, for where degenerates, slipshod operators, careerists, self-seekers, those without morals and others remain in the party, the counterrevolutionary-espionage-trotskyite-zinovievite has the ground for his work, finds his friends, organizes cadres for his counterrevolutionary, terrorist work.[26]

That Beria gave detailed evidence of ties between individuals and counterrevolutionary groups abroad indicated that plans to "expose" specific party officials had been underway for some time and that cases were now being prepared against them. Indeed the timing of this article was significant in that it appeared on the opening day of a Moscow show trial of former Politburo members Zinoviev and Kamenev, during which "Georgian deviationists" were implicated in the alleged conspiracy.[27]

Shortly thereafter, an important change occurred in the NKVD leadership in Moscow, when Nikolai Ezhov replaced Iagoda as NKVD chief, presumably as part of Stalin's effort to prepare the purge machinery.[28] At a CC plenum in early December 1936 Ezhov made a speech denouncing the prominent bolshevik theoretician Nikolai Bukharin. The latter had already been implicated in counterrevolutionary activity and now Ezhov accused him of being the ringleader, along with Aleksei Rykov, of a large conspiracy.[29] Eager to display his indignation in front of Stalin over Bukharin's alleged crimes, Beria jumped up no fewer than thirty-five times during Ezhov's speech with such interjections as "swine," "what a scoundrel," "that spy" and also added bits of information to strengthen the denunication. When it was Bukharin's turn to defend himself, Beria began interrupting him. Finally Bukharin turned to him in exasperation: "Good, Comrade Beria. But I didn't ask you. I am speaking for myself."[30]

In addition to Bukharin, whose arrest was imminent, the net was closing in on other prominent Bolsheviks, including Ordzhonikidze, now People's Commissar of Heavy Industry. Although he himself was in no immediate danger, Ordzhonikidze was under a great deal of pressure, as the NKVD had begun arresting his friends and relatives. Just a few weeks earlier, in late October 1936, the Georgian NKVD had arrested his brother Papulia. Sergo had heard about it while he was vacationing in Kislovodsk, in the North Caucasus, on the occasion of his fiftieth birthday. According to his wife, Zinaida, he was so upset that he refused to attend a special celebration in his honor. Bagirov happened to be present at the time and Ordzhonikidze conveyed to him his anger at Beria because of the arrest.[31]

Even after this incident, however, the formalities of friendship had been maintained. Beria, who had recently organized the publication of a special collection of Ordzhonikidze's writings, wrote a glowing birthday tribute to him, which appeared in *Pravda* just a few days after Papulia's arrest.[32] And Ordzhonikidze, for his part, did not seem anxious to break off relations with Beria completely. Indeed, he even turned to Beria for help on behalf of his younger brother, Valiko, just a few weeks later. Valiko, it seems, was fired from his job in the Tbilisi Soviet (Council) and expelled from the party for proclaiming the innocence of his brother Papulia. Ordzhonikidze apparently assumed that the decision to fire his brother had been made by the soviet and not on Stalin's orders, so he prevailed upon Beria as a last resort and telephoned him with a request for help. Beria responded right away, with a letter dated 25 December 1936:

> Dear Comrade Sergo!
> After your call I immediately summoned Valiko and he told me the story of his dismissal, confirming everything that the Chairman of the Tbilisi Soviet, Comrade Niogradze, sets forth in the enclosed explanation. On this very day Valiko was reinstated in his job.   Yours, L. Beria [33]

It may seem odd that Beria was willing to help Ordzhonikidze in this case, after having just presided over the arrest of his other brother. But the arrest could never have been carried out on Beria's own initiative. He must have been acting on orders from Stalin, who was moving against Ordzhonikidze on several fronts, and had no choice but to follow through.[34] When Beria had a little discretion, however, he was not averse to being helpful to someone if it suited his purposes. This episode epitomizes the surreal atmosphere of politics during the Stalinist period, where officials received important honors and medals just as warrants for their arrests were being prepared and where politicians toasted with Stalin at festive dinners while their closest family members were languishing in labor camps on his orders. A facade of "business as usual" and rational officialdom covered a torrent of violence and terror.

By late January 1937 Ordzhonikidze's situation had become desperate. He had been forced to stand by helplessly as his loyal deputy, G. L. Piatikov, was tried and executed. Then Stalin demanded that he prepare a speech, for the upcoming CC plenum, on sabotage in heavy industry, an obvious prelude to a purge of Ordzhonikidze's commissariat. This apparently was the last straw for Ordzhonikidze, who could foresee the impending terror and was not willing to be an accomplice to the persecution of his colleagues. On 18 February 1937, the day before the plenum was to open, Ordzhonikidze shot himself, following a heated argument with Stalin on the telephone.[35]

The suicide of such a prominent politician as Ordzhonikidze of course disrupted the outward political harmony and had to be hastily covered up by presenting it to the public as a heart attack. That evening, as part of the official ritual, Ordzhonikidze's party colleagues went to his home to offer their condolences to his wife, Zinaida. According to an eyewitness:

> Sometime later the Politburo members and a number of other high-placed offi-
> cials gathered in the dining room. Beria also appeared. In the presence of Stalin,
> Molotov, Zhdanov and the others, Zinaida Gavrilovna [Sergo's widow] called
> Beria a rat. She approached him and tried to slap him. Beria disappeared right
> after that and did not come to Sergo's apartment again.[36]

Beria skulked off, but he got his revenge. He later subjected Papulia to inhuman torture, forcing him to sign a confession saying that he had planned to kill Stalin, which Beria then delivered personally to the party leader.[37]

The CC plenum, which had to be postponed because of Ordzhoni-kidze's death, opened on 23 February. With Ordzhonikidze out of the way, it was easier for Stalin to silence all potential opposition to his plans for a massive attack on the party apparatus. Apparently several members of the Central Committee tried to persuade Stalin to abandon the purge and specifically to withdraw the charges of treason against Bukharin and Rykov, who were about to be arrested. But Stalin as usual managed to outwit his opponents and manipulate the proceedings to his advantage. In his speech to the plenum, which appeared in the press, Stalin portrayed Soviet society as swarming with spies and saboteurs, who pretended to be loyal to the party while actively working against it. He censured party officials for their lack of vigilance, their complacency and blindness, de-claring that these conspirators had to be ruthlessly smashed once and for all. Stalin was preparing the nation for widespread terror.[38]

Stalin also claimed that the time had come for more "intra-party de-mocracy," implying that dictatorial regional leaders should be replaced during upcoming party elections. He was outspokenly critical of party officials who cultivated a network of men personally loyal to them and who brought protégés with them when they were transferred to new posts. Stalin made it clear why he disapproved so strongly of this wide-spread practice of political patronage: "What does it mean to drag along with you a whole group of friends? It means that you gain some inde-pendence from the local organization, and, if you will, from the Central Committee."[39] Stalin evidently worried that such "family groups" in the regions away from Moscow would threaten his absolute power and that the loyalties among members of these groups would be obstacles to implementation of the terror. The solution to this problem was to introduce more "intraparty democracy" by having elections with secret ballots as a means of bringing in new people to replace the entrenched party bureaucrats.

Beria, with his extensive network of loyal protégés, must have been disquieted by Stalin's directive on intraparty democracy, which threatened to undermine his position. Furthermore, G. N. Kaminskii, People's Commissar for Health, was dredging up the old charge about Beria having been a spy for the Musavat government in 1920. Kaminskii was expelled from the party and arrested in June for being "untrustworthy," but nonetheless the accusation must have heightened Beria's vulnerability.[40]

TENSIONS WITH MOSCOW

The evidence suggests, not surprisingly, that Beria was unenthusiastic about "democratic" elections to party posts. Indeed, the turnover among Georgian party officials as a result of elections that took place in March–April 1937, in accordance with the instructions of the February plenum, was small. In a speech to the Tenth Party Congress of the Georgian Communist Party, held from 15–21 May, Beria reported that, although 25–30 percent of party committee members had been elected for the first time, no secretary of a *raikom*, *gorkom*, or *obkom* (district, city, or regional party committee) lost his post in the elections.[41] Georgia was not the only area where these secretaries remained in office.[42] The impact of the elections on the party apparatuses was not all that significant anywhere, so Beria was not alone in thwarting the apparent purpose of the elections.[43]

It is hardly surprising that there would be resistance to Moscow's directives. Although the electoral campaign was a separate process from NKVD purges in the sense that secretaries and members who were voted out were not necessarily arrested, the Central party leadership intended to use the elections not only to break up regional and republican party machines, but also to drop officials, including certain party chieftains, who were designated for arrest. The campaign for "democracy" was an obvious prelude to a broad witch-hunt for spies, traitors, and terrorists.

This may be why Beria urged restraint in his speech to the Tenth Congress. While he conceded that enemies of the people had not been completely destroyed, he went on to caution:

> We must act intelligently, so that one extreme does not lead to another. An indiscriminate approach to all former national deviationists and former

Trotskyites, of whom a few in the past turned up in their ranks and long ago honestly moved away from Trotskyism, can only harm the cause of the struggle with real Trotskyites, enemies and spies.[44]

Beria's resistance to Moscow, however subtle, was immediately noticed. The day after he made his remarks a highly critical article on the Georgian Congress appeared in *Pravda*.[45] The author, *Pravda*'s correspondent in Tbilisi (and thus a spokesman for the central party apparatus), attacked officials in Georgia for their complacency about faults within their organizations. Among those singled out for criticism was Beria's protégé Aleksei Argba, recently elected president of the Abkhazian government. The *Pravda* writer condemned the tendency to blame everything on past leaders who had long been removed, and complained that there were no ongoing efforts to eliminate poor methods of leadership. He observed sardonically that all those who spoke at the congress had ended with the traditional phrases honoring Georgian party leaders, which were followed by rote applause. Why, he asked, if these officials understood the directives of the February plenum, were they congratulating the leadership instead of demanding concrete results. The article ended by noting that the Georgian party had serious problems, which could only be solved by "ridding itself of the sickness from which, as the Congress had shown, several Georgian party leaders suffer."

Numerous other republican and regional party leaders were criticized in the press for similar shortcomings.[46] But this could scarcely have been a comfort to Beria, since most were about to be purged. Beria moved quickly to meet the threat, preparing a report for Stalin on the elections in Georgia as well as a response to the *Pravda* article, both of which were discussed at a meeting of the Georgian party bureau on 26 May. Beria then flew off to Moscow to put his case before Stalin. Apparently he assured Stalin that he would proceed full speed ahead with the purges because right after he returned to Tbilisi a large number of officials were removed from their posts for counterrevolutionary activities.[47]

That Beria managed to emerge unscathed from this dangerous situation was strong testimony to his political acumen. By 5 June he appeared to have weathered the storm. On that day he had an article published in *Pravda* on the results of the congress in which he adopted a tone that was far from contrite. Indeed, he used precisely those self-congratulatory phrases that the *Pravda* correspondent had found so offensive, stressing how much the Georgian party organization had accomplished in routing out spies and traitors. Toward the end of his report, however, he acknowledged the necessity for continued purges: "Georgian Bolsheviks will henceforth deal mercilessly and implacably with all enemies of the party and people, wreckers, diversionaries, spies and their accomplices."[48]

However much zeal he displayed publicly, Beria had little cause for enthusiasm about a widespread, violent purge in Georgia. It was one thing to get rid of enemies but quite another to decimate Georgia's party and state bureaucracy. Although he undoubtedly had few moral qualms about destroying innocent people, he had less to gain from doing so on a broad scale than Stalin had. One of Stalin's purposes was to ensure the total obedience of his subjects through fear. The purges enabled him not only to eliminate all possible opponents but also to instill in those who survived such intense anxiety that they posed no threat to his dominance. Stalin's security, as he saw it, depended on the insecurity of his colleagues, subordinates, and the public as a whole. For Beria, however, the situation was different. Although the general atmosphere of terror might deter potential challenges to his authority within Georgia, his fate was ultimately in the hands of Stalin. Beria had carefully and systematically built up a loyal following in Georgia, establishing a solid base for his rule there. The full-scale purge of 1937–38 was to create disarray and disorganization in the Georgian party and state apparatus, even forcing Beria to sacrifice some of his loyal henchmen. However amoral and sadistic Beria was, he was not, at this point at least, irrational. He did not suffer from the paranoia and megalomania that provided the ultimate motivation for Stalin to implement the "Great Terror."

SHOW TRIALS IN GEORGIA

Whatever his doubts about unleashing terror in Georgia, Beria had no choice but to proceed, and henceforth he exhibited no hesitation. A job was a job. Upon his return from Moscow after the June 1937 Central Committee plenum, Beria instructed Georgian NKVD chief Goglidze to call a meeting of all the city, district, and autonomous republican NKVD heads, who duly gathered together in the Georgian Central Committee headquarters on 9 July. Beria then declared that if those under arrest did not give the required confessions it would be necessary to beat them. He was following a Central Committee resolution, initiated by Stalin, that authorized physical torture.[49] Goglidze described the effect in Georgia:

> After this the Georgian NKVD began mass beatings of those under arrest. They were beaten at will. Testimonies against large groups of people appeared in the records and the numbers of those arrested as a result of having been mentioned in the testimonies grew, which led to falsification of cases and a distortion of reality.[50]

One of the first victims of the newly launched terror was the prominent Georgian Bolshevik Budu Mdivani. As was noted earlier, Mdivani had fought hard in 1921–22 against Stalin's efforts to form the Transcaucasian Federation, appealing to Lenin to protect Georgia's interests. Although Stalin had been close to Mdivani, he could not forgive him for this defiance and the two never reconciled their differences. Mdivani, for his part, lost few opportunities to make sarcastic digs at Stalin in the ensuing years. According to one account, for example, Mdivani liked to tell a joke about how Georgian workers urged Beria to set up an armed guard around the house of Stalin's mother in Tbilisi, not for protection, but so she would not give birth to another Stalin. Stalin, who heard about Mdivani's criticisms of him through Beria, did not take them lightly.[51]

To make matters worse, Mdivani had clung to his opposition to the Transcaucasian Federation. At a meeting of Tbilisi party activists held in June 1936 to discuss the new constitution and the consequent liquidation of the federation, Mdivani commented on how long it had taken for the worthlessness of the federation to be acknowledged.[52] Mdivani's outspokenness on this issue did not sit well with either Stalin or Beria, who had always presented the Transcaucasian Federation as a triumph for socialism. Within a few months Mdivani was dismissed from his post as deputy chairman of the Georgian Sovnarkhom (Council of People's Commissars) and a case was opened against him.

Mdivani himself courageously refused to "confess," as did another defendant in the case, Mikhail Okudzhava, which was presumably why the trial was held *in camera*. On 11 July 1937 *Zaria vostoka*, with the headline of "Death to Enemies of the People," announced the results. The Georgian Supreme Court found Mdivani, Okudzhava, and several other leading Georgian officials guilty of treason and other counterrevolutionary crimes (all covered under article 58 of the Criminal Code).[53] Mdivani, as the alleged ringleader, was accused of having established a secret "fighting group" armed with weapons and aiming to kill Beria and bring down the Soviet government. All were shot.

The day after the announcement of the verdict, *Zaria vostoka* reported on a meeting of Tbilisi party activists, at which Beria had spoken. Beria revealed the discovery of a widespread counterrevolutionary terrorist network within the Georgian NKVD. The culprits had been exposed and would be "obliterated into dust."[54] An NKVD employee, Suren Gazarian, who was arrested in July 1937, later revealed that at least seventeen high-level officials of his organization were charged with being members of this counterrevolutionary group, which was alleged to have ties with Mdivani's "national center." Among those arrested was Tite Lordkipanidze, former chief of the Transcaucasian GPU/NKVD, who had been working in the Crimea. Lordkipanidze eventually broke down under torture and "confessed," implicating several of his former subordinates, including Gazarian. Lordkipanidze and others were shot, and some committed suicide in prison, but Gazarian was lucky enough to be sentenced to ten years of imprisonment, from which he survived to recount his experiences.[55]

Among Beria's former police colleagues who fell victim to the purges were his former boss, Kvantaliani; Argba, who had worked in the GPU/NKVD before becoming party chief of Abkhazia; I. F. Stanskii, earlier a deputy chairman of the Transcaucasian NKVD; and A. N. Mikeladze, an old friend of Ordzhonikidze who served as police chief in Abkhazia from 1930 to 1937.[56] For the most part, however, Beria's Chekist protégés prospered as a result of the purges. Not long after the Mdivani trial and the ensuing sweep of arrests, *Zaria vostoka* published a list of Transcaucasian NKVD officials honored with awards for their "exemplary and selfless fulfillment of government tasks." Among those awarded were Georgian NKVD chief Goglidze; NKVD chief of Adzharia, a region in Georgia, M. A. Stepanov; and Georgian NKVD deputy chiefs Rapava, Kobulov, and Rukhadze.[57] These men planned the details of the public trials and conducted interrogations of the most prominent victims, while the overall direction was in the hands of Beria, who read the reports of the interrogations and gave instructions on who should be arrested.[58]

Of course Beria was operating according to guidelines established by Moscow, where the basic plans for the liquidation of the old party and state hierarchy were orchestrated. According to recently published archival documents, Stalin launched the purge officially with a Central Committee resolution on 2 July 1937. Then Ezhov followed up with more specific plans: in the next four months alone some 268,950 people were to be arrested and 75,950 shot immediately. In response to reports sent to him from regional and republican party leaders, Ezhov had set specific quotas for prisoners in each area, dividing them into category one (shot immediately) and category two (prison or labor camp). NKVD *troikas* (groups of three men) were set up to review cases and pass sentences. Beria's report to Ezhov did not appear among these documents, but that of Khrushchev, at the time Moscow party secretary, did. He not only recommended that 20,000 "kulak and criminal elements" be shot or arrested but he also requested, with no success, that he be designated a member of the troika. Other regional leaders fulfilled their plans and then wrote to Moscow asking permission to raise the quotas, opening the way for a flood of further arrests and executions.[59]

The almost monotonous similarity of the show trials in the various republics, with names and dates varied but charges and confessions strikingly alike, reflected the fact that republican authorities were following a formula prescribed by Moscow. The next big political trial in Georgia took place in August 1937. Because the Georgian NKVD had successfully wrested confessions out of the accused, the trial was public. The defendants, ten in all, were recently dismissed officials from the Signakhsk raion, accused of forming a counterrevolutionary terrorist organization. One of the leaders of the alleged organization, the former raion secretary A. D. Tsitlidze, gave lurid details of attempts to undermine agriculture and carry out terrorist acts against government figures. Similar "confessions" were given by other defendants.[60] This case was followed by a trial in September of eleven officials from Adzharia, with the leading defendant the former chief of the Central Executive Committee of Adzharia, Z. D. Lordkipanidze. The charges, by now familiar, ran the entire gammut of counterrevolutionary crimes: terrorism, treason, espionage, and so on. Lordkipanidze was accused of organizing a group that had ties with foreign agents abroad, with the goal of sabotaging Georgian agriculture, overthrowing the government, and killing Beria.[61]

At the end of October 1937 a trial of Abkhazian officials, including the brother of the deceased Nestor Lakoba, Mikhail Lakoba, opened in the city of Sukhumi. The charges involved counterrevolutionary crimes, including participation in a plot to kill Beria and Stalin, concocted by Nestor Lakoba. All the defendants confessed.[62] The irony of portraying Nestor Lakoba as having been the ringleader of this conspiratorial group was not lost on Stalin's biographer, Boris Souvarine: "Nestor Lakoba, accused of homicidal intentions with regard to Stalin, was actually the author of the pamphlet, *Stalin and Khashim*, in which he celebrated 'the greatest man of a whole epoch, such as history gives to humanity only once in one or two hundred years.'"[63]

Beria went after Lakoba's family with particular vengeance. Like Stalin, Beria could be especially cruel to those whom he knew well. Roy Medvedev reports that Lakoba's young wife was arrested shortly after his death. The Georgian NKVD led her away from her cell every evening for interrogation, and in the mornings she would be dragged back to her cell unconscious and covered with blood. The interrogators were trying to get her to sign a document saying that Lakoba had betrayed Abkhazia to Turkey, but she steadfastly refused, even when they threatened to kill her beloved fourteen-year-old son Rauf, who was beaten in front of her. Lakoba's wife finally died after a beating and her son was sent to a special labor camp for children. Sometime later Rauf reportedly wrote to Beria requesting that he and two comrades be allowed to continue their studies. After receiving the letter, Beria ordered the three boys to be brought to Tbilisi where they were shot. By this time almost all of Lakoba's family and friends had either been shot or imprisoned.[64]

Beria meted out similar punishment to one of the "ghost writers" of his book, E. D. Bediia, who had continued to devote himself to furthering the cult of Stalin in Transcaucasian history.[65] His career was cut short in October 1937 by his arrest on charges of participating in an anti-Soviet organization and preparing a terrorist act against Beria. Beria took a special interest in the Bediia case, reading all reports on the investigation and interrogations, just as he did with others who had worked closely with him in the past, such as Kartvelishvili and Kakhiani. Apparently he wanted to make sure that the confessions did not inadvertently implicate him. After being subjected to severe beatings, Bediia signed a confession, but for Beria that was not enough. He demanded a personal confrontation with the accused, possibly in the hopes that Bediia would give up any claims to the authorship of Beria's book. Bediia renounced his earlier confession when he met with Beria, who was extremely displeased. As a result, Bediia did not have a court trial; his fate was decided instead by an NKVD troika and he was shot on 2 December 1937.[66]

In fact those party officials who were tried publicly were in a distinct minority. The usual practice was a month or two of confinement, followed by a quick sentencing by the troika. In addition to the republican NKVD troika, which dealt with the most important cases, there were also troikas in the regional, district, and city NKVD branches. By mid-1937, judging from the correspondence between the party apparatus and the NKVD, the troikas were meting out sentences on a mass scale—handling thousands of cases every month.[67]

Not infrequently, however, prisoners died before sentencing as a result of beatings and torture at the hands of Beria's sadistic deputies or suicide. Rapava and Shota Tsereteli, who were members of the troika, actually murdered prisoners with their own hands. One prisoner, a former Georgian Komsomol secretary, ran to a window and jumped to his death as a result of what he had to endure during the interrogation.[68] A former NKVD officer later told how a subordinate, one Serebriakov, did not realize that he had beaten a prisoner to death during the interrogation:

> When I asked Serebriakov "how are things?" he replied that the prisoner was silent and would not answer his questions. I went over to the accused. He was dead. Then I asked Serebriakov what he had done with him and he showed me a wire whip thrown down, and a club of double thickness with which he had beaten the prisoner on the spine, not knowing that he was already dead.[69]

THE INTELLIGENTSIA RAVAGED

From the beginning of his party career Beria had taken a keen interest in the artistic and literary community in Georgia. At first some Georgian writers thought well of Beria because he permitted several of those who were out of official favor to be admitted to a newly organized Union of Georgian Writers in 1934. But Beria's true motives were revealed when he insisted on contributions from every writer to a collection of fawning lyrics for Stalin. By mid-1936 the writers' journal, *Literary Georgia*, had become "Beria's one-man weekly."[70] Beria voiced serious concern about Georgian literature at the Tenth Georgian Party Congress in 1937, singling out writers who had ties with "enemies of the people."[71] Shortly thereafter, on 27 May, the Presidium of the Georgian Writers' Union held the first of several closed sessions to discuss Beria's charges. A Western scholar who managed in 1989 to obtain verbatim minutes of the sessions, observed that they were conducted just like trials. Ironically, he notes, the writers who came under the heaviest attacks were those who had adhered most ardently to the official line: "It amused Beria to spare some of those who refused to lavish praise on him and to drive to their deaths those, like Paolo Iashvili [a well-known poet], who had publicly allied themselves to him."[72]

Despite their desperate attempts to extricate themselves by confessing their errors and reiterating their devotion to Stalin and Beria, the accused writers were doomed. On 22 July 1937, at a presidium session of the Writers' Union, Iashvili pulled out a gun and killed himself. Widespread arrests of others followed. According to Rayfield, about 25 percent of the Tbilisi branch of the union perished, while in other regions of Georgia the mortality rate was even higher.[73] Mikheil Dzhavakhishvili, one of Georgia's most popular writers, was arrested on Beria's orders and beaten to death in prison. Because of his popularity Beria deemed it necessary to justify the arrest by calling the presidium of the Georgian Writers' Union into his office and reading them a confession, written in Dzhavakhishvili's own hand and admitting to accepting money from foreign agents.[74]

Other cultural figures also perished. The young and talented orchestra conductor Evgenii Mikeladze was arrested in November 1937. Mikeladze was married to the daughter of Mamia Orakhelashvili, Ketevan, who was taken away by the police as well, though she had two small sons. The chief investigator in the case, Bogdan Kobulov, subjected Mikeladze to forty-eight days of interrogation, after which he was sentenced to be shot by the NKVD troika.[75] According to one account, Beria also questioned him. Although Mikeladze was blindfolded he recognized Beria, saying "You have covered my eyes, but my hearing is as good as ever." Beria then gave him such a blow to the head that he was rendered deaf.[76] The assault by Beria and his colleagues against Georgia's artists and writers was to have a devastating effect on Georgia's culture for years to come.

Beria's pretentions to being a patron of the arts led him to decide in 1937 to build an elaborate new museum as part of a jubilee celebration for the 750th anniversary of the famed Georgian writer Rustaveli. This entailed tearing down the ancient church at Metekhi, a treasured historical building. Dmitri Shevardnadze, a prominent Georgian intellectual and art collector, took a group of scholars and social activists to persuade Beria to save the church. Beria replied that it would surely be enough to preserve a scale model of the church so that people could see it in a museum, and then told Shevardnadze privately that if he gave up his efforts to save the church he would be appointed director of the future museum. Shevardnadze refused and was arrested within a week.[77] The Rustaveli celebration, the main ceremony of which took place in the Tbilisi Opera Theater, came at the height of the purges. As the writer Geronti Kikodze observed, "At that very time in Tbilisi and in the provinces dark pits were full of the intelligentsia and peasants." According to Kikodze, a portrait of Rustaveli had been moved, at great expense, to make room for those of Stalin, Ezhov, and Beria.[78]

THE CULMINATION

The number of victims in the upper echelons of the party by this time was staggering: of the 644 delegates to the Tenth Georgian Party Congress in May 1937, 425 had been arrested and shot.[79] According to official Soviet statistics, approximately 4,000 full and candidate members of the Georgian Communist Party (roughly 10 percent) were purged between January 1937 and January 1938, but most other sources place the number of victims in the party much higher.[80] Although there are no figures on the rates of arrests for nonmembers of the party, an idea of the magnitude is offered by a subsequent assertion that the Georgian NKVD troika during the time of its existence reviewed cases against 30,000 people, approximately a third of whom were shot.[81] But this figure presumably does not include cases reviewed by troikas at lower levels in the hierarchy. According to Geronti Kikodze:

> Many non-members of the party perished only because, for some reason, they had raised doubts among the Tbilisi triumvirate and its provincial branches, or some informer had come to envy their apartment or job. In 1937 the arrests and executions took place on such a massive scale that the trio in Tbilisi and their agents often did not concern themselves with compiling lists and conducting investigations: they judged guilty and innocent alike according to the law of the Holy Inquisition, and their decision had the power of God.[82]

On 2 December 1937 Politburo member Anastas Mikoian arrived in Tbilisi, meeting with Beria and Goglidze, presumably to discuss the progress of the purges.[83] Shortly thereafter a show trial, involving officials of the People's Commissariat of Agriculture, was staged. The press also reported that Enukidze and Orakhelashvili had been tried before a military collegium and shot on 16 December.[84] Orakhelashvili had kept his job as deputy director of the Institute of Marxism-Leninism in Moscow until April 1937, when his party card was removed on Ezhov's orders. He was soon arrested and transferred to Tbilisi. Subjected to intense torture, he signed a confession that included slanderous statements about his old comrade Ordzhonikidze. He was then tried by a Georgian NKVD troika and shot in front of his wife Maria, former deputy people's commissar of education in Georgia, who was herself subsequently executed.[85] With the exception of Kartvelishvili, who was not tried and shot until August 1938, the Georgian party Old Guard had been annihilated by the end of 1937.

By early 1938 the momentum of the purges was weakening. At a plenum on 14 January the Central Committee in Moscow issued a resolution, based on a report by Central Committee Secretary Georgii Malenkov, calling for measures to correct the errors and excesses committed by party leaders who had purged Communists without sufficient grounds.[86] By blaming regional party leaders for going too far, Stalin was able to shift responsibility for the purges from himself to those who had carried out his orders. At a plenum of the Georgian Central Committee held shortly thereafter, Beria duly reported on the resolution and spoke on the necessity of rectifying the mistakes that had occurred in Georgia.[87]

Stalin had evidently concluded that it was time to curtail the violence, but not before a final sweep of arrests and trials. At the end of January 1938 the Politburo issued a directive raising the quota on arrests, so as to authorize 57,200 more victims to be rounded up by the NKVD. According to the directive, Georgia was allocated an additional 1,500 arrests. All cases were to be dealt with and closed within two months.[88] The last show trial in Moscow was that of Bukharin, staged in March. In Georgia the last such trial—involving officials in the Animal Husbandry Institute—took place at the end of January 1938. Individual arrests continued throughout 1938, but on a much smaller scale.[89]

Mass arrests and executions had been occurring simultaneously in Armenia and Azerbaidzhan, where most of the party and state leadership was liquidated. Bagirov was the only leading Azerbaidzhan party official to escape being purged, presumably because he was protected by his friendship with Beria.[90] The party leader in Armenia, A. S. Amatuni, who had been in his post for little more than a year, was less fortunate. After a vist to Erevan by Georgii Malenkov and Beria in mid-September 1937 the leadership of the Armenian party apparatus was arrested and tried. The new first secretary was Beria's close associate, G. A. Arutinov, former head of the Tbilisi Party Committee.[91]

Throughout 1937 reports in the Georgian press on the exposure and punishment of counterrevolutionaries were interspersed with discussions about economic affairs and the arts, as well as with reports on routine

political developments. It was almost as if two separate Georgian socie-
ties existed simultaneously. During the autumn of 1937, while Georgian
prisons were filled beyond capacity with former party and state officials,
highly publicized preparations for elections to the USSR Supreme Soviet
were taking place. As their friends and neighbors were dragged off to
prison, candidates were delivering routine public speeches to their "con-
stituents." When Beria delivered his election speech in Tbilisi his tone was
less menacing than usual, but he left open the possibility of further arrests
by noting: "We cannot assume that all our enemies have been destroyed."[92] On 15 December *Zaria vostoka* published the election results,
along with a report of another indictment in a case of counterrevolutionaries. Not surprisingly, numerous members of Beria's entourage, including several NKVD delegates, featured among the newly elected Supreme
Soviet delegates.

It was fitting that 1937 closed with lavish celebrations honoring the
twentieth anniversary of the Soviet political police, the NKVD. *Zaria
vostoka* gave extensive coverage to the events, which took place in Tbilisi
as well as in Moscow.[93] NKVD Chief Ezhov, now a candidate member of
the Politburo, was accorded unprecedented prominence. His apparatus,
which had decimated the party, was now at the top of the power hierarchy. Robert Conquest has observed that regional and republic party secretaries no longer enjoyed supremacy in their areas, because police chiefs
were controlled by the center and could move against them at any time.
Beria's situation was somewhat different, however, because he had controlled the political police in Transcaucasia for a long time before becoming party chief. Somehow he had straddled the fence between police and
party, managing not only to survive, but to prosper. At the first session of
the USSR Supreme Soviet in Moscow in January 1938 Beria was elected
a member of the Supreme Soviet Presidium and also to the prestigious
Foreign Affairs Commission. When local papers reproduced pictures of
the session Beria was seated with the top leadership, right next to Ezhov.[94]
Within a short time the two would engage in a bitter power struggle, with
Ezhov the loser.

Chapter Five

MASTER OF THE LUBIANKA

> If a socialist society possesses so little inner elasticity that, in
> order to save it, one has to fall back on an omnipotent,
> universal, and totalitarian spy service, then things are
> in a bad way. . . . On whom are they to rely?
> On Beria? The bell will toll for him too.
> *(Trotsky,* Communism or Stalinism, *1939)*

BERIA'S DEFEAT OF EZHOV

AFTER THE PURGES had spent themselves by eliminating in a
frenzy a whole cadre of officials and large numbers of the general
public, the spring of 1938 witnessed a return to the appearance of
calm in Georgian political life. Beria and his colleagues seemed preoccupied with local elections and economic questions. In an article written for
Pravda in April 1938, Beria noted that the Soviet Union's internal enemies had been successfully defeated and then devoted his attention primarily to the Georgian economy.[1] His tone was similar in subsequent
speeches.[2] But, in fact, Beria was again in trouble by the late spring of
1938. He was subjected to slights by the press in terms of protocol. Instead of adhering to the rigorous rule of always listing him ahead of other
party figures in Georgia, *Zaria vostoka* slipped on at least two occasions
and placed Beria's name after lower-ranking leaders.[3] Another disquieting sign for Beria occurred at the end of May, when a protégé, Iuvelian
Sumbatov-Topuridze, was abruptly removed from his post as head of the
Azerbaidzhan NKVD, presumably on the orders of NKVD Chief Ezhov,
and replaced with an outsider.[4]

Ezhov, it seems, was preparing a case against Beria. In July 1938 he
ordered Georgian NKVD chief Sergei Goglidze to arrest Beria on charges
of involvement with the "Military-Fascist Center," whose case was already under investigation in Moscow. Instead of carrying out Ezhov's
orders, Goglidze was loyal to his patron, informing him of Ezhov's plans.
Beria said a tearful good-bye to his wife and son at the Tbilisi airport and
took a plane to Moscow (one source had him fleeing to Azerbaidzhan
first) where he appealed directly to Stalin.[5]

Beria reminded Stalin of his years of loyal, dedicated service and protested his innocence. Apparently his case was strengthened by the fact

that he had the support of Politburo member and People's Commissar of Heavy Industry Lazar Kaganovich, against whom Ezhov was also moving. Kaganovich was a seasoned Stalinist operative who was more than capable of fighting back, and somehow he and Beria managed to make Stalin see their side of things.[6] Stalin may have then decided that Ezhov had to be disposed of, but in his typical fashion he moved slowly, setting the stage for Ezhov's ultimate demise by forming a special commission to investigate the NKVD. The commission included CC Secretary Georgii Malenkov, Sovnarkom Chairman Viacheslav Molotov, USSR Procurator-General Andrei Vyshinskii, and Beria. According to Roy Medvedev, Kaganovich proposed that Beria be appointed a deputy chief of the NKVD so that he would have complete access to the materials needed for the investigation.[7]

With this in mind Stalin called together his subordinates, including Ezhov and Beria, summoned from Georgia. He declared that it was necessary to strengthen the NKVD by designating an assistant for Ezhov and asked Ezhov if he had any suggestions as to who should be appointed. When Ezhov did not offer any names Stalin suggested Beria. This caused Ezhov to start, but he restrained himself and answered: "He would be a good candidate. Comrade Beria can work, and not only as a deputy. He could even be people's commissar." Stalin replied disingenuously, "No, he isn't suited to be people's commissar, but he would make a good deputy."[8]

Beria was caught by surprise. According to Vsevold Merkulov, who wrote a lengthy report on Beria's career after the latter's arrest in 1953, Beria had not known why Stalin summoned him to Moscow and was dismayed when he learned he would have to be Ezhov's deputy.[9] Khrushchev had a similar impression, recalling that when he congratulated Beria on his new appointment the latter expressed displeasure.[10] Beria apparently did not realize then that Ezhov's days were numbered and that he was being groomed for Ezhov's powerful job. Or perhaps he was simply disinclined to serve again in the political police. In any case, he had no choice but to go along with Stalin's wishes and arrived in Moscow toward the end of August 1938 to take up his post as first deputy chairman of the USSR NKVD. The nature of his new appointment, confirmed by the USSR Sovnarkom on 22 August, was not mentioned in the press.[11] On 1 September 1938 *Zaria vostoka* simply announced that Beria had been relieved of his post as first secretary of the Georgian party organization in connection with a transfer to Moscow.[12]

Beria's replacement was Kandida Charkviani, third secretary of the Georgian Central Committee. Charkviani was not a member of Beria's clique and hence not Beria's preference for the post. Beria wanted his successor to be Valerian Bakradze, who had served as second secretary to

Beria in 1936 and 1937, before becoming head of the Georgian Sovnarkom. Bakradze, whose son was married to a niece of Nino Beria, was personally close to Beria and always went out of his way to please him. He organized a lavish banquet in Beria's honor before his departure for Moscow, and at a plenum of the Georgian CC on 31 August he was effusive in declaring his devotion to his former chief.[13]

Stalin probably rejected Bakradze's candidacy because he wanted the new party chief to be independent from Beria. But it soon became clear that Beria would manage to remain overlord of Georgia in absentia. After he left the republic the local press continued to pay homage to him with regular greetings from collective farms and industrial workers to the "devoted follower of the Great Stalin," along with photographs of him at high-level meetings and reprints of his speeches. At the Thirteenth Congress of the Georgian Communist Party in early 1940, republic leaders, including Charkviani, invoked Beria's name repeatedly, speaking about him in the most laudatory terms.[14]

Not surprisingly, Beria's appointment and the concommitant investigation into NKVD activities brought great consternation to Ezhov and his colleagues. Ezhov and Beria were outwardly friendly, and Beria was even a frequent guest at Ezhov's dacha during the first few months after his arrival. Ezhov continued to be treated normally in public, with no obvious signs of his imminent decline until after October 1938. But he was aware that he was being undermined—two of his deputies had been dismissed in early autumn—and began to fall apart under the strain, drinking heavily.[15]

Finally, the investigatory commission finished its report, which resulted in a secret resolution, adopted by the Sovnarkom and the Central Committee on 17 November 1938 and entitled "On Arrests, Supervision by the Procuracy and the Conduct of Investigations."[16] The strongly worded, lengthy resolution amounted to a complete renunciation of the purges. Directed at party, procuracy, and NKVD officials in the republics, it was highly critical of the "gross violations of legal norms" that had been committed during arrests and investigations, in particular the reliance on confessions extracted from the accused and the failure to keep records. Furthermore, the resolution stated, "the NKVD has gone so far in distorting the norms of the judicial process that very recently questions have arisen about giving it so-called 'limits' on the process of mass arrests." According to the resolution, "enemies of the people" who had penetrated the NKVD and the procuracy were falsifying investigatory documents and arresting innocent people.

The resolution forbade these organs from continuing their policy of mass arrests and exile. Henceforth, arrests were to be made only with the consent of the court or the Procurator; the notorious NKVD troikas, which decided cases on the spot, were to be abolished; the NKVD was to observe strictly the procedural laws on the conduct of investigations; and only "politically reliable" party members were to be appointed to NKVD posts. Finally, workers in the NKVD and the Procuracy were warned that they would face severe judicial sanctions for even the slightest infraction of Soviet law.

This resolution was the final nail in Ezhov's coffin. On 23 November he submitted a letter to Stalin requesting that he be relieved of his NKVD post and admitting that he bore full responsibility for all the NKVD's mistakes. His resignation was accepted by Stalin the next day and Beria took over as chief of the NKVD.[17] Ezhov's removal was a logical consequence of the winding down of the purges. Stalin needed a scapegoat for the mass terror that he had inflicted on the country and Ezhov was an obvious candidate.[18] Later, in the spring of 1939, USSR Procurator Vyshinskii also lost his job, which was not surprising given that he had conducted the highly publicized show trials. Fortunately for him, however, he was not arrested but simply transferred to a lesser post.[19]

BERIA TAKES OVER

Once in his new post, Beria set about "cleansing" the NKVD of undesirable elements. In other words, he initiated a full-scale purge of the Ezhovites, executing or imprisoning hundreds of officials. Even before his promotion Beria had moved against several NKVD officials closely associated with Ezhov, such as M. I. Litvin, Leningrad NKVD chief, and A. I. Uspenskii, NKVD chief in the Ukraine.[20] Another victim was Beria's old boss, Stanislav Redens, who was serving at the time of his arrest as head of the NKVD in Kazakhstan. Redens's wife, Anna, who was the sister of Stalin's deceased wife Nadezhda Alliluyeva, reportedly went to see Beria in an effort to save her husband, but Beria told her that she would be wise to forget about her marriage, which had never been registered.[21] Redens was shot shortly thereafter. Another victim was NKVD staffer Igor Kedrov, son of the old Bolshevik and former Chekist Mikhail Kedrov, who had complained about Beria in the early 1920s. After Beria's appointment as NKVD chief, both Kedrovs addressed their negative views of Beria directly to Stalin. Igor was arrested and shot immediately, and his father was killed a few months later.[22]

By early 1939 Beria had succeeded in arresting most of the top and middle-level hierarchy of Ezhov's apparatus, replacing these men with members of his Georgian group. It is possible to identify at least twelve Beria men—several of whom had been associated with him since the early

1920s—appointed to key NKVD posts between November 1938 and January 1939. Vsevold Merkulov became first deputy people's commissar and head of the Main Administration of State Security (GUGB) of the NKVD; Vladimir Dekanozov, head of the GUGB Foreign Department; Bogdan Kobulov, head of the GUGB Special Investigation Section; and Solomon Mil'shtein, chief of the GUGB Transport Department. Others who came into the USSR NKVD were Iuvelian Sumbatov-Topuridze, as head of the Economic Administration; Shota Tsereteli, as a deputy NKVD chief and head of the Guards Directorate; and Sardeon Nadaraia, appointed chief of Beria's personal bodyguard. According to Merkulov: "So many of us came [to Moscow] from Georgia that later Beria had to send some back, because Stalin had noticed it."[23]

Among Beria's associates who assumed republican and regional NKVD posts were Sergei Goglidze, appointed to head the Leningrad NKVD; Lavrentii Tsanava, who became NKVD chief in Belorussia; Grigorii Karanadze, NKVD chief in the Crimea; Aleksei Sadzhaia, in Uzbekistan; Amaiak Kobulov, the brother of Bogdan, in the Ukraine; and Mikhail Gvishiani, formerly a deputy chairman of the Georgian NKVD, who moved to the strategically important post of chief of the Far East NKVD.[24] Back in Georgia, the NKVD leadership was entrusted to Beria's loyal henchman Avksentii Rapava, with another protégé, Nikolai Rukhadze, serving as his deputy. This group of men, all of whom owed their allegiance to Beria, formed the core of his extensive power base within the NKVD.

As historian Robert Slusser has pointed out, previous heads of the security police—Dzerzhinskii, Menzhinskii, Iagoda, and Ezhov—had all lacked an autonomous power base before assuming their police posts and therefore were vulnerable to removal by the party leadership at any time. Beria, by contrast, with his long years of service in the Georgian police and party apparatus, had a well-established patronage network, which he transformed into the dominant elite of the NKVD.[25]

Why did Stalin permit Beria to convert the NKVD into his own fiefdom, as a direct extension of his Georgian power base? Slusser has suggested that he had little choice. As a result of the purges of the NKVD following the demise of Iagoda and then Ezhov, simply too few experienced police officials were left to administer this crucial component of the Soviet regime. Beria's ruthless team of former police comrades provided the kind of expertise necessary for the efficient functioning of the NKVD apparatus.[26] As Merkulov suggested, Stalin did at some point evince his displeasure when he realized how many officials had come from Georgia, causing Beria to retreat a bit. But this was a fairly mild reaction on Stalin's part, particularly given his strong dislike for "family circles" expressed in early 1937. Apparently, overriding political considerations kept him from clamping down hard on Beria at this point. Only later, after the war, did Stalin begin to take serious steps to limit Beria's power base.

Stalin continued, however, to let Beria know that he was being watched carefully and could not consider himself secure in his position or immune from reprisals. In other words, Stalin kept Beria on his toes. Thus, for example, at the very time of Beria's appointment as chief of the NKVD, Stalin brought up the vexed issue of Beria's alleged spying against the Bolsheviks in 1919. Beria turned for help to Merkulov, who had six years earlier been dispatched to Baku to retrieve (with Bagirov's assistance) documents in the party archives attesting to Beria's innocence. Beria had told Merkulov at the time that he was afraid his enemies would destroy the evidence if it was left in Baku. On Beria's instructions, Merkulov kept the papers, bringing them to Moscow with him in 1938. At the end of that year Beria asked Merkulov to produce the documents and also to write out an explanation to accompany them. When Merkulov had finished, Beria hurried off with the papers to Stalin's "nearby" dacha at Kuntsevo. Apparently Stalin was satisfied because, according to Merkulov, no more was heard of the matter.[27]

Although this episode must have caused him disquiet, Beria had Stalin's mandate to overhaul the NKVD and he forged ahead. His thorough "cleansing" of the NKVD and the fact that many of those purged were charged with criminal offenses, led Soviet people to hope that Beria's leadership would bring positive changes within the police apparatus. There was a general feeling that the NKVD would eschew the excesses of the Ezhov period, and people even began to talk about a "Beria thaw." According to one observer, "millions of prisoners wanted to see in Beria's move against these Chekists the beginning of their rehabilitation and of rational leadership, all the more so since Beria put a stop to physical torture and 'normalized' the regime in prisons and camps."[28]

In fact, torture continued to be applied to prisoners, but on a more selective basis. Beria ordered the release of several thousand prisoners who were still awaiting trial, while those arrested were treated somewhat less brutally, at least for a while. One source described the changes that came with Beria's appointment: "Previously the investigators would say to us: 'Come on, you gangster, write; or we'll make mincemeat of you.' Now they spoke differently: 'Come on, Vasily Ivanovich, write, write,' using the polite second person now; 'sign it, buddy; you'll get twenty years anyway.'"[29]

Arrests and executions continued, but on a smaller scale. Both Stalin and Beria realized that widespread terror was no longer necessary to subdue opposition within the country. This meant that the NKVD could enforce political control by less overtly repressive means. According to one former NKVD employee: "After Beria entered the NKVD, order was established."[30] In contrast to his predecessor, whose approach was crude and often hysterical, Beria brought a cold efficiency to his work, creating a feeling of purpose and stability among his subordinates. He did not bombard the population with news of plots and conspiracies, but attempted instead to establish a semblance of calm and "business as usual" within the country. Police powers did not diminish, they simply were less dysfunctional. As Robert Conquest put it: "In general Beria consolidated and institutionalized the system. From the *Ezhovshchina* [Ezhov's thing] developed, rather than an emergency operation against the people, a permanent method of rule."[31]

Within the NKVD Beria was apparently respected and considered deserving of loyalty. One reason for this was that he provided his subordinates with job security, as well as protection from physical destruction. With the wild excesses of the Ezhovshchina a thing of the past, the new group of NKVD employees could settle down to their work without constantly fearing for their lives. They also gained in material benefits; salaries of NKVD officials were doubled in November 1938.[32] According to Vladimir Petrov, who worked as a cypher clerk for the NKVD during the war:

> In NKVD circles Beria had the reputation of a good boss, who went to a great deal of trouble to look after the welfare of his staff. NKVD personnel who were transferred to Moscow and could not get accommodation could often put their case to Beria himself, who always saw to it that something was found for them. As a result of his forcefulness and drive we NKVD personnel had the best of what there was.[33]

In sum, Beria's assumption of the NKVD leadership by no means resulted in a weakening of the police apparatus. Rather, it became more effective and more firmly established as a stronghold of the regime.

The NKVD's prestige was particularly marked in comparison to the stature of other Soviet institutions, such as the Procuracy, which suffered a distinct decline in the wake of Andrei Vyshinskii's dismissal. His successor, Mikhail Pankratov, was no match for Beria, who soon managed to have the Procuracy under his thumb. Procuracy officials grew so dissatified with this situation that they wrote a collective letter to CC secretary Andrei Zhdanov in late October 1939, complaining about Beria. They said that he was ignoring the legal requirement that stipulated procuratorial supervision over the NKVD and was "cultivating a defense of the 'honor of the uniform' of NKVD personnel at all costs." NKVD employees earned double what they earned in the Procuracy. "Give us a director with a high degree of authority who can take on Beria," they requested.[34] It is not clear why the letter was addressed to Zhdanov, except that his party responsibility may have involved personnel appointments or legal affairs. In any case Zhdanov was in no position to move against Beria at this point, although he seems to have tried to do so after the war.

The political influence of the NKVD was apparent at the Eighteenth CPSU Congress in March 1939, when it was represented by no fewer than fifty-seven delegates, while eight NKVD officials were elected to candidate membership in the Central Committee, and Beria and Merkulov to full membership. Beria also achieved candidate membership in the Politburo, a status not reached by his predecessor, Ezhov, until over a year after he had become NKVD chief.[35] There was one anomaly, however, in the political stature of Beria and the NKVD. For some reason Beria's rank was not "General Commissar of State Security," like that of previous NKVD chiefs, but rather one grade lower, "Commissar of State Security, Grade 1." His subordinates, from Merkulov on down were also one rank lower than had been the case before. Beria did not become a General Commissar (equivalent to the army rank of Marshal of the Soviet Union) until January 1941.[36]

Perhaps Stalin thought it in keeping with the relaxation in repression to make some gesture toward reducing the public stature of the NKVD, particularly since the adulation of the police had gotten out of hand by the end of Ezhov's reign. With Ezhov's NKVD apparatus so recently discredited, it may have seemed appropriate to lower NKVD ranks as a sign of change. Beria himself, in his speech to the Congress, strengthened the impression that things were different at the NKVD and that it would no longer engage in a frenzied hunt for spies:

> It is a well-known fact that a great deal of harm was done by the Bukharin-Trotskyite saboteurs, wreckers and spies of foreign intelligence agencies who crept into our soviet, party and economic organizations. But it would be an error to explain the breakdowns that occurred in various segments of our national economy solely by the subversive activity of our enemies. These breakdowns are due, to a certain degree, to the unsatisfactory, unskilled work of a number of our Soviet economic leaders who have not yet mastered adequately the fundamentals of Bolshevik management.[37]

BERIA'S PERSONA: PUBLIC AND PRIVATE

In terms of Beria's own power and authority his "enlightened" approach was beneficial. Ezhov's reputation for cruelty and brutality had caused him to be despised by all, including those in the regime who profited from his purges. This made it easy for Stalin to blame him for the terror and then have him destroyed. Indeed most people wanted to blame Ezhov rather than Stalin because they had difficulty accepting that their leader could perpetrate such evil—hence the term *Ezhovshchina* in reference to the 1936–38 purges. Beria did not arouse such hatred among the general public, despite his reputation for extreme ruthlessness in Georgia. Evidently the details of his earlier police career and his subsequent role in implementing the Georgian purges were not widely known outside the republic. Even if stories of Beria's bloodthirsty exploits preceded him to Moscow, he probably did not look much worse than other members of the leadership, all of whom had abetted the Ezhovshchina.

That he was generally perceived as more rational and reasonable than the shrieking, dwarflike Ezhov doubtlessly enhanced Beria's effectiveness as NKVD chief, and hence also his overall political authority. His outward appearance—his head balding and his eyes encased in the familar pince-nez—together with the fact that he allegedly wrote a "scholarly" book, contributed to his image of respectability. According to a former NKVD employee who defected to the West: "Beria actually looked like a Jewish intellectual."[38] The outward manner he cultivated was one that stayed with him throughout his career, described by the British journalist Edward Crankshaw as "gentle and coldly, abstractly benign—the whole effect of that pedantic aloofness which makes people think of scholars when they should really think of fanatics of the most dangerous kind."[39] Noting that Beria's professorial appearance was deceptive, another Western journalist observed:

> When Beria was placed at the head of the NKVD in 1938 . . . a good many Soviet citizens, misled by the pince-nez and the book, raised hosannas on the assumption that Stalin had at last decided to put his cops in the charge of a history professor. The assumption only proved how little they knew. All his adult life Beria had been a Chekist.[40]

This benign impression did not always hold up to closer scrutiny. Some who had the opportunity to actually spend time with Beria, such as Svetlana Alliluyeva and the Yugoslav Communist Milovan Djilas, found him evil-looking and physically repulsive. Djilas, who met Beria after the war, described him as "somewhat plump, greenish pale, and with soft damp hands. With his square-cut mouth and bulging eyes behind his pince-nez, he suddenly reminded me of Vujkovic, the chief of the Belgrade Royal Police who specialized in torturing communists."[41]

Khrushchev claims that Beria's Russian was ungrammatical, and we know from other sources that he had a distinct Georgian accent.[42] But he had been around Stalin's Kremlin coterie enough to have a good idea of how he should best conduct himself among his new colleagues after arriving in Moscow. According to Antonov-Ovseenko: "Beria felt himself at home right away. He was clinking wine glasses with the crafty Mikoian, being photographed arm-in-arm with the simple-minded Voroshilov, listening attentively to the slow-witted Molotov. He amazingly quickly and naturally joined the entourage of this inner-circle."[43]

As far as Stalin himself was concerned, Antonov-Ovseenko observed: "Such a man did not make Stalin entirely comfortable. But like Beria himself, Stalin had never been able to experience complete peace of mind. The two were lone wolves. And their alliance was lupine."[44] Clearly Beria's well-established personal relationship with Stalin and the fact that the two could speak together in Georgian placed Beria in a more advantageous position than his predecessors. According to Svetlana Alliluyeva, after Beria moved to Moscow "he saw my father every day. His influence on my father grew and grew and never ceased until the day of my father's death."[45]

Alliluyeva was naturally anxious to emphasize the extent of Beria's influence on her father in order to justify her father's evil deeds. Thus, we must be cautious in considering her claim that Beria was a stronger character than Stalin, "a magnificent modern specimen of the artful courtier, the embodiment of Oriental perfidy, flattery, and hypocrisy who had succeeded in confounding even my father, a man whom it was ordinarily difficult to deceive."[46] Nonetheless, it is probably true, as Alliluyeva says, that Beria flattered Stalin shamelessly and "made up to him in a way that caused old friends, accustomed to looking on my father as an equal, to wince with embarrassment."[47] And, of course, Beria accommodated Stalin's innate suspiciousness by feeding him information about the perfidy of his minions.

As we have seen, these were practices Beria had already developed as Stalin's protégé in Georgia. Now, ensconced in Moscow and seeing Stalin daily, he had the opportunity to put his skills to even greater use. Khrushchev, although by no means unbiased, attested to Beria's continuous machinations and efforts to manipulate Stalin, which were to become more apparent in later years as Beria's influence became more pervasive. Stalin did not hesitate to put Beria in his place when he saw fit, however, as illustrated by an incident related by Gustav Hilger, counselor at the German Embassy in Moscow before the war. Hilger attended a dinner at the Kremlin given in late September 1939. Beria, who was seated next to him, kept trying to make Hilger drink more than he wanted to, a standard ploy, designed to disarm his interlocutors:

> Stalin soon noticed that Beriya [sic] and I were in dispute about something, and asked across the table: "What's the argument about?" When I told him, he replied, "Well if you don't want to drink, no one can force you."
>
> "Not even the chief of the NKVD himself," I joked.

Whereupon he answered, "Here, at this table, even the chief of the NKVD has no more to say than anyone else."[48]

Beria's aura of respectability masked his sexual debauchery, which apparently became more pronounced after he had been in Moscow for a while. After Beria's arrest his opponents produced a list, obtained from Beria's bodyguard, R. S. Sarsikov, of thirty-nine women with whom he had had sexual relations. They also had written testimony from Sarsikov, saying that Beria had contracted syphilis. Later Beria reportedly admitted to interrogators that he had undergone treatment for syphilis in 1943.[49] Another bodyguard, Nadaraia, confessed at his trial in 1955 that he and Sarsikov picked up young women off the streets and transported them to Beria's house, where he would rape them.[50] One victim's husband, a World War II pilot and Hero of the Soviet Union, claimed to have deliberately got himself arrested in order to draw attention to and protest Beria's repeated sexual aggressions against his young wife.[51] According to another source, young women in Moscow came to be terrified just by a glimpse of Beria's pictures in the press.[52] Stalin, who was a professed ascetic in sexual matters, must have heard what Beria was up to, but apparently chose to ignore it.[53]

It should be noted that these stories have been disputed by some who knew Beria. One former NKVD employee expressed strong doubts that Beria was raping young girls, noting that he was known in police circles as a man with exceptional self-control who worked extremely hard.[54] Nino Beria, in her 1990 interview, denied that her husband engaged in such practices: "Lavrentii was busy working day and night. When did he have time for love with this legion of women?"[55] And Beria's son, Sergo, made a similar disclaimer, though he allowed that his father did have another woman by whom he had a child.[56] Even if the stories circulating in Moscow were exaggerated they almost certainly had some foundation. They were corroborated by Edward Ellis Smith, a young American diplomat who was serving in the U.S. Embassy in Moscow after the war. Smith noted that Beria's escapades were common knowledge among embassy personnel at that time because his house was on the same street as a residence for Americans, and those who lived there saw girls brought to Beria's house late at night in a limousine.[57]

With this going on, it is hardly surprising that Nino Beria was not happy with her husband and increasingly built a life separate from his.[58] Stalin's daughter, who knew her well, claims that she hated living in Moscow and longed to be back in her native Georgia, where she had completed a degree in agricultural chemistry. Although she continued to work in her field, she gave most of her attention to her son, Sergo, who gained an excellent education, learning German and English, and was "gentle mannered and agreeable, like his mother."[59] Sergo graduated from the Military Electrotechnical Signal Academy in 1946 and, six years later, at the age of twenty-eight, obtained a doctorate in physical mathematics. He married Marfa Peshkova, granddaughter of the famous writer Maxim Gorkii.[60]

After moving to Moscow the Berias took over a dacha outside the city that had previously belonged to former vice chairman of the USSR Sovnarkom, V. Ia. Chubar, who had been arrested in the summer of 1938. Svetlana Alliluyeva visited Beria's dacha frequently:

> Beria's dacha was sumptuous, immense. The big white house stood among tall spruces. The furniture, the wallpaper, the lamps had all been made to the architect's designs—the same architect, Miron Merzhanov, who at one time used to build my father's dachas, until the day in 1949 when he was sent to prison and never returned. Nina [Russian for Nino] made the house seem cozier, being herself a sweet and cozy person. There was a movie-projection room in the house, but then such rooms existed in all the "leaders'" dachas.[61]

Svetlana Alliluyeva relates how on Sundays at his dacha Beria would amuse himself by shooting at targets. Then in the evening he would view American and German films, with his teenage son doing the translating, after which Beria would disappear, "no one knew where." They had a German woman living with them who took care of Sergo throughout his childhood and whom Nino protected from exile during the war. Svetlana Alliluyeva also mentions that the house was filled with foreign books and magazines, including many in German. This "German connection" may have contributed to the subsequent allegation that Beria had illicit contacts with Nazi Germany during World War II.[62]

BERIA'S NKVD AT WORK

In addition to purging the NKVD of Ezhovites, Beria devoted his energy to cleaning up loose ends left dangling by Ezhov. Several prominent party and government leaders, including Politburo members Chubar, S. V. Kossior (Khrushchev's predecessor as party leader in the Ukraine), and P. P. Postyshev, had been arrested some months earlier and were now awaiting trial as part of the "Military-Fascist Center." The investigator in the case, B. V. Rodos, subjected them to extensive torture, receiving detailed instructions from Beria.[63]

Beria himself took a personal interest in the case of one of the accused, Komsomol First Secretary Aleksandr Kosarev, apparently because Beria had a special grievance against him. Back in 1936 Kosarev had unwisely made the following toast in the presence of Beria's crony Bagirov, who happened to be his dinner guest, "Let's drink to true Bolshevik leadership of Transcaucasia, which we don't have now!" Of course Bagirov reported this back to Beria, who reproached Kosarev a couple of months later: "Sasha, what do you have against me? Am I really such a bad leader?" When the NKVD finally came to arrest Kosarev on the night of 28 November 1938, Beria was in attendance, a highly unusual occurrence since Beria normally did not deign to participate in these routine late-night round-ups. Kosarev's wife recalled that Beria was standing in the sitting room and, catching a glimpse of her, he shouted to his men to arrest her as well.[64]

Beria and his men, including the head of the Investigation Department, Bogdan Kobulov and his subordinate Major L. I. Shvartsman, devoted much effort to obtaining accusations against Kosarev from other Komsomol leaders who also were under arrest, but with little success.[65] Their failure to come up with testimony against Kosarev may have been one reason why the NKVD tried the Military-Fascist case *in camera*, rather than publicly. Another reason, as Robert Conquest suggests, may have been that the Soviet Union was already seeking better relations with Nazi Germany at this time and thus an antifascist trial was best avoided.[66] In any case most of the key defendants in the trial, which drew in some remaining fallen NKVD leaders as well, were quietly executed in February 1939.[67]

Beria also wound up a few cases involving the Red Army command. Ezhov had already carried out a devastating purge of the military, which had left the officer corps decimated. It is estimated that as many as forty thousand officers fell victim to the Ezhovshchina.[68] But Beria arrived in Moscow in time to personally conduct the interrogation of Marshal Bliukher, who was arrested in October 1938 while serving as Commander of the Far Eastern Army. A witness later recalled that during one session Beria and his colleagues beat Bliukher so badly that he lost an eye. Bliukher screamed out: "Stalin, can you hear what they are doing to me?" He died three weeks later, as a result of being either shot or tortured. Beria also interrogated Bliukher's wife, Glafira, who felt that he did this more out of "sadistic curiosity" than for any special purpose.[69]

There were more arrests in the artistic and scientific communities during 1939–40. The NKVD imprisoned the famous theater director Vsevolod Meyerhold in June 1939 and subjected him to intense beatings and torture. He died in early 1940.[70] In August 1940 Beria personally requested the arrest of the geneticist N. I. Vavilov. A prominent biologist D. N. Prianishnikov appealed to both Beria and Molotov to have him released and also prevailed upon Beria's wife, who knew Vavilov professionally, to obtain better conditions for Vavilov in prison, but to no avail. He eventually died in early 1943.[71]

Despite the NKVD's continued attacks on the intelligensia, Beria was not loath to support artistic endeavors when it suited his purposes. In early 1940 he established the NKVD Ensemble of Song and Dance to entertain Soviet troops fighting in the war against Finland. The ensemble, which drew upon the best artistic talent—including composer Dmitri Shostakovich and actor-director Yuri Lyubimov—performed throughout the war years.[72]

MOVING IN ON THE COMMISSARIAT OF FOREIGN AFFAIRS

In the spring of 1939 Beria and his colleagues turned their attention to foreign policy. The political police had, through its Foreign Department, long been involved in intelligence gathering and espionage abroad, but the advent of Beria's leadership marked an unprecedented expansion of the NKVD's foreign activities. Beria became leader of the NKVD at the very time that Stalin, disillusioned with the possibility of reaching an accord with the Western allies and fearful of German expansionism toward the East, decided that Soviet interests would be best served by an agreement with Germany. This fundamental shift in Soviet foreign policy brought new opportunities and tasks for the NKVD.

As a prelude to an agreement with Germany, Stalin decided that it was necessary to conduct a purge within the People's Commissariat of Foreign Affairs (NKID). Large numbers of diplomats and NKID personnel in the field had already disappeared under Ezhov, but the central staff in Moscow, led by the highly respected People's Commissar, Maxim Litvinov, had remained more or less intact. Litvinov, who had a British wife, was a skilled diplomat, closely associated with an anti-German interpretation of collective security. Getting rid of Litvinov and his staff paved the way for an agreement with Hitler and also offered Stalin and the NKVD a chance to eliminate veteran, independent-minded diplomats, replacing them with those who could be counted on to slavishly carry out instructions from the Kremlin.[73]

On 2 May 1939 a Central Committee Commission, consisting of Beria, Molotov, Malenkov, and Dekanozov, went to NKID headquarters and questioned staff members in Litvinov's office. Evgenii Gnedin, the NKID press officer was called in. Beria did not talk very much, but kept looking at him in a threatening way. When Gnedin mentioned his contacts with foreign correspondents, Beria suddenly shouted out: "We'll talk about that with you some more!"[74]

On the night of 3 May NKID headquarters were surrounded by NKVD troops. The next morning Beria, Molotov, and Malenkov arrived and informed Litvinov that he had been removed from his post. Litvinov promptly left Moscow and drove out to his dacha, which was surrounded by a small contingent of NKVD guards. He telephoned Beria and asked: "Why is this comedy with guards necessary?" Beria laughed and answered: "Maxim Maximovich, you don't recognize your own worth. You need to be protected."[75] At noon that same day Beria and Molotov called a meeting at the NKID to announce that Molotov was the new People's Commissar and Dekanozov his first deputy. Beria glanced around the room and his eyes fell on Pavel Nazarov, assistant to the chief secretary at the NKID. Nazarov's father, an old Bolshevik, had been arrested not long before. "Nazarov, why did they arrest your father?" asked Beria. "Lavrentii Pavlovich, you no doubt know better than I" was the response. Beria grinned and said, "You and I will talk about that." Soon Nazarov was arrested on charges of spying for Italy. The charge emanated from the fact that he had been born in Genoa, where his parents had fled to escape Siberian exile before the Revolution of 1917.[76]

Evgenii Gnedin was called in to see Dekanozov on the evening of 10 May and was promptly arrested, as were dozens of other leading NKID staffers. Bogdan Kobulov was in charge of interrogating them, apparently with the goal of gathering incriminating material against Litvinov, who remained at liberty. Gnedin recalled how he was taken to Beria's office after he had refused to confess to the espionage charges that Kobulov accused him of. When he continued to deny the charges, Kobulov, who weighed more than three hundred pounds, and his assistants began beating him on the skull as Beria sat complacently watching. Then Beria impatiently ordered Gnedin to lie on the floor, where he was kicked repeatedly by several prison employees. Gnedin had one final session with Beria, who at first adopted a thoughtful, cultured manner, asking Gnedin calmly if he had finally decided to confess. Again, when Gnedin steadfastly asserted his innocence, he was brutally beaten. Beria's last words to Gnedin were: "With such a philosophy and such provocations, you only make your situation worse."[77]

Despite the efforts of Beria and his men, Litvinov was never arrested and the case against him was dropped in October 1939. Perhaps Stalin decided that it would be too damaging to the Soviet Union's image to destroy such an internationally prominent figure. Or maybe he realized that Litvinov's services would be useful in the future, as they were in 1941, when the Soviet Union needed the support of the allies and Litvinov became Soviet Ambassador to the United States. Khrushchev claims that Beria had concocted a plan to kill Litvinov by staging an automobile accident on a road outside Moscow. If this is true, Stalin probably put a stop to it.[78]

The dismissal of Litvinov and the arrests of his subordinates, coming right after the extensive purges under Ezhov, caused complete chaos within the NKID, bringing, in the words of one Western scholar, "the normal functioning of Soviet diplomacy almost to a halt."[79] Poorly trained, inexperienced recruits replaced the well-educated, seasoned foreign service personnel, which led to a drastic change in operating style. The new recruits were hypercautious and reluctant to take any initiative whatsoever in their diplomatic dealings, abiding strictly by the directives from Moscow, a situation that did not benefit Soviet foreign policy. But it did provide the NKVD with the opportunity to move its own personnel into the Foreign Commissariat—Dekanozov being the most prominent example—and to use the Foreign Commissariat for clandestine purposes. Henceforth Soviet diplomats regularly carried out covert operations on behalf of the NKVD.[80]

The stifling atmosphere created by the presence of Beria's NKVD men at the NKID is illustrated by an episode involving V. N. Barkov, head of the Protocol Department in the late 1930s. Barkov had been instructed to meet with a foreign correspondent, but was required by the regulations to report first to Dekanozov. The latter, however, could not be found, so Barkov went ahead with the meeting anyway. When Dekanozov found out he not only gave Barkov a terrible dressing-down, he also had him arrested.[81] Episodes like this led to intense fear, on the part of Soviet diplomats and negotiators, of taking initiative. As one source described it: "Hemmed in by a predominating NKVD presence and distanced still further from policy-making than their predecessors by an autocratic Stalin, they were reduced to the level of a suppressed and isolated minority within the Soviet bureaucracy and the diplomatic community."[82]

A further example of the mentality of excessive secrecy and circumspection that Beria's men brought to Soviet foreign affairs appears in the memoirs of German diplomat Gustav Hilger. Beria himself, ever vigilant, told his men that they should follow Hilger's movements carefully because he was a dangerous person and could be spying.[83] In November 1940 Hilger was traveling with the German Ambassador and Molotov to Berlin, accompanied by Beria's security chief, Merkulov, who was supposedly along because he was responsible for Molotov's personal safety. When Hilger asked Merkulov innocently the name of the station at which they would be changing trains, Merkulov stubbornly refused to tell him, stating that it would be up to Molotov to decide. "In vain," Hilger wrote, "I argued that I could not be satisfied with his answer, since the place at which we had to change trains did not depend on Mr. Molotov's decision, but exclusively on where one gauge ended and the other began. He stuck to his position, and I could do no more than have patience for a couple of hours."[84]

As second-in-command to Molotov, Dekanozov played a key role in the negotiations with the Germans that led to the Nazi-Soviet Treaty of

23 August 1939. Subsequently, in December 1940, he became Soviet Ambassador to Berlin. He undoubtedly remained in close communication with Beria, who is said to have strongly favored the rapprochement with Germany, utilizing the efforts of the NKVD for this purpose.[85] In September 1939, shortly after the treaty had been signed, Beria managed to get another protégé involved in Soviet-German relations; Amaiak Kobulov, brother of Bogdan, became a counselor at the Soviet Embassy in Berlin.[86]

If we are to believe Khrushchev, however, Beria made at least one mistake in his efforts to influence the course of Soviet-German relations. In accordance with the Nazi-Soviet pact, the Germans sent over a battle cruiser to Leningrad in exchange for Soviet raw materials. Beria's agents tried to entrap a high-ranking German naval officer who had arrived to help outfit the ship, in order to compromise him and then enlist him into the services of the NKVD. But their efforts were discovered by the Germans, and Hitler personally "raised a rumpus." According to Khrushchev, Stalin was very angry with Beria about this.[87]

THE NKVD MOVES WESTWARD

The Nazi-Soviet Treaty, along with the Secret Protocols, which allowed the Soviet Union to move into Eastern Poland and the Baltic states, offered the NKVD new opportunities to extend its domain. Beria unleashed the NKVD upon hundreds of thousands of citizens of the newly occupied territories. Following the Soviet invasion of Eastern Poland in September 1939, the NKVD took over responsiblity for 200,000 Polish prisoners. In October 1939 about half these prisoners were freed and the others were placed in special NKVD prison camps at Staroblesk, Kozielsk, and Ostachkov. After war broke out between the Soviet Union and Germany 15,000 Polish officers and soldiers were still unaccounted for. Wladislav Anders, commander of the newly formed Polish army, who had just been released from Moscow's Lubianka Prison, requested information from Stalin about their fate. Stalin initially replied that they had escaped, but later said that they had all been released. In 1943 Polish officers organizing a new division to fight Hitler presented a list of recommended officers to Beria's deputy Merkulov, who responded by saying: "No, they are gone. We allowed a gross error to be committed in regard to them." Beria is then reported to have hastily corrected him, saying: "These persons are no longer in the Soviet Union, they went elsewhere."[88]

Now Russian authorities have publicly admitted that the mass grave of more than four thousand Polish officers discovered by the Germans in the Katyn Forest in 1943 was the handiwork of the NKVD, which carried out the massacre in the summer of 1940. The fate of the remaining Polish officers is still unclear, but it appears that close to four thousand were shot by the Kharkov NKVD.[89] Recently published correspondence between the NKVD leadership in Moscow and those in charge of the camps shows that Stalin, Beria, and People's Commissar of Defense Kliment Voroshilov were making most of the decisions on what to do with Polish army prisoners. And in October 1992 the Russian government handed documents over to Poland that included a 5 March 1940 execution order, signed by members of the Politburo.[90] Stalin reportedly decided to have them killed because he feared that they would stage an uprising and thwart the secret protocols he had agreed on with Hitler. Also he needed the camp space to house prisoners from the Baltic states.[91] The NKVD made a serious mistake, however, in not considering the possibility that this territory might fall into enemy hands. Since NKVD troops did not bother to remove the clothes and personal effects of the Polish officers, their identity and the approximate date of the massacre was clear to Hitler's army when it discovered the grave in April 1943. The vigorous denial by Soviet officials was not very convincing, especially since they had acknowledged as late as 1941 that they still held these Polish officers.[92]

In June 1940, after moving large numbers of troops into the Baltic states, the Soviets took the further step of staging elections there in order to replace the existing governments with regimes subservient to Moscow. Dekanozov, still first deputy foreign commissar, was dispatched to Lithuania to supervise the change of government there, while Vyshinskii, the former chief prosecutor, and Andrei Zhdanov, Leningrad party chief, were sent to Latvia and Estonia, respectively. It was the NKVD's job to make sure that Sovietization of these countries was carried out thoroughly. This involved arresting large numbers of Baltic citizens suspected of opposing the new pro-Soviet governments and recruiting NKVD agents from among the local populace. According to an NKVD official in the Baltics named von Neimann, whose diaries ended up in the West, State Security Chief Merkulov traveled to Riga on 23 July. He brought with him an order, signed by Stalin and Molotov, that called for the most rigorous punitive measures against those suspected of "counterrevolutionary activities."[93]

Von Neimann related how the NKVD decided on a policy, which was approved by Stalin, of mass deportation of the Baltic population to the interior of the Soviet Union. Deportees were to be former landowners, entrepreneurs, and members of the educated classes, while the poorer classes—factory workers and peasants—would remain. At the end of the summer von Niemann was received in Moscow by Stalin, who discussed the deportation plans with him, remarking, "Comrade Beria will take care of accommodations for our Baltic guests."[94] The operation, which began in the spring of 1941, involved the deportation of about 140,000 Lithuanians, Latvians, and Estonians to the Soviet Union, adding to the more than 400,000 Poles transferred to forced labor camps in 1940–41.[95]

BERIA'S EMPIRE

The NKVD's forced labor empire, under the authority of the Main Administration of Corrective Labor Colonies, or GULAG, was already massive as a result of the purges. There is still no expert consensus on camp population figures. One Russian scholar reported that on 1 March 1940 the GULAG itself consisted of 53 camps, 425 corrective-labor colonies, and 50 colonies for juveniles, containing a total of 1,668,200 inmates.[96] Economic historian Alec Nove argues, however, that one must include detainees in prisons and special settlements, which were also controlled by the NKVD. Using census figures, he estimates that the total number of detainees in 1939 was around 3.5 million.[97] Another Soviet source posits that by June 1941 there were 2.3 million persons in the GULAG.[98]

The most important economic activity of the NKVD was construction—of roads, railways, waterways, and power stations. Some projects were undertaken directly by the NKVD and some by GULAG workers contracted out to other commissariats. Mining of gold and nonferrous metals and lumbering were other key areas of production for the GULAG.[99] To have such a vast economic enterprise under his control was an awesome responsibility for Beria, although he left the day-to-day administration to such lieutenants as Iuvelian Sumbatov-Topuridze, head of the NKVD Economic Administration until 1940, and Bogdan Kobulov. According to most accounts, Beria's group was more effective in the utlilization of camp labor than Ezhov's had been. In an effort to raise productivity and more rationally exploit forced labor, Beria improved physical conditions in the camps and increased food supplies. As a result camp death rates declined from what they were under Ezhov, and forced labor became a more productive element of the national economy.[100] This is not to diminish, however, the extreme cruelties and hardships that GULAG prisoners continued to suffer under Beria. Recently published archival documents show that camp conditions were still intolerably harsh in early 1941, with prisoners lacking in even bare essentials such as soap, water, clothing, and nourishment, while they were forced to work more than twelve hours a day. These hardships increased markedly when the war began. The supply of food, heat, and other necessities deteriorated to the point where hundreds of prisoners, compelled to work even longer hours, were dying every day in each camp of malnutrition, exposure, and disease. In October 1941 alone, 1,474 prisoners died in the Pechora and Zapoliarny NKVD Railway Construction Camps.[101]

Under Beria, the GULAG began to operate on the principle that the prisoners' special abilities and qualifications should be utilized. Scientists with valuable expertise were not shot or sent to work on construction but were employed in laboratories. Thus, for example, the aircraft designer A. N. Tupolev, arrested by Ezhov in October 1937, was transferred in early 1939 to a special prison at Bolshevo, outside Moscow, where prisoners with a special expertise were kept. These prisoners worked for the "Special Technical Bureau of the NKVD." Tupolev himself was in frequent contact with Beria who, much to Tupolev's fury, gave him instructions from Stalin on what type of aircraft to design. Tupolev protested and finally had his way. Having been sentenced in 1940 to fifteen years in prison, Tupolev appealed personally to Beria to have the sentence revoked. He was released right after the German attack.[102] In another case, the physicist P. L. Kapitsa managed, after writing several letters to Stalin, Molotov, and Beria, to have his subordinate, the gifted physicist L. D. Landai, released to his custody on the grounds that his scientific work was essential to Kapitsa and other physicists.[103]

In addition to the vast GULAG, Beria's NKVD controlled the regular prisons, the militia or regular police, fire protection, border troops, internal troops, railroad troops, and convoy troops. As to the powerful Main Administration of State Security, which was responsible for counterintelligence, espionage, and internal political security, it was temporarily separated from the NKVD in February 1941 and transformed into a separate People's Commissariat of State Security (NKGB) under the leadership of Merkulov. It is not clear why this reorganization was initiated, but it may have been simply because the NKVD had so many functions and departments that it was more practical to create a separate state security organization. This arrangement was reversed once the war broke out and state security was again placed under the NKVD.[104] Meanwhile, at the time the reorganization was first announced in early 1941, Beria became a deputy chairman of the USSR Council of People's Commissars, the highest state body.

On the Brink of War

By this time the rapprochement with Germany that Beria and his deputies had promoted was deteriorating and Hitler was preparing an attack against the Soviet Union. Recent Russian sources have shown that Stalin and the party leadership received ample evidence that Hitler was preparing to attack the Soviet Union. Beginning in early 1940 both the NKID and NKVD produced a steady stream of reports on Hitler's plans, which were brought to the attention of Stalin and the Soviet leadership. One important source was Soviet Ambassador to Germany Dekanozov, who provided the main line of communication between the two countries. From February 1941 onward Dekanozov reported continuously to Foreign Commissar Molotov on German war preparations, leaving no doubt as to Hitler's intentions.[105] It is highly unlikely that Molotov failed to pass this information to Stalin, but he may well have been reluctant to press it on him too forcefully. Given his role in forging the alliance with Germany, Molotov had good reason to downplay Dekanozov's reports.

Of course Dekanozov could have urged Beria to do something about this information or even have taken it upon himself to convince Stalin of the impending invasion. His political stature had risen considerably since he became Ambassador to Germany. In February 1941, at the Eighteenth Party Conference, he was promoted to full membership on the Central Committee; at the traditional May Day parade three months later Dekanozov occupied a place right next to Stalin, which the German ambassador, in a note to the German Foreign Office, remarked upon as a sign of Dekanozov's prominence. (It was also correctly interpreted as evidence of how important diplomatic relations with Germany were to Stalin at this time.)[106] Later in the year U.S. Ambassador Steinhardt noted that Dekanozov was "probably more in Stalin's confidence than anyone else in the government."[107] But Dekanozov was a Chekist at heart and apparently did not want to risk his political position by attempting to dissuade Stalin of his conviction that Hitler would not attack. The German diplomat Hilger relates how in May 1941 he and the German Ambassador to the Soviet Union, Count Schulenberg, told Dekanozov at a secret meeting specifically of Hitler's plans to attack the Soviet Union and urged him to persuade Stalin to do something to forestall Hitler:

> From the very beginning we had told Dekanozov that we were acting on our responsibility and without the knowledge of our superiors. "You'll have to speak to the foreign minister," he kept repeating. Obviously, he could not imagine that we were knowingly and deliberately incurring the greatest danger for the purpose of making a last effort to save the peace. He must have believed that we were acting on Hitler's behalf and that we were trying to make the Kremlin take a step that would damage its prestige and its concrete interests.[108]

It is more likely Dekanozov knew that what they were saying was true but was reluctant to act on it. He finally did relay the news to Molotov, who in turn told Stalin. The latter's reaction was predictable: "We shall consider that disinformation has now reached the level of ambassadors."[109] Dekanozov was up against not only Stalin, but also Beria. When he informed Moscow on 21 June that the German attack would begin the next day, Beria's alleged response was to recommend to Stalin that Dekanozov be called to account for "bombarding" them with disinformation.[110]

It is difficult to explain Beria's reaction, particularly since he had other excellent sources of information about the impending invasion. As early as April 1940 he had many hours of conversation with an imprisoned Polish general, who gave him repeated warnings about German plans. Beria was particularly agitated at the suggestion that the Nazis would attack the Caucasus first because of the oil.[111] By early 1941 Beria's subordinates in the NKVD were producing daily communications, based on both military and political intelligence, about Hitler's war preparations; the military intelligence apparatus of the Ministry of Defense was coming up with equally forceful evidence.[112] All these reports reached Beria and other members of the leadership, including of course Stalin.

Some Russian historians have argued that Stalin did in fact realize what was happening but, knowing how ill-prepared the Soviet military was after the devastating purges, he continued to hold out for a diplomatic solution.[113] Even if this were so, his wishful thinking had the same effect: he operated on the assumption that an attack was not inevitable and therefore was adamant in his refusal to give credibility to the mounting evidence of Hitler's plans to invade. In mid-June 1941, for example, the chief of foreign intelligence, P. M. Fitin, forwarded a report to Merkulov from a well-placed source in the staff of the German air force, outlining the final steps that the air force had taken and noting that "all military preparations for an armed invasion of the USSR are completely finished and an attack might be expected at any time." Stalin had scribbled a response: "Comrade Merkulov, you can send your 'source' from the staff of the German air force to his ——— mother. This is not a 'source,' but disinformation."[114] Fitin later recalled that Stalin called him and Merkulov into his office the next day and made it clear that he would not trust any of their sources because they were not Communists.[115]

Nonetheless, the leaders of the intelligence organs might have gone further in pushing their case. Fitin recalls that his men actually wrote an in-depth analysis of their reports, drawing the appropriate conclusions, which was intended to be circulated among the leadership. But Merkulov refused to sign it, saying "those above us are better able to analyze than we are."[116] Merkulov was doubtless taking his cues from Beria, who apparently decided it was in his best interests to go along with Stalin at all costs. Beria may even have deluded himself into believing Stalin's line. He had been such a strong advocate of the collaboration with Hitler that he may, like Stalin, have found it hard to face up to the fact that this collaboration had proved disastrous and that diplomatic measures could not change German plans. This might explain why Beria was encouraging

Stalin in his incredible folly down to the last moments before the invasion. On 21 June, in addition to denouncing Dekanozov, Beria debunked a report from F. I. Golikov, head of military intelligence, who said that 170 German divisions were concentrated on the Soviet Union's western border. In a note to Stalin, Beria called Golikov a liar and expressed his faith in his chief: "My people and I, Iosif Vissarionovich, firmly remember your wise prediction: Hitler will not attack us in 1941!"[117] As was so often the case in Stalinist politics, neither Beria nor his subordinates suffered repercussions for their ill-fated actions. The war they had inadvertently helped to promote brought them new rewards, promotions, and prestige.

Chapter Six

THE WAR YEARS

> During the war Beria had become more brazen than ever.
> As Stalin lost control, and even lost his will during the
> period of our retreat from the Germans,
> Beria became the terror of the party.
> (Khrushchev Remembers, Vol. 1, 1971)

THE INITIAL STAGES

PREDICATING his strategic planning on the assumption that he could forestall a German attack, Stalin made some decisions on fortifying the border area, which was the responsibility of Beria's NKVD, that proved disastrous. Instead of preserving the old border defenses built during the 1930s, Stalin ordered the NKVD to build a new line of fortifications along the new borders to the West, incorporating the recently acquired western territories. But this was a slow process, particularly since the NKVD was apparently not providing enough labor for the construction (which came from the camps). Complaints from the military were reaching Stalin about the lamentable state of Soviet frontier defenses, but neither Stalin nor Beria did anything to rectify the situation. As a result, in June 1941 new border fortifications were still in the early stages of construction, while fortifications on the "old" border had been dismantled. Only 25 percent of the plan for building anti-tank ditches and anti-infantry obstacles had been completed by June 1941, making the Soviet border areas especially vulnerable.[1]

Compounding this problem was the fact that the NKVD ignored warnings from the military command and proceeded to rebuild a large number of airfields simultaneously. This meant that at the time of the German attack many were not operational and fighter aircraft were concentrated on the few functioning airfields, a situation that prevented the camouflage, maneuverability and dispersal of the aircraft. In addition, some airfields were built so close to the frontier that they were especially vulnerable to suprise attack. This resulted in staggering losses by the Soviet airforce in the first days of the war.[2] The vulnerability of Soviet defenses in the western region was heightened by the fact that German reconnaissance aircraft had been allowed with impunity to fly deep into Soviet airspace and survey Soviet frontier districts and interior areas. According to a Soviet history of the war: "The traitor Beria, as far back as March 1940, categorically forbade border troops to fire on intruding German planes, and also made sure that units of the Red Army and navy ships did not engage in combat with German aviation. He virtually opened Soviet airspace to enemy reconnaissance."[3] Of course, it was Stalin who steadfastly refused to acknowledge reports of German plans to attack and disallowed any moves against German aircraft on the grounds that it might be seen as a provocation.[4] But Beria zealously saw to it that Stalin's orders against any "provocatory" actions were observed to the letter. In early June 1941, for example, the commander of the Kiev Special Military District, Lieutenant General M. P. Kirponos, wrote to Stalin that the Germans were on the Bug River and that an attack was likely. He recommended that 300,000 civilians be evacuated from the frontier areas and that defenses be manned. The response from Moscow was that this would be a provocation, but on his own iniative Kirponos had already ordered some units to be moved closer to the borders. When the Ukrainian NKVD frontier troop commander learned of this and reported it to Beria, Kirponos was instructed to countermand these orders at once.[5]

The terrible disaster that befell the Soviet Union because of the failure to prepare for the German attack has been amply described. On the first day of the invasion, 22 June, the Germans smashed Soviet border defenses and wiped out most of the Soviet air force in the western regions. Within a few days German troops were well inside Soviet territory. Most historians have assumed that Stalin was so overcome by the news of the invasion that he was incapable of taking any action for several days. In fact, a diary of visitors to Stalin, recently reproduced from the archives, shows that this assumption was mistaken. However shaken he was, Stalin had eleven hours of meetings with party, state, and military leaders on the day of the attack, and he received visitors almost continuously for the next several days.[6] Beria, who undoubtedly was also greatly agitated, spent more time with Stalin than anyone else during this crucial period. He was the last to leave Stalin's office on the evening before the attack, at 11:00 P.M. He and Molotov were the first to show up, at 5:45 the next morning, after the invasion had begun, and the last to leave on that day. They were again the last to leave Stalin's office on 23 June.

While he was not paralyzed into complete inaction, Stalin was apparently in deep despair and unable to accept the full reality of the German attack. He was fearful that, having led his country into disaster, he had lost his credibility as a leader.[7] This is presumably why Molotov, rather than Stalin, announced over the radio that war had begun and appealed to the people to struggle against Hitler's army. Beria later recalled in front of Khrushchev what Stalin said at the time: "Everything is lost. I give up. Lenin left us a proletarian state and now we've been caught with our pants down and let the whole thing go to shit."[8] According to Beria, Stalin then announced that he could no longer be leader and left for his dacha. Beria, Molotov, Kaganovich, and Voroshilov followed him out and persuaded him to get a hold on himself and lead the country.[9]

It took Stalin until 3 July to regain enough composure to speak to the people by radio and even after that he apparently clung to the hope that diplomacy would stop the invading army. According to Pavel Sudoplatov, deputy chief of the NKVD foreign intelligence administration, Beria told him on 25 July 1941 to meet with the Bulgarian Ambassador to Moscow in order to convey through him an offer to Hitler to negotiate peace. Sudoplatov later claimed that this offer was not sincere, but was simply intended to buy time for the Soviet government. Khrushchev mentioned hearing from Beria about a similar offer, only he said that it had been made through a Bulgarian banker, an agent of Hitler, in the autumn of 1941. Whatever the case, nothing came of the plan.[10]

Meanwhile, the mechanisms for the wartime leadership were being established. On 23 June the USSR Sovnarkom and the Central Committee announced the creation of the General Headquarters of the Soviet High Command, called the *Stavka*, which consisted of Stalin and several military commanders and was headed by the People's Commissar of Defense, Marshal S. K. Timoshenko. Attached to the Stavka was a group of civilian advisors that included Beria.[11] Stalin himself assumed leadership of the Stavka and became People's Commissar of Defense three and a half weeks later.[12] On 30 June 1941, eight days after the German invasion of the Soviet Union, a five-man State Defense Committee (GKO) was created, with Stalin as its chairman. Other members included Foreign Affairs Commissar Molotov, as deputy chairman, Marshal Kliment Voroshilov, Central Committee Secretary Malenkov, and NKVD Chief Beria. This committee, which could be described as a war cabinet, had, as John Erickson put it, "a massive, consuming competence." All government, military, and party organs were subordinated to the GKO, which was responsible for economic and military production, all matters of state security and public order, and also supervised the "structure" of the Soviet armed forces. In addition, GKO members soon gained the right to sit in on meetings of the Stavka.[13]

As a member of the GKO, an advisor to the Stavka, and a deputy chairman of the Sovnarkom, Beria had wartime responsibilities that extended well beyond those of a peacetime NKVD chief. With Stalin increasingly devoting himself (after his initial period of inaction) to purely military matters, domestic affairs were left largely to Beria and Malenkov, who became, in George Kennan's words, a "sort of closed corporation."[14] Beria oversaw the enormous job of evacuating defense industries from western regions to beyond the Ural mountains and converting peacetime industry to war production. He was tasked with ensuring an uninterrupted supply of labor for the war economy, drawing on the vast GULAG, and with overseeing the movement of troops and equipment to the front. He was in charge of internal security, foreign intelligence of a nonmilitary nature, and counterintelligence and he oversaw the disposition of NKVD border and internal troops, which numbered several hundred thousand, performing both rear security and, in some cases, direct combat functions.[15] Like other members of the leadership, Beria threw himself into his tasks with the energy of desperation, motivated not so much by patriotism as by self-interest and fear. He could ill afford a Nazi victory over his country.

The NKVD's Punitive Arm

Of all Beria's roles, perhaps the most important in terms of his relationship to Stalin was that of policeman for the Red Army. Like most dictators, Stalin had a deep distrust of his military and, with the entire country subordinated to the war effort, he had even more reason to be concerned about its influence. Although he was commander-in-chief, Stalin still worried about being overshadowed by his generals, who rose to sudden prominence. His intense vanity and insatiable need for glorification made any other heroes intolerable to him. The obsequious Beria, himself no friend of the military, understood Stalin's feelings well and was able to show his devotion to his chief by making sure that the Red Army did not overstep its bounds.

Once Stalin took full charge of the war effort, his first reaction, probably encouraged by Beria, was to clamp down on the military and to restore the strictest discipline through drastic punitive measures. On 16 July the system of political commissars—whereby the party, through its representatives, shared dual command with the military—was reintroduced. On 20 July Stalin issued an order that all units be "purged of unreliable elements" and all officers and men escaping from German encirclement be rigorously investigated by the NKVD special sections (*Osobye otdely*), or OOs.[16] The OOs belonged to the Special Department of the NKVD's State Security Administration, which was responsible for military counterintelligence and for political security within the armed forces.[17]

So-called holding detachments were formed by NKVD troops with the purpose of keeping Red Army units in line. On 25 July they rounded up a thousand "deserters" and shot most of them.[18] Two days later the GKO issued an order imposing the death sentence on nine senior Soviet officers. Among them were Colonel General G. D. Pavlov, commander of the Western Front at the time of the German attack and his chief of staff, both of whom were made scapegoats for the rapid disintegration of the Soviet armies in the face of the sudden German onslaught. John Erickson described the effect of these coercive measures on the Red Army:

> Front, army and divisional commanders, who soon enough felt the weight of this new Stalinist direction, learned also what drastic measures lay hidden for those whom Stalin branded "coward." To these unfortunates, deprived of any defence, Stalin meted out death and demotion; in furious and vicious punishments they were scythed down by Beria, entrenched in the GKO as master of a swollen NKVD.[19]

Erickson notes further on: "The punitive right hand of Stalin had fallen, to salvage his own authority. . . . The Red Army, pounded by its external enemies, had now to face its internal foes, not least Beria and Mekhlis [head of the Political Administration]."[20]

The grim story of the OOs' persecution of the Red Army during the war has perhaps best been told by Alexandr Solzhenitsyn in *The Gulag Archipelago*, which is replete with examples of how innocent soldiers were shot or imprisoned and tortured by NKVD special sections. According to Solzhenitsyn:

> By the end of the summer of 1941, becoming bigger in the autumn, the wave of *the encircled* was surging in. These were the defenders of their native land, the very same warriors whom the cities had seen off to the front with bouquets and bands a few months before, who had then sustained the heaviest tank assaults of the Germans, and in the general chaos, and through no fault of their own, had spent a certain time as isolated units, not in enemy imprisonment, not at all, but in temporary encirclement and later had broken out. And instead of being given a brotherly embrace on their return, such as every other army in the world would have given them . . . they were held on suspicion, disarmed, deprived of all rights, and taken away in groups to identification points and screening centers where officers of the Special Branches started interrogating them.[21]

The novelist Konstantin Simonov described a tragic episode, based on fact, in which the NKVD disarmed a large number of Red Army soldiers who had fought their way out of German encirclement. As the soldiers were on the way to an NKVD screening center they were trapped again by Germans and, as they had no arms with which to defend themselves, were massacred.[22]

Although Beria had overall control, the immediate direction of the special sections was in the hands of the notorious Chief of the Special Department Viktor Abakumov. Abakumov, who had risen in the NKVD ranks and had been head of the Rostov Oblast NKVD before assuming his new post in 1940, was not directly associated with the Beria group.

He therefore was able to maintain some independence, which kept Beria on his guard. Abakumov soon gained notoriety for his extreme ruthlessness and cruelty. Solzhenitsyn says that Abakumov personally participated in the beating and torture of prisoners: "He was not averse to taking a rubber truncheon in his hands once in a while."[23] Nor, according to Solzhenitsyn, was Abakumov's deputy, M. D. Riumin, who would have the Persian carpet in the office where he conducted interrogations covered with an old, blood-spattered runner before he began his beatings.[24]

CLASHES WITH THE MILITARY

As attested to by military memoirs, both Beria and Abakumov were despised and feared by the Red Army, with good reason. In addition to directing the punitive operations of the special sections, they were continually interfering in military matters, trying to "throw their weight around" and intimidate the officer corps. Riumin was no less a menace. When his flagrant abuses in running the counterintelligence section of the Northern Fleet in 1942 were finally reported to Abakumov by the procurator's office, Abakumov's response was to promote him.[25]

On one occasion, just before the German offensive against Moscow in October 1941, the Moscow District aviation commander, Colonel N. A. Sbytov, relayed a report from two pilots that a massive, two-column German motorized and armored formation was approaching the town of Iukhnov, not far from Moscow. Having learned this information, which proved to be accurate, the military council of the Moscow Military District began preparations to move against the German columns, but then Beria interfered, calling these preparations "provocations." K. F. Telegin, a member of the council, recalled how Beria suddenly telephoned him and asked about the source of the report on the German advance. Following Telegin's response, Beria said in a sharp voice: "Look here, do you take every bit of nonsense as the truth? You have evidently received information from panic mongers and provocateurs."[26]

Sbytov was then called to see Abakumov, who demanded to know the source of the report of the German advance and then asked Sbytov to produce photographs of the reconnaissance. Sbytov had no photographs, but pointed out that the pilots, who were flying at only two hundred to three hundred meters, were reliable sources. Abakumov sent Sbytov back to staff headquarters after trying unsuccessfully to get him to deny the report by threatening to put him before a military tribunal. After hearing about this incident, Telegin interceded on Sbytov's behalf, telephoning an unnamed Central Committee secretary, who was able to put an end to the interference by Beria and Abakumov.[27]

On another occasion Colonel General of Artillery N. N. Voronov was ordered by Stalin to transfer a fully equipped artillery corps to one of the army groups. In response to Voronov's request for nine hundred trucks to transport the troops, Stalin directed Beria and Malenkov, who were present at the time, to see about obtaining them. Outside Stalin's office, Beria and Malenkov had a sharp exchange with Voronov, trying (unsuccessfully) to force him into accepting only half the number of trucks needed.

Voronov also recalled an incident when he was going over a distribution list of armaments and munitions with Stalin, who queried an NKVD request for fifty thousand rifles. Stalin summoned Beria immediately and asked why he needed so many rifles. When Beria tried to explain in Georgian, Stalin interrupted him with irritation and ordered him to answer in Russian. Then Beria said that the rifles were for newly formed NKVD divisions. Stalin responded that twenty-five thousand rifles would be sufficient, but Beria kept insisting on more. This irritated Stalin so much that he finally approved only ten thousand rifles for the NKVD. Voronov recalled Beria's reaction: "When we left Stalin's office, Beria overtook us and said malevolently: 'Just wait, we'll fix your guts!' "[28]

Beria did get back at Voronov, according to Admiral I. S. Isakov, who served as first deputy commissar of the navy during the war. Isakov frequently attended meetings of the Stavka, at which Beria was usually present. Although those who attended always sat quietly in a designated chair, Beria, as Isakov recalls, behaved as he saw fit. He would pace the floor, whistling and evincing no interest in the discussion. Then he would frequently say things to Stalin in Georgian, addressing him as "Koba." At one meeting Voronov did not show up as expected. Stalin asked where he was: "Lavrentii, he's not at your place, is he?" Beria, who was pacing the room as usual, responded nonchalantly that he was and that he would be back in two days. At the Stavka meeting two days later Voronov did indeed reappear: "This time the tall, spare artillery officer was sitting in his place, having lightly powdered the dark bags under his eyes."[29]

Early in the war Beria also clashed with Army General Georgii Zhukov, chief of the General Staff. In mid-July 1941 Beria began spreading information, which proved to be false, about enemy paratroopers having landed in the region of the town of Belyi, the right flank of the 24th Army, commanded by Lieutenant General S. A. Kalinin. When Zhukov telephoned Kalinin to ask about the presence of these German paratroopers, Kalinin replied that he knew nothing about it. He was relieved of his command the next day, even though he had been correct in saying that the rumor had no basis. As it turned out, Beria, apparently irritated by not having his information confirmed, had brought about Kalinin's dismissal. He had asked Zhukov what sort of man Kalinin was and when Zhukov replied that he hardly knew him, Beria retorted in a menacing voice: "If you hardly know him, why did you agree to his appointment as commander?" He walked out of Zhukov's office without waiting for an answer and Kalinin's fate was sealed.[30]

Zhukov was to have further unpleasant encounters with Beria thoughout the war. Both Beria and Stalin were jealous of Zhukov's popularity, which rose sharply after Soviet victories in the Battle of Moscow in early 1942. So Beria took it upon himself to gather compromising materials about Zhukov, as well as to undercut his authority. In the spring of 1942, Beria had Major General V. S. Golushkevich, Zhukov's chief of operations on the Western Front, arrested in the hopes of getting testimony from him that would harm Zhukov, but Golushkevich did not cave in.[31] Eventually, however, Beria was to prove successful in damaging Zhukov's career.

FURTHERING THE WAR EFFORT

British journalist Alexander Werth claimed that by late 1941 Stalin had learned his lesson from the bitter defeats suffered by the Red Army under the strong arm of the NKVD and decided to loosen up police controls. According to Werth, the role of the NKVD was reduced and, although army officers continued to be subjected to NKVD surveillance, the NKVD interfered much less than it had before.[32] Although the actions of Beria, Abakumov, and others, gave little indication that the NKVD had loosened the reins on the military by this time, it is possible that the grave threat faced by the Soviets brought about a subtle change in the posture of the NKVD as a whole. The U.S. Ambassador in Moscow at the time, Laurence Steinhardt, observed in a note to the secretary of state that at the traditional celebration of the anniversary of the Bolshevik Revolution, on 7 November 1941, the official slogans were devoted only to the war and the usual slogan praising the NKVD had been omitted.[33] It is perhaps no coincidence that, in *Pravda*'s picture of the leaders standing on top of Lenin's tomb for the occasion, Beria is shown at the far end, short in stature and the only one not saluting the passing military parade.[34]

Nonetheless, whatever his dislike for the Soviet military command, Beria's chief concern was to repel the Nazi invasion of his country. Throughout the summer of 1941 he was monitoring the continuous stream of NKVD intelligence on the German advance toward Moscow and the situation in areas under attack.[35] By October 1941 the Germans had come so close to Moscow that the leadership decided to evacuate the government, including the NKVD, to the city of Kuibyshev. Stalin and the GKO remained in Moscow, however. Because of the German bombing,

Beria moved his office from the Lubianka to the basement of no. 2 Dzerzhinskii Street, where there was an air-raid shelter. One of his tasks at this time was to supervise the evacuation of armaments factories to the East, with the aid of NKVD internal troops. In the event that German troops entered the city, Beria and Moscow Party First Secretary A. S. Shcherbakov were responsible for blowing up all enterprises that could not be moved.[36] Later, with the beginning of the Soviet counteroffensive in early 1942, it was possible to halt the evacuation and bring some factories back from the East. Such wholesale transfers of factories caused tremendous disruption and a variety of organizational problems. It was not until the autumn of 1942 that Soviet armaments production was able to satisfy the demands of the front armies.[37]

Beria shared responsibility for defense production with other members of the GKO. Together they coordinated the needs of the front with production capacity and directed the planning of the various commissariats.[38] Beria himself oversaw the operations of the Commissariats of Armaments and Munitions, headed by D. F. Ustinov and B. L. Vannikov, respectively. We have no way of knowing to what extent he actually involved himself in the operations of these commissariats, although he made every effort to ensure that his own NKVD troops were well supplied. According to Victor Kravchenko, an official in the defense industry who later defected: "The nominal Commissars . . . would have preferred a quick death to the righteous anger of Beria and his organization. Everyone in the plants and offices and institutions directly or indirectly connected with armaments and munitions was gripped by dread fear. Beria was no engineer. He was placed in control for the precise purpose of inspiring deadly fear."[39]

Beria's NKVD played a crucial role in defense production by providing forced labor from its vast GULAG and from special settlements. Although close to a million prisoners were conscripted into the Red Army during the first three years of the war, new arrests compensated for these losses, preventing the depletion of the ranks of forced labor.[40] The NKVD provided thirty-nine thousand laborers to produce weapons and ammunition and forty thousand for aviation and tank production. During the first three years of the war NKVD prisoners produced more than seventy million units of ammunition, valued at 1,250 million rubles. NKVD forced labor was also used extensively to mine coal and metals and to construct defense industry enterprises. Close to 448,000 NKVD prisoners, for example, were detailed for railway construction.[41]

The productivity of forced labor during the war was remarkably high, despite the extreme hardships that prisoners and exiles endured. In March 1944 Beria informed Stalin that the NKVD had fulfilled on time an order from the GKO to construct a coal mine in the Karaganda Basin, which could produce 1.5 million tons of coal annually. A month later he proudly reported that the NKVD had completed construction of a metallurgical factory capable of producing 400–450,000 tons of cast iron a year.[42] Such achievements were reached at great human cost. The suffering in the camps was so severe that the USSR Procuracy's Department for Oversight of Places of Detention took it upon itself to write to Beria about the harsh conditions that prisoners had to endure. One source has estimated that more 620,000 NKVD prisoners died during the war as a result of the cold, hunger, or disease.[43]

THE NKVD IN COMBAT

In April 1942 a special NKVD Administration for Guarding the Rear was created, consisting of border and internal troops. In addition to preventing desertions, these troops performed a variety of tasks, such as uncovering enemy agents who had penetrated the front and liquidating small enemy groups and armed detachments. In 1942 alone rear security troops are said to have caught more than fifteen hundred spies and diversionists and destroyed more than 135 groups of bandits and three thousand enemy "sympathizers and accomplices." They also guarded prisoners and performed garrison duty in cities and towns liberated from the Germans, rebuilt bridges, and lay railroad track. In many cases NKVD divisions, which served as a reserve force for the regular military units, participated directly in combat.[44] The fact that NKVD troops were under the dual subordination of the General Staff of the Red Army, which directed their maneuvers at the front, and the NKVD, which had overall control over the disposition of the troops and their transfer from one front to another, led to further clashes between the Beria group and Red Army leaders.

For all his meddling in military matters, Beria himself stayed far away from the fighting. As far as is known, he visited the front on only two occasions. In August 1942 Beria arrived on the Transcaucasian Front as a representative of the Stavka. The situation was particularly serious at this time because the Germans were advancing over the Caucasian Mountains toward the Black Sea while to the southeast they were driving toward the vital oil fields of Groznyi and Baku. Stalin was worried about the loyalty of the Caucasian peoples, particularly the Moslems in the mountain areas, whom the Germans had been courting, so he had sent Beria there to hold the population in line.[45]

The 1952 edition of the *Great Soviet Encyclopedia*, published when Beria was still in favor in the Kremlin, portrayed him as the military hero of the Caucasian defense: "On Stalin's instructions in these days of grave danger for the people, L. P. Beria led the defense of the Caucasus. L. P. Beria closely coordinated the work of the rear and the front and ensured the brilliant execution of Stalin's plan to smash the German-Fascist troops in the Caucasus."[46] How Beria managed this victory, when he remained in the Caucasus for only a few weeks and the Germans were not repulsed from the area until early 1943, is not explained.

The generals in command of the Transcaucasian Front presented an entirely different picture of Beria's role there, as do sources from military archives. According to these sources, Beria arrived with a large retinue of his henchmen, including Kobulov, Mil'shtein, Tsanava, Lev Vlodzimir-skii, chief of the USSR NKVD Investigation Department, Rukhadze of the Georgian NKVD, and Grigorii Karanadze, head of the Dagestan NKVD. Also accompanying Beria was his eighteen-year-old son Sergo, who had been spared from fighting at the front by joining a special group of radio technicians, and S. M. Shtemenko, a young officer from the General Staff, who was to become Beria's protégé.[47] Beria immediately began to throw his weight around, issuing orders in the name of the Stavka and demanding that they be carried out to the fullest. According to I. V. Tiulenev, commander of the Transcaucasian Front, Beria and Kobulov exceeded their authority, going over the head of the front command and disorganizing its work. They clashed straight away with one general, who somehow offended them, and even threatened him with arrest.[48]

Armed with unlimited authority from Stalin, Beria established a Northern Group of the Caucasian Front, headed by NKVD General I. I. Maslennikov, for the defense of the Transcaucasian Mountains. This effectively denied Tiulenev's headquarters staff and the staff of the 46th Army, which manned the passes, control over mountain operations. Maslennikov, who was inexperienced in combat, took it upon himself to ignore the orders of the front commander and demanded the regrouping of troops on his own.[49] Furthermore, in place of reinforcements that Tiulenev had requested from the Stavka, Beria ordered in new NKVD units, which could not be used for active combat. Later, when Tiulenev was in Moscow, he asked Stalin to have some NKVD units transferred to his command. Beria, who was present at the time, objected sharply, hurling abuse at Tiulenev. Only when Stalin insisted did Beria reluctantly agree to place a certain number of troops at the disposal of the front command. Tiulenev summed up his impression of Beria's visit to the Caucasus:

> Throughout his brief stay at the front, Beria did not once display a serious interest in the defense system elaborated by the Military Council of the front and approved by the Stavka. . . . Beria's trips to the defense lines in the area of Makhachkala, Groznyi, Vladikavkaz and Sukhumi boiled down to showiness

and noise, to the creation of a facade of concern about the organization and strengthening of defense. In fact with his criminal attitude and conduct he only disorganized, hindered and disrupted our work.[50]

In March 1943 Beria made another trip to the Caucasus, again accompanied by Shtemenko, in order to direct supplies at the North Caucasian Front, but only remained there for ten days.[51]

THE PARTISAN MOVEMENT AND
INTELLIGENCE GATHERING

Following the German invasion the NKVD organized, together with the party, a movement for partisan warfare in areas overrun by the Germans. In July 1941 party and NKVD officials began establishing partisan detachments, which paralleled the existing territorial structure of the party. Already in June Beria had ordered local NKVD organizations to form home defense units, known as "destruction battalions," designed to prevent sabotage and diversion by German parachutists, but in July the NKVD transformed those battalions near the front into partisan units.[52] On 8 August 1941 Beria sent a communication to Stalin in which he reported that partisan detachments had been formed from NKVD units in all regions along the Western Front. In the Ukraine alone, for example, NKVD personnel had formed three fully armed detachments, numbering one thousand to two thousand men each. In addition, several destruction battalions, numbering nine thousand men in all, had reorganized into partisan units. In Belorussia more than a thousand NKVD and militia employees had formed fourteen partisan detachments. According to Beria's report, the partisans were successfully sabotaging the enemy in the rear and were also providing the Red Army with important intelligence.[53]

The NKVD soon created an agency directly responsible for partisan activities, the Fourth (Intelligence-Sabotage) Administration, headed by Deputy Commissar of Internal Affairs Pavel Sudoplatov. Although the main control over the partisan movement rested with the party, the NKVD screened persons under consideration for membership in partisan units. Also, for a brief initial period, NKVD special sections were responsible for the military utilization of the partisans. By the beginning of 1942, the framework of control over the partisan movement had all but disintegrated and the Red Army assumed much of the direction of partisan bands. Then, in May 1942, the Stavka created a Central Staff of the Partisan Movement, which was attached to the party's Central Committee. Although the NKVD's formal authority over the partisans had declined by this time, it continued to exercise control through NKVD special sections in every partisan operative group. NKVD influence at the higher levels was also maintained by the prominent role of NKVD officials in the movement.[54]

As John Armstrong, author of a study of the partisan movement, pointed out, the NKVD never came close to controlling the partisans as a "private empire," because the NKVD was divided against itself. While the Fourth Administration consisted mainly of Beria loyalists, such as Sudoplatov, NKVD officials in the republican and regional partisan groups often came from the border guards, which had a history of friction with the political police. Thus, for example, the chief of staff of the Ukrainian partisan movement, former border guard, and subsequently deputy chief of the Ukrainian NKVD, T. A. Strokach, became a bitter opponent of Beria. Strokach's partisan organization operated with great success and apparently enjoyed the special favor of the central staff of the partisan movement in Moscow.[55]

Beria had close ties with the Belorussian partisan movement through his Mingrelian crony Lavrentii Tsanava, who had headed the NKVD there since 1938. Tsanava, who was jokingly referred to as "Lavrentii the Second," later wrote an extensive history of the partisan movement in which he credited Beria with providing enormous practical help to the Belorussian partisans.[56] But other Belorussian partisans were antagonistic to Beria and the NKVD. Kiril Mazurov, who eventually served as a leading party official under Brezhnev, claimed that during the war Beria did everything to suppress the partisans, attempting to transform the movement into diversionary detachments subordinated to the NKVD.[57]

By late 1942 the partisans had been drawn more closely into the Soviet intelligence network and a formal chain of command had been worked out through which they could supply both the Red Army and the NKVD with military, political, and economic intelligence. The Foreign Intelligence Department of the NKVD's State Security Administration, headed by Lieutenant General P. M. Fitin, was making a large-scale effort to procure intelligence on the organization and functions of the German occupation force and was sending masses of agents into German-occupied territory.[58] Within the Foreign Department—or in some way connected to it—was a sabotage department, which was charged with carrying out myriad intelligence and sabotage functions and conducting liaison with the partisan movement. The head of this department, A. P. Osipov, was collaborating with Brigadier George A. Hill, who had come to Moscow as a representative of Britain's SOE (Secret Operations Executive). The NKVD had a similar mission for liaison with the SOE in London. Osipov and Hill prepared a handbook for partisan operations which laid down their functions and purpose and established regulations for coordination with the Red Army. In addition to writing the handbook, they tackled the problem of conditioning the Red Army Command to make full use of the partisans, a difficult task given the military's distaste for the latter.[59]

In early 1942 Hill had a personal meeting with Beria. Hill recalled that Beria's office was large, with thick carpets, and several deep, leather-covered easy chairs. The walls were bare except for an enormous framed painting of Stalin in uniform. Beria was badly briefed about the SOE and had to be constantly prompted by Osipov. As they sat drinking liqueurs and smoking Russian cigarettes, Beria quizzed Hill on poisons and silent firearms. "How silent could an automatic pistol really be?" he asked. He then wanted to know whether the SOE would agree to its promise to drop NKVD agents behind enemy lines, to which Hill replied that SOE would do so to the limits of possibility. "As he put the question," Hill observed, "all his ruthlessness came to the fore, and I realised the power that he had within him, power that has brought him to, and kept him at, the top. . . . The more I saw of him, the less I liked him; an evil, sinister creature."[60]

William Donovan, head of the OSS (U.S. Office of Strategic Services), went to Moscow in late 1943 to arrange an exchange of missions with the Soviet security services. He met with both Fitin and Osipov, but not with Beria, perhaps because by this time the intelligence apparatus was no longer subordinated to the NKVD (see below). In fact no exchange of missions between the OSS and Soviet intelligence organs was ever established, because Federal Bureau of Investigation Chief J. Edgar Hoover reportedly felt that too many Soviet agents were in the United States already (and he was proved right). But on Donovan's initiative the cooperative relationship continued right up until the time that the Soviets reached Berlin. Documents, special equipment, and secret intelligence, including valuable cryptographic materials, were sent from the OSS to the Soviets in considerable quantities, in order to aid the Soviet Union in defeating Germany. Donovan developed a genuine liking for Fitin and was much encouraged by the spirit of cooperation that existed between the services. Had he met Beria, or Fitin's immediate superior, Merkulov, perhaps he would not have been so well disposed toward the Soviets.[61]

Recently released Soviet documents indicate that the NKVD's intelligence-gathering network was quite successful. Thus, while Beria still controlled the intelligence services, they had managed to obtain detailed information on Hitler's former deputy Rudolph Hess and his dramatic flight to England in May 1941. Beria sent Stalin a top-secret memorandum, dated 2 October 1942, in which he wrote that the British knew of Hess's plans to fly to England well in advance.[62] British intelligence apparently intercepted a letter from Hess to the Duke of Hamilton, on whose estate he landed, and continued to correspond with him in the

Duke's name. According to Beria's memorandum: "In this correspondence all the questions of organization of the flight were discussed in detail. However, Hamilton himself did not take part in the correspondence." Beria went on to point out that, according to his source, a colonel in the Czechoslovak military intelligence, Hess's letters clearly laid out German plans to attack the Soviet Union. By the time he received this information Stalin was preoccupied with far more pressing matters and it was of little practical use, but he nonetheless must have been impressed with the abilities of Beria's intelligence-gathering apparatus.

DIVISION OF THE NKVD

On 16 April 1943, with the tide of the war having turned in favor of the Soviets, the NKVD was again divided into two parts. The Main Administration of State Security (GUGB) of the NKVD was transformed into a separate People's Commissariat of State Security (NKGB), under the leadership of Vsevold Merkulov, who became, like Beria, a people's commissar. As part of this reorganization the Special Department for Military Counterintelligence was removed from the state security organs and transformed into a Main Administration for Counterintelligence, or SMERSH (Death to Spies), which was placed under the General Staff of the Army. Now Abakumov was no longer Beria's (or Merkulov's) subordinate and Beria's NKVD had relinquished its control over military counterintelligence to the Armed Forces.

These changes undoubtedly diminished the formal power of Beria as NKVD chief. It is not clear, however, that they were motivated, as some have suggested, solely by Stalin's desire to rein in Beria. That they were first instituted in early 1941 and then reversed after the German attack suggests that, had Beria's broad powers been a serious concern for Stalin, he would not have postponed the division of the NKVD for almost two more years. It may be that the NKVD, with its own army of several hundred thousand troops, had simply become too large and had too many functions to be efficiently controlled by one commissariat. The Soviets had made large territorial acquisitions since 1939 and with the German retreat they would be controlling even more territory and people. This meant expanded police operations and a larger labor camp population. From an organizational standpoint it made sense to streamline the police and security apparatus in this way.[63]

As for military counterintelligence, it was apparently transferred to the authority of the Red Army because of the need to improve its effectiveness.[64] For example, the head of German intelligence on the Eastern Front, Reinhardt Gehlen, had managed, through his skill in working with

Russian prisoners of war, to infiltrate agents behind Soviet lines and gain information on Soviet military decision making at the highest levels.[65] Stalin may well have decided that a separate military counterintelligence organization, with at least formal subordination to the Red Army command, would enable the Soviets to combat German spy networks more vigorously.[66]

Beria's loss of direct control over the security apparatus was mitigated by the fact that Merkulov remained at the helm as the new NKGB commissar, allowing Beria to exert his influence. Beria also retained his followers in key positions below Merkulov. Bogdan Kobulov was first deputy people's commissar of state security, and Solomon Mil'shtein was chief of the third directorate. Sergei Goglidze, Mikhail Gvishiani, Amaiak Kobulov, Lavrentii Tsanava, and Avksentii Rapava, to name a few Beria supporters, were in charge of republican state security administrations. According to Merkulov, Beria would have preferred a Caucasian, like Bogdan Kobulov or Vladimir Dekanozov, in the top security post but Stalin would have objected, so Beria put forth Merkulov instead.[67] Sometime in 1943 Dekanazov was shunted off to Bulgaria as Soviet ambassador, but he returned in 1945 to serve as Molotov's assistant in the Foreign Affairs Commissariat.

Within the NKVD itself, Beria had his longtime protégé Stepan Mamulov (Mamul'ian) as head of the NKVD Secretariat and Iuvelian Sumbatov-Topuridze as chief of the NKVD's Economic Administration. This is not to mention police officials who did not rise up the career ladder in Georgia but may have formed a bond with Beria after he took over the USSR NKVD in 1938, such as Vlodzimirskii. Beria's new first deputy, Sergei Kruglov, was not part of his Georgian clique either. He had been recruited into the NKVD in 1939, at the age of thirty-two, after working in the cadres (personnel appointments) department of the People's Commissariat for Heavy Industry. But he became, by all evidence, a dedicated NKVD loyalist until he switched ranks in 1953 and allied with Khrushchev to oppose Beria. The same was true of Kruglov's deputy Ivan Serov, a military officer who joined the NKVD at the same time as Kruglov. Although they eventually betrayed him, neither Kruglov nor Serov showed any reluctance to support Beria's agenda, participating actively in all the NKVD's brutal repressions.[68] Beria's power was reinforced by the fact that he was a member of the GKO, the supreme wartime authority, with supervisory responsibilities for both the police and intelligence apparatuses. Thus he remained the superior of both Abakumov and Merkulov. In May 1944 he was promoted to deputy chairman of the GKO and his authority was strengthened. In short, although the division of the police apparatus may have been a setback for Beria, he was holding his own.

THE NKVD ON THE OFFENSIVE:
DEPORTATIONS AND ARRESTS

The tremendous upheaval caused by the war meant that Beria's vast army of NKVD troops was called on to fulfill broad functions. The precise number of troops under the NKVD at this time is unknown but most estimates, both Soviet and Western, range between 600,000 to 700,000, including border, internal, and other specialized troops.[69] Once the war had begun, NKVD troops were unleashed on national groups within the Soviet Union that had fallen under suspicion for potential disloyalty to the regime. In August 1941, for example, the Volga German Autonomous Republic was abolished and hundreds of thousands of Volga Germans were forcibly uprooted and exiled to remote regions of Siberia and Kazakhstan. Germans in the Ukraine, Crimea, Kuban, and Transcaucasia were also rounded up and shipped off, leaving all but a few of their possessions behind. Beria was in charge of these operations.[70]

A new wave of deportations began after the German retreat. All Soviet citizens who had lived under German occupation were considered suspect, and the NKVD, with Beria at the helm, took it upon itself to rid the formerly occupied regions of any possible opposition elements. Thousands were arrested for alleged collaboration with the Nazis and entire national groups were deported under the most difficult physical conditions to barren special settlements in Central Asia and Kazakhstan. The first to be uprooted, in November 1943, were 68,938 Karachi people from the North Caucasus. They were followed by 93,139 Kalmyks in early January 1944. Beria was personally supervising these grisly operations and sent regular communiques to Stalin and the GKO on their progress.[71] On 20 February, accompanied by his deputies Ivan Serov, Stepan Mamulov, and Bogdan Kobulov, he arrived in the city of Groznyi by special train to oversee preparations for the deportation of the Chechens and Ingush. Some nineteen thousand NKVD, NKGB, and SMERSH personnel, with the assistance of a hundred thousand NKVD troops took part in the effort, which began three days later. By 7 March Beria was able to report to Stalin that close to 500,000 Chechens and Ingush were in transit to Kazakhstan and Kirgizia.[72] As Beria's letters to Stalin reveal, he was not merely executing the latter's orders but was assuming responsibility to single out additional national groups to be deported. On 24 February 1944 Beria wrote to Stalin with the suggestion that the Balkars be included among the deportees from the North Caucasus. He also asked permission to assign the NKVD troops carrying out operations in Chechnia to this task: "If you give your consent," he wrote, "I will be able to make all preparations necessary for the deportation of the Balkars on the spot, before returning to Moscow."[73] The proposed operation was carried out on 8–9 March, resulting in the deportation of 337,103 Balkars. Beria also initiated deportations from the Crimea. On 10 May 1944 he wrote to Stalin saying that, in view of the "traitorous actions" of Crimean Tatars against Soviet people and the consequent undesirability of having them in the border regions, the NKVD recommended that they be deported. The next day Stalin signed a GKO decree ordering the NKVD under Comrade Beria to resettle all Crimean Tatars in Uzbekistan by 1 June. On 18–20 May, more than 180,000 Tatars were shipped off in trainloads. Beria was apparently overseeing events from Moscow, with Kobulov and Serov on the spot. In June 1944, again at Beria's instigation, more than 33,000 Bulgarians, Greeks, and Armenians living in the Crimea were added to the list of deportees.[74]

Beria's matter-of-fact reports of course reveal nothing of the human suffering that was wrought by this "mini-holocaust." Tens of thousands—including women, children, and old people—perished while they were being transported like cattle in overcrowded railway cars without water or food. Mil'shtein informed Kobulov that, in the process of shipping the Chechens and Ingush, the NKVD had decided that it could make do with fewer railway cars by crowding forty-five instead of forty persons into each carriage—a perfectly reasonable decision, he observed, since almost half the contingent were children. He added that they also had been compelled to do without sanitation facilities, and consequently an epidemic of typhus had broken out.[75] One of those who survived the trip later described it: "In 'cattle cars' filled to overflowing without light or water, we traveled for almost a month to our destination . . . Typhus was having a heyday. There was no medicine . . . During the short stops at lonely, uninhabited stations we buried our dead near the train, in snow that was black from engine soot (it was forbidden, with punishment of death, to go more than five meters from the train)."[76] Many more died of famine and disease once they had reached their destination.[77]

For Beria this suffering apparently had no meaning. It was all part of a day's work: "The deportations were a routine, successful NKVD operation, for which he [Beria] might receive an additional portion of approval from his leader."[78] Indeed, the only credible explanation for Beria's enthusiasm in initiating these deportations was that he wanted to please Stalin, since he himself can hardly have believed what he told his chief—that entire national groups were guilty of collaborating with the Germans. Beria saw to it that his subordinates would receive some of the glory. In December 1944 he wrote to Stalin asking that the NKVD-NKGB officers who distinguished themselves in these operations be honored. Stalin complied, and 413 NKVD members received awards.[79]

As the Red Army moved westward in 1944 "liberating" German occupied territory, NKVD troops were charged with conducting operations against rebellious nationalist groups and enforcing law and order. Beria's troops and agents rounded up large numbers of liberated Soviet prisoners of war for repatriation. By October 1944, 354,590 Soviet soldiers who had been captured by the Germans had fallen into the hands of the NKVD. After screening, 36,630 were subsequently arrested by SMERSH.[80] The NKVD also screened, processed, and conveyed to resettlement or imprisonment masses of suspect people from Eastern Europe and the Baltic states. As a result of these operations, the population of the GULAG began to swell in 1944–45.[81]

A formal agreement on the mutual repatriation of Soviet and American soldiers and civilians was drawn up and signed at Yalta in February 1945. Although nothing in the agreement required American and British commanders to forcibly repatriate Soviet citizens against their will, the Soviets insisted on it and the Western allies complied, shipping trainload after trainload of former prisoners of war back to the Soviet Union. A special organization for repatriation of Soviet prisoners had been set up under the Sovnarkom, headed by Colonel General F. I. Golikov, but in fact Beria took charge of the process. As John Erickson observed, "Beria struck first."[82]

By 1944, with the Germans in retreat, the party began to tighten its reins on the military again. Stalin had grudgingly allowed the military to take precedence in order to defend the Soviet Union successfully, but he would not countenance this situation for long. Stalin himself had mastered military affairs sufficiently to become deeply involved in military strategy and, as chief of the Stavka and commissar of defense, presided directly over the Red Army's war against the Germans. Now he set about putting the military in its place. In November 1944 Stalin removed Kliment Voroshilov as his deputy commissar of defense, replacing him with a political commissar—and also a former Chekist—Nikolai Bulganin. This was a blow to the prestige of the Red Army and a symbol of the reassertion of party predominance.

One of the first victims of Stalin's efforts to cut the military down to size was Marshal Zhukov, whose brilliant military successes had earned him tremendous public admiration and popularity, thus arousing Stalin's ire. Beria, always adept at kindling Stalin's jealous suspicions, was in on the behind-the-scenes moves against Zhukov. In May 1945, after his army marched into Berlin, Zhukov was put in command of the Soviet military administration there. Beria managed to get his deputy Ivan Serov appointed as Zhukov's assistant, serving as chief of the civilian administration in the Soviet zone of Germany. Henceforth, reports began to trickle back to Stalin about Zhukov—that he was boasting about his victories and even that he was planning a military conspiracy against Stalin.[83] Beria's men also did all they could to keep important information hidden from Zhukov. It turns out, for example, that he was not told that Hitler's body had been found. He did not know that autopsies were carried out and an investigation launched to confirm the identity, as well as the cause of death. All this was done by SMERSH and the NKVD, with both Beria and Serov privy to the information but not the commander of Soviet forces in Berlin.[84]

During the summer of 1945 accusations against Zhukov began to grow, fed by Serov's transmissions back to Moscow, where a case against Zhukov was being prepared, apparently under Beria's direction. In late 1945 Stalin denounced Zhukov at a large Kremlin gathering, from which Zhukov was absent, for ascribing to himself all the war victories. Then in April 1946, following a clash with Viktor Abakumov, who had come to Berlin and was arresting Soviet officers, Zhukov was summoned home. He was called before a session of the Stavka and accused by Stalin, Beria, and Kaganovich of conspiratorial activities. Apparently Stalin had planned to arrest Zhukov but he sensed the strong solidarity of the military leaders and their support for Zhukov, so instead he demoted Zhukov to the post of commander of the Odessa Military District and removed him from the Central Committee.[85]

The names of other prominent wartime commanders also ceased to be mentioned in the Soviet press. As Roy Medvedev noted, "Stalin was determined not to share his military glory with them."[86] With Beria's connivance, Stalin had succeeded in dealing the military a blow to its prestige and public stature. Henceforth the party, led by Stalin, would again be the dominant force in the Soviet system, with the security apparatus not far behind. In keeping with this change, in July 1945, members of the police and security forces were given military ranks, and Beria himself became a marshal of the Soviet Union, the highest rank below that of generalissimo, which Stalin appropriated.[87] Beria would later pay a heavy price for confronting the military, however. In 1953 Zhukov and other generals were more than willing to assist Khrushchev in arresting him.

IN DIPLOMATIC CIRCLES

Despite Beria's role in the GKO and the importance of the NKVD's awesome powers, Beria himself remained an enigmatic, behind-the-scenes character to Western observers throughout the war. Those with access to Stalin's inner circle, of course, were aware of how powerful Beria was and how much influence he had with Stalin. But, unlike the generals, whose activities were the object of constant press reports, or figures like Molotov, who as foreign commissar was frequently in the limelight, Beria received little public mention. Considering Stalin's intense jealousy when he felt that other members of the leadership were gaining too much prominence, Beria's relative obscurity was probably fortuitous for him.

Although Beria attended wartime diplomatic dinners and was present at important conferences of the allied forces, including the Teheran Conference in November 1943 and the Yalta Conference in February 1945, foreign diplomats had little occasion to interact with him. He remained on the sidelines and is scarcely mentioned in Western diplomatic accounts of allied meetings.[88] Some diplomats realized that the Soviet attitude toward the West, which was so difficult to fathom, was not solely attributable to Stalin, no matter how powerful he appeared. George Kennan, writing from Moscow in September 1944, observed:

> In the case of Stalin's relations to the Western world the role of his political intimates must—in view of his own ignorance, his extreme seclusion and his suspicious Georgian nature—be little short of decisive. . . . it is here, in the relations between Stalin and his advisors, that we must seek the explanations for the puzzling, often contradictory manifestations of the Soviet attitude toward Western nations."[89]

In considering what Stalin's advisors were like and what advice they gave, Kennan could only conclude grimly that, with little knowledge of the world abroad, these men viewed events in terms of their own xenophobic preoccupation with internal security and domestic concerns. "It is possible," wrote Kennan, "that the conceptions of these men might occasionally achieve a rough approximation to reality and their judgments a similar approximation to fairness; but it is not likely."[90] Kennan's assessment could not have been far off the mark. Despite his wartime experience, Beria's interaction with the world outside the Soviet Union had been very limited. Moreover, his main preoccupation was with the byzantine world of Kremlin politics. It would take a few more years for Beria to view foreign policies in more rational and objective terms.

Judging from his behavior at Teheran, Beria was intensely suspicious of the Western allies. Nicholas Kviatashvili, a Georgian by birth whose family had emigrated to England, accompanied the British delegation as a military officer and left a vivid account in his memoirs of his impressions of Beria.[91] Kviatashvili recalled that, when the conference participants were invited to a dinner at the British Embassy, the NKVD, led by Beria, insisted on a thorough search of the building beforehand, minutely inspecting every room and even going up on the embassy's roof. The inspection lasted for nearly two hours.

Beria may also been engaging in a bit of intelligence-gathering for the Soviet side. Indeed, the Soviets were actively spying on their allies at the conference. According to Beria's son, Sergo, who was also at Teheran, the Soviets had bugs in several rooms of their residence there, where Roosevelt was staying. Beria, reportedly at Stalin's behest, had arranged for Sergo to take on the job of translating tapes of secretly recorded conversations of Roosevelt and Churchill. (Sergo was fluent in both English and German.) He then would deliver a daily report to Stalin on what they had said.[92]

According to Kviatashvili, Stalin's NKVD bodyguards at Teheran, about ten or twelve in all, were mostly Georgians. Their chief was Shota Tsereteli who, ironically, given his bloodthirsty reputation in NKVD circles, came across as "good-looking, highly intelligent and courteous," impressing all the British and American officers who met him. As for Beria, Kviatashvili was awed by him:

> Beria made a tremendous impression on me right from the first meeting. In the next few days I met him several times and had several conversations with him, both personal and during discussions of security matters. And that impression did not diminish but on the contrary grew. There simply cannot be any doubt that he was an extremely intelligent and shrewd man with tremendous willpower and ability to impress, command and lead other men. He may have been too sure of himself. He seemed to completely disdain any opposing view, was quite intolerant of anybody else's opinions and became very angry if anyone strongly opposed any of his proposals. Not that any of the Soviets dared—they behaved like slaves in his presence.[93]

Churchill, who later remarked in his memoirs on how thoroughly the NKVD had searched the British Embassy in Teheran, did not underestimate Beria's significance.[94] The American diplomat Charles Bohlen recalled in his memoirs a telling incident regarding Churchill and Beria, which took place at a dinner held by Stalin during the Yalta Conference. The British Ambassador, Archibald Clark-Kerr, was apparently getting on well with Beria, having amicably carried on a discussion with him at luncheon earlier in the day about the sex life of fish. At dinner Clark-Kerr rose and said that, after all the toasts to such spiritual things as comradeship and friendship, he was proposing a toast to the "man who looks after our bodies," meaning Beria. Churchill was not amused. According to Bohlen, he leaned forward in his chair and growled, "No, Archie, none of that."[95] Kathleen Harriman, who had come to Yalta with her father, Ambassador Averell Harriman, also recalled the incident, noting that instead of clinking glasses with Clark-Kerr, Churchill shook his finger at him and warned, "Be careful, be careful."[96] In Churchill's eyes Beria, with his vast police empire, no doubt symbolized the darkest side of Stalin's regime, serving as a reminder of the limits of the Western alliance with the Soviet Union, limits that were soon to become all too apparent.

Chapter Seven

KREMLIN POLITICS AFTER THE WAR

> Turned into a deity, Stalin became so powerful that he ceased
> to pay attention to the changing needs and
> desires of those who had exalted him.
> *(Milovan Djilas,* Conversations with Stalin*)*

BERIA AND THE ATOMIC BOMB PROGRAM: THE FIRST STEPS

THE COLD WAR between the Soviet Union and the West that Churchill foresaw well before Hitler had been defeated escalated quickly once the Soviets joined the race to develop an atomic bomb. Having surmounted incredible obstacles and endured inconceivable hardships to achieve a victory over the Nazis, the Soviets felt they deserved "superpower" status. But in order to attain this status, they had to catch up with the United States, which by the end of the war had successfully developed a bomb. Beria was the logical person to take on this daunting task, for it required someone skilled in the operations of intelligence, security, and police coercion, key elements behind the Soviet strategic weapons program. Beria's leadership of this program from 1945 to 1953, which offered him the opportunity to exert his direct influence over the most crucial area of Soviet military policy, was highly successful. The evidence indicates that his considerable administrative and organizational skills and his vast web of connections in the Soviet bureaucracy enabled him to be a very effective "atom bomb tsar." Indeed, he threw himself into the job with complete dedication, even following scientific developments closely, though he had no technical training.

Soviet scientists had been working on atomic energy well before Beria came on the scene and were fully informed about theoretical and experimental developments in the West in the years preceding the war. In 1940, at an autumn session of the Soviet Academy of Sciences, the physicist A. I. Kurchatov gave a report on the possibility of bringing about a chain reaction that would create an enormous amount of nuclear energy. And in October 1941, in an address to a meeting of fellow scientists, physicist Petr Kapitsa discussed the destructive potential of an atom bomb.[1] But the German invasion put a temporary stop to research in this area, and the expertise of Soviet scientists was directed toward the more immediate cause of the war effort.

By late 1942, as the outlook for the Soviet Union in its struggle against the Germans began to improve, Stalin again directed attention to atomic research. At this time the Soviets were receiving valuable information from foreign intelligence agents about work on the atomic bomb in the United States, Britain, and Germany. Much of this highly sensitive strategic information came initially to Beria.[2] Toward the end of October 1941 he received a telegram from the NKVD's foreign intelligence station in London saying that top secret documents indicated that the British and Americans were hurrying to develop a bomb using an explosive nuclear reaction of uranium-235. Two months later Beria received evidence—based on papers found on a German POW—that German scientists were also developing an atomic bomb. A subsequent coded message from London on British-American cooperation in an atomic project convinced Beria of the importance of this information, which he then presented to Stalin.[3] According to I. N. Golovin, a direct participant in the bomb project, as well as a deputy to Kurchatov and subsequently his biographer, Stalin called a meeting of four leading scientists, including Kapitsa, in November 1942, and asked them whether it was scientifically feasible to build an atomic bomb. They replied in the affirmative and emphasized the crucial importance of such a project. This apparently convinced Stalin, who then began to consider who would be placed in charge of the scientific work. At first Kapsita and another well-known physicist were discussed, but Stalin thought it preferable to have someone younger and not so famous. Kurchatov, director of Laboratory no. 2, was designated to head the newly established atomic weapon project.[4]

Meanwhile Beria had been continuing with his program of collecting intelligence on foreign efforts to build a bomb. He had a small room set aside for him in the Kremlin where he could pass on information from his intelligence sources to Kurchatov and other physicists. Then he would have their requirements forwarded to his agents abroad. Thus, for example, Beria's deputy Fitin, who was directly in charge of foreign intelligence, sent out a coded message, on 14 June 1942, to his agents in London, Berlin, and New York, requesting that they obtain information on "the theoretical and practical aspects of the atomic bomb projects, on the design of the atomic, nuclear fuel components, the trigger mechanism, various methods of uranium isotope fission," and on the policies and governmental structures of bomb development in Germany, Britain, and the United States.[5]

A key source of secret information for Moscow was Klaus Fuchs, a highly respected physicist who had emigrated to Britain from Germany in the mid-1930s. He first approached the Soviets with an offer to spy for them in the autumn of 1941 and began passing information through channels of Soviet military intelligence. By 1943 he was dealing directly with the state security apparatus. As a top nuclear physicist, Fuchs was invited to the United States to work on the top secret "Manhattan Project" at Oakridge and then at Los Alamos. He was then able to provide data to the Soviets on all aspects of the U.S. bomb program, including details of the construction of plutonium and uranium bombs. Working with a Soviet agent named A. S. Feklisov, he continued to supply the Soviet intelligence apparatus with reports until shortly before his arrest in early 1950.[6] Another important source was the New York-based espionage network of an American communist couple, Morris and Lona Cohen. Morris Cohen, who had been recruited by the Soviets during the Spanish Civil War, passed secret information from an American physicist on to Vasilii Zarubin, head of the Soviet intelligence station in New York from 1941 to 1944.[7]

The Americans and the British first learned about Soviet espionage activities when the cipher clerk at the Soviet Embassy in Ottawa, Igor Guzenko, defected to Canadian authorities in September 1945.[8] Guzenko's information revealed that the Soviets had a substantial network of agents whose goal was to obtain secret information about atomic weapons programs in the West. But the extent to which the Soviets relied on intelligence gathering to develop their own bomb has only recently come to light, in materials from Soviet archives. On 4 March 1943, Kurchatov sent a report to M. G. Pervukhin, a deputy chairman of the Sovnarkom, in which he noted that intelligence from the West had enabled him and his colleagues to "by-pass many laborious phases involved in tackling the uranium problem." The information had led them to revise their views on fundamental issues and to adopt new methods of research.[9] And later Kurchatov wrote a letter to the Soviet security organs in which he discussed the invaluable help they had provided in the creation of the atomic bomb.[10]

General oversight for the atomic bomb project was initially the responsibility of Molotov rather than Beria. But Kurchatov was dissatisfied with Molotov's leadership and toward the end of 1944 or in early 1945 wrote a letter to Beria complaining that a year had passed without prospecting for deposits of uranium, without which little could be done toward developing an atomic bomb. Why was the letter addressed to Beria? In Golovin's words: "Now, of course, everyone knows that he [Beria] was a bloody hangman. But at that time Kurchatov turned to a member of the Politburo, a man with great authority, who had influence over Stalin."[11] In fact, Beria did not become a full member of the Politburo until March 1946. But since he was in charge of intelligence-gathering for atomic research and also was the GKO member responsible for armaments and munitions, he was the logical person to whom Kurchatov would turn. Apparently Stalin also recognized Beria's special qualities, for by mid-1945 he assigned Beria to replace Molotov as overall director of the fledgling program.

After Hiroshima

Despite ongoing scientific research, a full-scale effort to produce an atomic bomb in the Soviet Union did not begin until after the American bomb was dropped on Hiroshima on 6 August 1945. Truman had told Stalin at the Potsdam Conference in July that the United States had a bomb that was highly destructive and Stalin knew the details from Beria, but the implications of this new weapon were not brought home to him until the bombing of Hiroshima. The next day Stalin reportedly summoned Kurchatov and several other leading nuclear physicists to the Kremlin, along with the Commissar of Munitions B. L. Vannikov, and ordered them to catch up with the United States as fast as possible, no matter what the cost.[12] The lines of command and the organization of the program are not entirely clear, but Stalin set up a Scientific-Technical Council under the Sovnarkom (since 1946 the Council of Ministers), which consisted of scientists and economic managers, to administer the program. He appointed Vannikov chairman of the council, with Kurchatov and Pervukhin, commissar of the chemical industry, as his deputies. In 1946 the council's work was supplemented by the First Administration of the Council of Ministers, which Vannikov also took charge of.[13]

Meanwhile a so-called Special Committee on the Atom Bomb, headed by Beria, was organized on 20 August 1945. In addition to Beria, the committee included eight members: Kurchatov, Vannikov, Pervukhin, Kapitsa, Malenkov, the State Planning Committee (Gosplan) chief Nikolai Voznesenskii, and two deputies of Beria in the NKVD, A. P. Zaveniagin and V. A. Makhnev. It is not clear exactly how this committee was connected to the Scientific-Technical Council, but since Beria had the ultimate authority (aside from Stalin himself) for the atom bomb program, Vannikov was subordinated to him.[14] Having supervised munitions and armaments production throughout the war, Beria had worked closely with many of the industrial managers who were participating in the project, including Vannikov. And, of course, he had under his command the vast prison labor force that was employed in the nuclear industry. Much of the construction of buildings and installations was done by NKVD (since 1946 MVD) prisoners, as was the mining of uranium and radium. Prisoners were also used for atomic energy research, 50 percent of which was done in special NKVD centers called *sharashi*, such as those described in Solzhenitsyn's *The First Circle*, where highly trained specialists worked in captivity.[15] Finally, that the bomb project was developed in conditions of utmost secrecy made it practical to have the NKVD responsible for administrative tasks, as well as for guarding installations.

By all accounts, Stalin gave the atomic energy program the highest priority, with no resources spared to ensure its success. With such an enormous responsiblity on his shoulders Beria could not administer the atomic program from afar; he became actively involved in the day-to-day decision making, reporting back to Stalin, who showed intense interest.[16] Beria seems to have clashed straight away with the physicist Kapitsa, whom he enlisted to join the Scientific-Technical Council in September 1945. Having already run up against Beria when he was trying to save his assistant from arrest in 1939, Kapitsa resented Beria's constant interference in scientific matters, as well as his imperious manner. He also opposed the idea of copying Western technology rather than relying on the development of Soviet science. In October 1945 he took the bold step of writing to Stalin to complain about Beria and to request that he be released from the special committee:

> Now, having clashed with Comrade Beria about the Special Committee, I feel especially clearly how intolerable is his attitude toward scientists.
>
> When he enlisted me in this work he simply ordered his secretary to call me to his office. (When Witte, the Minister of Finance [under the Tsar], recruited Mendeleev to work in the Office of Weights and Measures, he went himself to Dmitrii Ivanovich.) On 28 September I was in the office of Comrade Beria and when he decided it was time to end the conversation he just stuck out his hand and said "Well, good-bye." These are not mere trifles, but symbols of respect to a person, to a scientist.[17]

Stalin showed the letter to Beria, who was disturbed enough to call Kapitsa on the telephone and ask him to come over for a talk. Kapitsa refused. Beria, who apparently wanted to make amends, then went himself to see Kapitsa, bringing with him a magnificent present, a double-barreled Tula rifle.

The relationship between the two men did not improve, however, and a month later Kapitsa again wrote to Stalin:

> Comrades Beria, Malenkov and Voznesenskii conduct themselves in the Special Committee as if they were supermen. Especially Comrade Beria. To be sure, he holds the baton in his hands. . . . Comrade Beria's basic weakness consists in the fact that the conductor must not merely wave the baton, but also understand the score. In this Beria is weak.

I told him straight out: "You don't understand physics. Let us scientists judge these matters." And to that he retorted that I knew nothing about people.[18]

Kapitsa's relations with Beria had become so bad, he wrote, that he was again requesting dismissal from the Special Committee and the Council. A month later Stalin released Kapitsa from his position on the Special Committee, but this was not the end of the matter. Kapitsa was punished for his recalcitrance a few months later by losing all his scientific posts and being placed under virtual house arrest for the next eight years.[19]

Other scientists working on the atomic bomb project also had to endure Beria's haughtiness and disrespect, but none dared complain as Kapitsa had done. According to a colleague of Kurchatov, A. P. Aleksandrov: "Beria was a terrifying man, vile. We all knew this. Our very lives depended on him."[20] Aleksandrov once had a meeting with Beria and his assistant General Makhnev to discuss Aleksandrov's proposal to build a special factory for producing deuterium (an isotope of hydrogen). Beria had doubts about the proposal because there had already been an explosion during experiments in obtaining deuterium. He completely ignored Aleksandrov, addressing his questions to Makhnev: "Does he know," asked Beria referring to Aleksandrov, "that if the factory blows up he will have hell to pay?" Despite Beria's admonitions, Aleksandrov stuck to his guns and the factory was built and operated successfully.[21]

Not all the nuclear scientists shared these negative assessments of Beria, however. Kurchatov and his deputy Golovin apparently got on well with Beria and considered him a good leader. According to Golovin: "For us Beria's administrative abilities were obvious. He was unusually energetic. Meetings did not last for hours, everything was decided very quickly. The largest burden of the work was in the years 1945–47, during which we always felt his operational leadership. He read our written reports quickly, for example, and returned them with questions and requests for clarifications."[22] Others concurred with this assessment of Beria. According to one source: "The scientists who met him could not fail to recognize his intelligence, his willpower and his purposefulness. They found him a first-class administrator who could carry a job through to completion."[23]

The Nobel-prize winning physicist Andrei Sakharov, who was recruited to work on the bomb project in 1948, attended meetings at Beria's Kremlin office on numerous occasions. Once Sakharov went alone to see Beria, who wanted to ask him about a proposal involving the development of a magnetic thermonuclear reactor. After listening to Sakharov's reply Beria asked him if he had any questions. Without thinking Sakharov asked why the Soviet Union lagged so far behind the West in technology. Beria answered matter-of-factly: "Because we lack R&D and a manufacturing base. Everything relies on a single supplier, *Elektrosyla*. The Americans have hundreds of companies with large manufacturing facilities." Only when Beria offered Sakharov his "slightly moist and deathly cold" hand did Sakharov realize that he was "face-to-face with a terrifying human being."[24]

In addition to providing Soviet scientists with the secrets of Western atomic technology, Beria made great efforts to ensure that uranium and other materials were in adequate supply. When plants and industries were being dismantled in the Soviet zone of Germany he demanded top priority for the First Administration of the Council of Ministers, often running into conflicts with other government officials. Thus, for example, after winning a row with Kaganovich, commissar for the construction materials industry, Beria had the MVD appropriate excavators at two factories in Nordhausen, which were then shipped to the Volga-Don MVD for mining uranium.[25]

The limited availability of raw materials for atomic energy was a serious problem for the Soviets in 1945. Mining operations were begun in late 1945 in Czechoslovakia and Bulgaria and somewhat later in Germany and Poland, but initially the prospecting was not all that productive. Later, however, the exploitation of deposits in the satellite countries and in the Soviet Union proved more successful. By 1948 the Soviets were devoting tremendous effort to uranium mining, so that production increased dramatically and continued to do so throughout 1949 and 1950.[26]

Beria took an active role in the recruitment and utilization of German scientists for atomic research. In the summer of 1945 two groups of scientists arrived in the Soviet Union, one headed by Baron Manfred von Ardenne and the other by Gustav Hertz. After talks with Beria in Moscow, the scientists were flown to a settlement near Sukhumi, in Abkhazia (close to Beria's birthplace), where a laboratory and other buildings had been constructed. The Sukhumi installation was under the direct control of the MVD, which imposed strict security on the German scientists. Deputy MVD Chief Zaveniagin, who headed the MVD Bureau for Research, Development, and Production on the Military Use of Atomic Energy and supervised prison labor for atomic purposes, was one of those in charge of the German scientists. Their immediate supervisor at Sukhumi was MVD General A. I. Kochlavashvili, a Georgian and Beria's personal representative. Beria himself visited often, since his own village was nearby.[27]

The German scientists found the regime at Sukhumi dispiriting, to say the least. They could go nowhere without an escort, were forbidden contact with Russians, and had almost no communication with the outside world, aside from a weekly supervised visit to the market in Sukhumi. Hertz complained to Kochlavashvili, who responded with anger and apparently did little to improve the situation. In October 1948 the German scientists were flown to a top-secret research installation near Sverdlovsk in the Urals for a meeting with members of the Scientific and Technical Council. Beria presided. Dressed casually in a gray pullover sweater and a gray jacket, he is said to have resembled, with his pince-nez glasses and his big head, a large old owl. He told the Germans that he wanted their help in correcting the false notion spread by the Western press that progress on the atomic bomb should be credited to Germany rather than to the Soviet Union. To Beria's great surprise Hertz spoke up and told Beria how disillusioned the men in his group were, how their isolation and lack of freedom had made them passive and apathetic toward undertaking new obligations. Beria then asked for the MVD representative at the Sukhumi installation. General Kochlavashvili stood up like a lightning bolt and identified himself, whereupon Beria ordered him to improve the conditions for the German scientists and promised them more privileges. After this encounter life at the Sukhumi installation did become more bearable for its inhabitants.[28]

Beria was an eyewitness to two of the most important events in the history of Soviet atomic research. The first was on 25 December 1946, when Kurchatov started up an atomic reactor for the first time. Beria was extremely enthusiastic and wanted to go inside the building that housed the reactor but he could not because of the radioactivity. He asked Kurchatov many questions about the materials used for the reactor. The operation of the first Soviet reactor boosted the confidence of those engaged in the atomic program and enabled the Kremlin to take a new, more positive line, reflected in public hints that the U.S. monopoly on atomic energy development would be short-lived.[29]

Beria was also present at the control center when the first Soviet atomic bomb (plutonium) was exploded, on 29 August 1949. He was extremely nervous before the countdown, expressing his doubts that it would work. After the explosion Beria embraced and kissed Kurchatov, saying: "It would have been a great misfortune if this had not worked out successfully." Then he suddenly became concerned again and wanted to know if the Soviet explosion resembled the American blasts and quickly telephoned someone who had seen an earlier U.S. explosion at Bikini. Beria was greatly relieved to discover that the blast had been similar. He then telephoned Stalin to tell him the news but Stalin, in his inimitable way, replied abruptly that he had already heard and hung up. Beria was extremely agitated by Stalin's reaction, which destroyed his euphoria. Pounding his fists into the officer who had put through the call, he said: "You have put a spoke in my wheel, traitor, I'll grind you to a pulp."[30]

Obviously Beria had been under a great deal of pressure to ensure that the atomic bomb project was successful and that the Soviets would catch up with the Americans in the shortest possible time.[31] In fact, the Americans were surprised that the Soviets had succeeded so early in detonating an atomic bomb. Just a year earlier, in July 1948 Central Intelligence Agency (CIA) Director R. H. Hillenkoetter had sent a memorandum to President Truman, assuring him that the earliest date by which it was remotely possible for the USSR to complete its first atomic bomb was mid-1950 and suggested that the most probable date was mid-1953. A year later, just a few weeks before the Soviets exploded their first bomb, Hillenkoetter reiterated these estimates, but added that one method the Soviets appeared to be following suggested that their first atomic bomb would not be exploded before mid-1951.[32]

Thus, insofar as Western governments were concerned, the Soviet atomic program made unexpected strides, causing the West extreme disquiet and intensifying the cold war. Whether the pace was fast enough for Stalin is another question but, since Beria continued to supervise the atomic energy program until 1953, Stalin cannot have been dissatisfied with his performance. Ironically Beria's arrest in June 1953 prevented him from reaping glory from one of the most momentous achievements in Soviet atomic energy development, the explosion of the first hydrogen bomb on 12 August 1953.

SHAKE-UP IN THE SECURITY APPARATUS

In early 1946 extensive personnel and organizational changes occurred in the Soviet leadership, including the police and intelligence apparatus. The Soviet press announced in mid-January that Beria had relinquished his post as head of the NKVD to his deputy, Kruglov.[33] Then in March, as part of a general changeover to a ministerial system, the NKVD and NKGB became the MVD and MGB, respectively, while a Council of Ministers replaced the Council of People's Commissars.[34] As far as Beria was concerned, his release from his police post was a positive change because it relieved him of day-to-day supervision over this organization and allowed him to spend more time on the bomb project. He did not lose his authority over the police and intelligence apparatus because he continued to oversee this area in his capacity as a deputy chairman of the Council of Ministers. And, in discarding his formal association with the police, he gained the stature of an all-around statesman. As George Kennan observed: "I believe that this change signifies an advance rather than reverse in the political fortunes of Beriya. . . . Kalinin [Soviet President] being now old and not very active it is indeed probable that Beriya is the most important figure in Russia after Stalin and Molotov."[35] The fact that in

March 1946 Beria gained full membership in the Politburo (along with Malenkov) apppeared to confirm Kennan's assessment.[36]

Nonetheless, Beria's situation was not perfect. Kruglov could not be considered a protégé and Beria's loyal deputy Merkulov was replaced by Viktor Abakumov as head of the MGB late in the summer of 1946. This change was not instigated by Beria, who was distressed to lose Merkulov, but by Stalin, apparently with the intention of limiting Beria's pervasive influence on the security organs. According to Merkulov, Abakumov had "wormed his way into Stalin's confidence," and had been intriguing against him (Merkulov) for some time. Instead of defending Merkulov, Beria backed off, even encouraging him to try to establish better relations with Abakumov: "Beria was scared to death of Abakumov and tried at all costs to have good relations with him, although he knew Abakumov was dishonest. . . . Beria met his match in Abakumov."[37] This of course made Merkulov, who was dispatched to work in Germany, deeply resentful. But apparently Beria did not want to risk arousing Stalin's displeasure by standing up for Merkulov against Abakumov.

The following months witnessed numerous changes in both the MVD and MGB as several new deputies arrived, apparently under the auspices of Abakumov and Kruglov. These changes may also have been influenced by the arrival of a new CC secretary, A. A. Kuznetsov, who took over party supervision of the police. With the exception of Stepan Mamulov, a longtime Beria crony who became a deputy minister in the MVD, none of the new men were part of Beria's "Georgian mafia," although most had been in the security or internal affairs organs for a long time.[38]

Despite his setback with the police apparatus, Beria's political standing showed no signs of decline. In the protocol ranking of the leadership, he usually held the position of third-in-line, after Stalin and Foreign Minister Molotov. Thus, for example, he stood third when names of nominees to the USSR Supreme Soviet were presented in early 1946. At the funeral of Soviet President Mikhail Kalinin in June 1946 Beria and Malenkov had equal status, but when portraits of Soviet leaders were displayed at V-J Day celebrations on September 1946 Beria assumed greater prominence. His picture appeared on one side of Stalin and that of Molotov on the other, with the remaining Politburo portraits, including those of party secretaries Malenkov and Zhdanov, conspicuously far behind. The same pattern was followed at the anniversary celebration of the Bolshevik Revolution in November 1946.[39]

According to Khrushchev, then party first secretary in the Ukraine, Beria enjoyed considerable influence in matters of foreign policy: "Stalin jealously guarded foreign policy. The one person able to advise Stalin on foreign policy was Beria, who used his influence for all it was worth."[40] Khrushchev cites as an example how Beria "harped" at Stalin continuously about the return of certain territories in the eastern part of Turkey that had earlier belonged to Georgia. Stalin finally gave in and sent a memorandum to Turkey in which he pressed Soviet territorial claims. But these demands backfired, causing Turkey to accept offers of support from the United States and its allies, who set up military bases near the Turkish border with the Soviet Union.[41] As overlord of Transcaucasia, Beria had a special concern about the security and territorial integrity of this area. When Ambassador Walter Bedell Smith sought in 1946 to persuade Stalin to withdraw Soviet troops from northern Iran, he refused on the grounds of protecting Baku's oil fields and remarked to Smith: "Beria and others tell me that saboteurs—even a man with a box of matches—might cause us serious damage. We are not going to risk our oil supply."[42]

Beria's star was especially bright in his native Georgia, which he continued to preside over from afar. When he "campaigned" for election to the USSR Supreme Soviet in early 1946, as a delegate from the Tbilisi-Stalin District, he was portrayed as a national hero, whom the enthusiastic Georgian crowds thronged to get a glimpse of. Throughout January 1946 enlarged photographs of Beria filled the pages of Georgian newspapers, accompanied by effusive words of praise and greetings to Beria, the "beloved son of the Georgian nation." Beria was hailed for his "iron will and strong hand" in organizing the Georgian people for the defense of their homeland and for his enormous work in developing the Georgian economy. In the words of one worker: "The prosperity of all branches of our country's economy is tied to Beria's name."[43]

Poems and songs were composed in Beria's honor. One, entitled "A Song about Beria," celebrated his role in defending Georgia during the war:

He, son of beloved Georgia,
whose name is glorified by all,
brought the will of the leader:
hold out, meet the enemy's strength.

He closed off decisively, tightly
the paths, the mountain passes,
So that the black facist hordes
would not penetrate Georgia.

The enemy forces were turned back
Again the sky shines clearly.
The snowy mountains withstood,
to praise the valor of our hero.

We sang joyously with them,
believing firmly in victory:
"Let our defender Beria
thrive for many years."[44]

In his election speech, Beria in turn praised his countrymen for their courage in resisting the German advance. He also discussed at great length the measures necessary for Georgia to recover economically, which suggested that he was still very much involved in Georgian affairs.[45]

MALENKOV AND ZHDANOV

Beria's closest ally in the leadership at this time was CC Secretary Malenkov, whose primary responsibility was overseeing the industrial ministries. In this capacity Malenkov headed a powerful Committee for the Rehabilitation of the Economy of Liberated Areas. Formed in late 1944, the committee aimed at depriving East Germany of economic strength and military potential by dismantling its industry. At the same time Soviet industry and agriculture could be revived using appropriated German equipment.[46] The committee became a focal point for rivalry among the various Soviet ministries, which were vying with each other for the bounty from Germany. Some members of the leadership, including CC Secretary Andrei Zhdanov and Foreign Trade Minister Anastas Mikoian, were opposed to the committee and its aims. They wanted to leave Germany in a condition to pay extensive reparations and they also felt that German economic matters should be placed in the hands of Gosplan, headed by Zhdanov's ally Nikolai Voznesenskii, which would work through Mikoian's Ministry of Foreign Trade.[47]

Beria's position on the question of postwar German industry was not as clearly defined as Malenkov's. He supported the latter's committee in that he advocated dismantling the industrial infrastructure of the Soviet zone to provide equipment for Soviet industry. But at the same time he wanted to preserve enough equipment in Germany for use in the mines in Saxony, where much of the uranium ore for the atomic bomb project was being extracted. In June 1946 Beria sent over an assistant, Major General A. M. Maltsev, to supervise the extraction and processing of Saxony ore. He remained there for the next four years.[48]

A rivalry between Zhdanov, who represented the interests of the party bureaucracy, and Malenkov, who was seen more as a spokesman for the economic ministries, had been growing for some time. As far back as the late 1930s they had disputed over the proper role for the CC Secretariat. Malenkov advocated its close involvement in economic management, whereas Zhdanov wanted the Secretariat to concentrate on personnel matters and party-political work.[49] The German issue fueled their deep-seated animosity further. Whatever his policy views, Beria was Malenkov's ally and he could not easily remain neutral; he came down firmly in the Malenkov camp. That Beria himself had never been on good terms with Zhdanov may have strengthened his resolve.[50]

Beria's support was not enough to prevent Malenkov from falling under a political shadow as a result of his feud with Zhdanov, however. Malenkov was suddenly dropped from the CC Secretariat in May 1946 and replaced by N. S. Patolichev, a protégé of Zhdanov. He remained in the Politburo, as a deputy prime minister, but was shunted off to serve in Central Asia. Beria then "step-by-step" raised the question of Malenkov with Stalin and the latter finally brought him back to Moscow in early 1947.[51]

The dispute over what to do with German industry had led to an official inquiry into Malenkov's committee in the summer of 1946. The commission that conducted the inquiry, under Zhdanov's influence, recommended that economic disarmament of Germany cease. The functions of Malenkov's committee were then transferred to the Administration for Soviet Property Abroad (also referred to as the Reparations Administration) under the Soviet Military Administration in Germany. For Beria this was not an entirely negative development because Merkulov became chief of the Administration for Soviet Property Abroad sometime in 1946 or early 1947. Then Dekanozov left the Soviet Foreign Ministry to become Merkulov's assistant. Dekanozov had considerable experience working with Germany prior to the war, which doubtless proved valuable in his new job. He had also been conducting lengthy negotiations with American diplomats on various aspects of Soviet policy in Europe.[52]

Meanwhile, Beria's former deputy Ivan Serov was still in Germany as a deputy commander of the Group of Soviet Forces, a post he retained until early 1947. And sometime in 1948 Bogdan Kobulov showed up as an official in the Soviet Military Administration there. With close associates in these key positions Beria was able to protect his own interests, in particular the atomic bomb project. He ensured a steady flow of materials and equipment from Germany to support his project by insisting that his priorities take precedence.[53]

However powerful and influential Beria was, he could ill afford, in the cut-throat world of Kremlin politics, to be complacent as he watched Zhdanov's ascendancy in the leadership during 1946–47. That Stalin was often absent and was apparently in declining health made the rise of Zhdanov and his associates all the more threatening. Stalin reportedly had suffered a slight stroke in late 1945 and a second one in 1947. Diplomats who met him noted that his mind was still sharp, but he was spending much less time at the Kremlin and delegating more work to others. During 1947–51, Stalin's annual Black Sea vacations lasted from late August until late November or early December. Although he received foreign diplomats and carried out administrative tasks while he was in the South, much of the day-to-day management of foreign and domestic affairs was in the hands of his lieutenants.[54]

Left to their own devices, these lieutenants naturally competed among themselves for primacy and the stakes were high. The struggle was over power but it was carried out in the arena of policy. In 1946 Zhdanov launched a campaign against "decadent" Western influences in the arts and letters, which earned the name "Zhdanovshchina." He was able to push successfully for a tough, militant line domestically; ideological orthodoxy was the order of the day. Soon the effects of the Zhdanovshchina were reflected in foreign policy, which became more ambitious in its goals of spreading communism abroad. In September 1947 the Communist Information Bureau, or Cominform, was established, uniting European communist states. Zhdanov and Malenkov both attended the founding conference, but Zhdanov gave the major policy speech.[55]

Not surprisingly, given the rigorous observance of the practice of presenting a united front to the outside world, there were no overt signs that anyone in the Kremlin disagreed with the Zhdanov line. And since Stalin apparently backed Zhdanov's policy, the others had no choice but to go along with it. As far as Beria was concerned, there was little reason to assume that he had any objections in principle to the Zhdanovshchina. But the problem was that having his policies adopted made Zhdanov too powerful and hence a threat, or a perceived threat, to those who had similar ambitions. Beria was not like Molotov, Voroshilov, or Kaganovich, who managed to survive by carving out their own areas of responsibility and avoiding, insofar as was possible, "stepping on others' toes." For Beria, simple survival was not an aim; his sights were set on a leadership position second only to that of Stalin, and Zhdanov was undoubtedly aware of this.

The changes in the CC Secretariat that accompanied Malenkov's dismissal from that body did not bode well for Beria. Both new secretaries, Patolichev and Kuznetsov, were close to Zhdanov. As noted above, Kuznetsov, who had been party chief in Zhdanov's stronghold of Leningrad, was placed in charge of the police. It is not clear just how much supervisory power he had, but the mere fact that such an area of responsibility had been deliniated and that a Zhdanov man was in charge must have been a substantial irritant to Beria.[56] Stalin must have consented to this move, even if it was Zhdanov's idea. From Stalin's standpoint it was a good idea to have a party outsider keeping Beria's police empire in line. And he may well have relished the intense animosity that this new arrangement created among his subordinates.

A further annoyance for Beria was the appointment in the summer of 1946 of N. I. Gusarov—also tied to the Zhdanov clique—to the post of inspector in the CC Secretariat. Gusarov took his new job seriously and began criticizing regional party officials, including Beria's friend Azerbaidzhan Party Chief Bagirov, who was accused of "unpartylike behavior." The latter reportedly called Stalin and complained. Stalin's reaction is unknown, but in the spring of 1947 Gusarov was transferred to the post of party chief in Belorussia for the purpose of tightening up central party control. There he clashed with Beria's crony and fellow Mingrelian Tsanava, chief of the Belorussian MGB, who apparently ruled the republic with an iron fist.[57]

THE ANTI-SEMITIC CAMPAIGN: FIRST SIGNS

By themselves these swipes at Beria's domain might have seemed trivial and easy to ward off. But in the autumn of 1946 another development was unfolding that had deeper, longer-term ramifications for Beria. This was the subtle, but nonetheless unmistakeable, campaign against the Jews. During the war the Soviet leadership had tolerated moderate expressions of nationalist feelings with a view toward uniting all Soviet peoples against the Germans. Once Germany had been defeated, however, the unrelenting struggle against all forms of "nationalist deviation" was resumed, with Zhdanov as the chief spokesman. Although the campaign was not directed at Jews per se, the anti-Semitic undertones were apparent. A series of articles began appearing in the Soviet press in mid-1946, criticizing Jewish writers, poets, and playwrights for being apolitical and for romanticizing Jewish history and the Jewish way of life. A simultaneous campaign against "cosmopolitanism," or Western influence, in various fields of literature and scholarship was also implicitly directed at the Jews, since they were heavily represented among intellectuals and scholars. Many Jewish intellectuals were singled out for criticism.[58]

In addition, the wheels of a purge of the Jewish Antifascist Committee (JAC), an officially sanctioned body established to recruit the support of world Jewry for the war effort, were set into motion. On 12 October 1946, not long after Abakumov became MGB chief, the MGB submitted a note to the party leadership and the Council of Ministers "On the nationalistic manifestations of some workers of the Jewish Antifascist Committee." A few weeks later a proposal was put forth to Stalin from the CC Secretariat recommending the dissolution of the JAC.[59] Under Abakumov's direction the MGB began collecting incriminating evidence against JAC members, which was carefully monitored in the Secretariat. CC Secretary Zhdanov had a key role in the campaign, initially at least. Malenkov was under a cloud, working in Central Asia, so much of the critical information gathered about the JAC from 1946 to early 1948 was addressed to Zhdanov.[60]

The anti-Semitic intentions of the Kremlin leadership became ominously clear in January 1948, with the murder of Solomon Mikhoels, director of the Moscow Yiddish Theater and chairman of the Jewish Antifascist Committee. More than any other figure in the Soviet Union, Mikhoels symbolized the Jewish cause. Mikhoels had traveled to Minsk, in Belorussia, with Jewish theater critic V. I. Golubov-Potapov. According to the official report, the two were summoned from their hotel to an urgent meeting and were killed en route by a truck, which then disappeared.[61] After Stalin's death, however, Beria managed to get the true story, which he related in a letter to Malenkov.[62] On questioning Abakumov, who had been imprisoned by Stalin in 1951, Beria learned that Stalin had ordered Abakumov to have Mikhoels killed, a task carried out in Minsk by Deputy Minister of State Security S. I. Ogol'tsev and Belorussian MGB Chief Tsanava. Mikhoels and his companion were lured into a car and taken to Tsanava's dacha outside Minsk, where they were murdered. Their bodies were then dumped on the side of a road. When Beria learned of Tsanava's complicity, he ordered his arrest, along with that of Ogol'tsev.

Many had assumed that Beria was responsible for the murder, since he oversaw the police apparatus, but this letter indicates that the plot was carried out behind his back. In fact he had little to gain from the murder. He had supported the idea in 1942 of creating the Jewish Antifascist Committee in order to harness the war efforts of Soviet Jews at home and abroad and had maintained direct contacts with JAC leaders after that.[63] Indeed, he seems to have been sympathetic to their cause. In May 1944 Mikhoels wrote a letter to Molotov complaining about discrimination against Jews in liberated Ukraine. On receiving a copy of the letter, Beria issued instructions to Ukrainian Party Chief Khrushchev to "take the necessary measures to improve the living and working conditions of Jews in the newly liberated areas."[64]

Beria was often described as looking like a Jew and it was even rumored that he was. Although these rumors seem to have no foundation, their appearance may have connected Beria with Jews in the public mind. There is also reason to believe that he was helpful to Jews in Georgia. The American journalist Harrison Salisbury, who visited Georgia after the war, discovered that Beria, as Georgian party leader, had instigated the establishment of a program for rehabilitating Georgian Jews. The program included a Jewish charitable society and a Jewish ethnological museum in Tbilisi.[65] It might be added that Beria's sister's husband was a Jew and that Beria had several Jews in his retinue: Mil'shtein, Raikhman, Mamulov, Sumbatov-Topuridze, and N. I. Etingon, to name a few. Although many Jews lost their jobs in the late 1940s as a result of the anti-Semitic campaign, these men survived.

This is not to say that Beria always went out of his way to defend Jews. He had, after all, obeyed Stalin's order to deport tens of thousands of

Polish and Ukrainian Jews to Siberia in 1940 and 1941. And he was not above making anti-Semitic comments about his Jewish colleagues. According to Molotov, Beria referred to Kaganovich behind his back as "Lazar, that Izraelite."[66] But he had, perhaps for reasons of calculated expediency, pursued policies that associated him with a moderate attitude toward Jews, in comparison with Zhdanov, for example.

That Beria was not a party to the Mikhoels murder is indicated by the fact that he eventually became a target of the anti-Semitic campaign that the murder inaugurated, a campaign that culminated in the announcement in early 1953 that a so-called Doctors' Plot had been uncovered. The case implicated both Jews, including Mikhoels, and state security employees in a conspiracy against the leadership. Not only did Beria denounce the Doctors' Plot as a hoax after Stalin's death, he also took it upon himself to attempt a revival of Jewish culture immediately after Stalin died.[67]

It may not be a coincidence that, in addition to First Secretary Gusarov, another Zhdanovite was in the Belorussian CC Secretariat at the time of the Mikhoels murder: S. D. Ignat'ev, who was to replace Abakumov as USSR MGB chief in mid-1951.[68] Ignat'ev later helped to fabricate the case against the doctors. Thus, although Stalin may not have planned in early 1948 to use anti-Semitism as a weapon against Beria, the campaign against the JAC could not be seen as a favorable development for him. At this time, depositions were being collected against JAC members by the MGB and on 26 March 1948 Abakumov forwarded a report to the Central Committee, with copies to Stalin, Molotov, Zhdanov, and Kuznetsov, saying that JAC leaders, including Mikhoels, had conducted anti-Soviet nationalist activities. On 20 November 1948 the Politburo adopted a resolution approving a decision of the Council of Ministers to disband the JAC.[69]

It should be pointed out that this resolution was adopted after Zhdanov's sudden death in August 1948 and that the campaign against Jews continued to gain momentum in late 1948 and early 1949, with the arrests of the leadership of the JAC, so we cannot assume that Zhdanov was the sole impetus for it. By 1949 several party leaders had lent their support to the policy of anti-Semitism. Khrushchev, for example, first secretary in the Ukraine, favored the dissolution of the Union of Jewish Writers in Kiev and the closure of a Jewish literary journal.[70] And Malenkov apparently took part in the questioning of one JAC leader before the latter was arrested in 1949.[71] But they could hardly be expected not to go along with a program that was advocated by Stalin himself. Beria too, for that matter, must have given his formal sanction to the anti-Semitic campaign.

It is worth noting that by the time of the Mikhoels murder Beria's political standing was slightly lower than what it had been in 1946 and early 1947. He had dropped to number four, below Molotov and Zhdanov, in the leadership ranking.[72] There were also signs that Beria's domination of Georgian politics was no longer unchallenged. At a plenum of the Georgian Central Committee held 15–17 April 1948 two of Beria's longtime associates, Georgii Sturua and Avksentii Rapava, both Mingrelians, were removed from the party bureau. Sturua, the old Bolshevik who had supported Beria in his early years in the party, also lost his post as president of the Georgian Supreme Soviet and Rapava was moved from the powerful job of Georgian MGB chief to become the republic's minister of justice.[73] Georgian First Secretary Charkviani himself had reportedly tried to protect Sturua, who was charged with economic illegalities, but to no avail.[74] He did not regain his post until Beria reinstated him in April 1953, after Stalin's death.

A month later another Mingrelian associate of Beria, P. A. Shariia, was removed in disgrace from his post as Georgian CC secretary for propaganda. Shariia had for years worked closely with Beria in the Georgian party apparatus and had helped in the creation of Beria's famous book. In 1945 he traveled to Paris on Beria's (and Stalin's) behalf in an effort to recover Georgian museum treasures that had allegedly been taken by the Mensheviks when they left Georgia in the early 1920s. He had talks with Georgian émigré leaders about their returning to Georgia and managed to organize the repatriation to Georgia of Nino Beria's nephew, Teimuraz Shavdiia, who had been captured by the Germans in 1942 and had served in the so-called Georgian Legion, organized to combat resistance to German occupation forces.[75] As a result of Shariia's efforts, the CPSU Politburo passed a resolution on 26 May 1947 allowing for the return from France of fifty émigré families to Georgia.[76]

A year later Shariia was in trouble. His sin, it seems, was that on the occasion of his son's death in 1943 he wrote a lengthy poem that had a deeply religious theme and was therefore "ideologically harmful." Thanks to Beria's intervention, Shariia was not expelled from the party and was later able to go to Moscow to become Beria's speech writer.[77] Why the Georgian party bureau had waited five years to punish Shariia was not explained. It may be that his friendship with Beria prevented the bureau from taking action against him in 1943, but later certain Georgian leaders—encouraged by Stalin and others in Moscow—decided it was time to put Beria's power over Georgia to the test.

To the outside observer, of course, none of these negative signals were evident and Beria seemed to enjoy his usual prominence. His picture even appeared on the cover of *Time* magazine in March 1948, with the caption

"The Cop at the Keyhole Is King." *Time*, apparently unaware that he was no longer chief of the security police, portrayed Beria as the embodiment of the police state expanding westward across Europe. Unlike his predecessor, *Time* said, Beria seemed to be sane and well balanced, a symbol of the new Soviet man, for whom it was as "easy to kill on the party's orders as to drink a glass of water. . . . More and more power gravitates toward Beria, not merely because he is an ambitious intriguer, but because power brings more power."[78]

It was indeed a fact that the Soviet security police was extending its domain westward. With the reduction of regular Soviet military forces, the police assumed the main role in the Sovietization of Eastern Europe. Immediately after the war extensive security police networks were set up in all the satellite states. Their officials were handpicked by Beria and his men and directly responsible to Moscow.[79] But Beria's foreign policy role may have been limited somewhat after 1946 by the fact that MGB Chief Abakumov was not dependent on him. Also, in the autumn of 1947 an Information Committee (KI) was created under the Council of Ministers, incorporating the MGB's Foreign Intelligence Directorate and military intelligence. This was part of an effort to streamline intelligence gathering and make it more responsive to foreign policy needs, as well as to counter the newly formed CIA. Molotov and later Vyshinskii headed the KI. Little is known about the KI, so it is not clear to what extent this organizational change represented a true loss of authority for the MGB. In any case, as with so many other of Stalin's postwar rearrangements in the party apparatus, the change was short-lived. By 1948 some of the KI's responsibility, including liaison with satellite countries, returned to the MGB and by 1951 the KI was disbanded altogether.

Meanwhile Zhdanov, responsible for foreign policy in the Secretariat and the moving spirit of Cominform, was attempting to dominate this area and to use foreign policy as a weapon in domestic power stuggles. Although Malenkov was Zhdanov's principle enemy, Beria too must have been relieved when Zhdanov suffered a physical decline and in July 1948 was incapacitated by heart disease, from which he died in late August. As was so typical of Kremlin politics, some of Zhdanov's policies were already being undermined before he died. In particular, relations with Yugoslavia, which Zhdanov had done so much to cultivate, had begun to deteriorate several months earlier.[80] But the overall impression is that the struggle between the Zhdanov and Malenkov factions was more over power than policy. This is indicated by the fact that, aside from the Yugoslav question, the "Zhdanov line" continued to be adhered to in several areas even after his death. Advocates of Trofim Lysenko's pseudo-biology prevailed, for example, and official anti-Semitism became even more virulent.

BERIA'S REVIVAL

Zhdanov's death resulted in an upsurge of influence for both Beria and Malenkov, who alternated in the number three position in the formal leadership lineup during late 1948 and 1949. With Stalin's apparent sanction, or perhaps even at his direction, they set about erasing Zhdanov's influence by fabricating criminal charges against his protégés. These charges resulted in the sensational "Leningrad Case," which eventually implicated close to five hundred people connected with Zhdanov and Leningrad. The details of the case are still murky, but Beria and Malenkov enlisted MGB Chief Abakumov to have several leading political figures, including CC Secretary Kuznetsov, Politburo member and Gosplan chief Voznesenskii, and Leningrad First Secretary P. S. Popkov dismissed from their posts and arrested in early 1949. The charges ranged from separatism (trying to usurp Moscow's power by creating a separate party base in Leningrad) to treason (collaboration with Yugoslavia).[81]

Another victim was B. M. Kedrov, editor of the journal *Voprosy filosofii* (Questions of philosophy) and son of the Chekist M. S. Kedrov, who was said to have denounced Beria years earlier. The younger Kedrov was attacked in the press and lost his job in 1949 but was not arrested.[82] The case also extended to Belorussia, where several leading political figures from the Zhdanov group were arrested. S. D. Ignat'ev was shunted off to serve in Uzbekistan.[83]

Voznesenskii was a major target of the Leningrad case and his demise was especially dramatic. According to one source, the police originally charged him with losing secret documents, but he managed somehow to defend himself and the case was dropped.[84] He was arrested again in late 1949 and executed along with other defendants in the Leningrad Case in the autumn of 1950. Although Voznesenskii's alliance with Zhdanov was clearly an important factor in his fall, that Stalin was bitterly opposed to his economic policies was also a cause. Molotov later claimed that Beria, who was jealous of Voznesenskii and viewed him as a competitor in the Council of Ministers, persuaded Stalin to remove Voznesenskii from his post.[85] But Stalin had sufficient incentive to move against Voznesenskii anyway. In fact, Beria's role in the Leningrad affair was not as important as that of Malenkov, who seems to have run the entire case behind the scenes.[86]

By late 1949 the Zhdanov faction had been all but eradicated and Beria and Malenkov were Stalin's uncontested favorites. As for Molotov, who seems to have stayed out of the fray with Zhdanov, he remained the number two man in the formal leadership hierarchy but was abruptly relieved of his post as Foreign Minister and replaced by Andrei Vyshinskii in

March 1949.[87] At the same time Anastas Mikoian lost his job as Minister of Foreign Trade. Though both men remained in the Politburo, they were clearly out of favor with Stalin. The latter had even gone so far as to have Molotov's Jewish wife, Polina Zhemchuzhina, arrested in early 1948 as part of his anti-Semitic campaign.

With Zhdanov out of the way Beria had more opportunity to use his personal sway with Stalin. Discussions between Stalin and his subordinates took place mainly during the interminable, late-night dinners at Stalin's dacha, dinners that Khrushchev, for one, found excruciating. Although Stalin's favorite Georgian dishes were the usual fare, Beria often brought his own food—eel, hominy, corn, cheese, and "greens."[88] According to Khrushchev: "Stalin's old retainer Matryona Petrovna used to serve Beria and say in her thick nasal voice, 'Well, Comrade Beria, here's your grass.' We all used to get a big laugh out of that. Beria really did eat greens, just as they do in Central Asia, and sometimes he stuffed them into his mouth with his fingers. Every now and then he used a fork, but usually he ate with his fingers."[89]

Stalin by this time was constraining his consumption of alcohol, but he continued to press it on others, apparently because he enjoyed seeing them get drunk and embarrass themselves. He therefore would not countenance any restraint on the part of his dinner guests. Beria typically took it upon himself to enforce Stalin's wish and ensure that all the guests drank to excess. When Khrushchev once pleaded that he had a kidney ailment and should be exempt from drinking, Beria spoke up and said that he too had a kidney ailment, but that he drank nonetheless and it did him no harm. This of course left Khrushchev without an excuse.[90]

Often those present at Stalin's table became so drunk that they would have to be carried away by bodyguards in the early hours of the morning. According to Stalin's daughter, who observed these revelries firsthand, Beria more than once reached this state, but he never allowed himself to become the butt of the humiliating practical jokes that were played on the guests. A tomato slipped onto a chair before the person sat down or salt poured into someone's glass of wine would produce uproarious laughter. Beria was usually the instigator of these pranks, but "no one ever dared slide a tomato under him."[91] Perhaps, unlike Khrushchev, Beria actually enjoyed these dinners. They gave him an opportunity to "show off" in front of Stalin, gratifying Stalin's sadism by humiliating and demeaning the others. Although Stalin's subordinates had little choice but to endure these episodes good-naturedly, outsiders sometimes reacted differently. Milovan Djilas, who was heading a delegation from Yugoslavia, attended a dinner at Stalin's dacha in 1949:

> The evening could not go by without vulgarity, to be sure, Beria's. They forced me to drink a small glass of *peretsovka*—strong vodka with pepper. . . . Snig-

gering, Beria explained that this liquor had a bad effect on the sex glands, and he used the most vulgar expressions in so doing. Stalin gazed intently at me as Beria spoke, ready to burst into laughter, but he remained serious on noticing how sour I was."[92]

On 29 March 1949 the USSR Supreme Soviet commemorated Beria's fiftieth birthday by awarding him the Order of Lenin "for outstanding service to the Communist Party and the Soviet people." Observers at the American Embassy in Moscow concluded that this award was not significant, since other officials had received the same award on similar occasions. But the fact that it was accompanied by a special communique conveying congratulations and best wishes from the Council of Ministers and the Central Committee was seen as an indication of Beria's close relationship with Stalin.[93] As Ambassador Smith noted: "Beria has also been one of Stalin's closest associates for many years and his personal loyalty to his chief is unquestioned. In return, Stalin has demonstrated his complete confidence in Beria on so many occasions that Beria's prestige in the inner party circle cannot be doubted."[94] Smith came to the conclusion that when Stalin died power would probably be divided among his three immediate subordinates: Molotov, Malenkov, and Beria and that "no struggle is likely to occur that is in any way commensurate with the battle of giants which took place after Lenin's death."[95]

Smith was probably correct in his assumption that there was little infighting among those whom he saw as the "big three." Molotov was by now accepting the role of an old Bolshevik who enjoyed prominence largely because of past achievements and whose influence with Stalin had waned.[96] He did not appear to be competing with Beria and Malenkov. The latter had a formidable alliance. According to Svetlana Alliluyeva: "Until March 1953, one could always see Malenkov and Beria walking arm-in-arm. They always moved as a couple and as such used to come to my father at his dacha, in appearance of closest pals."[97] But in terms of power the two were not equal. The small, plump, "three-chinned" Malenkov was an archetypal party bureaucrat with little imagination or initiative—a "typical office clerk and paper-pusher," as Khrushchev put it contemptuously.[98] Although he could be sly and devious, Malenkov did not come close to Beria in terms of intelligence and political acumen. Once the skillful and ambitious Zhdanov was out of the way, Beria was a top contender for Stalin's mantle. His only drawback was that he was a Georgian.

It may true, as Smith said, that Beria's loyalty to Stalin was still strong in 1949, but the assumption that Stalin had complete confidence in Beria was incorrect. With the benefit of hindsight it seems that Stalin, by the time of his seventieth birthday in December 1949, had become deeply paranoid. He was not facing his old age and eventual death with equanimity. Unlike other leaders, such as Mao Zedong, for example, who felt secure enough to designate a successor, Stalin could not tolerate the idea of an heir apparent.[99] However much faith he had had in Beria in the past, the prospect of his eventually taking over as leader—either alone or in a power-sharing arrangement with Malenkov—could not have been palatable to Stalin. It undoubtedly aroused in him the concern that an attempt would be made to usurp his powers while he was still alive.

Even if Beria was aware of Stalin's distrust, and he probably was, he could do little to disabuse him of his suspicions. Like his Kremlin colleagues, Beria gave a glowing tribute to Stalin on the latter's seventieth birthday. His speech, filled with such phrases as "Comrade Stalin's name stands among the names of the greatest geniuses of mankind," could not have been more effusive in its praise of the leader.[100] But by this time little could satisfy Stalin's insatiable appetite for glory and affirmation; the slightest incident could plant the seeds of suspicion within him. Beria, who for years had nurtured and played on these traits of Stalin for his own advancement, was now about to fall into the net of Stalin's delusions that he himself had helped to cast. Zhdanov's demise eliminated a key rival but, in bringing Beria to the forefront, it made him the main object of Stalin's pathological fear of betrayal.

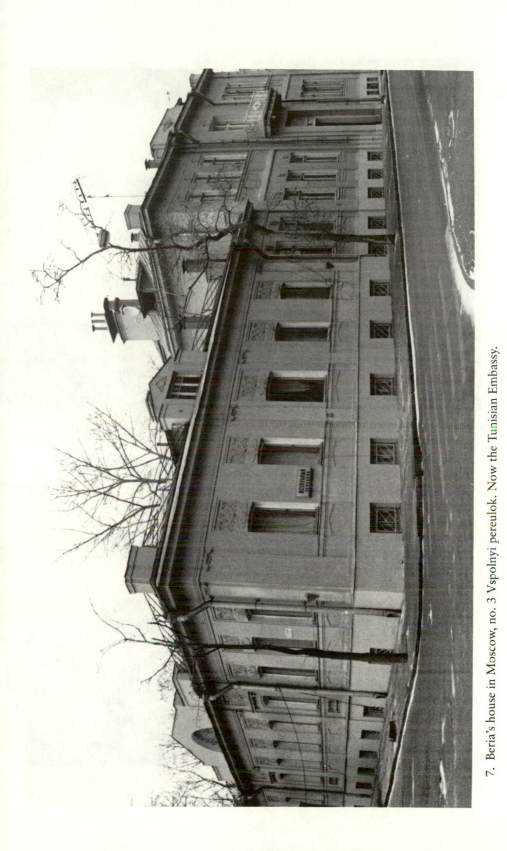

7. Beria's house in Moscow, no. 3 Vspolnyi pereulok. Now the Tunisian Embassy.

8. Beria's most powerful Kremlin colleagues in the immediate postwar period: Molotov (*top left*), Malenkov (*top right*), and Zhdanov (*bottom*).

TWENTY CENTS   MARCH 22, 1948

TIME

THE WEEKLY NEWSMAGAZINE

COMMUNISM'S BERIA
The cop at the keyhole is king.

$6.50 A YEAR   (REG. U. S. PAT. OFF.)   VOL. LI NO. 12

9. Beria on the cover of *Time* magazine, March 1948.

10. Beria in a touched-up photograph, around 1950.

11. Molotov, Beria, and Malenkov standing on Lenin's Tomb, watching the May Day Parade, 1953.

12. Malenkov (left front) and Beria (right front) as pallbearers at Stalin's funeral.

Chapter Eight

BERIA UNDER FIRE: 1950–1953

> Russia today is a country of terror and wild rumour.
> *(Edward Crankshaw,* The Observer, *January 1953)*

ENTER KHRUSHCHEV

IN KEEPING WITH his strategy of playing off his subordinates against one other, lest one should become too powerful, Stalin made a key personnel change in December 1949. Khrushchev, at the time first secretary of the Ukrainian Republic, was tranferred to the post of first secretary of the Moscow City and Regional Party Committees, replacing G. M. Popov. The transfer gave Khrushchev exceptionally wide powers. In addition to being head of the Moscow party apparatus, he was a full Politburo member and a Central Committee secretary, so he had both regional and functional responsibilities. More to the point, Stalin saw in Khrushchev a counterbalance to the Beria-Malenkov alliance and thus encouraged his rise in the Kremlin hierarchy. As Khrushchev observed:

> Upon taking my job in Moscow I could see that my arrival on the scene got in the way of Beria and Malenkov's plans. I even began to suspect that one of the reasons Stalin called me back to Moscow was to influence the balance of power in the collective and to put a check on Beria and Malenkov. It seemed sometimes that Stalin was afraid of Beria and would have been glad to get rid of him but didn't know how to do it. Naturally, Stalin never told me this, but I could sense it. He seemed to trust and value me.[1]

With Stalin's apparent support, Khrushchev embarked almost immediately on two important projects: a purge of the Moscow party apparatus and a reorganization of the collective farm system. In early 1950 Khrushchev personally presided over the removal of several Moscow officials, replacing them with his own candidates. He then turned to agriculture, managing to push aside A. A. Andreev, the Politburo member who supervised this area, and to initiate a new program.[2]

Khrushchev's initiative was based on the idea of consolidating *kolkhozes* into super collectives, called agro-towns, to administer the farming system. In a series of articles and speeches in 1950–51 he advocated this policy and also criticized the link, or small-team system of agricultural production, promoted by Andreev. Khrushchev favored instead the idea of large brigades to carry out agricultural work. Malenkov, who was closely involved with agricultural policy, resented Khrushchev's intrusions and worked to undermine him by attacking his proposals for amalgamating collective farms. Agricultural policy, long a subject of controversy in the Kremlin, became the battleground for the contending factions below Stalin.[3]

Beria's direct responsibilities did not encompass agriculture and he said little on the subject publicly, except insofar as it related to Georgia. Although he refrained from taking a stand on the question of agro-towns, he did acknowledge, in a March 1950 speech for election to the USSR Supreme Soviet, that Georgia's collective farms lagged far behind in wheat production, thus suggesting a need for change.[4] Beria's protégés jumped into the fray, however, and attacked Khrushchev's proposals. Armenian Party First Secretary Arutinov, speaking at the March Congress of the Armenian Communist Party, criticized those who sought to resettle small villages into agro-towns. And in a May 1951 address, Azerbaidzhan party chief Bagirov disavowed attempts to forcibly consolidate small villages.[5] Thus Khrushchev's comment that he was "constantly running up against Beria and Malenkov" was not without foundation.[6]

Unquestionably Soviet agriculture was plagued with problems. Aside from the weather, which created tremendous uncertainty, the system of collective farming itself was not conducive to high productivity. Moreover, misappropriation of collective land and farm equipment by local officials became widespread after the war. This situation eventually gave rise to a Kremlin campaign against "localism" and "departmental interests." On 5 September 1949, *Pravda* called for the strongest sanctions against "plunderers of socialist property" and the imposition of tighter controls from the center. The reintroduction of the death penalty— abolished from the criminal codes in 1947—in January 1950 underscored the regime's determination to use severe repression for economic crimes.

Insofar as the campaign against economic abuses involved all regions and republics, it could not have been seen at the time as specifically aimed at Beria's Georgian fiefdom. (Nor was it initiated under Khrushchev's auspices, since it began before he arrived in Moscow.) Nonetheless, the appearance in September 1950 in the Georgian language paper *Komunisti* of an article that discussed the problem of *shevsto* (the dominance of local bosses) indicated that Georgia was among the targets of the campaign.[7] The article, written by A. I. Mgeladze, party secretary in Abkhaziia, claimed that such bosses protected "their people," placing them in important positions even if they were incompetent. These criticisms were later said to have been intended as a signal to Charkviani to curb such practices, but they could have been directed at Beria as well. Another target was Bagirov. Sometime in 1950, Stalin ordered the Minister of State Control, Lev Mekhlis, to send a commission down to Azerbaidzhan to investigate complaints about him. Bagirov turned to Beria and the two managed to involve certain members of the commission in a scandal, which discredited them and ended the investigation.[8] Stalin then brought Merkulov back from Germany to replace Mekhlis in October 1950. Nonetheless, it was becoming clear that Beria's power base in Transcaucasia was no longer secure from attacks by the center.

Whatever Khrushchev's role in these events, he was irritated by the fact that Beria used his Georgian connection to gain influence with Stalin, so he was probably happy to see Beria's fiefdom under criticism. Khrushchev complained in his memoirs that Beria made sure that Stalin's household staff was composed entirely of Georgians who were personally known to Beria. Not only did Stalin have a Georgian chef and Georgian kitchen help, his housekeeper until after the war was a cousin of Nino Beria.[9] According to Khrushchev this eventually caused Stalin considerable unease, because he was losing his trust in Beria—a process that Khrushchev may well have encouraged. So Stalin ordered all the Georgian help to be thrown out and replaced with Russians.[10]

Unfortunately Khrushchev does not relate the timing of this episode, or Beria's reaction. Beria's official standing in the leadership was still high in 1950, the year that volume 5 of the *Great Soviet Encylopedia* appeared with a glowing biographical sketch of him.[11] Beria was described as "one of the most prominent leaders of the Communist Party and of the Soviet state, a loyal disciple and companion-in-arms of I. V. Stalin." By comparison, the recently demoted Andreev was presented in volume 2, which also appeared in 1950, as only a "prominent man."[12] Beria also remained a part of Stalin's retinue right up until the latter's death. Though Stalin distrusted him, he regularly attended Stalin's late-night dinners—from which Molotov, Mikoian, and Voroshilov were excluded by 1952—behaving, according to Khrushchev, as brazenly as ever.[13] But this of course was the inexorable logic of politics in the Kremlin under Stalin. No one, no matter how favorably he was treated by the leader, could be sure that he would not lose his job, and perhaps his life, the next day.

Although Beria continued to oversee the police and security apparatus, it was no longer packed with his supporters. As for Abakumov, he had cooperated with Malenkov and Beria in moving against the Zhdanovites, but Beria was wary of him, especially given the intense rivalry that existed between Abakumov and Merkulov. He clearly could not count on Abakumov, who often worked directly for Stalin, bypassing Beria entirely. Indeed, in the late spring of 1951 Stalin ordered Abakumov to concoct a conspiracy case against several of Beria's Mingrelian associates, including Belorussian MGB chief Tsanava. Later Stalin reportedly told him to "go after the big Mingrelian" (Beria).[14] Just as the wheels of the case had been set in motion, however, Stalin removed Abakumov from his MGB post and had him arrested in June 1951. Merkulov later revealed that he had written a note to Stalin denouncing Abakumov.[15] Abakumov's deputy, M. D. Riumin, provided Stalin with an additional motive: he informed Stalin that Abakumov had known about a Jewish bourgeois nationalist plot, linked to American spies, and had for some reason kept it a secret. Furthermore, he had allegedly murdered a prisoner, a Kremlin physician arrested early in 1951, who was the source of important information.[16] But Stalin may have needed no motive. He may have simply decided that the time had come to get rid of Abakumov, just as years earlier he had disposed of Iagoda and Ezhov.

Beria probably had no regrets about Abakumov's departure from the scene. He ignored Abakumov's many letters describing how he was being tortured and begging Beria to help him get out of prison.[17] Even after Stalin's death, when Beria had numerous individuals released, he allowed Abakumov to languish. (Of course he learned by this time that Abakumov had organized the Mikhoels murder.) Nonetheless, things did not turn out in Beria's favor in the summer of 1951. Abakumov's replacement was none other than Semen Ignat'ev, the former associate of the Zhdanov group whom Beria and Malenkov had managed to remove from the Belorussian Secretariat in 1949. This was a distinct blow to Beria and may explain why, when Merkulov came to see Beria after Abakumov's arrest expecting a favorable reception, Beria refused to see him.[18] In August 1951, after Ignat'ev's appointment, several new men, all associated with Khrushchev, suddenly appeared in the MGB: A. A. Epishev, a party secretary in the Ukraine, and I. T. Savchenko, also from the Ukrainian party apparatus, became deputy ministers of State Security; V. E. Makarev, a former Moscow party official during Khrushchev's tenure there in the 1930s, became chief of the MGB Personnel Department. In addition, a lesser official named N. R. Mironov, who had served in the Ukrainian party apparatus under Khrushchev's protégé Leonid Brezhnev, was brought to Moscow to work for the MGB.[19] These men had been military-political officers during the war and thus had an additional career bond. Moreover, at this time several military-political officers joined the Central Committee's Administrative Organs Department, which vetted appointments to the police apparatus.[20] The arrival of these new men indicated an effort by Stalin, with the help of Khrushchev, to inject party blood into the security apparatus. Indeed, Epishev later recalled that he was brought in to make personnel changes and thereby "strengthen party control over the MGB."[21] In October 1951 Lavrentii Tsanava was abruptly dismissed from the MGB in Belorussia, as were Abakumov associates A. G. Leonov and M. T. Likhachev, the chief and deputy chief, respectively, of the MGB's Investigation Department for Especially Important Cases. Tsanava was allowed to come to Moscow and work in some capacity for Beria, but the other two were arrested and later tried with Abakumov. Riumin, who had denounced Abakumov to Stalin, was placed in charge of the investigation department.[22] The influx of party officials into the MGB continued well into 1952.[23]

TROUBLE IN GEORGIA

Beria was still the overlord of Georgia in the early 1950s. He remained a full member of its top leadership body, the Georgian party bureau, and returned to the republic to preside over important functions and ceremonies. For this purpose he continued to maintain his residence on Machabeli Street in Tbilisi. At party and government meetings in the republic, greetings were routinely sent to Beria, and the press commemorated his birthdays with great fanfare. Furthermore, his name was still attached to myriad public places and enterprises. In short, he continued to enjoy a real cult of his personality in his native republic, though he had been in Moscow since 1938. As one Western historian pointed out, Beria's influence was substantial enough to enable him to impose his own policy preferences on Georgia, even in cases where they diverged from policies decided in Moscow.[24]

One reason for Beria's continued influence in Georgia was his extensive patronage network. Many leading party, government, and cultural officials owed their jobs to him. As long as they demonstrated their loyalty to him, they could be secure in their posts, enjoying the privileges and benefits of an elite class without fear of reprisal for the occasional wrongdoing. Those from Beria's home region of Mingrelia, to which Beria was fiercely loyal, were especially well off. He had always shown special consideration to his fellow Mingrelians, who were heavily represented in top party and state posts, thus arousing resentment on the part of Georgians from other regions.

When Beria came back to Georgia for vacations at his dacha in Gagra he was treated like royalty, with republican officials ready to serve him at a moment's notice. According to one account, the dacha was lavishly appointed with a swimming pool, tennis courts, a movie theater, and a volleyball court. Beria had played football in his youth and was still good at volleyball, though he had become rather overweight in the war and postwar years. He also enjoyed classical music and had a large Steinway piano for visitors to play. His favorite composers were Chopin, Berlioz, and Rachmaninoff.[25]

One story, related by a Mingrelian comrade who occupied the post of deputy minister of culture in Georgia, offers a revealing and chilling picture of how Beria related to others and they to him. Beria invited this official to Gagra for a visit and took him out for a ride in his cherished speedboat, purchased from Germany, which Beria drove at 80 kilometers an hour. While out at sea they came upon a young woman swimmer, who was a member of the Dinamo sports society and was training for a competition. Beria stopped the boat and insisted that she come aboard. Almost immediately he began making lewd suggestions and indicating his desire to seduce her, despite her obvious terror of him. He then turned to his Mingrelian friend and, saying that he wanted to be alone with the woman, ordered him to jump off the boat and swim back. When the latter replied that he could not swim, Beria pushed him overboard. If it had not been for Beria's bodyguards, who were watching from the shore and quickly sent out a boat to rescue him, the official would have drowned. Yet he never dared to reproach Beria and continued to be his guest at the dacha.[26]

This story, if accurate, shows that Beria's lust for young women had become even more desperate as he grew older and that little could stand in the way of his desires, even another human life. He reportedly had a special proclivity for sportswomen and insisted on having his pick of the female athletes who traveled from Georgia to Moscow every year for the annual Day of Physical Culture.[27] The story also illustrates the incredible degree of subservience that Beria was able to command, a result of the ironclad rules of the patronage system in Georgia and of Beria's power to punish disobedience.

It might seem from the above account that no one in Georgia would dare risk opposition to Beria. But there were Georgian politicians who did not like him and resented the special favors he granted to Mingrelians. Given the right signals from Moscow, they were prepared to take part in efforts to undermine him. By the autumn of 1951 these signals had begun to arrive. On 9 November Stalin, without consulting the Politburo, personally dictated a Central Committee resolution on a so-called Mingrelian nationalist conspiracy.[28] A purge of the Georgian party and state apparatus followed. On 18 November 1951 *Zaria vostoka* reported that, as a result of disclosures of embezzlement in a major Tbilisi construction trust, the Georgian Central Committee had dismissed Second Secretary M. I. Baramiia, Minister of Justice Rapava (until 1948 Minister of State Security), and Procurator V. Ia. Shoniia and expelled them from the party. Rapava and Shoniia had been arrested on criminal charges.[29] All three officials were Mingrelians and Beria protégés. Baramiia, a member of the party bureau since 1943, had expressed particular devotion to

Beria in a speech to the Georgian Party Congress in January 1949.[30] In addition, two Central Committee department heads lost their jobs.

Meanwhile, the USSR Supreme Soviet had initiated some organizational changes that directly affected Georgia. On 5 November 1951 two new *oblasts* (regions), Tbilisi and Kutaisi, were created, thus subdividing the territory not already included in so-called autonomous oblasts. The stated purpose of these changes was to "strengthen party and state leadership over agriculture and industry," which in practice meant that the central party apparatus in Moscow could bypass the republic administration and exercise control directly through the oblasts, undercutting the power of republican party leaders.[31] Similar reorganizations took place in other republics, as part of a more general move against the powers of republican party leaderships, but in Georgia the repercussions were especially significant. In mid-January 1952, "in connection with the formation of new *oblasts*," Georgian Party First Secretary Charkviani lost his post as head of the Tbilisi city party committee (*gorkom*).[32] This was rather surprising, since Charkviani had only taken over this post a month earlier. With the first secretaryship of the newly created Tbilisi *obkom* (regional party committee) also in new hands, Charkviani's control was diminished considerably.

By December 1951 further dismissals had been announced in Georgia. The CC secretary for propaganda, R. S. Shaduri, lost his job suddenly with no explanation, and another official, G. N. Zambakhidze, was dropped from the party bureau. Then, in mid-January 1952, the press announced that the first secretary of the Georgian Komsomol, I. S. Zodelava, another Mingrelian, had been purged.[33] Two weeks later, Georgian First Secretary Charkviani presided over a meeting of the Tbilisi party committee where large-scale abuses and embezzlement in various ministries were discussed. Charkviani demanded a "resolute and final extermination of bribery—one of the most scandalous phenomena still with us as a survival of the old order."[34]

Charkviani cannot have relished the job of cleansing the republican party apparatus through a campaign against corruption. Whatever satisfaction he may have felt in getting rid of Beria's Mingrelians, it was marred by the fact that some of his own appointees had to be purged as well. Having been head of the republic since 1938, Charkviani had responsibility for what went on there and the more corruption and scandal that was revealed, the worse it reflected on him. His downfall was inevitable by early 1952.

In March 1952 Stalin pushed through a second resolution on the "Mingrelian conspiracy," which added momentum to the Georgian purge.[35] This time he drew Beria directly into the affair, dispatching him to Tbilisi to preside over a Georgian CC plenum on 1–2 April that removed Charkviani from his post. His successor was A. I. Mgeladze, the party official who had criticized the practice of patronage in 1950.[36] A brief announcement of the plenum appeared in *Zaria vostoka* but with no details.[37] Charkviani had never been a part of Beria's clique and he may have attempted to build up his own power base in the republic independently of Beria.[38] Nonetheless, the two had a long and relatively tranquil association and Beria, as Charkviani's de facto superior, bore some responsibility for the latter's failings.

A session of the Georgian Supreme Soviet held on 5–6 April 1952 revealed that Charkviani had simply "left the republic," but Baramiia was under criminal prosecution, an ominous sign.[39] Additionally, V. B. Gogua, a Mingrelian, lost his job as chairman of the presidium of the Georgian Supreme Soviet and Grigorii Karanadze, who had headed the Georgian NKVD/MVD since 1943, was dismissed. Karanadze's association with Beria dated back to 1929, when he joined the republic OGPU.[40] In sharp contrast with previous occasions, only one Supreme Soviet delegate conveyed greetings to Comrade Beria in his speech.[41]

Further details of the 1–2 April plenum emerged when *Zaria vostoka* published a report on a Tbilisi party conference held on 15–16 April.[42] In his speech before the conference, newly elected Georgian Party First Secretary Mgeladze said that the past leadership had been given a chance to clean house after the November 1951 plenum, but had accomplished little in the struggle against bribery and corruption.[43] Former leaders, he went on, had grossly flouted the principles of intraparty democracy by persecuting critics from lower levels of the apparatus who had exposed serious violations of legality. Moreover, the party leadership had become so intoxicated with its economic successes that it had grown complacent about deficiences. Mgeladze pointedly reminded his audience that, "as far back as 1937 at the February-March plenum of the VKP(B) Central Committee, Comrade Stalin warned the party of the dangers of intoxication with success." It might be recalled that one object of Stalin's warning in 1937 had been Beria's leadership in Georgia, which had subsequently been accused of bragging about its achievements and not being sufficiently self-critical. Beria was brought to heal and forced to remedy the situation with large-scale purges. Now Mgeladze was pointedly dredging up past "sins" of the Georgian party leadership under Beria.

Mgeladze made a point of stressing that Beria himself had presided at the recent plenum, which revealed abuses so serious that they led to the infiltration of "enemy elements" into the leadership. As he portrayed it, the situation had deteriorated to the point where hostile elements had already done damage—before Beria, designated overseer of the republic, sought to correct things! As if to dispel any doubts about Beria's responsi-

bility for Georgia, *Zaria vostoka* published a front-page declaration from
the plenum to Comrade Beria, promising that serious shortcomings
would be overcome in the shortest possible time. The declaration referred
to Beria as the leader who had educated the current cohort of officials and
"instilled in them so many traditions during the many years he had presided as head of the party there."[44] (In other words, these men had operated according to Beria's principles!) A similar message was sent to Beria
from a meeting of the Tbilisi *Obkom* at the end of April and again from
the Komsomol congress held in May.[45]

Immediately following the Tbilisi Conference a meeting of the Georgian Komsomol—presided over by Mgeladze—removed the remaining
four Komsomol secretaries and approved a new bureau of its Central
Committee. Then, on 23 April, *Zaria vostoka* announced that almost the
entire Kutaisi city party committee had been removed.[46] The changes
were dizzying. By the end of April, only two officials from the "old leadership" remained: a republican Central Committee secretary and the secretary of the Tbilisi city party committee. The purges were not limited to
Beria's Old Guard; they even extended to some who had recently been
promoted.[47]

The only positive development for Beria was the sudden dismissal of
Georgian Minister of State Security Nikolai Rukhadze in late June
1952.[48] Rukhadze, who had been promoted to full membership in the
republic party bureau only seven months earlier, had been in the forefront
of the attack against Beria's Mingrelians. Although Rukhadze himself
had a long relationship with Beria, dating back to his enlistment in the
Georgian GPU in 1926, he had evidently turned against his former mentor. Rukhadze's replacement was A. I. Kochlavashvili, who had worked
as an MVD major general in the atomic energy program under Beria.[49]

Judging from events at the Fifteenth Georgian Party Congress, however, the situation was still highly threatening to Beria. Mgeladze's speech
to the September 1952 congress sharply attacked the previous party leadership in Georgia.[50] Charkviani, he said, had "entrusted all organizational work, the selection of personnel and checkup on fulfillment, to
alien persons, to people who had penetrated into the apparatus of the
Central Committee and pursued aims hostile to the party." He went on to
point out:

> If this anti-party practice of "localism" and "patronage" had not received its
> due rebuff from the party, "patrons" would have appeared, wishing to take
> "their" special areas "under their high protection" and to shield persons who
> had gotten into trouble there, seeking in this manner to increase their authority
> as "patron" among the "masses." If this had happened, Georgia would have
> been split up into a number of "provincial duchies" which would have

possessed "real" authority and nothing would have been left of the Communist Party of Georgia and the government of the Georgian SSR.[51]

This was a rather astonishing admission of just how far the practice of patronage and the expression of separatist tendencies had gone in Georgia. Moreover this was happening at a time when, Mgeladze claimed, the Americans were using Turkey, which had recently joined NATO, as a base for stirring up trouble near the Turkish-Georgian border. Thus, he implied, the development of localist tendencies was especially grave for the security of the republic. And, of course, foremost among those who practiced patronage and demonstrated nationalism were the Mingrelians. Though Mgeladze sought to assure the congress that these practices had for the most part been overcome, he did issue an ominous word of warning: "All those who try to dismantle Georgia, to 'exercise patronage' over her separate 'provinces' or to set them one against the other will be crushed."[52]

Although Mgeladze was probably exaggerating the threat of separatism in Georgia, it is true that nationalist feelings ran high in the Transcaucasian area and that unrest was a problem among several ethnic minorities in the Georgian republic. (Indeed, the ethnic violence that erupted in Georgia after it became an independent state in 1991 shows just how intense these nationalist sentiments remained.) In 1948 local people sabotaged mines in Abkhaziia, for example. In June 1949 concern over disloyalty toward the Soviet regime led the authorities to deport "tens of thousands" of residents of Greek, Turkish, Iranian, and (non-Soviet) Armenian origin from the Black Sea areas of Georgia. Further, in April 1950 the Georgian press revealed that people from a number of local villages in those areas had been "resettled."[53]

Beria himself indicated concern about such unrest when he went out of his way in several speeches to contrast "the prosperity of the national republics of the USSR" with the "backward agrarian countries" of Iran and Turkey.[54] And he may have been particularly worried about Turkey, if it was true, as Khrushchev asserted, that his prodding of Stalin to make territorial claims on Turkey had been an element that pushed it toward an alliance with the West. But his real worry was probably Stalin's view of the situation, since Stalin had apparently linked the Mingrelians with sympathies toward Turkey.[55]

THE NINETEENTH PARTY CONGRESS

At the time of this congress, which began on 5 October 1952, the purges in Georgia were still progressing at full force, coming close in extent to those in 1937–38. It was later reported that, in the period from April to

December 1952, party secretaries and department heads were replaced in 427 *oblast*, city, and *raion* committees. Furthermore, the turnover at the lowest level, the party cell, was a startling 20 percent.[56] In his speech to the congress, Mgeladze never mentioned Beria's name, an unprecedented omission. Yet he was excessive in his praise of Stalin, on whose "personal instructions" the Georgian party was eliminating its defects.[57] Beria, then, was no longer credited with ordering a cleansing operation in that republic.

Significantly, at least twenty-three speakers at the congress condemned "bourgeois nationalism," an accusation to which Beria's stronghold in Georgia was particularly vulnerable. Yet Beria's speech, much of which was devoted to the nationalities question, gave no indication that this was a problem. As one Western scholar pointed out, Beria approached this issue in a way that deviated significantly from the tenets Stalin had established. [58] He discussed, for example, the evils of "Great Russian chauvinism," describing how the tsarist system had oppressed non-Russian nations and denied them rights, including the use of their native languages in administration. This was a subject that the Stalin regime, which continued to enforce Russian domination on non-Russian peoples in the most oppressive manner, avoided mentioning. Beria continued: "In the struggle against enemies of Leninism the Party defended the Leninist-Stalinist national policy and ensured the complete and final overthrow of great-power chauvinism, bourgeois nationalism and bourgeois cosmopolitanism." That Beria listed great-power (i.e., Russian) chauvinism first among the three "national deviations" and then claimed that all three had been overcome clearly ran counter to the views of other speakers at the congress, who were calling for a vigorous attack on bourgeois nationalism among non-Russians and against bourgeois cosmopolitanism (expressions of Jewish identity). Moreover Beria did not use the phrase "Great Russian people," but referred instead to "the peoples of central Russia," a clear departure from the accepted practice of acknowledging the superiority of Russians over other national groups.[59]

In sum, Beria seemed to be openly defying the Kremlin line on nationalities, a line that decried any assertions of national or ethnic identity, other than that of Russians. What motivated him to take this seemingly bold stance, particularly when his own political position was so precarious? If he was advocating the interests of non-Russians as a means of gaining their support, was he not taking a grave political risk by offending Stalin? One possible explanation for Beria's action is that Stalin at this point was not focusing attention on policy debates. Although present at least for some parts of the congress, he played a very low-key role. He had, after all, only a few months to live and his health was in serious decline. He only managed to climb up on the podium at the end of the congress to give a short speech. Khrushchev says in his memoirs that, while Stalin had the idea of convening the congress and assigned the reports to be given, he never actually read them, but instead instructed Khrushchev, Malenkov, and Beria to look them over.[60] Under these circumstances, it is not so surprising that Beria would take a more offensive tack, playing the nationalities card for all it was worth.

CONFLICT BEHIND THE SCENES

Beria was already aware by now that he was an object of Stalin's suspicions, so he might also have seen little point in adhering slavishly to the Kremlin line. Stalin was losing his grip, not only physically but also mentally, and the slightest mistake could arouse his distrust. By all accounts he was consumed with thoughts about plots against him. He suspected Molotov, Mikoian, and Voroshilov, for example, of being agents of Western governments, excluding the former two entirely from his inner circle by late 1952. In December 1952 he dismissed his loyal private secretary of many years, A. N. Poskrebyshev, for "passing secret documents" and had his longtime bodyguard, N. S. Vlasik arrested. As Khrushchev put it: "It all depended on Stalin's fertile imagination, who was an agent of what imperialistic country from one day to the next."[61]

At this time Stalin was apparently planning a massive purge of the party, extending to several members of the top leadership. As part of this plan, Stalin disbanded the Politburo right after the congress and created in its place a much larger body, a twenty-five-man Presidium, thus diluting the powers of its members. But he also created an informal "bureau" of the Presidium, which consisted of himself, Beria, Malenkov, Khrushchev, Voroshilov, Kaganovich, Saburov, Pervukhin, and Bulganin. Beria's inclusion in this group was not necessarily a sign that he had regained Stalin's favor. It was characteristic of Stalin to treat his subordinates well just as the axe was about to fall.

Khrushchev himself managed to remain above suspicion—as did his rival Malenkov—and thus was in a strong position to encourage Stalin's intrigues against Beria and perhaps to take some initiatives on his own.[62] To further his goals, Khrushchev not only brought protégés into the MGB, he also gained a foothold in the Central Committee Department for Party, Trade Union, and Komsomol Organs (Cadres Department), which selected personnel for leading party posts. Sometime in 1952 Malenkov's protégé N. N. Shatalin, who headed this department, was pushed out. He was replaced first by N. M. Pegov and then, after the congress, by A. B. Aristov. The latter was closely associated with Khrushchev and continued to be for many years thereafter.[63]

Thus by 1952, or perhaps even earlier, Khrushchev had devised a means of directly influencing personnel appointments, thereby making it difficult for Beria to uphold his Transcaucasian fiefdom. Nonetheless, as his performance at the Nineteenth Party Congress indicated, Beria was holding his own, and he had some fairly powerful resources at his disposal. Despite the extensive purges in Georgia, he managed to protect many of his protégés from arrest, moving some to lesser posts rather than seeing them dismissed entirely. Also, his most important allies, Bagirov and Arutinov, remained party leaders of Azerbaidzhan and Armenia and were reelected to full membership in the Central Committee at the Nineteenth Congress. Although Dekanozov and Gvishiani were inexplicably dropped from membership in the latter body, Goglidze, Bogdan Kobulov, and Merkulov were all elected candidate members along with three other Beria allies.

As for the police apparatus, the picture was mixed, suggesting an intense struggle. Beria managed to retain some influence, staving off a purge of his supporters. Deputy MGB Chief Epishev recalled that his own recommendations (probably made at the behest of Ignatiev or Khrushchev) were often ignored and that appointments to leading MGB positions were made without consulting him: "There were many signs that someone did not want me in the job."[64] That "someone" was probably Beria, with Malenkov backing him up whenever possible. Malenkov, as a Central Committee secretary, was involved in making personnel appointments and he may have resisted the efforts of the Ignat'ev group to pack the MGB. In May 1952, for example, CC department chief Pegov sent Malenkov a note saying that Ignat'ev wanted to appoint one R. E. Mel'nikov, second party secretary in Uzbekistan (where Ignat'ev had recently served) to the post of deputy minister of state security. Malenkov wrote back to Pegov: "Explain this business—make a report to me." The proposed appointment then fell through.[65]

Among the Beria supporters who remained in leading MGB posts throughout this period were: Solomon Mil'shtein, Stepan Mamulov, Amaiak Kobulov, Pavel Sudoplatov, Boris Obruchnikov, Lev Vlodzimirskii, and L. F. Raikhman.[66] And of course Beria had managed to get rid of Georgian MGB chief Rukhadze, who had betrayed him. Furthermore, in February 1952 Sergei Goglidze, one of Beria's closest protégés, came to Moscow as a deputy minister of state security and chief of the third directorate of the MGB.[67] This directorate carried out political surveillance of the military, so it was a key post. Nonetheless, at least two high-level police officials connected with Beria were arrested after the Nineteenth Congress—N. I. Eitingon, a Jew, who was then implicated in the Doctors' Plot, and S. F. Kuz'michev, who had served in Stalin's personal bodyguard and then as deputy chief of the MGB Guards Directorate.[68] Probably others were arrested as well, since at this time Stalin, possibly with Khrushchev's encouragement, was launching a new attack on the Beria camp, and one of its key targets was Beria's stronghold in the MGB.

The influx into the MGB of officials from the party's military-political department and the simultaneous appointment of Goglidze as head of military counterintelligence suggest that two forces were at work in a Kremlin power struggle that also involved the military establishment. A case in point is the demotion of Army General S. M. Shtemenko, who was close to Beria. Given his responsibilities during the war and his subsequent job as "atomic bomb tsar," Beria must have been in constant contact with members of the military establishment. Although, as we know, he had alienated many of Stalin's generals, he had cultivated good relations with some, including Shtemenko, who had accompanied Beria to the Caucasus in 1942 and 1943. It was at Beria's instigation that Stalin appointed Shtemenko chief of staff of the Soviet Army in 1948.[69] According to a letter that Shtemenko wrote to Khrushchev after Beria's arrest, Beria had seen Shtemenko frequently during the years 1948–52, apparently making his influence felt on key strategic questions.[70]

In late 1951, at the time the Georgian purge began, three of Shtemenko's colleagues—Marshal of Artillery N. D. Iakovlev, Deputy Minister of Defense I. A. Mirzakhanov, and Colonel General I. I. Volkotrubenko—were suddenly dismissed from their posts and placed under criminal investigation because of alleged defects in certain antiaircraft weapons. This case, which resulted in the arrests of these officials in February 1952, cast a shadow on Shtemenko. At the end of May Beria called him and asked how things were going at the Ministry of Defense. Shtemenko reported that since the arrests things had become difficult and his recommendations were not being followed. Beria told him to write to Stalin and explain that the special bureau of the Council of Ministers, which oversaw the military and the defense industry, was being bypassed in the decision-making process (apparently by the CC Secretariat). Shtemenko and his boss, Defense Minister Vasilevskii, wrote to Stalin, but a day or two later Shtemenko went to the hospital for an operation and nothing came of it. Shtemenko lost his job as chief of staff in June 1952 and was sent off to Germany.[71]

Beria apparently could not intercede on Shtemenko's behalf, although he clearly would have liked to. This is indicated by the fact that right after Stalin died Beria brought Shtemenko back to the General Staff and released the other generals from prison.[72] Shtemenko's revival, however, was short-lived; he again lost his job after Beria's fall in June 1953 and was forced to write a humiliating recantation to Khrushchev, begging him for work. This episode shows that by early 1952, Beria was no longer able to influence Stalin directly. Though he managed to have his protégé Goglidze appointed to a top MGB post, responsible for criminal investigations of the military, this was at the very time that Shtemenko's colleagues were arrested. We know that Goglidze was a "Beria man" par excellence, so he surely cannot have sanctioned the arrests. Evidently someone higher up—possibly Ignat'ev—had taken charge of this case.

THE "DOCTORS' PLOT": STALIN'S LAST VENDETTA

Stalin's anti-Semitism grew more virulent toward the end of his life, when he was obsessed with the idea of a Jewish conspiracy. Although arrests of some high-level Jews had been occurring as far back as 1949, the first sign that this might develop into a widespread purge came on 27 November 1951, with the arrest of Rudolph Slansky, general secretary of the Czechoslovak Communist Party, and his deputy Bedrich Geminder, both Jews and both associated with Beria and the MGB. Indeed, acting with Beria's sanction, they had made Czechoslovakia a center for funneling aid and weapons to Israel in its conflict with the Arabs after the war. With Stalin's favorable stance toward Israel now completely changed, Slansky and Geminder were accused, among other things, of "cosmopolitanism," "Zionism" and the pursuit of an anti-Arab policy.[73]

The case had been prepared by Abakumov, who in 1949 sent two MGB subordinates, V. I. Komarov and M. T. Likhachev, to Prague to supervise an investigation into charges of an international conspiracy in Czechoslovak governing circles. They were soon recalled, and subsequently arrested in the wake of Abakumov's demise. Another MGB advisor, V. A. Boiarskii, replaced them, but in the autumn of 1951 (immediately following the change of leadership in the MGB) he was criticized for obstructing an investigation of Slansky and was recalled. His replacement was Aleksei Beschastnov, an MGB officer who had worked with Khrushchev's protégé Leonid Brezhnev during the war.[74] Beschastnov, who was to enjoy a successful career in the security police under Khrushchev and Brezhnev, pursued the Slansky case with vigor. It took more than a year to prepare the trial, which took place during 20–27 November 1952 and featured fourteen defendants, eleven of whom were Jewish. Slansky, Geminder, and nine others, depicted as "apprentices of Zionism," were sentenced to death on charges of high treason and espionage. Later, after Beria's fall, Slansky was depicted as a Beria man and denounced for introducing Beria's methods in Czechoslovakia.[75]

The Prague trial can be seen as a forerunner of the subsequent Doctors' Plot trial in Moscow. In fact, the charge of political murder by doctors introduced in Prague was to be a central theme, along with Zionism, of the Doctors' Plot. There is also evidence that some of the testimony and witnesses in the Slansky case were to be used again in the Doctors' Plot trial.[76] Meanwhile, the public campaign against Zionism and "cosmopolitanism" in the Soviet Union intensified. In May–June 1952 the military collegium of the USSR Supreme Court examined the case of fifteen people connected with the Jewish Antifascist Committee. Ignat'ev had forwarded the prosecutor's findings to Stalin on 3 April with an attached letter suggesting execution for all defendants except one, L. Shtern. The major proof of guilt was a proposal submitted by the JAC leadership to Stalin in February 1944 to establish a Jewish republic in the Crimea. The military collegium sentenced thirteen people to death in July 1952.[77] Then, late in November the Ukrainian press announced that several Jews in Kiev had been sentenced to death by a military tribunal for "counter-revolutionary wrecking."[78] This was followed in early January 1953 by an ominous article, written by the second secretary of the Leningrad party committee, Frol Kozlov, in the authoritative party journal *Kommunist*.[79] Kozlov mentioned the conspirators who had been uncovered among Eastern European party leaders, including Slansky. He urged vigilance against similar enemies in the Soviet Union, while at the same time making a pointed reference to a Jewish Communist who had been exposed as a "provocateur" years earlier.

On 13 January 1953 the official announcement of the Doctors' Plot, which was later revealed to have been fabricated by Ignat'ev and his deputy, Riumin, appeared in the Soviet press.[80] It alleged that a terrorist group of doctors, "who made it their aim to cut short the lives of active public figures in the Soviet Union by means of sabotaged medical treatment," had been uncovered "sometime ago." According to the announcement, among the victims were the deceased party leaders Zhdanov and Shcherbakov, who had allegedly been prescribed drugs that were contraindicated for their serious ailments. The doctors also had allegedly sought to undermine the health of several leading military officers, but their arrest had disrupted their plans. Although the announcement did not specify that six of the nine accused doctors were Jews, the latter were singled out as having conspiratorial conections with the JAC, which was labeled as a bourgeois Jewish nationalist organization established by American intelligence. The announcement, which was followed by further arrests of Jewish doctors, set off a frenzy of anti-Semitism in the Soviet Union. Large segments of the Soviet population, it seems, were willing to believe this fantasy of medical murders and a Jewish-led conspiracy.[81]

There is little doubt that the announcement was a harbinger of mass arrests and deportations of Soviet Jews, who were saved only by Stalin's death. But Jews were not the only ones with reason to be fearful. Beria and his MGB allies had equal cause to intrepret the announcement as a blow, for it was accompanied by an editorial that pointedly criticized the security police: "The state security organs did not uncover in good time the wrecking terrorist organization among the doctors. However, these organs should have been especially vigilant."[82] Indeed, Stalin had already drawn the connection between the MGB and the Doctors' Plot in early December 1952, when he had the Central Committee Presidium issue a directive, "On the Situation in the MGB and on Sabotage in a Medical Case," which called for tighter controls on the MGB.[83] This cast a shadow on Beria because he had overall responsibility for the MGB and because his protégé Merkulov had been MGB chief at the time that Shcherbakov died, in 1945. Furthermore, Beria had been associated, however tentatively, with the JAC. Although Ignat'ev was now MGB chief, he was blameless because the plot had been discovered "sometime ago" and he in fact was in charge of the investigation.

The announcement also implicated Stalin's recently arrested body-guard, N. S. Vlasik, although his name was not mentioned. From 1947 to the time of his arrest in mid-December 1952 Vlasik had been chief of the MGB Guards Directorate, which was responsible for protecting all state leaders. Thus he had presumably "lacked vigilance" in allowing doctors to harm Zhdanov in 1948. Moreover, according to the materials on his indictment (published for the first time in 1989), one of the charges against him was that of passing secrets to certain Jewish plotters.[84] Vlasik, who had served in Stalin's guard since 1931, was not a "Beria man," but his immediate subordinate in the Guards Directorate, S. F. Kuz'michev, who was arrested a month later, was. Beria released Kuz'michev after Stalin's death and made him chief of the Guards Directorate.[85] As for Vlasik, one source refers to his presence in the Kremlin on the night of Beria's arrest, so he might have been released after Stalin died, but Mer-kulov gives the impression that Beria did little to help him.[86]

Observers in Moscow at the time deduced that the plot was aimed at least in part against Beria, even though they of course had no way of knowing that Beria would later declare the case a fabrication and release those under arrest after Stalin's death.[87] Khrushchev later discounted this idea, claiming instead that Stalin had engineered the case because he wanted an excuse for a mass purge. Though he acknowledged Stalin's growing distrust of Beria, Khrushchev never mentioned Beria as an in-tended victim of the plot in his subsequent memoirs. To be sure, Khrushchev wanted to portray Beria in the worst possible light, as an evil perpetrator, not a victim. But another reason for covering up this aspect of the Doctors' Plot might have been that Khrushchev himself had en-couraged Stalin to pursue the case.

Clearly the anti-Semitic campaign had begun well before Khrushchev came on the scene in Moscow. Stalin was, if not the mastermind, than a keen advocate of the campaign. Given Stalin's intense prejudice against Jews, as well as the anti-Semitism latent in Russian society, this group was the logical focal point for elaborating a conspiracy, particularly since it could be extended to "bourgeois nationalists" (non-Russian nationalists) both at home and abroad, as well as to the security services, which Stalin distrusted. Nonetheless, the way in which the affair had developed by late 1952 suggests that others in the leadership were at the least egging him on. Indeed, it is even possible that Stalin may have lost his grip in his last years and actually believed, in part at least, the absurd charges against the doctors. Robert Conquest considers this unlikely, pointing out that "during the early purges he showed himself capable of carrying out liquidation on a colossal scale without really believing the charges as made public."[88] But there is growing evidence that the Stalin of 1952–53 was a very different man from the Stalin of the 1930s, having deteriorated both physically and mentally. As was argued above, he had always been psychologically unbalanced. In his later life this trait became aggravated by physical infirmities. According to one of the doctors who examined Stalin's body after his death in March 1953, Stalin had been suffering from severe hardening of the arteries for some time:

> The serious hardening of the cerebral arteries that we saw during the post-mortem examination of I. V. Stalin may raise the question of how the disease, which had undoubtedly developed over the previous several years, might have affected Stalin's condition and his character and his actions in those years. . . . I suggest that Stalin's cruelty and suspiciousness, his fear of enemies, loss of adequacy in assessing people and events, and his extreme obstinacy were all created to some extent by the arteriosclerosis of the cerebral arteries. . . . An essentially sick man was managing the state.[89]

It is thus not unreasonable to suggest that Stalin's innate suspiciousness had grown into such an intense paranoia that he was receptive to the idea that Kremlin doctors were plotting against him. We know that he had a terrible fear of death and that he had lost all confidence in the doctors that took care of him. When V. N. Vinogradov, one of the few physicians permitted to see Stalin, had examined him in early 1952 and recommended that he take a rest, Stalin was furious. Vinogradov was arrested later that year as part of the Doctors' Plot.[90]

Khrushchev says that the initial impetus for the case against the doctors came from a Dr. Lydiia Timashuk, who wrote Stalin a letter suggesting that, on the basis of Zhdanov's electrocardiograms, it appeared that his illness had been mis-diagnosed. Timashuk was reportedly a secret informer for the police at the Kremlin Hospital and was in direct contact with Ignatiev's deputy, Riumin.[91] Khrushchev claims that the letter led Stalin to the conclusion that a group of eminent Kremlin doctors were plotting against the Kremlin leadership. He called his subordinates to a meeting shortly after the Nineteenth Party Congress to tell them about the letter and his orders for the arrests of the doctors.[92]

It is hard to imagine that Timashuk wrote this letter of her own accord. Indeed, Khrushchev admits that "she was probably influenced or ordered by someone" and implies that the someone was in the MGB. Yet even if it was Riumin who communicated with her directly, neither he nor his boss, Ignat'ev, would have taken the initiative in concocting the case. They must have been guided by someone higher up in the leadership. Some historians have suggested that this was Poskrebyshev, chief of the "Special Section" of the Central Committee, in addition to being Stalin's personal secretary. Boris Nicolaevsky argued, for example, that "Poskrebyshev was the only one able to appoint a candidate like Ignat'ev as Minister of State Security and allow him to pursue a policy that was, apart from everything else, directed against the mighty and influential Beria."[93] But we now know that Poskrebyshev was demoted in late 1952 and lost his personal access to Stalin so, although he may have taken part in initial efforts to go after Beria, his involvement in the fabrication of the Doctors' Plot is unlikely.[94] Nor does it appear that Malenkov was the mastermind, although he would never have dared to oppose it. His long-standing feud with Zhdanov would have discouraged him from calling attention to the latter's suspicious death and he was too closely associated with Beria to benefit by his demise.

It is possible that Khrushchev was somehow behind the case of the Doctors' Plot. By late 1952, as we know, several men with close connections to Khrushchev had been brought into the MGB. Both MGB Chief Ignatiev and Deputy Minister Epishev were protégés of Khrushchev and he protected them long after the Doctors' Plot had been denounced as a fraud and Beria had fallen. Khrushchev's account of the Doctors' Plot in his memoirs seems disingenuous, to say the least. He presents the events as an innocent outsider who observed firsthand Stalin's vendetta against some Jewish doctors. But in fact, as one analyst says, the doctors were "no more than pawns in a major operation directed against Khrushchev's colleagues, an operation which was also intended to involve Soviet Jewry in a wholesale pogrom."[95]

If Khrushchev was encouraging Stalin, what were his motives? It is evident from Khrushchev's memoirs that he despised Beria, although this did not become clear until after Stalin's death when, as will be discussed in the next chapter, Khrushchev actively recruited his colleagues in a plot to get rid of him. In fact, Khrushchev admits that he began to view Beria as an enemy much earlier: "In the late forties I was already convinced that when Stalin died, we would have to do everything possible to prevent Beria from occupying a leading position in the Party."[96] Beria's arrogance and his special access to Stalin clearly irritated Khrushchev. He also resented Beria's closeness with Malenkov, watching "with great interest as this 'friendship' between the two rogues developed," and did his utmost to undermine their relationship, telling Malenkov privately how much Beria distained him.[97]

Khrushchev was also strongly anti-Semitic, so he would have had few qualms about the Doctors' Plot. As party leader of Ukraine during the 1940s, he not only kept silent about the massacre of Ukrainian Jews by the Nazis at Babi Yar but he must have assisted in the deportation of Jews from the Ukraine in the late 1940s. As was pointed out above, Khrushchev has allowed living conditions of surviving Jews in liberated Ukraine to become so intolerable by the spring of 1944 that Beria had to give him special instructions on remedying the problem. Khrushchev often made disparaging remarks about Jews, apparently unwittingly, and in the early 1960s, as party leader, he initiated a campaign against corruption that seemed aimed primarily at Jews.[98]

One rather puzzling aspect of the Doctors' Plot was the inclusion of members of the military—marshals A. M. Vasilevskii, L. A. Govorov, and I. S. Konev, and army generals G. I. Levchenko and S. M. Shtemenko—among the alleged victims of the doctors' machinations. If being a victim was meant as a sign of prestige then why was Shtemenko listed, rather than his successor, V. D. Sokolovskii? What about Marshal G. K. Zhukov and Admiral N. G. Kuznetsov? Both had recently been elected to the Central Committee, yet were not on the list of victims. Again, we can only conclude that several forces were at work here.[99] We do know, as Khrushchev later revealed, that Marshal Konev, commander of the Carpathian Military District, who served as a general in the Ukraine during the war and knew Khrushchev well, had sent a long letter to Stalin claiming that he was being poisioned by doctors, thereby fanning Stalin's distrust.[100] Konev's star rose after Beria's arrest in June; he served as a chairman of the special military tribunal at Beria's trial. In 1955, presumably as a reward for his support, Khrushchev appointed him commander in chief of the Warsaw Pact Forces. Thus Konev may have been encouraged by Khrushchev to write the letter.

That Khrushchev was keenly interested in the case of the doctors is clear from the correspondence of the CC Secretariat that was written shortly after the plot was announced and is now available in the Russian archives. Khrushchev carefully monitored public reaction to the announcement through reports from local party officials, forwarded to him by Aristov, chief of the party cadres department.[101] The reports showed that a wave of virulent anti-Semitism had gripped the country, with people demanding that Jews be removed from their posts and shot. The reports also indicated that party officials were purposely encouraging this sentiment with calls for vigilance, apparently on directions from the Moscow leadership. A widely expressed fear was that Stalin's life had been endangered by Jewish doctors. "The workers are all very worried about Stalin's health," Aristov observed in one commentary on the reports. Though others in the Secretariat, including Malenkov, were sent such information too, the majority of the reports were directed to Khrushchev. His reaction is not known, but apparently he did nothing to discourage the public reaction against Jews, which bordered on mass hysteria. When Stalin died suddenly a few weeks later, many people wondered whether the Jewish doctors were to blame.[102] But Beria was quick to dispel such rumors by announcing that the entire plot was a hoax, thus ending the bitter vendetta against the Jews that Stalin had launched.

Chapter Nine

THE DOWNFALL OF BERIA

> Beria, we are told, fell because he was the chief author of the
> new policy of concessions. If this is so, then like Cawdor
> in Shakespeare's Macbeth, nothing in his life
> became him like his leaving it.
> *(Abe Stein, The New International, May–June 1953)*

STALIN'S DEATH

DESPITE THE emergence of much new material on the Stalin period as a result of *glasnost'*, the details surrounding Stalin's death on 5 March 1953—an event that set off one of the most bitter and dramatic power struggles in Soviet history—remain unclear. Aside from the brief official communiques reporting Stalin's illness and then his death, we must rely on the personal accounts of Khrushchev, Stalin's daughter, and a few other witnesses, which diverge on certain important points. Under normal circumstances such discrepancies might seem unimportant. But Stalin died in the midst of a witch-hunt for medical conspirators and Jewish collaborators, a witch-hunt that threatened to turn into a purge of some of his closest subordinates. Thus the movements and behavior of those around him in those last days have special significance. Did his lieutenants hasten his death, as some have suggested?

Although he was clearly in bad health, Stalin managed to get about until the end. On 27 February he attended, without his Kremlin subordinates, a performance of *Swan Lake* at the Bolshoi Theater. The following evening he watched a movie at the Kremlin with Beria, Malenkov, Khrushchev, and Bulganin, after which they all retired to Stalin's nearby dacha at Kuntsevo for a late evening meal. Khrushchev's account of what occurred after this is as follows.[1] The meal lasted until five or six o'clock in the morning of 1 March. Stalin was quite drunk, but seemed in a good mood, so they all went home cheerfully. The next day was a Sunday and Khrushchev stayed home, expecting a late night call from Stalin. He finally went to bed, only to be awakened in the night by a call from Malenkov, who had been notified by Stalin's guards that something was amiss. Malenkov had already telephoned Beria and Bulganin. Khrushchev drove to Stalin's dacha and met his colleagues there. The "Chekists," as the guards were called, said they had sent Stalin's aging maid, Matryona Petrovna, to check on him. She had found him sleeping on the floor, so the guards had lifted him up and laid him on the sofa in the next room. Khrushchev implies that they had assumed Stalin was drunk: "We decided that it wouldn't be suitable for us to make our presence known while Stalin was in such an unpresentable state. We separated and all went home." Later that night Malenkov called again to say that the "Chekists" were worried that something was seriously wrong with Stalin. They all met again at the dacha, having arranged for doctors to come as well. His condition was diagnosed as grave and they set up a vigil at his bedside.

One of Stalin's bodyguards, A. T. Rybin, tells things quite differently.[2] Citing the firsthand account of the deputy commissar for the dacha, Lozgachev, he says that Khrushchev and others left Stalin's dacha at 4 A.M. on 1 March, after drinking only fruit juice, and were escorted out by the MVD officer on duty, Colonel I. Khrustalev. Stalin then told his guards he was going to bed and that they should as well. At midday on 1 March the guards were slightly concerned that there was no movement in Stalin's quarters, but at approximately 6:30 that evening lights were turned on in his office and hallway. They awaited a summons from Stalin, but there was none. At 10:30 P.M. they decided that someone had to check on Stalin, but they argued over who should do it. Finally the mail arrived, which gave Lozgachev an excuse to go to Stalin's quarters. There he saw Stalin, sprawled on the carpet near the table, unable to speak, but conscious and able to nod in agreement when they asked if they could move him. The guards, who noticed Stalin was cold and concluded he must have been lying there since at least seven or eight o'clock that evening, lifted him onto a couch and hurried off to call MGB chief Ignat'ev. According to this account, Ignat'ev "showed himself lacking in courage" and referred them to Beria—a curious reaction in view of the fact that Ignat'ev was Beria's archenemy. Apparently they chose to call Malenkov instead. The latter called them back, saying he could not find Beria, that they should try to reach him. A half hour later Beria himself telephoned the guards, ordering them not to tell anyone about Stalin's illness.

Lozgachev sat with Stalin alone, awaiting the arrival of medical help, which he assumed Malenkov had summoned. At 3:00 A.M. on 2 March Beria and Malenkov arrived. Stalin at this time appeared to be sleeping soundly and snoring. Beria berated the guards for having made a fuss over nothing and, despite Lozgachev's protestations that Stalin was ill, left with Malenkov. At 7:30 A.M. Khrushchev arrived and announced that medical help was on the way. Meanwhile, another guard called Molotov, who said he would come over right away. The doctors arrived between

8:30 and 9:00 A.M., immediately diagnosed a cerebral hemorrhage, and began giving Stalin injections and oxygen, as well applying leeches. By this time Beria and all other members of the leadership were present.

The Rybin account makes no mention of Matronya Petrovna, nor does it indicate that Khrushchev was with Malenkov and Beria at the time of their first visit to the dacha in the middle of the night. Whereas Khrushchev says that Malenkov was called again by the guards after this visit because they had become worried about Stalin, Rybin says that the guards knew that Stalin was seriously ill from the moment they had first found him (apparently around 11:00 P.M.) and does not refer to a second call to Malenkov.

To complicate matters further, a recent article, based on the unpublished manuscript of one of the doctors who attended Stalin at his deathbed, says that Stalin had been seen by a guard (looking in through a peephole) working at his desk as late as 3:00 A.M. on 2 March, and that it was not until 7:00 A.M. in the morning that the guard had checked again and found Stalin unconscious on the floor.[3] So, it would seem, the doctors who were summoned to care for Stalin were told that he was not discovered ill until much later than was the case.

In her memoirs, *Twenty Letters to a Friend*, Svetlana Alliluyeva added little to Khrushchev's account, except to confirm that her father's body was found on the floor at 3:00 A.M. on 2 March. She herself was not called to the dacha until late that morning. Recently, however, Alliluyeva, on the basis on information later conveyed to her by a member of the household staff at Kuntsevo, raised serious questions about the way her father's illness was handled.[4] Alliluyeva states that Stalin's maid found him unconscious on the floor late in the day of 1 March and requested that the doctor from the building next door be called immediately. Instead the officers of the guard decided that their bosses had to be informed first and began to argue about what to do. This took several hours, during which time Stalin lay on the floor with no help whatsoever. Finally, the Kremlin leaders arrived to establish whether something was wrong with Stalin. Alliluyeva notes:

Doctors were not called in for the next 12–14 hours, while a drama was played out at Kuntsevo: the servants and the guards rebelled, demanding that a doctor be called, but the leaders assured them that there was "no need to panic." Beria himself contended that "nothing has happened. He is sleeping." And with this verdict, the leaders left, only to be called back again a few hours later, since the entire guard at the dacha and all the staff by now was furious over this trick. Finally the members of the leadership demanded that the patient be carried to another room, moved and placed on the bed--*still* without doctors—which was impermissible from a medical point of view. Patients with a trauma (a hemorrhage in the brain) should not be moved about and carried. And in addition, doctors who were nearby had not been called upon for a specific diagnosis.[5]

Alliluyeva states that doctors did not arrive at Kuntsevo any earlier than 10:00 A.M. on 2 March. Stalin's medical records, with notations from the imprisoned Vinogradov, were nowhere to be found. Then immediately after her father's death, she says, Beria ordered Kuntsevo to be evacuated. All those who had pressed for doctors to be brought in at the onset of Stalin's illness were dismissed. Everyone was told to be silent. The dacha was closed up and the doors barred. As Alliluyeva notes, the official press announcement said that Stalin had been stricken in his Moscow apartment, rather than at Kuntsevo.[6] This was done, she says, so that if anyone at the dacha later revealed what had happened before Stalin died that person's story could be discredited.

The above accounts, despite their discrepancies, suggest strongly that members of the leadership may have deliberately delayed medical treatment for Stalin—probably for at least ten or twelve hours—when they knew he was seriously ill. They then covered up this delay. (Whether Stalin would have died anyway is of course a matter of conjecture.) Though Alliluyeva seems to blame Beria above all for this, her account does not absolve the other members of the leadership who were also present. She does not say who these men were, but implies that at least three others—Malenkov, Khrushchev, and Bulganin—were there, which Khrushchev attests to. Why Rybin does not mention Khrushchev's presence is puzzling, especially since he notes that the first to be notified of Stalin's illness was Khrushchev's protégé Ignat'ev, who most certainly would have informed Khrushchev before anyone else. It is hard to imagine that Khrushchev would not have been anxious to be on the scene as soon as possible.

It is not difficult to come up with motives that Stalin's subordinates might have had in denying him medical treatment for so long. They might have been uncertain as to what to do with him for fear they would be held responsible for any mistakes in his treatment. If he had lived, but with paralysis, for example, they might have been charged with medical conspiracy. Then, of course, they may have wanted him to die. Stalin had, after all, become a demanding and capricious tyrant, whose paranoia all but incapacitated him. Even those in Stalin's good graces, such as Malenkov and Khrushchev, could not be sure that they would avoid becoming objects of Stalin's vengeance at any moment.

Though the decisions regarding Stalin were probably made collectively, among the top four leaders, some had more to gain by his death than others. This was especially true of Beria, who most surely would have been arrested if Stalin had lived longer. Khrushchev claims that after

Stalin fell ill, Beria started "spewing hatred against him and mocking him
. . . but, interestingly enough, as soon as Stalin showed these signs of
consciousness on his face and made us think he might recover, Beria
threw himself on his knees, seized Stalin's hand, and started kissing it."[7]
Stalin's daughter describes his behavior similarly:

> There was only one person who was behaving in a way that was very nearly
> obscene. That was Beria. He was extremely agitated. . . . He was trying so hard
> at this moment of crisis to strike exactly the right balance, to be cunning, yet
> not too cunning. It was written all over him. He went up to the bed and spent
> a long time gazing into the dying man's face. From time to time my father
> opened his eyes but was apparently unconscious or in a state of semiconscious-
> ness. Beria stared fixedly at those clouded eyes, anxious even now to convince
> my father that he was the most loyal and devoted of them all.[8]

Both Alliluyeva and Khrushchev recall that Beria could not conceal his
triumph when he drove off in his car after Stalin finally died, a reaction
that is hardly surprising in view of the circumstances. As for Khrushchev,
he was apparently thrown into a state of panic. As long as Stalin had been
alive Beria was restricted in his ability to respond to moves against him.
Now, however, he was free to fight back and Khrushchev was more than
a little apprehensive. "More than by his death itself," Khrushchev recalls,
"I was disturbed by the composition of the Presidium which Stalin left
behind and particularly by the place Beria was fixing for himself. . . . I
wasn't just weeping for Stalin. I was terribly worried about the future of
the country. I already sensed that Beria would start bossing everyone
around and that this could be the beginning of the end."[9]

The other leaders, however, did not view Beria as such a threat. Indeed
some, especially Malenkov, were on close and friendly terms with him.
Thus Khrushchev's first task was to persuade his colleagues that Beria
was dangerous and that they must join forces against him. Even before
Stalin died, during their vigil at Stalin's bedside, he appealed to Bulganin,
warning him that Beria would take over the security forces and then destroy the other leaders. Bulganin was apparently receptive, but Malenkov
would not even agree to talk to Khrushchev privately after Stalin died,
retorting that he should wait until the entire Presidium met.[10]

KHRUSHCHEV VERSUS BERIA

Because Stalin had designated no heirs and there were no institutionalized
procedures for transferring power, a great sense of uncertainty prevailed
among the leaders about how they would carry on without Stalin. Although Khrushchev claims they did not meet to make decisions until after

Stalin died, in fact the bureau of the CC Presidium—consisting of Beria, Bulganin, Voroshilov, Kaganovich, Malenkov, Pervukhin, Saburov, and Khrushchev—met during the night of 4–5 March. They decided at this meeting to do away with the enlarged CC Presidium and smaller bureau, reverting to the earlier practice of having only a Presidium.[11] The next evening a joint session of the Central Committee, the Council of Ministers, and the Presidium of the Supreme Soviet took place to confirm this decision and to decide on positions in the new leadership. The meeting lasted from 8:00 to 8:40 P.M., ending just an hour and ten minutes before Stalin died.[12]

As Khrushchev had feared, Malenkov and Beria took the initiative at the meeting. Beria immediately proposed Malenkov as chairman of the Council of Ministers, while the latter then moved that Beria be named one of his first deputies (the others being Molotov, Bulganin, and Kaganovich). Malenkov also proposed the merger of the Ministries of Internal Affairs and State Security (MVD and MGB) into a single Ministry of Internal Affairs with Beria as its chief. None of this sat well with Khrushchev, but there was little he could do. As indicated by the public announcement of these changes on 7 March, which spoke of preventing disarray and panic, the leadership was nervous about possible political unrest and therefore was at great pains to present an image of unity.[13]

Given the short duration of the joint session, there cannot have been much discussion about the proposed changes. Most decisions had probably been made the night before by the Presidium bureau and were simply approved at the larger session. This might explain why the composition of the new Presidium was identical to that of the Presidium bureau, except that it now included Molotov and Mikoian. Thus the Old Guard no longer had its formal powers diluted by the group of younger *apparatchiks*, several of whom were connected with Khrushchev.[14] As for Khrushchev himself, he was forced to relinquish his post as Moscow party first secretary, so he could concentrate on his duties in the CC Secretariat. Surprisingly, however, Khrushchev's replacement, N. A. Mikhailov, was able to retain his post on the Secretariat, as was Malenkov, though he was at the same time head of the government. Also detrimental to Khrushchev was the removal of his protégés L. I. Brezhnev and N. G. Ignatov (not to be confused with S. D. Ignat'ev) from the Secretariat.

Despite the fact that the changes announced on 7 March seemed to favor Malenkov and Beria, there were indications of a compromise. While Beria's crony Bagirov became a candidate member of the Presidium and Malenkov's protégé Shatalin a member of the Secretariat, Khrushchev also managed to promote an ally: former MGB chief Ignat'ev became a CC secretary, though he was a bitter enemy of Beria.[15] During the first days after Stalin's death a cult of Malenkov's personality emerged and he seemed to have assumed Stalin's mantle. But this was less a reflection of Malenkov's power than a desire on the part of the nervous Kremlin leadership to convey to the Soviet people that Stalin's death had not resulted in a power vacuum and that there would be continuity at the top.

At Stalin's funeral the impression was more of a triumvirate, consisting of Malenkov, Beria, and Molotov, who all gave eulogies of Stalin.[16] Earlier Beria had called Merkulov to his office to make corrections in his speech. When he arrived Beria was sitting with his MVD cronies, Mamulov, Liudvigov, and Ordyntsev, joking and laughing.[17] Even at the funeral Beria did not attempt to feign grief. Although Molotov reportedly seemed genuinely shaken by Stalin's death and devoted the bulk of his speech to Stalin's accomplishments, Malenkov and Beria were more sanguine, discussing the future course of Soviet policy. According to Soviet writer Konstantin Simonov, who was at the funeral, they did not exhibit "even a trace of personal sorrow, regret or upset, or a feeling of loss—in this sense both speeches were totally cold. . . . Beria's speech, with his accent and his sharp, sometimes croaking intonations, displayed this absence of grief the most obviously. But in general the mental state of both orators was that of people who had come to power and were pleased about it."[18] Beria even went so far as to be disrespectful of Stalin. He omitted mention of Stalin's Christian name and patronymic when he spoke of him and was much less effusive in praising him than the other two were.[19] Beria also indicated an intention to move away from Stalinist policies, particularly regarding the nationality issue. He repeatedly stressed the multinational nature of the Soviet state as if to emphasize the necessity of preserving its diversity.

Beria made a point in his eulogy of mentioning favorably the decision to appoint Malenkov chairman of the Council of Ministers. Since Malenkov was still his closest ally, Beria benefited from boosting his authority, without having to worry about Malenkov becoming so powerful that he would be a threat. By all accounts Malenkov lacked the will and the political acumen to become a real dictator and he was easily steered by Beria. As Nino Beria later observed: "He [Beria] had a practical mind and understood that it would be impossible for a Georgian to become leader after Stalin's death. Therefore he approached someone that he could use, someone like Malenkov."[20] The two remained inseparable, creating a formidable political team.[21] It was this partnership, buttressed by the highly visible MVD troops in Moscow, that presented Khrushchev with his greatest obstacle. If he was to succeed in undermining Beria's power he would have to draw Malenkov away from him.

However strong they were as a team, Beria and Malenkov could not disregard the views of others. Apparently there was such dissatisfaction with the hasty imposition of Malenkov as leader of both party and state that he and Beria made a strategic retreat. By 13 March *Pravda* had ceased using a dual title for Malenkov and the number of his quotes diminished. Instead of stressing Malenkov as party leader the press began to emphasize the Central Committee as a whole. Although it was not reported publicly until 21 March, a meeting of the party leadership convened on 14 March and relieved Malenkov—"at his own request"—of his position on the Secretariat.[22]

Malenkov's retreat entailed some concessions from the Khrushchev forces, however. Moscow Party First Secretary Mikhailov and Khrushchev ally Aristov, former head of the CC party organs department, were also dropped from the Secretariat on the fourteenth and shortly thereafter Ignat'ev was dismissed. Thus the balance of forces within this body was kept relatively even. Although Khrushchev was now the senior secretary, he had to contend with Shatalin, who was in charge of party appointments. Moreover, the Secretariat was now reduced to four men— Khrushchev, Shatalin, Suslov, and Pospelov—a sign that the party apparatus was losing ground to the state, in particular to the Council of Ministers. Just as with the earlier struggle between Zhdanov and Malenkov, the rivalry here was between representatives of the party apparatus (led by Khrushchev) and those of the state (Beria and Malenkov). Malenkov had in the past straddled the fence between the two bureaucracies, but Beria's stronghold at the national level lay solidly with the Council of Ministers, now headed by Malenkov. Among the four first deputy prime ministers (Beria, Molotov, Bulganin, and Kaganovich), Beria came first in the order of precedence and he sought to emphasize his personal prominence, especially at the expense of Khrushchev. At the 15 March session of the Supreme Soviet, Beria rather than Khrushchev put forth Malenkov's name as chairman of the Council of Ministers. Molotov later said that he had tried to dissuade Beria from doing this beforehand, on the grounds that the party's senior secretary by tradition made personnel recommendations, but to no avail. Furthermore, although it had long been the custom for the senior secretary to sign his name to the protocols of CC Presidium meetings, suddenly they were signed by the "Presidium of the Central Committee," thus diluting Khrushchev's authority.[23]

BERIA THE REFORMER

That the new leadership arrangements were not reached by peaceful compromise, but by bitter power brokering, left the situation highly volatile. Neither Khrushchev nor Beria could afford to be complacent. Beria quickly seized the initiative with a series of moves designed to strengthen his power base. Not surprisingly, he first concentrated on his all-union

MVD, which now incorporated the security apparatus (formerly the MGB), the regular police, and a significant body of troops. Beria dismissed Riumin (soon to be arrested) and Epishev from their police posts, along with Ignat'ev. Kruglov, Serov, and Bogdan Kobulov became his first deputies. He promoted Sudoplatov to deputy chief of the First Directorate (internal security); Obruchnikov took charge of MVD personnel appointments; another longtime associate, N. S. Sazykin, became chief of the Fourth Directorate; and Eitingon and Kuz'michev were released from prison to become a deputy department chief and head of the Guards Service, respectively.[24] Beria conducted a wholesale purge of the foreign intelligence directorate, dismissing its chief, S. R. Savchenko, and recalling at least two hundred foreign agents to Moscow.[25] He also made sweeping personnel changes in the republic-level MVD and below. On 16 March he presented Khrushchev with a list of eighty-two new appointments to be confirmed.[26] The amalgamation of the MVD and MGB necessitated some of the changes, but in the process Beria was ensuring that the new appointees would be his men.

Interestingly Beria set about streamlining the MVD to rid it of functions that had no political significance. On 6 March he instructed Kruglov to work out procedures for handing over MVD construction units to various other ministries and the vast GULAG to the Ministry of Justice. The MVD was to retain, however, special camps for political prisoners and prisoners of war. Later, he requested the CC Presidium to approve restrictions on the powers of the infamous Special Board, the police tribunal.[27]

These policies were part of a broader program of liberalization and de-Stalinization that Beria embarked on in order to win popular support. Under Stalin it had hardly been necessary for Kremlin political figures to consider public opinion, since the regime's legitimacy rested on Stalin's cult, which was buttressed by terror. But now there was genuine concern within the leadership about maintaining authority in the country without using force. For Beria this was an opportunity both to win support for the regime as a whole and to change his own public image from that of policeman to liberal statesman. Beria's colleagues, including Khrushchev, wanted to turn away from Stalin's reign of terror and institute some sort of liberalization. But Beria, who was the first to dissociate himself from Stalin, took matters in his own hands, carrying the process farther than his colleagues wished to see it go. Reform followed reform in dizzying succession.

As a first deputy chairman of the Council of Ministers, Beria had responsibilities that extended beyond the police apparatus, and into the economic realm. Here he tried to eliminate inefficient Stalinist practices that made little economic sense. On 21 March he introduced a proposal to stop several grand-scale construction projects on the grounds that they would have little practical benefit. The construction of around twenty such undertakings, including the Volga-Baltic Canal and a large hydro-electric system along the lower Don River, was halted.[28] Beria also became openly critical of the agricultural policies advocated by Khru-shchev, especially the agro-towns which had caused considerable discon-tent among peasant farmers.[29]

On 24 March Beria sent a document to the CC Presidium requesting amnesty for a large category of prisoners. According to the document, of the 2,526,402 inmates in labor camps, only 221,435 were "especially dangerous state criminals," confined to the MVD's special camps. The majority of prisoners posed no serious danger to state or society. On 27 March the Presidium approved a decree freeing all those serving sentences of five years or less, women with children under ten, pregnant women, and young people under eighteen—approximately one million prison-ers.[30] Even before the amnesty a distinct relaxation took place in the camps. According to a young Austrian serving in Siberia, prison regula-tions were eased considerably shortly after Stalin's death, even among politicals. Prisoners suddenly were permitted writing materials, parcels from home, and visits from relatives.[31]

The most sensational reform, announced in *Pravda* on 4 April, was the repudiation of the Doctors' Plot and the rehabilitation of the arrested doctors. Significantly, the announcement came in the form of a communi-que from the MVD, thus making it clear that Beria was behind it. Accord-ing to the communique:

> It was established that the testimony of the arrested, allegedly confirming the accusations against them, was obtained by officials of the investigatory depart-ment of the former Minister of State Security through the use of impermissible means of investigation which are strictly forbidden under Soviet law. . . . The persons accused of incorrect conduct of the investigation have been arrested and brought to criminal responsibility.

Ignat'ev was criticized for "political blindness and heedlessness," while Riumin and his assistants were arrested.[32]

The message from the MVD was that Stalinist-type justice was a thing of the past and arbitrary police terror would no longer be permitted. There was talk of reforming the criminal codes in order to protect individ-uals from arbitrary police persecution. And at Beria's instigation the cult of personality was swiftly eroded. Stalin's name was mentioned less and less frequently in the press. The emphasis was on collective leadership rather than Stalin's legacy. For example, on 9 May, on Beria's initiative, the CC Presidium passed a resolution prohibiting the display of leaders' portraits during holiday demonstrations.[33] Unbeknownst to the general public Beria went even further in de-Stalinizing. According to Konstantin Simonov, he gathered documents revealing Stalin's complicity in the Doc-tors' Plot and displayed them for Central Committee members to read in

special rooms in the Kremlin. Among the documents was written testimony from Riumin about how Stalin urged him to conduct more
interrogations and how Stalin wanted to use the Doctors' Plot against
Beria.[34]

Beria did not confine his reforms to internal policy. He also took distinct steps to reduce international tensions. According to the Moscow-
based journalist Harrison Salisbury:

> The most astonishing thing that happened after Stalin died was the quickness
> with which symptoms of a thaw appeared. Go back to those days, and they
> strike you with their dramatic rapidity. I don't think Stalin had been dead a
> week, when a young man in the Foreign Office called up the American Embassy
> and said, "You know, if you don't want to move out of your Embassy on
> Moldavia Street"—as Stalin had ordered them to do—"it's alright with us, you
> can stay there." . . . A week or so later, there were hints circulating through the
> diplomatic corps that the Russians were talking very reasonably and frankly.[35]

Moscow also began to exert its influence to bring about a truce in Korea
and on 2 April armistice negotiations were resumed. On 25 April *Pravda*
gave a favorable assessment of a speech by Eisenhower, expressing the
Kremlin's readiness to settle differences with the United States. The impetus for the new foreign policy course came directly from Beria. In fact, he
was later accused of taking initiatives on his own and implementing policy through the MVD, even trying to arrange a secret meeting with Tito
to discuss a rapprochement with Yugoslavia.[36] Significantly, the Secretariat ceased altogether to discuss foreign policy, which from March onward
was under the sole purview of the Council of Ministers.[37]

Other signs indicated that party control over the state machine was
weakening. On 26 April *Pravda* announced that ministers had been
granted a new right: "to determine the use of materials and funds within
the competence of their ministry and to decide without reference to others
all important questions relating to the activity of the enterprises and institutions under their control." In other words, these decisions could be
made without party approval. A few weeks later *Pravda* urged that ministries be given more independence and greater rights.[38] Because he was
chairman of the Council of Ministers Malenkov had little reason to resist
efforts to extend ministerial powers, but Khrushchev must have found
this trend disquieting, to say the least.

BERIA'S NATIONALITIES POLICY

Beria carried out his political program on two fronts: in addition to promoting the powers of the state over those of the party, he emerged as a
defender of non-Russian nationalities against the Russian-dominated

center. Turning first to Georgia, he swiftly reversed many of the changes that the purges of 1951–52 had wrought. At his instigation, the CPSU Central Committee passed a resolution, on 10 April, declaring the Mingrelian nationalist conspiracy a fabrication and ordering a rehabilitation of all those accused. On 14 April a plenum of the Georgian Central Committee fired Mgeladze, who had been first secretary of Georgia since the previous April, and replaced him with A. I. Mirtskhulava, a Mingrelian. The CC bureau was drastically purged: of the eleven full members elected in September 1952, all were dismissed except two officials and they were demoted to candidate status.[39] The new bureau was packed with Beria men, including Dekanozov and Mamulov (sent from Moscow as Beria's personal representatives), Sturua, Baramiia, and Zodelava (the last two having been released from prison). According to one of those present at the plenum, "When Beria came to Georgia in April 1952 he was acting on instructions from the Central Committee in Moscow, but this time he was acting on his own."[40]

The next day the Georgian Supreme Soviet confirmed a host of government changes.[41] Z. N. Ketskhoveli was replaced as chairman of the Georgian Council of Ministers by Beria's close friend Bakradze. Given the shift of power from party to state, this post was now the most powerful in the republic.[42] Baramiia became minister of agriculture; Rapava was released from prison to become minister of state control; Zodelava became first deputy chairman of the Council of Ministers; and Dekanozov assumed the highly important post of minister of internal affairs. On the party side, Mamulov was placed at the head of the cadres department, which made him responsible for party appointments. In a speech to the Supreme Soviet Bakradze praised Beria in glowing terms (while barely mentioning Stalin) and then went on to explain that Baramiia and others had been victims of a "falsified, provocational 'case' involving non-existent nationalism, framed up from beginning to end by the enemy of the people and party, the former Minister of State Security Rukhadze."[43]

A witch-hunt ensued for those who were close to Stalin and had supported the arrests of Mingrelians, as denunciations from those anxious to be in the Beria camp flowed into the CC. Mgeladze, for one, was investigated for bribery committed when he was party secretary in Abkhazia and was pronounced guilty by the CC on 10 June.[44] Beria, quite naturally, wanted to take credit for exposing the frame-up and to appear as a champion of Georgian rights. With this in mind he had written a long report, in his name, and instructed Bakradze to read it at the 14 April Georgian plenum along with other documents. Bakradze, however, had only presented the resolution of the CPSU Central Committee declaring the Mingrelian case a hoax. When Beria found out, he was furious and berated Bakradze for his "political stupidity."[45] Beria wanted to do more than simply reconstitute his apparatus in Georgia when he exposed the Mingrelian case. He wanted to curb "Great Russian chauvinism" and assert the rights of indigenous nationalities. This explains why *Zaria vostoka*, now controlled by Beria's men, made a point of declaring that both the Mingrelian case and the Doctors' Plot had been based on false charges of racial and national bias, thereby signaling that attacks against "bourgeois [non-Russian] nationalism" would no longer be countenanced.

The struggle between the Khrushchev and Beria forces became especially bitter when Beria applied his nationality policy to the Ukraine, Khrushchev's bailiwick. In early April Beria appointed his henchman P. A. Meshik to head the Ukrainian MVD, with longtime protégé Solomon Mil'shtein as his first deputy. The two men immediately began replacing MVD chiefs in the oblasts and preparing for an overhaul of the party and state apparatus. The goal was to remove Russians from leading posts and install Ukrainians, so as to give the indigenous nationality more influence over republican politics. This was part of a broader program that Beria was promoting in all the republics to strengthen the position of non-Russian minorities.[46]

Western Ukraine was the focal point of Beria's efforts. Sometime in April Meshik ordered T. A. Strokach, internal affairs chief in Lvov, to collect data on the ethnic composition of party officials in the region and to find out the extent to which the Ukrainian language was used in schools and in the press. He was also told to assess the problem with underground nationalist groups in Western Ukraine. According to Strokach's subsequent account, he thought this order was unusual, so he told Lvov Party Chief Z. T. Serdiuk, who in turn told Ukrainian Party First Secretary L. G. Mel'nikov. The latter was disturbed by the request but apparently unwilling to go against Beria, so he told Serdiuk, "You look into this information, maybe it was ordered by Beria and we have to come up with it."[47] Serdiuk, who had worked closely with Khrushchev for many years, did not cooperate and was consequently arrested, apparently on Beria's orders.[48] Beria then managed to obtain the necessary information from the republican MVD and used it as a basis for a report on the situation in Western Ukraine that was highly critical of local officials for their brutal policies of Russification, which had in the past resulted in thousands of deaths. The report called for the promotion of ethnic Ukrainians into the leadership and the use of Ukrainian language in conducting official business.[49] As a result of the report, the CPSU Central Committee passed, on 26 May, a resolution on Western Ukraine that criticized the nationalities policies of the Ukrainian party and called for Mel'nikov's dismissal. A plenum of the Ukrainian Central Committee met on 2–4 June and duly relieved Mel'nikov of his post, replacing him with a Ukrainian, A. I. Kirichenko. According to a subsequent report on the plenum, Mel'nikov and the Ukrainian party leadership "committed in their practical work distortions of the Leninist-Stalinist national policy of our party; these distortions took the form of the shameful practice of promoting to leading party and Soviet posts in the Western regions of the Ukraine mostly people from the other regions of the Ukrainian SSR and of introducing teaching in Russian at Western Ukrainian universities."[50] The sudden change in Moscow's policy was greeted warmly in Western Ukraine. According to a note sent to Khrushchev by Kirichenko on 16 June, the majority of participants at regional party plenums voiced strong support for Beria's recommendations.[51]

As it turns out, Beria was taking other steps to extend national rights in Western Ukraine, including the promotion of religious freedom. He brought to Moscow the primate of the Greek-Catholic (Uniate) Church, Metropolitan Yosyf Slipyi, who was serving an eight-year sentence in a Mordovian prison camp. Beria's emissaries then began secret negotiations with Slipyi about the normalization of Soviet relations with the Vatican and the legalization of the Greek-Catholic Church in Western Ukraine.[52] This was the complete reversal of a policy that Khrushchev had promoted when he was party leader of Ukraine and had in 1945 forced a group of clergy from the Greek-Catholic Church to join their church with the Russian Orthodox Church.[53] The talks ended abruptly after Beria was arrested and Slipyi was sent into administrative exile.

Beria intended his nationalities program to be applied in other republics as well. He issued memorandums on this question for Belorussia, Lithuania, Latvia, and Estonia, calling for the return of non-native officials to Moscow and the appointment of ethnic cadres to key leadership posts in these republics, as well as for the widespread use of the native language in official business.[54] After Beria's arrest the first secretary of Lithuania, A. Iu. Snechkus, claimed that Beria's deputy had traveled twice to Lithuania, incognito, in order to collect information for Beria's memorandum, which then "grossly exaggerated" the popular strength of nationalist underground groups in the republic. Beria, he said, had tried to stir up tensions between Russians and Lithuanians to a dangerous level.[55] In Belorussia Beria ousted the Russian MVD chief, Mikhail Baskakov, along with nine other oblast internal affairs chiefs, replacing them with Belorussians. He then designated Mikhail Zimianin, a Belorussian, to replace the Russian party leader there, Nikolai Patolichev. At a stormy party plenum that opened in Minsk on 25 June, reports were delivered in Belorussian for the first time, and the way in which national questions had been handled by Patolichev and other Russian officials was criticized.[56]

It hardly needs to be pointed out that Beria's radical approach to nationalities policy marked a sharp departure from the Stalinist line. The implications for center-periphery relations were far-reaching, to say the least. For the first time since the creation of the Soviet Union non-Russian nationalities were encouraged to assert their own cultural and political identities and the traditional policy of Russification was thrown into question. Western historians have generally considered Beria's appeal for support from non-Russians to be a sort of desperate, foolhardy gambit. Now, with the hindsight gained by seeing the strength of nationalist sentiment in the former Soviet Union, it appears as a promising, though risky, strategy for consolidating political power. Stalinism represented not only despotism, but also domination by Great Russians over other national groups. As Beria realized, an attempt to gain credibility by de-Stalinization required some recognition of national rights.

Khrushchev had good reason to resent the imposition of Beria's nationalities policy, particularly in Ukraine, where it struck directly at his power base. But he was compelled to go along with it for the time being. As he put it:

> It so happened that Beria's position on this question was correct and that it coincided with the position of the All-Union Central Committee. . . . Everyone knew that this was right and that it was consistent with the Party line, but at first people didn't realize that Beria was pushing this idea in order to aggravate nationalist tensions between Russians and non-Russians, as well as tensions between the central leadership in Moscow and the local leadership in the republics."[57]

Other members of the Presidium, it seems, were more open-minded about Beria's program and did not view it as such a threat. Thus it was necessary for Khrushchev to bring them around and persuade them to oppose Beria. With this purpose in mind Khrushchev took Malenkov aside and said, in his words, "Listen Comrade Malenkov, don't you see where this is leading? We're heading for disaster. Beria is sharpening his knives."[58] According to Khrushchev, Malenkov was initially reluctant but was eventually persuaded to join forces with Khrushchev and move against Beria.

While uneasiness about the nationalities policy may have caused Malenkov to lean in Khrushchev's direction it is by no means clear that this was the deciding factor. We have only Khrushchev's account to go on and he undoubtedly did not relate all the machinations he carried out to break up the Beria-Malenkov alliance. He does describe one telling incident that took place sometime in the late spring of 1953. Beria had suggested to the other Presidium members that they all have dachas built, at government expense, in the Georgian city of Sukhumi near the Black Sea. He sang the praises of Sukhumi and even went so far as to have building plans drawn up. Apparently Malenkov initially thought this was a good idea until Khrushchev began to persuade him that it was a cynical plot. Khrushchev told Malenkov that since people would have to be thrown out of their homes in order for his dacha to be built, this would cause great public resentment and he would be forced to resign. "Don't you see?" Khrushchev told him, "Beria says he's going to have plans drawn up for a dacha of his own, but you'll see, he won't have it built. He'll build one for you and then use it to discredit you." Malenkov was incredulous: "How can you say that? Beria talked it all over with me." But, Khrushchev notes, "This conversation started Malenkov thinking."[59]

CRISIS IN EAST GERMANY

Khrushchev might have found it difficult to win over Malenkov and the others if it had not been for Beria's policy toward East Germany, which had an unfortunate outcome for the Kremlin. The situation in East Germany was a source of grave concern to the Kremlin at this time. The economy was in a shambles, with serious shortages of consumer goods and foodstuffs. As a result, close to 500,000 East German citizens had fled to West Germany since 1951. The main cause of this economic crisis was the overambitious program of rapid industrialization and forced collectivization pursued by Communist party leader Walter Ulbricht. When Ulbricht appealed to Soviet leaders for economic relief at Stalin's funeral and afterward, they refused, urging him instead to slow the pace of the "construction of socialism." But Ulbricht resisted. In mid-May the Central Committee of the SED (German Communist Party) announced a 10 percent increase in industrial work norms for the GDR, which meant further sacrifices on the part of the people.[60]

On 27 May 1953 the Presidium of the Soviet Council of Ministers met to discuss the German situation—the Secretariat, as mentioned above, no longer had authority for foreign policy—and produced, on 2 June, a document entitled "Measures to Improve the Political Situation in the GDR." The document, drafted and signed by Beria, made the following recommendations to East German leaders: (1) abandon the policy of forced construction of socialism; (2) work for the creation of a united, democratic, peace-loving and independent Germany; (3) stop forcing the creation of agricultural cooperatives, which have met with great resistance from the peasants; (4) end the policy of eliminating private capital, which is premature, and draw private capital into different areas of the economy, including agriculture; (5) introduce broad steps to improve the financial system; and (6) take broad measures to ensure individual citizens' rights and put an end to unjust and cruel judicial treatment; review cases of those already in prison.[61]

The Soviet leadership did not reach agreement on the document without controversy. Reportedly Beria tried to introduce a recommendation

that the GDR stop building socialism altogether, but Molotov objected
and the final version advised against the "forced construction of socialism." Soviet diplomat Andrei Gromyko, who was present at one of the
Presidium meetings, claims that Molotov and others resented Beria's cav-
alier attitude toward the GDR and reproached him for not supporting its
existence as a separate state.[62] Khrushchev and Molotov later denounced
Beria's program at the July 1953 plenum, accusing him of turning against
socialism and playing into the hands of the West by trying to create a
united neutral, bourgeois Germany.[63] But this was after the fact. The Presidium did end up supporting Beria's program, however reluctantly,
presumably because its members realized that something had to be done
before the East German economy collapsed.

On 2–4 June the Kremlin leadership held a meeting in Moscow with
East German Communist party leader Walter Ulbricht and two of his
colleagues. The East Germans, reluctant to push forward with changes,
presented a more modest plan for dealing with their problems. To this
Kaganovich retorted: "Our document amounts to a revolution, yours to
reform." The discussion became so heated that Beria was shouting at
Ulbricht. (Later Ulbricht was to recall that "Beria was indignant when I
opposed his policy in regard to the German question in 1953.")[64] Finally
the Germans were compelled to support the "Beria Document," as they
called it, presenting it to the Politburo of the German Communist Party
(SED) in Berlin on 5–6 June.[65]

Meanwhile, on 28 May, Moscow announced that East Germany had
been placed under civilian control. Marshal V. I. Chuikov, commander of
Soviet forces in Germany, was recalled to Moscow and replaced by a
civilian commissioner, Vladimir Semenov, who had previously been a political advisor to the Soviet Control Commission in East Germany. Semenov reportedly had worked in the NKVD and was close to Beria.[66] He
was to oversee the new course in East Germany and make changes in the
party leadership. It was rumored that the Ulbricht group would be replaced by a more liberal one, led by Rudolf Herrnstadt, in the near future.
Herrnstadt, editor of the Communist party daily, was supported by Beria
and had been charged with elaborating reforms based on the Beria Document. Herrnstadt was working closely with Wilhelm Zaisser, chief of the
security police and directly answerable to Beria. These men, joined by
East Berlin party leader Hans Jendretsky, were using the reform issue to
push Ulbricht out of the SED leadership.[67]

On 10 June the East German Politburo announced the "new course"
publicly, enumerating a long list of liberal measures in the press. They
would reduce crop quotas for peasant farmers along with the amount of
fines for nondelivery of quotas. They promised peasants who had fled to
West Germany that their farms would be returned if they came back.

Shop owners and traders were offered inexpensive loans, and some retail prices were to be lowered immediately. Significantly, no mention was made of the "construction of socialism."[68] On 13 June the government enacted an amnesty for hundreds of prisoners and the press urged that individual rights be protected by the constitution. Furthermore, the official Russian newspaper in East Germany criticized the Soviet Military Control Commission—the symbol of ironclad Soviet rule—for having committed serious errors.[69] The announcement of these sudden reversals of government policy created an atmosphere of heightened expectations among the East German people and uncertainty in the ruling elite.

Ulbricht and his supporters, however, continued to resist the extension of concessions to workers. In particular, they gave no indication that they would rescind the proposed 10 percent rise in labor norms, which was the source of intense dissatisfaction. Contradictory statements on this question by party and government officials confused the issue and fueled public discontent to the point where workers took to the streets of East Berlin in protest on 16 June. By the next day protests had spread to all of East Germany and were no longer limited to economic aims but included political objectives, such as the removal of Ulbricht. This was a real crisis for Moscow. As one observer put it: "The entire weight and authority of the Russian imperial power had to be brought to bear in support of the feeble shadow power of satellite regimes if the demonstrations were not to turn into the first stages of revolution."[70]

By midday on 17 June, Soviet tanks were crushing the uprising. The repercussions in Moscow must have been felt immediately, although the Soviet press said little about it in the days that followed. Having pushed the policy of liberalization in East Germany that had such catastrophic consequences, Beria bore the most responsibility, especially since his surrogates—Semenov and Zaisser—had contributed to the leadership conflict that prompted the rising. Of course, if the Moscow leadership had been more in agreement about the "new course" and had pushed Ulbricht harder, then perhaps the East German leadership would not have vacillated so much and the disturbances might not have occurred. But Beria's Kremlin colleagues preferred to overlook this factor and to blame him for the crisis, denouncing him at the July plenum for pushing liberalization in East Germany too far. Moreover, a few weeks after the rising, Soviet party leaders sent a letter to the SED Politburo accusing Beria of forcing a policy of compromise that might have led to the abandonment of East Germany.[71]

Although it has long been known that Beria took a relatively liberal line after Stalin's death, the full extent of his bold initiatives has only recently come to light, with the publication of the documents cited above. He was advocating sweeping reforms that, had they succeeded, would not only have changed the nature of the Soviet system but would have opened the way for a partial dismantlement of the Soviet bloc. Of course Beria did not want to restore capitalism, as his colleagues later claimed. Nor did he want to introduce true democracy. But he did recognize the urgent need to back away from rigid Stalinism, to take a strategic retreat from ideological precepts in the name of practicality and to initiate policies that had popular appeal. In this respect he was more practical and forward-looking than most of his colleagues. That Khrushchev himself later adopted some of Beria's programs, including de-Stalinization, demonstrates that he and the other Presidium members understood that some reform was necessary to the survival of the Soviet system. But Beria, it seems, was too precipitous in pushing for change. And he failed to anticipate the destabilizing effect that sudden liberalization would have in East Germany. The East German crisis provided Khrushchev with a pretext for rallying opposition against Beria.

The Plot against Beria

According to most accounts, Beria was arrested at a hastily convened Presidium meeting on 26 June 1953, nine days after the East German uprising. During this period Khrushchev had been working feverishly to gather forces against his opponent. This was no easy task, since Beria still enjoyed support within the party Presidium. Moreover, as head of the vast police and intelligence apparatus, he was a difficult man to arrest. Khrushchev still had to bring Malenkov, whose collaboration was essential to the success of the plot, around to his way of thinking. But he found this difficult: "As anyone who knew Malenkov will tell you, after Stalin's death he was completely without initiative and completely unpredictable. He was unstable to the point of being dangerous because he was so susceptible to the pressure and influence of others. It was no accident that he had fallen into Beria's clutches."[72] Khrushchev was eventually able to turn Malenkov's malleability to his own advantage and persuaded him to write up agendas for Presidium sessions so that they included issues on which Beria would be defeated when they were voted on. This demonstrated to Malenkov that Beria could be outmaneuvered when they put forth their arguments "on a firm party position."[73]

Seeing that he was being challenged, Beria must have realized that Khrushchev was recruiting forces against him, so he too sought support behind the scenes. According to Molotov:

> Beria called me and asked me to support his group. I told him to the contrary, he should support our position. But he would not listen, and hung up on me.

He thought it would be easy to get even with Khrushchev's group, but Khrushchev turned out to be more clever. If Beria had listened to me, history would have had a different outcome.[74]

It is not clear what Molotov meant when he spoke of "our position," but he may have been referring to the East German question. Judging from his comments, Molotov was not ill-disposed toward Beria: "Beria was a most clever man, inhumanly energetic and industrious. He could work for a week without sleep . . . As far as the accusations that Beria was an agent of a foreign country are concerned, they are untrue. He was loyal to the Soviet Union to a fault."[75] But the debate over East Germany had caused Molotov to side with Khrushchev and the subsequent crisis there led him to go along with Beria's arrest, however reluctantly.[76]

Khrushchev had little trouble persuading Minister of Defense Bulganin to back him in his plan to oust Beria. Having worked with Khrushchev in the early 1930s in Moscow, he was on friendly terms with him and he apparently had little use for Beria. When Bulganin disagreed with Beria over the German question Beria had threatened to have him fired. Khrushchev also says that Gosplan Chairman Mikhail Saburov readily agreed with the plot. But the remaining Presidium members—Pervukhin, Mikoian, Voroshilov, and Kaganovich—presented problems. It was left to Malenkov to talk to Pervukhin, with whom he was on close terms. The latter was reluctant to go along, saying only that he would think it over. But time was running out, since the plot had already been set in motion so, Khrushchev says, he himself went to see Pervukhin and was more successful.[77]

Voroshilov and Mikoian were strong supporters of Beria. When Khrushchev went to see Voroshilov, the latter immediately began "singing Beria's praises." Khrushchev recalled: "After Voroshilov had greeted me in this way, I couldn't possibly talk to him frankly about Beria."[78] Although Khrushchev implies that Voroshilov finally agreed to go against Beria at the eleventh hour, Mikoian was not even informed of the plot, presumably because he would have told Beria. As for Kaganovich, he was out of town and did not return to Moscow until the night before Beria's arrest. Subsequently, at the July plenum, he gave the impression that he had nothing to do with the plot and made a point of thanking Malenkov, Khrushchev, and Molotov for organizing the operation against Beria.[79]

The decision to oust Beria from the Presidium was by no means, then, a unanimous one and his arrest must have taken some leaders by surprise. Although Khrushchev persuaded Malenkov, Molotov, and Bulganin to take an active role, other members of the leadership were either enlisted at the last minute, or left in the dark completely. What provided Khrushchev with the strength to carry out this dangerous and daring operation? How was he able to overcome Beria, who had the support of a powerful police and security apparatus behind him? The key to Khrushchev's success, it seems, was support from certain elements in the military. Soviet generals had traditionally remained outside of Kremlin politics, particularly after their ranks had been decimated by the purges in the thirties. As a political group, they had much less influence over policy than other Soviet institutions had. The military was not apolitical, however, and given the longstanding animosity between the military and the police, some Soviet generals had viewed the rise of Beria and the MVD after Stalin's death with disquiet. The East German crisis fueled their dislike of Beria and gave their opposition a concrete cause. Having watched him dismantle Soviet military control there and replace one of their generals with a civilian and former policeman, they now blamed him for a policy of appeasement and demanded a tougher line as they were called on to rescue the situation. Khrushchev, who had established close relations with several generals when he was a political commissar during the war, was able to capitalize on this resentment of Beria and use it to his advantage.

Nonetheless, Khrushchev again faced obstacles. Beria himself, as chief of the MVD, had his own forces at his disposal. Two MVD divisions, politically reliable and trained especially for dealing with internal unrest, were stationed in Moscow, while the Kremlin itself was guarded by MVD troops.[80] There was no question of these troops defecting. They were loyal to Beria, as were most other MVD members. Khrushchev had no more popular support or legitimacy than Beria, so the coup against Beria had to be kept secret, or else the entire regime might topple. Moreover, not all elements of the military could be counted on to move against Beria. The commander of the ground forces in the Moscow Military District, Colonel General P. A. Artemev, for example, had been an NKVD troop commander in the war and was known to be sympathetic to Beria.[81]

Khrushchev's strategy for this highly risky operation, which was apparently decided on at the very last minute, was to select military officers that he knew personally and to promise them rewards for their support. At 9:00 A.M. on 26 June he called K. S. Moskalenko, commander of Moscow's Air Defense and asked him to enlist several of his most trusted men for a special task. Moskalenko had served during the war on the Stalingrad, Voronezh, and Ukrainian fronts, where he was in frequent contact with Khrushchev and the latter had recommended him highly to Stalin.[82] Moskalenko in turn enlisted Major General P. F. Batitskii, chief of staff of the Air Force, who had earlier been his deputy in the Air Defense Force, and three of his (Moskalenko's) subordinates in the Air Defense Command: Colonel I. B. Zub, chief of the Political Directorate;

Major General A. I. Baskov, chief of staff; and Major V. I. Iuferev, his officer for special operations. Both Moskalenko and Batitskii received promotions after Beria's arrest and all five officers received military awards in December 1953.[83]

Khrushchev's call was followed by one from Bulganin, who told Moskalenko to bring his men, armed, to his office at the Ministry of Defense. Khrushchev says in his memoirs that Malenkov had decided the night before the arrest to widen the circle of officers to include Marshal Zhukov and others, but Moskalenko's version is different. He claims that when he and his men arrived at Bulganin's office that morning, Bulganin informed him that he was to arrest Beria and asked him if he could get some additional men without delay. Moskalenko suggested Zhukov, who happened to be at the ministry at the time, and four others with whom he and Khrushchev had fought on the Ukrainian Front during the war: Brezhnev, at the time first deputy chief of the MPA (Main Political Administration), M. I. Nedelin, an artillery commander, A. L. Getman, commander of a tank division, and S. S. Shatilov, deputy chief of the MPA. Colonel General A. M. Pronin, a member of the military council of the Moscow Military District, was also summoned.[84]

No one in the second group had had time to get weapons, so Bulganin gave Brezhnev his pistol and the rest were unarmed. At 11:00 A.M. the hastily convened group of military officers—those with weapons concealed them under their jackets—entered the Kremlin gates in two official cars, one belonging to Bulganin and the other to Zhukov. The car windows were darkened, so they could not be seen clearly by the MVD guards. They gathered in the waiting area outside Malenkov's office, where a meeting of the Central Committee Presidium was soon to take place.[85]

Bulganin and Khrushchev (and, according to one version, Malenkov and Molotov) came out of the office and told the men that on receiving a given signal—conveyed through Malenkov's assistant—they were to enter the room and arrest Beria. They explained that Beria was an enemy of the people and was trying to destroy the party. Beria arrived shortly thereafter, dressed casually in a worn-out suit and not wearing a necktie. He apparently suspected nothing, having seriously underestimated Khrushchev. Outside, in the reception area, sat fifteen or so assistants and guards belonging to Beria. [86]

The official record of the Presidium meeting has been declared missing from the archives; the only firsthand account of what transpired next comes from Khrushchev who has given conflicting versions and so cannot be accepted as totally reliable.[87] (In fact, as is discussed below, Beria's son Sergo claims that the planned Presidium meeting never took place and that Beria was confronted at his home).[88] Khrushchev claimed in his memoirs that, although Malenkov chaired the session, it was he who took the floor to denounce Beria. When Khrushchev stood up and began, Beria looked at him with a startled expression and said: "What's going on, Nikita? What's this you're mumbling about?" Khrushchev started with the old accusation that Beria had spied for Musavat counterintelligence in Baku, and then went on to discuss Beria's recent policies toward the non-Russian republics, accusing him of deliberately stirring up antagonisms to undermine the unity of the Soviet state. He also brought up the amnesty for camp inmates, claiming that Beria was "trying to legalize arbitrary rule" and that "no honest Communist would ever behave the way he does in the Party."

Bulganin then took the floor to agree and after him Molotov. Both "expressed the proper party position on the matter." Mikoian, however, continued to defend Beria. At this point Malenkov, as chairman, was supposed to sum things up, but he lost his nerve and could not speak. When Khrushchev then proposed that Beria be released from all his posts, Malenkov went into a state of panic and instead of putting the motion to a vote pressed a secret button to call the generals from the next room.

At approximately 1:00 P.M. Zhukov, Moskalenko, and the four armed officers entered Malenkov's office. Malenkov, still overcome with fear, announced Beria's arrest in a faint voice and Moskalenko, brandishing his pistol, ordered Beria to put his hands up, while Zhukov searched him. From the subsequent accounts of Zub and Moskalenko it is clear that some leaders knew nothing of Beria's arrest beforehand. According to Zub: "When we came in, some members of the Presidium jumped from their seats, evidently unaware of the details of the arrest. Zhukov immediately reassured them all: 'Take it easy comrades! Sit down.'"[89] Moskalenko recalled: "Aside from Bulganin, Malenkov, Molotov, and Khrushchev, no one knew about or expected Beria's arrest."[90] And, of course, Beria too had been caught completely off guard. When they searched him they found a paper with the word "alarm" scribbled several times in red letters. Apparently he had written this during the session, hoping to somehow get it passed to his men.[91]

The officers led Beria back into the waiting room and within a few minutes the Presidium session ended and all participants left, including Zhukov. Beria's captors had to wait until dark, which came late in the evening, this being June, before taking Beria out of the building since Beria's men were still guarding the Kremlin. Beria was nervous and kept asking to go to the toilet, apparently with the idea of somehow signaling his guards, but he was not successful. Around 10:00 or 11:00 P.M. Army General Maslennikov, a first deputy chief of the MVD, and Vlasik, who had apparently been released from prison after Stalin died, suddenly arrived in the reception area. They began shouting and demanding to know what was going on. Moskalenko hastily put them through on the telephone to Bulganin, who somehow persuaded them to leave.[92]

Finally, around midnight, Moskalenko managed to obtain five government cars with signal lights and sent them to the headquarters of the Moscow District Air Defense on Kirov Street. There they picked up thirty armed officers commanded by the chief of the operations department, and brought them back to the Kremlin. These officers, apparently without incident, replaced Beria's guards, so that Moskalenko and his four men were able to convey the prisoner out of the Kremlin (through the Spassky Gates). Followed by another car containing Brezhnev and his group of officers, they took Beria to the garrison guardhouse at Lefortovo Prison.[93]

Although Khrushchev had apparently managed to persuade the Presidium to go along with Beria's arrest, it is clear that his account of the episode—in which he portrays his colleagues, with the exception of Mikoian, as having been in full agreement beforehand—was inaccurate. Several of them were taken by complete surprise at the 26 June plenum and might well have resisted the move if they had known in advance. Judging from the fact that the plot was kept secret from all but a select group of officers (who were enlisted at the very last minute), Khrushchev did not feel he could rely on the military either. According to Moskalenko's account, Khrushchev approached another, unnamed marshal of the Soviet Union before coming to him but the officer in question refused to join him. Moreover, when it was suggested to Bulganin beforehand that he enlist his deputy, Marshal A. M. Vasilevskii, in the operation, Bulganin hastily dismissed the idea, presumably because he did not trust him.[94]

Beria's arrest was, then, a highly risky operation that succeeded more by luck than anything else. The coup plotters, improvising as they went along, were in considerable danger for the next few days, until the Beria forces could be subdued and any potential challenges resisted. Although they tried to keep the arrest a secret, word was doubtlessly getting around and they could not be sure what the repercussions would be. As a precaution, Khrushchev and his allies ordered additional military forces into Moscow. According to a report from the U.S. Embassy in Moscow, on the afternoon of 27 June, twelve armored personnel carriers, thirty-six motorcycles, twenty T34 tanks, twenty-three SU 100 self-propelled guns and twelve maintenance vehicles could be seen moving along Bol'shaia Sadovaia Street. These same vehicles were seen leaving Moscow two days later.[95]

Although the military could be expected to accept Beria's arrest as a fait accompli, the MVD was a different matter. Khrushchev's men began arresting Beria's closest associates right away—his bodyguards, Sarsikov and Nadaraia, were caught while Beria was on his way to the Presidium meeting. But it would hardly have been practical, or even feasible, to arrest all of the senior staff, so some MVD officials, Kruglov and Serov in particular, were co-opted by the Khrushchev forces. As one incident shows, this proved to be a complicated maneuver. On 27 June Serov and Kruglov arrived at Lefortovo Prison and demanded to see Beria. Khrushchev, it seems, had told them that they could participate in the "investigation" of Beria's crimes. Moskalenko, who had misgivings about the idea of Beria's deputies investigating him, insisted that one of his men sit in on the questioning. Serov and Kruglov adamantly rejected this proposal and a heated argument ensued.

Moskalenko then tried to contact Malenkov and Khrushchev, finally reaching them at the Bolshoi Theater, where they were attending, along with other Presidium members, a performance of *The Decembrists*. (Ironically, this is an opera about an attempted coup d'état by a group of military officers.) Malenkov told Moskalenko, Serov, and Kruglov to come to the theater, where, rather comically, they met with the Presidium in a small room between acts. Responding to the complaints of the two MVD officers that Beria was not being treated properly, Moskalenko said: "I am not a jurist, or a Chekist. I don't know what is right or wrong in dealing with Beria. I am a military man and a Communist. You have told me that Beria is an enemy of the party and the people. Therefore we, including myself, treat him like an enemy. But we won't let anything harm him." Finally the dispute was resolved and Serov and Kruglov left. Moskalenko sat down with the party leaders and drank a toast to a "good, successful and, as Malenkov said, clean job."[96]

Chapter Ten

THE AFTERMATH

> There is of course elementary justice in the fate of Beria and his
> GPU [sic] associates, but it would have been more
> fitting if retribution had been meted out by his
> victims rather than his accomplices.
> (U.S. Ambassador to Moscow Charles Bohlen to the
> Secretary of State, December 1953)

FURTHER ARRESTS

FOR REASONS OF security Beria's captors decided to move him
from Lefortovo to an underground bunker at the staff headquarters of the Moscow Military District on Komissariat Lane, near the
embankment of the Moscow River. The two-story bunker had been built
under an apple orchard as a temporary command post during the war
and few people knew of its existence. Moskalenko, having replaced Artemev as chief of the Moscow Military District, remained in charge of Beria
with the group of men who had carried out his arrest. Not surprisingly,
Beria was under heavy guard.[1]

Meanwhile, the leadership was rounding up all of those close to Beria
in the MVD and elsewhere. His wife and twenty-eight-year-old son,
Sergo, were placed under house arrest at a dacha outside Moscow and
subsequently moved to different prisons, Nino to Butyrka and Sergo to
Lefortovo. Sergo, by this time married with two daughters and a son on
the way, was working in the field of weapons development as a physical
mathematician.[2] According to Nino, they had no idea what had happened: "At first we thought that a revolution had occurred and anticom-
munist forces had taken over the state." Then an interrogator began visiting Nino in Butyrka Prison, demanding evidence from her about her husband: "I told him that I would never give him any information, bad or
good. They didn't bother me again after this. I was in prison for more
than a year."[3]

On 29 June the CC Presidium met again and passed a resolution "On
the Organization of the Investigation in the Case of the Criminal, Anti-
party and Anti-state Activities of Beria."[4] Although formal charges under
the criminal code had not been made, the case was clearly a political one.
Therefore, according to the legal formalities to which even Stalin's judi-

cial system adhered, it was under the joint investigative purview of the USSR Procurator-General and the organs of state security, now part of the MVD. The Presidium, however, apparently decided that the MVD should have no formal authority for the case and that instead the USSR Procurator-General and Marshal Moskalenko would conduct the investigation. This was unusual, since Moskalenko was not in the judicial or legal apparatus and the military as such had no powers of criminal investigation.[5] The Procurator-General at the time, G. N. Safronov, had worked closely with Abakumov and was apparently not considered reliable, so he was dismissed.[6] As Khrushchev put it: "We had no confidence in the ability of the State Prosecutor to investigate Beria's case objectively, so we sacked him and replaced him with Comrade Rudenko."[7] R. A. Rudenko had been chief procurator in the Ukraine since 1944 and he knew Khrushchev well. It was hardly a coincidence that the two men in charge of the Beria case were linked to Khrushchev, since he was running things behind the scenes.

According to Khrushchev, the Presidium had initially decided to let Beria's close associate Merkulov remain free because he could be useful for the investigation. When they called him in for a talk, Merkulov, hoping to avoid arrest, agreed immediately to help the Central Committee with its investigation. He wrote two long letters to Khrushchev, dated 21 and 23 July, in which he provided detailed information on Beria's career, while at the same time trying to present himself in the best possible light by stressing his differences with Beria. "With every day, the more I think about the case, I remember the name Beria with great indignation and disgust, indignant that such a high-standing man could stoop so low," Merkulov wrote.[8] Khrushchev was especially interested in evidence that Beria had spied against the Bolsheviks in 1919. But Merkulov's reports offered nothing to support these charges. Indeed, Khrushchev found them "absolutely worthless . . . like a piece of fiction." Merkulov was then charged as an accomplice in Beria's crimes.[9] All of Beria's MVD protégés were arrested as well, including Vlodzimirskii, the Kobulov brothers, Goglidze, Sudoplatov, Kuzmichev, Sazykin, Eitingon, and Raikhman in the USSR MVD, and Meshik and Mil'shtein in the Ukraine.[10]

Of course the Georgian MVD was hit the hardest, because Beria's men dominated the organization there. Although rumors about Beria's fate had been flying in Moscow ever since he had failed to appear at the Bolshoi Theater on 27 June, those in Georgia apparently suspected nothing. Shortly after Beria's arrest, Iurii Krotkov, a playwright and journalist with close ties to many prominent Georgians, received an urgent midnight telephone call from Nora Tigranovna Dekanozova, the wife of Georgian MVD Chief Dekanozov. She was living in Moscow and had just learned that not only had Beria disappeared but that his close assistant Shariia and the head of his secretariat, Boris Liudvigov, had been arrested. She had tried to warn her husband in Tbilisi but was not successful. The next day he flew to Moscow with Bakradze and some other Georgian leaders for a conference and was arrested at Vnukovo airport, right in front of his wife.[11] Dekanozov's assistants—Karanadze, Tsereteli, and others—were then arrested in Tbilisi, along with party bureau member Mamulov and Georgian Minister of State Control Rapava.

Kruglov and Serov were not only spared but were promoted to chief and first deputy chief of the MVD, respectively. Although both had worked under Beria for several years and were on good terms with him, they were not part of his Georgian mafia and thus could dissociate themselves from him. Having had no knowledge of the plot against Beria beforehand, they were persuaded to cooperate in exchange for these promotions. Their cooperation may have been helped by the fact that Serov had worked in the Ukrainian NKVD when Khrushchev was there and had known him well. In early 1954, Khrushchev demonstrated his trust in Serov by appointing him to head the new security apparatus, the KGB, which was separated from the MVD and made an independent organization. Kruglov, whom Khrushchev says he hardly knew, lasted in his MVD post only until 1956 and then was removed.[12]

Kruglov and Serov had to keep rank-and-file MVD officers in line during this tense initial period, countering opposition to Beria's arrest. By all accounts Beria had enjoyed considerable support in the MVD. According to one source: "It must be said that many state security workers idolized Beria and were ready to go through fire and water for him. After all, for years he had ensured that they had a special standard of living, practically making them into 'supermen.'"[13] Concern over stability and morale within the MVD may have motivated the party leaders to avoid a large purge of this organization, limiting arrests and dismissals to senior officials close to Beria. Even in this group not everyone suffered. Mikhail Gvishiani, chief of the NKVD in the Maritime region was simply pensioned off and retired to his native Georgia.[14]

The July CC Plenum

The arrests of Beria and his supporters could not be publicized without the formal sanction of the Central Committee. Thus from 2 July to 7 July the approximately 216 full and candidate members of this body met in a secret session to hear Khrushchev and his colleagues explain their move against Beria eleven days earlier. The "top secret" stenographic report of this historic plenum remained locked in the party archives until it was published for the first time in early 1991.[15] It provides a fascinating and revealing picture of the events surrounding Beria's arrest, making it clear that Beria's opponents were still on very shaky ground at this point and were thus "pulling out all the stops" to contrive a criminal case against Beria and persuade Central Committee members that they had done the right thing.

The plenum was chaired by Khrushchev, but he left it to Malenkov to introduce the question of Beria and launch into the case against him. For Malenkov this must have been a difficult and awkward task, given that he had been closely associated with Beria for more than ten years. He explained rather feebly that, after Stalin's death, "we members of the Presidium began to be convinced that Beria was dishonest and, as became clear later, he used our desire for unity, for friendly work in a collective leadership, for his criminal purposes." He then went on to describe Beria's transgressions, including his use of the MVD to collect information on party members in the Ukraine, his efforts to normalize relations with Yugoslavia, and his stance on the German question.[16]

Why, Malenkov asked rhetorically, did they allow such behavior to go on for almost four months without doing anything? "Beria's true colors had to be discovered and descried. Everyone had to see how he was a destroyer and underminer of the unity of our Central Committee." He implied that, though they realized that Beria was acting wrongly, they were cautious because they wanted to preserve party unity. Malenkov went on to claim that when they confronted Beria with his wrongdoings on 26 June he had acted in a cowardly manner and avoided taking responsibility for them. So the Presidium decided to remove Beria from his posts and to revoke his party membership. Then realizing that they should not "stop halfway" with such an adventurist, they arrested Beria as an enemy of the party and the people. Malenkov did not attempt to explain how they justified this, given that the Presidium was not authorized to arrest anyone.[17]

Khrushchev, taking the floor after Malenkov, presented a similar rationalization for Beria's arrest, though he brought up additional accusations, such as Beria's spying on behalf of the Musavat, his alleged efforts to undermine the collective farm system, and so on. Khrushchev also denounced the MVD, which he said had gained vast, unjustified powers and had usurped the party's role. He allowed that even before Stalin died they could see that Beria was a "great intriguer," but he had great sway with Stalin and it would not have been a good idea to destroy the unity of the leadership by speaking out against him. Later Khrushchev defended the seemingly close relationship that he and Malenkov had had with Beria:

Some said: "How is it that Malenkov often walks arm-in-arm with Beria? Probably they're together, talking about me." And others probably said "Khrushchev also goes with him." [laughter]. This is true. They went out and I went along. Viacheslav Mikhailovich Molotov even said: "You go around and are always discussing something." I answered: "Nothing worthwhile, he says vile things, it's disgusting even to listen."[18]

Khrushchev went on to explain that these outings served a purpose, recounting an incident on the night before Beria's arrest:

On Thursday [June 25th] we—Malenkov, Beria and I—went home in one car, although we knew that he was an intriguer, trying to get me to scheme against Malenkov, and against others, but mainly Malenkov. Saying good-bye, he squeezed my hand, and I responded with a warm handshake: well, I thought, you fraud, this is the last handshake. Tomorrow at two o'clock we will be waiting for you. [Laughter] We won't shake your hand, we'll put your tail between your legs.[19]

As if to dispel doubts in his audience, Khrushchev claimed that this was the only way to deal with a "provocateur" like Beria. If they had told him beforehand that they did not like what he was doing, he would have inflicted reprisals on them. They had no choice but to feign friendship and then surprise him at the Presidium meeting. Khrushchev made a point of saying that the entire leadership had agreed on the Beria question— "Comrades Malenkov, Molotov, Bulganin, Kaganovich and all other comrades." Khrushchev dismissed the concern voiced by some that the news of Beria's arrest would appear as a sign of weakness in the party leadership, insisting that the outside world would see it as evidence of strength.[20] Khrushchev's words conveyed a distinct sense of insecurity. Whatever justifications he came up with for the sudden ouster and arrest of Beria, he was clearly aware that he and his colleagues were treading on thin ground when they presented this as a fait accompli to the Central Committee.

The next speaker was Molotov, who criticized the decisions that Beria had imposed on the Presidium after Stalin's death but was not quite as derisive toward his former colleague as Khrushchev had been. Although Molotov claimed that the 26 June Presidium meeting lasted for two and a half hours, during which time Beria was asked to explain his recent actions, he made it clear that the Presidium, or certain members thereof, had decided in advance to arrest him: "During this period [since Stalin's death] Beria was unrestrained and unduly presumptuous. As a result it was easy to expose him, arrest him and put him into prison."[21]

Not surprisingly, Molotov focused on Beria's foreign policy, in particular his handling of the German question and his efforts toward rapprochement with Yugoslavia. Beria, he said, had tried to conduct foreign policy independent of the Presidium, relying on the MVD instead. It seems that Beria had written a personal letter to A. Rankovich, Tito's immediate subordinate in the government of Yugoslavia, in which he re-

quested a secret meeting with Rankovich and Tito to normalize relations
between the Soviet Union and Yugoslavia. The letter was found in his
briefcase when he was arrested and held up as proof that Beria was, in
Molotov's words, an "agent of the class enemy."[22]

Bulganin went even further when he took the floor, claiming that Beria
was a spy who had been collecting information on the defensive capabili-
ties of various branches of the armed forces with the aim of passing it on
to the Soviet Union's enemies. He then urged that the MVD's powers be
reduced and its leading personnel purged. Moreover, the MVD should be
a civilian, not a militarized, ministry. Why, he asked, was it necessary for
the MVD to have armed troops? Was it not enough that the government
had a regular army, with generals, officers, and soldiers?[23] This suggestion must have evoked a favorable response from the military men in the
audience.

The next Presidium member to speak, Kaganovich, took up where Bulganin left off: "We are not talking about political deviation from the
party line, but about a dangerous, counterrevolutionary, adventurist plot
against the party and government." This was the first time that the term
counterrevolutionary had been used to describe Beria's actions, thus indicating to Central Committee members that Beria was to be charged with
treason. Apparently the Presidium had decided to present the accusations
against Beria gradually, in order to test the reactions of the Central Committee. Though Kaganovich launched into a scathing denunciation of
Beria, he pointedly disassociated himself from the decision to arrest him,
making it clear that Malenkov, Khrushchev, Molotov, and Bulganin were
the instigators and that he was in the Urals at the time these plans were
made. This prompted Malenkov to interrupt him hastily with a reminder:
"But when we told Comrade Kaganovich he unconditionally, immediately accepted the decision, like we all did."[24] Perhaps Kaganovich was
hedging his bets, in case the Central Committee opposed the Presidium's
action against Beria, though this was unlikely.

As might be expected, given his opposition to Beria's ouster, Mikoian
was not called on to speak until late in the proceedings, by which time the
accusations against Beria had been drummed into the audience repeatedly. Whatever his views on Beria, Mikoian had no choice but to go along
with the Presidium decision. It would have been unthinkable for him to
do otherwise. So he dutifully contributed some additional information to
back up the case against his former comrade. He said that when he first
heard the charge that Beria had worked for the Musavat at a 1937 CC
plenum he had assumed that Beria was carrying out an assignment for the
Bolshevik party. He realized now, however, that the charge was probably
true, especially since Beria had never been able to come up with proof that
he was actually working for the Bolsheviks. But Mikoian was equivocal
on this issue, even noting at one point, "We do not yet have direct facts

that show whether or not he was a spy, whether or not he received instructions from foreign bosses."[25]

Mikoian also discussed how Beria interfered with economic agreements made by the Soviet Union with Czechoslovakia and India and how he deliberately tried to prevent the Kremlin leadership from taking measures to improve agriculture. But he again seemed vague. The latter charge was to figure in the official indictment of Beria, though how Beria did this was not specified. Mikoian mentioned that the Presidium was anxious to raise agricultural output and recognized that this would have entailed increasing prices so as to give peasants an incentive to produce more. But, he claimed, when they discussed various proposals Beria blocked them. Probably they disagreed about how much to raise prices, with Beria pushing for more concessions to the countryside. This would have been consistent with his attitude toward collectivization in East Germany.

A host of other party and government figures were called forth to testify about Beria's evil deeds, often painting the most lurid of pictures. CC Secretary N. N. Shatalin discussed evidence found in a search of Beria's office of his relations with women: women's garments, letters, and so forth. He cited testimony from Beria's former bodyguard, Sarsikov (neglecting to mention that he was in Butyrka Prison), noting that Sarsikov had a long list of women with whom Beria was having sexual relations. He also could prove that Beria had fathered several illegitimate children and had contracted syphilis.[26] As for the charges that Beria raped young girls, these were not mentioned at the plenum but came up later at the trial.

Among those who spoke were Beria's protégés, including Bakradze, the recently appointed chairman of the Georgian Council of Ministers. Though he had been a strong follower of Beria, singling him out for fulsome praise at the April 1953 plenum of the Georgian Central Committee, this did not prevent him from denouncing his mentor in an effort to save his own skin. Beria, he said, had achieved the top party post in Georgia in 1931 by intriguing against others and by currying Stalin's favor. When he left the republic to take up his position in Moscow he placed his "understudies" Shariia and Rapava in charge. Bakradze claimed that Beria knew full well that the so-called Mingrelian conspiracy was a fabrication, but he did nothing until it suited him. On the contrary, he "added fuel to the fire" by appearing at the April 1952 Georgian party plenum. When he did decide to expose the plot, after Stalin died, he rehabilitated several persons who were actually criminals, like Shariia.[27]

No matter how strongly Bakradze denounced Beria, his association with him doomed his political career. He would soon be dismissed from his post and expelled from the party, along with other Georgian colleagues. But at least he was spared the ordeal of imprisonment and a public trial. This was not the case with Bagirov, who also attacked Beria at the plenum but was eventually arrested. Bagirov, whose name had been uttered in the same breath as Beria's for years, spoke at the plenum only briefly and was clearly on the defensive. He began by saying that he had been uneasy about what had occurred since Stalin's death and that when he learned from Khrushchev on 2 July that the Presidium had arrested Beria he felt greatly relieved. Beria, he said, was a chameleon, an enemy of the party and the people and so clever and sly that Bagirov had been unable to see his criminal nature even though they had known each other for more than thirty years: "I cannot explain it other than because of my unwarranted trustfulness and the dulling of my party, communist vigilance towards this double-dealer and scoundrel. This will serve as a serious lesson for me."[28]

Bagirov had little to reveal about Beria, except that he had been planning to establish, without the knowledge of the Central Committee, new awards to be given to republican officials. Bagirov was contrite, but he also tried to show that he had not been under Beria's thumb, as most party officials had assumed:

> During the fifteen years that Beria lived here, in Moscow (I don't want to deny my responsibility for my failure to see through this man, I am not trying to justify myself) I was at his home only once and that was with Comrade Stalin, and the rest of the time I met with Beria, as with other members of the Presidium, either at Stalin's place or at work. . . . I did not consider Beria the boss of Azerbaidzhan, although he tried to be.[29]

Bagirov's words were met with scornful rejoinders from the audience and finally Malenkov admonished him: "Comrade Bagirov, you are trying to justify yourself. You were close to Beria, but that is not the issue under discussion."[30] Bagirov then ended his testimony with an impassioned declaration of his devotion to party principles, but it was to be of little use. His fate was already decided.

Another of those who jumped on the anti-Beria bandwagon was G. A. Arutinov, first secretary of Armenia since 1937. He had been a Beria man par excellence, showing obeisance to his mentor by naming regions, squares, and buildings after him throughout Armenia and dutifully accepting his recommendations for party and state appointments. Now he tried to pretend that he had never been close to Beria. Arutinov admitted he had worked under Beria in Georgia during the 1930s, but he made a point of saying that he had not met with Beria for the past seven or eight years—a highly unlikely proposition considering they were both members of the CPSU Central Committee. After noting that he had detected negative traits in Beria many years earlier, Arutinov made an unexpected reference to the purges: "It is well known how many good party cadres Beria killed in Georgia in 1937, only because many of them would not recognize him."[31] This was a topic that Khrushchev and his colleagues had assiduously avoided, focusing instead on Beria's wrongdoings in his early career and after March 1953. They could hardly bring up the 1937–38 purges without raising questions about Stalin and about their own roles. Was this a subtle reminder to the leadership that they should not go too far in purging Beria's associates, lest they implicate themselves?

Although he had been Beria's deputy and had worked closely with him for years, Kruglov, now Beria's successor in the MVD, was reasonably confident when he spoke out against Beria. After thanking Khrushchev and his colleagues for exposing Beria as an enemy, Kruglov said that he had been concerned about Beria's behavior since Stalin's death. Before this, he explained, officials like himself, Serov, and Maslennikov had had little to do with Beria, since the MGB was separate from the MVD, where they worked. This of course was disingenuous.[32] During the war years all three of these men had worked directly under Beria in the NKVD, helping him to carry out a variety of operations, including mass deportations. But for the moment this had to be overlooked and when Kruglov's remarks evoked a cynical rejoinder from General S. K. Timoshenko, Malenkov broke in to remind him: "The Central Committee knows Comrade Kruglov, he came from the party apparatus. He had to put up with a lot. When the Central Committee needed something, he always obliged."[33]

Central Committee members could hardly ignore the glaring inconsistencies and outright untruths in the testimonies of the speakers who were marched up to the podium to say what they had been told to say. They must have realized that all this was simply an ex post facto attempt by Khrushchev and his colleagues to justify Beria's illegal arrest and to portray it as a moral victory for the party. As Konstantin Simonov, who attended the plenum, observed:

> Khrushchev told about how they had caught Beria on the very eve of his preparations to seize power. The word "caught" suited the character of Khrushchev's story, his temperament and the awful pleasure with which he related all this. . . . It was completely obvious to me when I listened to him that Khrushchev was the initiator in this red-handed catch, because he was shrewder, more talented, energetic and decisive than the others. On the other hand, he was helped by the fact that Beria underestimated Khrushchev, his qualities—his deeply natural, pure masculinity, his tenacious cunning, his common sense and his strength of character. Beria on the contrary, considered Khrushchev a round-headed fool, whom Beria, the master of intrigue, could wrap around his finger.[34]

Simonov went on to observe that it never would have entered anyone's head to take issue with what Khrushchev said. These Central Committee members were seasoned *apparatchiks* and bureaucrats, inured to the falsehoods that governed official Soviet life and accustomed to going along with pretenses for the sake of their political survival.

No one asked the Presidium members on whose authority they had arrested Beria or why they did not seek the prior approval of the Central Committee, as the rules dictated. Were they not guilty of the very same offense—circumventing the authority of the Central Committee—of which Beria was accused? No one questioned the legal basis of the charges against Beria or asked for proof of the accusations that were made. And no one inquired as to why Beria's perfidy and treachery had not been unmasked earlier, during the many years that Malenkov, Khrushchev, and the others had been on the closest of terms with him. It must have seemed strange that, during the months following Stalin's death, Beria was able to impose an array of new policies with no apparent obstacles. If they had all found Beria's program so objectionable, why had they done nothing about it? Surely the plenum participants realized that Beria's policies had not been opposed by the entire Presidium and suspected that the opposition to him was of recent vintage. But this was a docile group, trained in the best tradition of Stalinist obedience to the party line.

On 7 July 1953 the Central Committee unanimously approved a resolution calling for Beria's expulsion from the party and for his trial on criminal charges. They also passed resolutions expelling Bogdan Kobulov and Sergei Goglidze from candidate membership in the Central Committee, reinstating Semen Ignat'ev, an apparent perpetrator of the Doctors' Plot, to full membership and elevating Marshal Zhukov from candidate to full member, a reward he had earned in the Beria operation. The resolution on Beria took the form of a secret letter from the Central Committee to lower party organs stating, after a lengthy introduction, that Beria had been unmasked by the Presidium as an "agent of international imperialism." The letter enumerated the criminal acts that Beria allegedly committed: he had tried to promote his own power by discrediting his colleagues in the leadership; he had tried to place the MVD above the party; he had ordered the MVD, without the party's knowledge, to fabricate materials on party members; he had tried to foment animosity and hostility among the various national groups; he had tried to steer the GDR off the course of socialism and make it into a bourgeois state; he had tried to establish personal ties with Tito and Rankovich in Yugoslavia; and, in 1919, he had served as a spy for the Musavat intelligence service, later hiding this from the party.[35]

REACTIONS AND REPERCUSSIONS

The first news the outside world heard of Beria's fate (though there was much speculation by this time) came on 10 July, when *Pravda* reported briefly that a Central Committee plenum had taken place "recently" and that, following a report by Malenkov on the "criminal anti-Party and anti-state activities of L. P. Beria," the Central Committee had decided to expel him from the party ranks. *Pravda* went on to report that the Presidium of the USSR Supreme Soviet had resolved to remove Beria from his ministerial post and to transfer the criminal case against him to the USSR Supreme Court. The announcement did not specify what charges had been leveled against Beria under the Criminal Code.[36] The next day *Pravda* published an editorial endorsing the resolution and citing positive reactions from local party organizations. *Pravda* reported on further response to the arrest on 16 July, when it gave a brief account of a meeting of party activists in the Ministry of Defense, who had unanimously approved the actions taken by the Central Committee against Beria. This, of course, not only demonstrated military solidarity with Khrushchev and the anti-Beria forces, but it also gave the military new prominence by acknowledging that it had a say in party politics, an impression reinforced by Marshal Zhukov's promotion to the Central Committee. This prominence, it seems, was the quid pro quo exacted from Khrushchev by the generals in return for their support.

Although much of the military leadership may have welcomed Beria's fall, this feeling was not necessarily shared by all members of the party and government. Of course Beria was not popular and, according to Simonov, some people had worried that he had accumulated too much power after Stalin's death and were therefore relieved to hear he was ousted.[37] But his reform policies had also won him support, particularly from those in the non-Russian republics, many of whom had benefited by receiving promotions. Further, the announcement of his sudden arrest undoubtedly aroused doubts about the stability of the Kremlin leadership.

Khrushchev and his colleagues were deeply concerned about the response from rank and file party members and from the population as a whole. After announcing Beria's arrest they ordered party activists at all levels to organize meetings to denounce Beria. Khrushchev and Malenkov took great pains to monitor the reactions, pouring over reports that came in from party officials throughout the country. Although many voiced support for the CC decision, many were also skeptical. According to one report, some party workers expressed doubts about the truth of the charges against Beria, asking "who can we believe?" Some felt he was arrested because of his Georgian nationalism, rather than because he was a traitor. In Moscow itself, according to Moscow's party secretary Mikhailov, party workers were asking a lot of questions and did not seem to believe the official explanations.[38]

Whatever their views on Beria, party and state functionaries had no choice but to follow the dictates of the leadership. Immediately after his arrest was announced, all vestiges of Beria's role as a political leader disappeared. His portraits were swiftly removed from public places and his name erased from official publications. Prisoners in MVD camps, where pictures of Beria had been especially prominent, reported that the pictures were taken down on the day his arrest was announced.[39]

The reaction of the average Soviet citizen to the news about Beria was difficult to gauge, given the reluctance of most people to express views on politics, but apparently skepticism was prevalent. According to Western intelligence reports anxiety was widespread in the first few days, as rumors spread of a military coup and a possible purge. When things settled down, many Soviet citizens expressed indifference to Beria's arrest, attributing it correctly to yet another power struggle at the top. Few believed that the charges against him had substance, with the possible exception of his attempts to use the MVD to increase his own power. But they did not feel that his fate would have much effect on their lives. They were primarily concerned with their struggle to maintain themselves economically. Although Soviet citizens had noticed a general relaxation in the regime's policies after Stalin's death, along with an increase in the availability of consumer goods, few attributed these policies specifically to Beria. This is hardly surprising, since only those in the upper echelons of the party and government could be expected to have any grasp on the inner workings of the leadership. And Beria's long association with the dreaded Soviet police made him an unlikely reformer in most people's eyes.[40]

In Georgia, however, where Beria had been revered as a national hero, the reaction was different. According to a Russian student who was vacationing in a small Georgian village at the time, the news about Beria had a noticeable impact:

> His portraits, as was the custom in Georgia, had hung everywhere: at the post office, the cafeteria, even the store. On the morning of 10 July I set out for the famous wine-making *sovkhoz* [state farm], Salkhino. And on the bus the first thing to strike my eyes was a gaping empty place next to the portrait of Stalin. . . . A Georgian sitting alone in the bus, having caught my startled expression and noticed my smile, looked at me with hostility and turned away. On the way back, at six in the evening, I changed from a small bus that went around the mountain roads to a large one, that went on the highway. The driver, a Georgian, half turned to me, and looking off into a corner, asked "Sad?" "Sad," I answered. "They took away." He didn't say what they took away, but I decided that the time had came to be daring and affirmed: "They took away." He rung his hands hopelessly: "The last support of the Georgian people has fallen." And he didn't say another word for the whole trip.[41]

The next day the village square, normally filled with Georgians drinking and arguing, was empty and an aura of uneasiness prevailed. A day or two later things were back to normal on the surface, but "traces of the

Beria affair struck one's eyes everywhere in Georgia that summer." On the signboard for the Beria Sovkhoz of Youth Culture near Gagra, Beria's name had been erased but one could still faintly make it out. Beria Streets were now Malenkov Streets, yet Malenkov's name appeared in bright paint, while no one bothered to repaint the word *street*, which had been written years ago and was by contrast dull and worn.[42]

In Tbilisi, according to foreign diplomats, everything appeared normal and quiet on 10 July. The only noticeable change was the removal of Beria's name and picture from places all over the city. When asked about Beria, Georgians were closemouthed, though they undoubtedly had much to say in private.[43] To be sure, Beria was not beloved by the Georgian people. The bloody purges over which he had presided were still strong in their memories and his name continued to evoke fear. But he was their countryman and his public disgrace tarnished the image of Georgia. Moreover, however ruthless he had been, he may have been seen by some as their spokesman, the representative of Georgian interests in Moscow. In short, just as some Georgians had accepted Stalin as their hero and absorbed the legend built around him, so too had they accepted Beria, albeit to a lesser extent. Evidence to support this hypothesis came almost three years later, in March 1956, when riots and demonstrations broke out in Tbilisi as a protest against Moscow's rule, and portraits of both Stalin and Beria were seen waving in the crowds.[44]

Among those Georgians who had been personally associated with Beria, the reaction was panic and disavowal. Iurii Krotkov recalled one particularly telling incident:

> I telephoned the Moscow-based Georgian dramatist, Georgii Mdivani. Speaking Russian with a strong accent, though he considered himself a "great Russian writer," he shouted furiously into the receiver when I asked him, "Well, Georgii, how is your Lavrentii Pavlovich getting along?" "*My*, why *my*? What rubbish! I always said that Beria was an abomination, a fraud, a scoundrel, a bandit and a seducer of young girls! That villain should be shot!" Not long before this Mdivani had lauded Beria at every opportunity as the greatest student of Lenin and Stalin and the most outstanding communist of our time. He called him an "unswerving Chekist," and always bragged about his acquaintance with Beria, claiming that he could call him anytime at the ministry and ask to see him.[45]

Georgian Prime Minister Bakradze continued to take the lead in denouncing Beria, giving the main report on his alleged crimes at a joint session of the Georgian Central Committee and the Tbilisi Party Committee, held on 13–14 July 1953.[46] Bakradze assailed Beria as a "foul criminal" and an "agent of international capitalism," for whom no punishment would be too severe. Others who spoke at the plenum, presumably against Beria, were First Secretary Mirtskhulava and bureau members Baramiia, Sturua, and Zodelava, all of whom had been brought back into the party leadership—and in the case of Baramiia, released from prison—under Beria's auspices in April. These men, it seems, were allowed to remain in their posts long enough to purge Beria's MVD "accomplices" (all under arrest) from the Georgian party apparatus. According to certain unnamed speakers at the plenum, Beria "pushed forward workers of the MVD on the basis of their personal devotion to him, selecting suspicious individuals, alien to the party," types such as Rapava (whom Bakradze had vindicated in a speech to the Georgian Supreme Soviet on 15 April), Rukhadze, Mamulov, Dekanozov, Shariia, Kobulov, and Mil'shtein. The plenum removed Dekanozov and Mamulov from the Central Committee bureau and, as a sign of the army's new influence, elected Major General P. I. Efimov a member of that body.[47]

The reprieve was brief for Bakradze and the other erstwhile Beria associates who had joined the ranks of his opponents. On 20 September 1953, a Georgian CC plenum, attended by CC CPSU Secretary Shatalin, removed Bakradze, Mirtskhulava, Baramiia, Zodelava, and Sturua from the CC bureau and expelled them from the CC. Mirtskhulava's replacement as first secretary, V. P. Mzhavanadze, though a Georgian, was from the Khrushchev camp. He had been a political commissar in the Soviet Army since the early thirties and after the war had served in Ukrainian military districts.[48] Mzhavanadze was joined in the Georgian CC bureau by two other military men: A. I. Antonov, commander of the Transcaucasian Military District (replacing Efimov, who was unexpectedly dismissed) and A. N. Inauri, a regimental commander during and after the war, who had become head of the MVD.[49] This was an unprecedented display of military presence in the political arena.

Those who had lost their jobs in April 1953 when Beria exposed the "Mingrelian Affair" were quick to appeal to Moscow for reinstatement. On 18 July former Georgian party chief Mgeladze wrote a personal letter to Khrushchev, claiming that his relations with Beria had always been distant and that he had never followed Beria's instructions. Noting that he had been out of work a long time, he begged Khrushchev to give him a job. A few weeks later, apparently desperate, Mgeladze sent Khrushchev a telegram asking him what he had decided to do. On 18 August, Khrushchev came through and Mgeladze received a job as director of a state winery in Georgia.[50] Two other victims of Beria's revenge, Z. N. Ketshoveli and V. D. Budzhiasvili, wrote to Khrushchev and Malenkov in July to report what they knew about Beria's evil deeds and asked to be readmitted into the party, which they were.[51]

Meanwhile, the purge of Beria's followers spread throughout the Georgian party hierarchy. New secretaries were appointed to head the organizations in Abkhazia, Adzharia, and Tbilisi. By February 1954,

3,011 apparatchiks who were in republican, regional, and city party committees in September 1952 had been expelled.[52] These were not, however, Stalinist-type purges, in that they did not involve widespread arrests and executions. Only those with close ties to Beria were imprisoned and most simply lost their jobs and party cards.[53]

The purges extended to other parts of Transcaucasia, since the entire area had been Beria's fiefdom. On 18 July 1953 a joint plenum of the Azerbaidzhan CC and the Baku Party Committee dismissed Bagirov from the CC.[54] He was charged with a "shameful style of leadership" and "crude, dictatorial management"—fairly innocuous offenses considering the charges leveled against other Beria men. Bagirov, who had recently traded his party position for that of chairman of the Azerbaidzhan Council of Ministers, was shunted off to be the deputy chief of an oil drilling combine in the Kubyshev district of Azerbaidzhan.[55] It is not clear when he was arrested, but it may not have been for another year or so. His trial did not take place until April 1956.

Armenian Party First Secretary Arutinov lost his job in August 1953, and was later expelled from the party for his alleged failure to purge Beria followers from the Armenian party apparatus, as ordered by Moscow.[56] Unlike Bagirov, Arutinov was spared a public trial. Indeed, he may not have been imprisoned at all; he was reported as being the head of a state farm in Armenia in December 1954.[57] Although Kremlin leaders had taken their time in moving against Bagirov and Arutinov, this did not reflect ambivalence about whether they deserved reprisals. In fact, Khrushchev had apparently instructed Ignat'ev to collect evidence against both Bagirov and Arutinov as far back as March 1953. After the July CC plenum the investigations were stepped up and damning materials against both men began pouring into the CC Secretariat.[58] But Moscow had to be cautious, since the immediate arrests of these non-Russian republican leaders could have stirred up nationalist resentment and made the new regime look too uncompromising on the nationalities issue. Also, their real crimes were that they had presided over the purges that had decimated native elites in the 1930s. But, for the reasons mentioned above, Khrushchev and his allies wanted to avoid the issue of the purges. It was only after February 1956, when Khrushchev gave his secret speech denouncing Stalin, that the Kremlin's policy changed and the 1937–38 terror was openly discussed.

THE IMPACT ABROAD

Not surprisingly Beria's fall also had strong repercussions in the MVD's foreign intelligence directorate. A new chief, A. S. Paniushkin, was brought in to replace the man Beria had appointed three months earlier,

V. S. Riasnoi. Paniushkin was no stranger to foreign operations; he had served in diplomatic posts, including that of ambassador to China and to the United States. But he was not linked to the Beria group.[59] The news of Beria's arrest reportedly caused dismay among Soviet agents abroad. In late July 1953, for example, U.S. observers in Vienna reported a "more than usual grim-visaged appearance" in the Soviet delegation to the Allied Council, which included MVD officers under diplomatic cover. The deputy commissioner, Kudriavtsev, who had earlier been involved with the Canadian atomic-spy ring, lacked his usual self-assurance and another suspected MVD agent was said to have been exceptionally churlish. Significantly, the Soviet military did not share the despondency exhibited by the civilian personnel.[60]

Vladimir Petrov, an MVD agent in Australia at the time, recalled a similar reaction among his colleagues at the Soviet Embassy in Canberra:

> We had a Party meeting in the Canberra Embassy at which all these charges were solemnly read out. No one commented. . . . What is certain is that Beria was the loser in a naked struggle for supreme power, which is not yet ended. Beria, by seniority, record, abilities, achievements, was the most natural successor to Stalin among the leaders who remained.[61]

Petrov and his wife defected in Australia as a result of Beria's fall: "It had a direct and decisive influence on my own fate and my decision to escape from the Soviet service." And he was not the only MVD agent to make such a decision. One of his colleagues defected while in Japan for similar reasons.[62] In order to prevent such defections the Kremlin recalled a number of MVD agents from abroad. In the Soviet Embassy in Rome, for example, several foreign agents were sent home immediately after Beria's arrest and replaced by "Kruglov men."[63]

The impact in Soviet satellite states was no less profound. In East Germany, according to the communist official Heinz Brandt, the news of Beria's arrest was at first hailed with satisfaction, even by those party officials who favored reform:

> We cracked our bad jokes about him without even remotely suspecting that with Beria's fall the scales had been tipped against Herrnstadt and Jendretzky and the new course and for Walter Ulbricht. Although only a few people knew it, Beria, along with Malenkov, had been the principal initiator of the new course as a policy of coexistence, so the German reformers were now doomed along with their master in the Kremlin.[64]

Zaisser and Herrnstadt were expelled from the Politburo and the Central Committee, accused of having pursued a policy of compromise that threatened communism in East Germany, and Jendretsky was removed from the Politburo. Ulbricht, who had opposed the "new course" was now secure in his position as party leader, although he was prevented by Moscow from throwing his opponents into jail and from abandoning the policy of relaxation.[65]

In Hungary, Communist party leader Matyas Rakosi tried to use Beria's fall as a pretext for putting a stop to the "new course," which had been imposed by Moscow. But his efforts were successfully resisted by government leader Imre Nagy and others, apparently with Moscow's support. This suggests that Kremlin leaders, although reluctant to go as far and as fast as Beria proposed, were not against some reform in Eastern Europe.[66] Beria's arrest also caused a shake-up in the North Korean Communist Party. At the beginning of August 1953 no fewer than ten party leaders were purged, and shortly thereafter a top government leader committed suicide.[67] Czechoslovakia, on the other hand, whose leaders had managed to resist reforms after Stalin died, was much less affected by the events in the Kremlin. Political trials and repressions continued unabated throughout 1953.[68]

As for the noncommunist world, the Beria affair caused a tremendous shock wave. It dominated the headlines in virtually every leading Western newspaper and gave rise to intense speculation among journalists and government officials. U.S. Ambassador to Moscow Charles Bohlen, for example, who was vacationing in France when the news broke, immediately flew back to Washington to confer with Secretary of State John Foster Dulles.[69] Coming so quickly after Stalin's death and so unexpectedly, Beria's fall led most observers to conclude that the Soviet regime was weak and unstable. Yet many disagreed about what policy course the Kremlin would follow in the future. Those who connected Beria with the recent "soft policy" at home and abroad, worried that the Kremlin would adopt a much stiffer attitude, while others argued that the new leadership could not afford another policy shift. No one took the charges against Beria seriously; most realized that he was the victim of a power struggle. Yet few Western analysts deduced that Khrushchev had been Beria's chief opponent. Instead they attributed his ouster to Malenkov and assumed that the latter was the strong man at the helm.[70] In fact, Malenkov's power had increased very little because Khrushchev had now emerged to fill the vacuum left by Beria's departure. He was to be no less ambitious and forceful in pushing through his agenda than Beria had been.

THE TRIAL OF BERIA AND HIS MEN

In the months that followed the announcement of Beria's arrest, his name was barely mentioned in the Soviet press. At an August session of the USSR Supreme Soviet, which approved the official decree removing Beria, few references were made to him. Bakradze, still trying to save his own skin, was the only deputy to bring up the affair. Malenkov's speech, delivered on 8 August, was devoted primarily to economic questions.[71] He discussed several new measures to improve the lot of the collective farmer and raise productivity in the countryside, thus continuing with the policy of concessions that Beria advocated. A few theoretical articles in legal and party journals mentioned the charges against Beria, but nothing was said about when the case would come to trial.[72]

Behind the scenes, however, the party leadership was feverishly gathering information to buttress its case. In addition to commissioning reports from Beria associates—such as Merkulov, Shtemenko, and Zimianin—they had undoubtedly instructed interrogators to question Beria's imprisoned comrades day and night. And the CC Secretariat was amassing denunciations of Beria from a variety of sources.[73] Though they put up a wall of silence, Kremlin leaders were clearly preoccupied with the Beria case.

Suddenly, on 17 December 1953 the Soviet press announced that the USSR Procurator-General had completed its investigation and turned Beria and his six "accomplices" over to the Supreme Court for trial by a special judicial session in accordance with the procedural law of 1 December 1934. (This law applied to cases of "terrorism" and provided that neither defendants nor counsel were permitted in the courtroom; no appeals were allowed; and the sentences were to be carried out immediately after the verdict was pronounced.[74]) According to the announcement, Beria had forged a treacherous group of conspirators—codefendants Merkulov, Dekanozov, Kobulov (Bogdan), Goglidze, Meshik, and Vlodzimirskii—with the criminal aim of using the organs of the MVD, both central and local, "to seize power and liquidate the Soviet worker-peasant system for the purpose of restoring capitalism and the domination of the bourgeoisie."[75]

The announcement went on to say that Beria had tried to undermine the collective farm system, to cause food shortages in the country, and to sow discord among the peoples of the USSR. He had also, in 1919–20, committed treason by serving as an intelligence agent for the Musavat government and then establishing secret contact with Mensheviks. The indictment charged that in subsequent years Beria had established secret, criminal contacts with foreign intelligence services and with Georgian Mensheviks abroad. In addition he had persecuted Ordzhonikidze and his family and, along with his accomplices, had murdered the Chekist M. S. Kedrov because he possessed materials on Beria's criminal past. Beria and the six others were indicted for treason, terrorism, and participation in a counterrevolutionary, conspiratorial group, crimes enumerated in articles 58-1, 58-8 and 58-11, of the RSFSR (Russian Republic)

Criminal Code. In addition, Beria was charged with having been a secret agent of a counterrevolutionary government during the civil war period (article 58-13). The punishment for these crimes, for those with military ranks, which all the defendants had, was death by shooting.

Khrushchev had in fact already sent the text of the indictment in the Beria case to local party leaders on 15 December 1953. Anxious about how the party rank and file would react, he wanted local leaders to do groundwork by calling meetings to discuss it.[76] Once the indictment was published, the press launched into a campaign of denunciations against the Beria group. In a spirit reminiscent of the purges of the thirties, headlines such as "Ever Higher Rises the Wave of National Anger" and "No Mercy to Beria and His Gang" featured in the papers, which reported on popular meetings and demonstrations against the accused traitors. Party officials sent their impressions of these meetings and the general public reaction to the announcement to Khrushchev.

Meanwhile the trial, which lasted from 18 to 23 December and was held *in camera*, was already underway. The head of the Special Judicial Panel that heard the case was Khrushchev's comrade Marshal Konev, who had helped to stir up the "Doctors' Plot" by claiming that he had been poisoned. Others on the panel were Moskalenko; N. M. Shvernik, chairman of the All-Union Central Council of Trade Unions; E. L. Zeidin, first deputy chairman of the USSR Supreme Court; N. A. Mikhailov, secretary of the Moscow Oblast Party Committee; L. A. Gromov, chairman of the Moscow City Court; K. F. Lunev, first deputy minister of internal affairs, and M. I. Kuchava, chairman of the Georgian Council of Trade Unions.

The composition of the Special Panel was unusual, to say the least. It was neither a military tribunal—a special court comprised of military officers—nor a proper Soviet court. As Stalin's biographer Isaac Deutscher observed, it was a "political tribunal par excellence."[77] Aside from Zeidin and Gromov, the panel members had no judicial expertise. The presence of Konev and Moskalenko was presumably designed to demonstrate military support for the trial, but it is nonetheless curious that Moskalenko would serve both as investigator and judge, which even by Stalinist standards was a flagrant violation of judicial procedure. Moreover, according to Moskalenko's reminiscences, he worked day and night for six months investigating the case, together with Rudenko, yet he was commander of the Moscow Military District at the time.[78]

Shvernik, who was also close to Khrushchev, had been removed from his post as chairman of the USSR Supreme Soviet at Beria's instigation after Stalin died, so he had a strong incentive to serve as Beria's judge.[79] Lunev was another Khrushchevite. He had worked under Khrushchev in Moscow in the late forties and was now keeping an eye on things for

Khrushchev at the MVD.[80] As for Mikhailov, he was considered by most to be a Malenkov man, so perhaps he was included on the panel as the latter's representative.[81] Finally, Kuchava was the "token Georgian," an obscure party official in Georgia until he was suddenly made Trade Unions chief there after the Beria affair broke.[82] The verdict was reported in the press on 24 December. The Special Panel confirmed all the charges in the indictment and sentenced all the accused to the highest criminal punishment. They were shot that very evening. According to the transcript of the trial, which emerged from the archives of the military procuracy and was published in excerpts in 1989–91, Beria and his codefendants were present during the proceedings and even testified. Yet the procedural law under which they were tried (article 58-1) specified that neither the accused nor his representative should be allowed in court. Moreover, the brief press reports of the trial that appeared at the time did not mention the participation of the defendants, nor did Moskalenko's account.

These anomalies led some observers to suggest that Beria was already dead at the time of the trial. Khrushchev himself contributed to this speculation by giving conflicting versions of Beria's death. In May 1956 he told a delegation of French socialists that Beria had been killed at the Presidium meeting on 26 June. He repeated this story to Italian communist leaders in September 1956, claiming that Beria had been strangled by Presidium members when they confronted him. Then two days later he changed his story and reverted back to the official version. He even played parts of a taped transcript of the trial to bolster this version, but the Italians regarded the transcript as a fake.[83] Svetlana Alliluyeva later claimed, on the basis of information from the chief army surgeon, A. A. Vishnevsky, that Beria was executed a few days after his arrest, following a hurried, staged trial.[84] Rumors that Beria had been killed in June 1953 circulated widely in Moscow, fueling additional stories in the Western press.[85]

Of course, speculation about the Beria case was not discussed in the Soviet press until the era of *glasnost* began in the late 1980s. The publication at that time of excerpts from the transcript of the trial may have been intended to quell doubts about the official version, but it did not. Georgian journalist Georgii Bezirgani, for example, questioned the authenticity of the trial transcripts, pointing out one puzzling aspect of the official version of Beria's fate. The trial reportedly took place in the bunker of the staff headquarters of the Moscow Military District, where Beria had been held secretly since June. Here, too, he was shot and his body burned. Yet the other six were said to have been shot in the Lubianka. Why, asked Bezirgani, would the authorities deem it necessary to transport them all the way across town to execute them? Why were they, too, not shot in the military bunker?[86]

As Bezirgani argued, it is difficult to understand why the new leadership would wait six months to kill Beria and his supporters. It could hardly have been to render justice by gathering and analyzing the facts of the case. As with earlier political trials under Stalin, the verdict was decided on well beforehand and the charges were largely unfounded. Whatever Beria's many crimes, they did not include spying for foreign governments or sabotaging agriculture. Furthermore, Bezirgani pointed out, it was politically dangerous to keep Beria alive:

> Let us remember that this was a tense time. The political barometer could begin at any moment to waver in any direction. Did it make any practical sense to keep this "marshal in cast-off soldiers clothes" in the basement of the district staff headquarters? The Bolsheviks—let's give them their due—were above all pragmatic, practical, hard realists. They didn't care the slightest rap about any procedures or formalities. Moreover, I am sure that as long as Lavrentii Beria was living, even under the heaviest guard in the brick army bunker, neither Malenkov, Khrushchev, Molotov, nor Mikoian could sleep peacefully at their private dachas.[87]

Beria's son Sergo also believes that his father was dead before the trial. He recalled that on 26 June he heard from a friend that there was gunfire at his father's house. When he arrived a guard told him that he had seen a body carried out on a stretcher. Sergo assumed this was his father, shot dead. Some years later, he claimed, Shvernik, one of the above-mentioned judges at his father's trial, told him he had never seen Beria alive after 26 June.[88] If Sergo Beria's account is accurate, which is by no means certain, or if Beria was interrogated for several days or weeks and then executed, the transcripts of the trial had to have been falsified or put together from doctored tapes. The alleged trial testimony would have come from statements made by the defendants during the investigation. What about the supposed eyewitness accounts of the trial? I. G. Zub, for example, who was part of the arrest party and allegedly sat in on the trial, mentioned Beria's presence in an interview in 1987.[89] Kuchava, a member of the Judicial Panel, was interviewed in 1990, at age eighty-four, and offered a brief account from his diary, claiming that Beria was present at the trial:

> Not only in Georgia but throughout the country there is a legend that Beria was not at the trial, that it was someone made up as Beria. This lie has no basis. Beria was at the trial, gave testimony and on 23 December said his final word. . . . I and all those others present could see perfectly clearly that it was actually Beria and not his double who sat on the bench of the accused.[90]

Aside from a short comment on Beria's behavior at the trial—"He manifested nervousness, stubbornness, deviousness. Unlike the other defendants he asked the court many times to spare his life, to give his request to Khrushchev"—Kuchava's observations added nothing new and seemed to be taken directly from the case records.

Although it is feasible that the accounts of both Zub and Kuchava were fabricated, one additional piece of evidence suggests that a trial took place and that Beria was present. Members of the diplomatic colony in Moscow discovered that a building on the banks of the Moscow River was under intensive guard by infantry units during the time that coincided with the latter sessions of Beria's interrogation and with his trial.[91] As mentioned above, the staff headquarters of the Moscow Military District was on the river embankment, so this could have been the building in question.

If Beria was still alive in December 1953—something we can never be sure of until the archives on his trial are opened—this does not explain why the leadership devoted so much effort to documenting the case, putting together forty volumes of evidence and testimony, when the verdict was a foregone conclusion. The verdict made no mention whatsoever of Beria's real crimes, the murder and repression of thousands of innocent victims during the purges and after. Yet, judging from the published excerpts from these volumes, these crimes were a focal point of the investigation, which provided detailed descriptions of how Beria and his colleagues ordered beatings, torture, and executions. It is possible that Khrushchev intended early on to have a public trial of Beria and to use these materials to expose the excesses of the purges with a view to eventually discrediting the Old Guard—Malenkov, Molotov, Kaganovich, and others—but then he decided that this was politically inexpedient.

However much Khrushchev had depended on the military to help in defeating Beria, he cannot have relished the idea of turning the entire investigation over to the generals, so the MVD had been drawn in behind the scenes. Serov had signed orders for the arrests of Beria's colleagues and for the searches of their premises, while Kruglov had collected evidence from Beria's detractors.[92] The majority of those arrested ended up in the Lubianka or Butyrka, both MVD prisons. The MVD also carried out the investigations of other Beria associates, whose criminal trials took two and a half years to complete, apparently because members of the Old Guard were resisting a public exposure of their crimes. The first trial was that of Riumin, sentenced to death by shooting in July 1954 for, among other crimes, "unjustified arrests of a number of Soviet citizens."[93] Then, at the end of December 1954, the verdict in the trial of Abakumov and four of his former MGB deputies was announced. They were charged with various state crimes and conspiratorial acts, but the most significant charge was that of falsifying the "Leningrad Case," at Beria's behest. This case had not been mentioned in Beria's trial and that it was brought up at this point was an ominous sign for Malenkov, who had been deeply involved.[94]

Rapava, Rukhadze, and six other former Georgian police officials were tried publicly almost a year later and pronounced guilty of high treason, terrorism, and participation in counterrevolutionary organizations—under the direction of Beria. Here, for the first time, the indictment mentioned victims of the Georgian purges: Bediia, Orakhelashvili, and a few others. All the defendants were shot except one former interrogator, who was sentenced to twenty-five years in prison, and Beria's bodyguard, Nadaraia, who for some reason got off with a sentence of only ten years.[95]

The final trial was that of Bagirov, which took place from 12 to 26 April 1956 in open session in the city of Baku. The charges were familiar—treason, terrorism, participation in a counterrevolutionary organization. Bagirov and five other defendants were found guilty and all but two, former MVD officials S. F. Emelianov and A. S. Atakishev, were shot.[96] A new dimension emerged here, however, in that a long list of victims of repression in Azerbaidzhan was presented in the announcement of the verdict. The acknowledgment that there had been widespread purges in the Stalin era was no coincidence, since Khrushchev had just given his famous secret speech on Stalin's crimes two months earlier. As it turned out, he later used de-Stalinization to expose the part his colleagues played in the purges and even tied them to the Bagirov case. Malenkov, Molotov, and Kaganovich were accused at the Twenty-second Party Congress in 1961 of having given protection to Bagirov.[97]

The trials of Abakumov, Rukhadze, Rapava, and Bagirov were not conducted according to the draconian procedural law of 1 December 1934, although the Supreme Soviet did not repeal this law until 19 April 1956. Judging from the public announcements, these trials were open and defense and counsel were permitted to attend. Of course it made little difference, because the accused were deemed guilty beforehand, but at least the new leadership showed an inclination to discard some of the most repressive features of the Stalinist system.

Another sign of moderation was that the families of those shot in connection with the Beria case were treated rather mildly in comparison with the Stalinist days. Most, including Dekanozov's family, were sent off to Central Asia for a year or two and then allowed to return home.[98] Only Nino Beria and her son had been imprisoned. She recalled that, although the interrogators left her alone after her refusal to give testimony, they did finally institute charges against her. One charge was that of using state transport for personal reasons because she had had a box of dirt from the black earth region flown to her in Moscow so that she could study the soil content as part of her work at the Agricultural Academy. A second charge had to with employing foreign labor: she had brought a tailor to Moscow from Tbilisi to make her clothes. The authorities released Nino Beria after a year and exiled her and Sergo to Sverdlovsk. They had little money, but Sergo was finally able to find work in his specialty. Later they were told they could live anywhere but in Moscow. Sergo Beria settled in Kiev, where he still lives, working in the field of anti-aircraft defense technology. His wife, Marfa, remained in Moscow with their children.[99]

Nino immediately moved back to her native town in Mingrelia, but she was barely settled when the authorities told her she could not reside in Georgia. She then went to live near Sergo in Kiev, where she died on 7 July 1991 at age eighty-seven, bitter, sad, and terribly homesick for her native Georgia. In her only interview given to a journalist she lamented the fate of Beria, Stalin, and other Georgian political figures of their time: "They at least believed that they were fighting for some goal, on behalf of humanity. And what came of it? Not one of them did their own nation and motherland any good and that second nation also did not recognize their work. These people were left without a country."[100]

It is doubtful that Stalin and Beria ever deluded themselves into believing that they were fighting "on behalf of humanity." The world of Beria and Stalin was, after all, a world where moral values and democratic humanism played no role, where the heroic mythology of Marxism-Leninism had given way to autocratic cynicism. The interests of humanity, as determined by their egocentrist conceptions of life, were defined solely in terms of preserving their own political power.

Chapter Eleven

BERIA RECONSIDERED

I N COMPARING the fates of Stalin and Beria it can hardly be said that historical justice prevailed. Though he may not have received timely medical treatment, Stalin was at least allowed to die a natural death, followed by a state funeral with all the honors befitting a leader. Beria, by contrast, was imprisoned, tried, and executed. Subsequently he became the scapegoat for all the negative phenomena of the Stalin period. Stalin continued to have admirers and apologists, even after Khrushchev's revelations about him, but Beria remained the consummate embodiment of evil in the public mind.

There is of course good reason for Beria having borne much of the blame for the excesses of the Stalin period. Soviet leaders have traditionally made their defeated opponents scapegoats for past errors in order to legitimize their successions. Because Beria was a lesser figure than Stalin in terms of his political authority and public persona, his evil deeds could be recognized without disgracing and discrediting the entire Stalinist system. Stalin had been the object of public adulation for so long and was so closely tied to the patriotic illusions shared by Soviet citizens that to acknowledge his crimes fully was to question the regime's legitimacy. Stalin's successors recognized this, which is why the full truth about the purges could not emerge until the Soviet system began to unravel.

Beria's fate brings to mind that of Hermann Goering, creator of the Gestapo, commander-in-chief of the Luftwaffe, and Hitler's most powerful deputy. He, too, became the object of his leader's wrath after years of loyal service. In 1945 Hitler turned on Goering and ordered that he be arrested and killed. Though he escaped death at the time because the allies invaded Germany, Goering subsequently underwent a trial for his crimes while Hitler lay peacefully in his grave. Indeed, it is ironic that the prosecutor in Beria's case, Rudenko, had served on the war crimes tribunal at Nuremberg, sitting in judgment of Goering.

Goering was questioned at great length by prison psychiatrists, anxious to gain insight into the psychology of evil. Although he differed from Beria in that he shrank from personal torture and hands-on violence ("I've never been cruel, I've been hard"), his chilling exposition on the needs of ordinary citizens might have easily been expressed by Beria:

> "Why of course the *people* don't want war," Goering shrugged. "Why would some poor slob on a farm want to risk his life in a war when the best he can get

out of it is to come back to his farm in one piece? Naturally the common people don't want war; neither in Russia, nor in England, nor in American, nor for that matter in Germany. That is understood. But after all it is the *leaders* of the country who determine the policy, and it is always a simple matter to drag the people along, whether it is a democracy or a fascist dictatorship. . . . Voice or no voice, the people can always be brought along to do the bidding of the leaders."[1]

This arrogance and cynicism was evident in Beria from the beginning of his career in Georgia and it doubtless motivated most of his actions as a leader. To some extent it also led to his downfall, because his innate sense of superiority toward Khrushchev blinded him to Khrushchev's political cunning. Yet, unlike Goering, who became a crazed morphine addict, and whose views were discounted by other German leaders in the last years of the war, Beria remained supremely rational and purposeful to the end. It is this aspect of his career that historians, particularly those in the former Soviet Union, have been loath to recognize. Beria may have been boorish, disgusting, and totally without principle, but he was not out of his mind.

Beria came very close to inheriting Stalin's mantle as leader of the Soviet Union, perhaps to remain in power for several years. Indeed, it was by no means a foregone conclusion that Khrushchev would be successful in ousting Beria and arresting him. The details that have emerged about the coup make it clear that it was hastily planned and haphazardly executed. Only luck and circumstance prevented the plot from failing. If Beria had not fallen, he might well have continued with the pragmatic program of de-Stalinization and liberalization that he had pursued in the first three months after Stalin's death. Beria was, after all, a hard-working, efficient, and effective administrator, who was admired and respected by those who worked under him. It is not all that hard to imagine him as a "policeman-turned-liberal" in the same genre as Iurii Andropov, Brezhnev's successor as party leader in 1982. After serving for a decade and a half as a sinister and ruthless KGB chief who sent talented writers to labor camps and perfected the strategy of placing troublesome dissidents in psychiatric hospitals, Andropov was praised as a liberal, especially in the West, and credited with starting the process that led to *perestroika*. As was the case with Beria, Andropov was in a good position to press ahead with reform because he had already proven that he was "tough." He was therefore less vulnerable to accusations of being "soft" or lacking resolve. Moreover, like Beria, he was practical enough to realize that the outmoded, rigid bureaucracy fostered by his predecessor was leading the Soviet Union down the road to decay. Andropov was not driven by a moral or ideological imperative, but by the insights gained from his years of amassing information, as head of the police, on all aspects of Soviet society.

Having been in charge of the police for many years, Beria was similarly "enlightened" and he energetically set about putting his ideas to work after Stalin died, motivated above all by the desire to further his own power. Two aspects of Beria's program might have had especially far-reaching implications for the Soviet system. First, he wanted to reduce the power of the party apparatus and free the government from party interference in administration and decision making. This was of course heresy from the Leninist point of view, but it might have eventually led to a less ideologically cumbersome and more efficient bureaucracy. Second, he planned to give the non-Russian minorities a greater role in decision making and to recognize, on a limited basis, their national and cultural identities. This marked a reversal of the consistent policy of Russification and Sovietization that had been in force since the early days of the Soviet regime. To question the dominance of Great Russians over other nationalities was to question the very essence of Stalinism. Yet, as the nationalist ferment in the Gorbachev era and the subsequent dissolution of the Soviet Union has shown, the nationality question was of tremendous political importance, even in the early 1950s. The idea of making concessions to the republics was much more prescient than it appeared at the time.

Khrushchev did of course adopt many of Beria's policies and he can be credited with pushing for de-Stalinization despite opposition from the Old Guard. But on the whole his record of reform was less than successful. This was partly because of the fundamental dilemma faced by all reformist leaders in the Soviet Union, including Gorbachev: the difficulty of changing the system without destabilizing it and threatening its very existence. Khrushchev was also impeded by his indebtedness to the military as a result of its support in the Beria coup, an indebtedness that was increased by his reliance on Marshal Zhukov to help him defeat a challenge by the "antiparty group" in 1957. Though Khrushchev managed to get rid of Zhukov, he was not strong enough to prevent the military from defending its priorities and exerting its influence on policy-making, a phenomenon unheard of in the Stalin era. Pressure from the military hindered Khrushchev's efforts to reduce defense spending and make more substantial investments in agriculture and the consumer sector. It also undermined his attempts at improving relations with the West.

Above all, Khrushchev was incapable of making substantial reforms because he was too deeply cast in the Stalinist mold. Although he no longer relied on police terror, he quickly adopted the highly personalized, capricious and autocratic style of leadership that had characterized the Stalin period and never focused on the deeply rooted institutional problems. Khrushchev has been "rehabilitated" in recent years, emerging as a relatively positive leader in historical assessments. But in some respects this seems unwarranted. Although he did not join the Politburo until

1939, after the purges had wound down, he profited directly from the deaths of his senior colleagues. And archival documents have shown that he willingly carried out directives from the center in 1937–38. After Khrushchev came to Moscow in 1950, he acted as Stalin's avid supporter during the dark era of the anti-Semitic campaign. If Khrushchev had the slightest compunction about subjecting innocent people to unwarranted suffering, he would not have promoted Kruglov and Serov, who had rounded up whole nations to be sent to Siberia or put to death.

Khrushchev did not have Beria arrested because of the crimes he had committed under Stalin during the purges; rather, it was because Beria had accrued too much power and was imposing reformist policies on other members of the leadership. Without doubt Beria had more blood on his hands than other members of the leadership, except Stalin himself. But it was all a matter of degree and to say that Beria was any more evil that Molotov, Malenkov, or even Khrushchev is to obscure the fact that they all bore responsibility for the crimes of the Stalin period. Stalin did not rule in a vacuum. He was surrounded by sychophantic lieutenants who competed for his favor:

> They trembled at his manic behavior, but at the same time, they inflated and encouraged his suspicions. As his loyal followers and protectors, as it were, for the purpose of winning his affection, they allowed accounts or whisperings to get through to him of various enemies secretly bent on harming the country and him. It may be assumed that by this cunning bit of work they wanted not only to make themselves safe from him in the present, but also to assure themselves a part in the legacy, for the struggle of the gods over it in the Red Olympus began when Zeus himself was still alive.[2]

Stalin relied heavily on those below him, to whom he doled out his patronage in return for their support. As historian Graeme Gill has argued, the Soviet state early on became dependent on a system of personalized networks that made political institutions instruments of powerful figures rather that organs governed by set rules and norms. The result was a distinctly patrimonial power structure:

> The entire Stalinist political system was patrimonial in nature. . . . Through the power of appointment and his ability to remove sub-national leaders, Stalin effectively granted them a secular benefice, a share of the institution he headed. In return, they acknowledged his authority and deferred to him, but within their own backyards they were in a similar situation to Stalin: they could bestow favours on others.[3]

This patrimonial power structure bred tyrants. For every Beria at the top there were little Berias in the republics, districts, and towns, fostering their own personality cults and imposing their arbitrary wills.

It is thus not surprising that a man like Beria emerged in the leadership, however tempting it might be to view him as an aberration. To portray him as an exception, who rose to a powerful position because of a fluke, is to misrepresent the very nature of the Soviet system during the Stalinist period. If Beria was an exception, it was not because he was amoral, sadistic, and cruel. Rather, it was because he was intelligent, astute, and devoted to achieving power. He was also adept at the kind of court politics that prevailed in the Kremlin and below. His deviousness and two-faced behavior was an asset in this environment, particularly in dealing with Stalin. Beria never ceased to maintain his flattering tone—"As usual, you have hit the nail on the head, Iosif Vissarionovich"—though by the end he was heaping scorn on Stalin behind his back.

Even if Beria had managed to outmaneuver Khrushchev and retain his dominant position in the leadership he might, in the long run, have had little more success than Khrushchev in creating a viable and effective system of government because he, too, was deeply ingrained in the Stalinist tradition. But historians would probably have provided a more balanced assessment of him, going beyond the legend of Beria as the arch-villain of the Stalinist period to examine his career in a broader historical context.

The habit of blaming everything on specific individuals rather than looking for the deeper causes of a corrupt and dysfunctional system dies hard in the former Soviet Union. Indeed the official portrayal of the August 1991 coup attempt reflects this tendency. The plotters, who included the head of the KGB, were declared traitors for "attempting to seize power"—the same charges leveled at Beria—though they were simply resorting to the well-established methods of settling power struggles that their predecessors used. The failure of the coup was hailed as a victory for democracy, which to some extent of course it was. But, as the case of Beria reminds us, it takes more than simply getting rid of a few "villains" at the top to change a political system. The long history of rule by dictatorial methods in the former Soviet Union has left an enduring legacy, which, despite the continued progress toward democracy, could affect its political evolution for years to come.

NOTES

In citing works and archival sources, the following abbreviations have been used:

BSE	*Bol'shaia sovetskaia entsiklopediia*
d.	delo
DDQ	*Declassified Documents Quarterly*
f.	fond
KVS	*Kommunist vooruzhenikh sil*
l.	list
op.	opis
RTsKhIDNI	Rossiiskii tsentr khraneniia i izucheniia dokumentov noveishei istorii
TsGA	Tsentral'nyi gosudarstvennyi arkhiv
TsGIA	Tsentral'nyi gosudarstvennyi istoricheskii arkhiv
TKhSD	Tsentr khraneniia sovremennoi dokumentatsii
VIZ	*Voenno-istoricheskii zhurnal*
ZV	*Zaria vostoka*

INTRODUCTION

1. As one scholar points out, "The fact that Beria continues to appear in fiction, stylised, hyperbolised, parodied and conflated with coevals, says something about the hold which this figure still has over the public in the late 20th century. None of Beria's predecessors in office is the subject of any comparable public interest." Kevin Windle, "From Ogre to 'Uncle Lawrence': The Evolution of the Myth of Beria in Russian Fiction from 1953 to the Present," *Australian Slavonic and East European Studies* 3, no. 1 (1989): 15.

2. See, for example, Leonard Schapiro, "What Is Fascism?" *The New York Review of Books* 14, no. 3 (February 1970): 14. As Schapiro put it: "Each is able to act only until the moment when the leader chooses to declare his will."

3. See, for example, Gustav Bychowski, "Joseph V. Stalin: Paranoia and the Dictatorship of the Proletariat," in Benjamin B. Wolman, ed., *The Psychoanalytic Interpretation of History* (New York: Basic Books, 1971), pp. 115–149; Robert C. Tucker, *Stalin as Revolutionary. 1879–1929: A Study in History and Personality* (New York: W. W. Norton, 1973); and Daniel Rancour-Laferriere, *The Mind of Stalin. A Psychoanalytic Study* (Ann Arbor: Ardis, 1988).

4. T. H. Rigby has argued that Stalin actually demonstrated a high degree of "objective loyalty" toward his closest subordinates, in that, unlike those at lower levels, most were allowed to remain in their positions throughout the Stalin era. But, as he observes, Stalin had ensured their obedience by instilling fear in them, so there was no need to continually purge the leadership at the top. See T. H. Rigby, "Was Stalin a Disloyal Patron?" *Soviet Studies* 38, no. 3 (July 1986): 311–324.

5. Ronald Grigor Suny, "Beyond Psychohistory: The Young Stalin in Georgia," *Slavic Review* 50, no. 1 (Spring 1991): 48–58. Suny argues here that at-

tempts to understand Stalin have focused too narrowly on psychological factors, while the important role of his Georgian heritage has been neglected.

6. Suny, "Beyond Psychohistory," p. 54.

7. Robert C. Tucker, "Svetlana Alliluyeva as Witness of Stalin," *Slavic Review* 27, no. 2 (June 1968): 306. Tucker has been one of the few historians to recognize Beria's importance. "The time has come," he wrote here, "when we must revise the general view that Beria was no more than one of the many tools of Stalin's dictatorship, although he was a tool" (p. 306).

8. As one source expressed it: "Veneration and remembrance of the dead lie at the core of basic Georgian traditions and values, the cornerstone of their historic survival." See Julie Christensen, "Tengiz Abuladze's 'Repentance' and the Georgian Nationalist Cause," *Slavic Review* 50, no. 1 (Spring 1991): 166.

9. Milovan Djilas, *Conversations with Stalin* (New York: Harcourt, Brace and World, 1962), p. 151.

CHAPTER ONE
EARLY LIFE AND CAREER

1. Karl Kautsky, *Georgia. A Social-Democratic Peasant Republic. Impressions and Observations*, trans. H. J. Stenning (London: International Bookshops, 1921), p. 14.

2. David Lang, *A Modern History of Soviet Georgia* (New York: Groove Press, 1962), pp. 18–19.

3. This issue was raised recently in media discussions of the acclaimed Georgian film *Repentance*, an allegory about the Stalinist purges in Georgia. See Elizabeth Walters, "The Politics of Repentance: History, Nationalism and Tengiz Abuladze," *Australian Slavonic and East European Studies* 2, no. 1 (1988): 113–142.

4. Ronald Grigor Suny, *The Making of the Georgian Nation* (Stanford, Calif.: Hoover Institution Press, 1988) p. 4; Nino Salia, ed., *Georgia. An Introduction* (Paris: Centre National de la Recherche Scientifique, 1975), pp. 17–18.

5. Lang, *A Modern History of Soviet Georgia*, p. 18.

6. Suny, *Making of the Georgian Nation*, p. 20.

7. Ibid., p. 55.

8. Ibid., pp. 140–171; Firuz Kazamzadeh, *The Struggle for Transcaucasia, 1917–21* (New York: Philosophical Library, 1951).

9. Several brief Soviet biographies of Beria appeared before his 1953 arrest. See *ZV*, 15 November 1931, p. 1; *Malaia sovetskaia entsiklopediia* (Moscow, 1937), p. 857; and *BSE*, 2d ed., vol. 5 (Moscow: Gosudarstvennoe Nauchnoe Izdatel'stvo, 1950), pp. 22–23.

10. Peoples and Languages of the Caucasus, Language and Communication Research Center, Columbia University, 1955, p. 3; Stephen Jones, "The Mingrelians," *Encyclopedia of World Cultures*, G. K. Hall, 1993.

11. Jones, Ibid.

12. Suny, *Making of the Georgian Nation*, p. 97.

13. Ibid., p. 77. Gourials, another ethnic group in that region, are presently called Gurians.

14. Kautsky, *Georgia*, p. 23.

15. Some information on Beria's family appeared in a report compiled by Georgian party officials after his arrest in 1953, located in TsKhSD, f. 5, op. 15, d. 448, ll. 246–248.

16. S. Danilov, "K biografii L. Beria," *Na rubezhe* (Paris), nos. 3–4 (1952), pp. 31–32.

17. This autobiography was reproduced in the third of a series of articles on the Beria trial: B. S. Popov and V. G. Oppokov, "Berievshchina," *VIZ*, no. 1 (1990): 70–72.

18. TsKhSD, 5, op. 15, d. 448, ll. 246–248. Beria seems to have been the only one in the family to distinguish himself in any way as a Bolshevik. In 1953, for example, one cousin was working as a seamstress and her husband was a schizophrenic; another was a former Menshevik who had been arrested numerous times for writing anti-Soviet articles.

19. Danilov, "K biografii L. Beria"; TsKhSD, f. 5, op. 15, d. 448, ll. 246–248.

20. Popov and Oppokov, "Berievshchina," pt. 3, p. 70.

21. After Beria's arrest in 1953 he was accused of lying about when he joined the party. But a Soviet publication, in the course of offering biographical information on all those elected to the Central Committee of the Communist party in 1934, confirms the date of Beria's membership as March 1917. See *Izvestiia TsK KPSS*, no. 12 (1989): 88.

22. Popov and Oppokov, "Berievshchina," pt. 3, p. 70.

23. On the development of the revolutionary movement in Transcaucasia, see Kazemzadeh, *Struggle for Transcaucasia*, pp. 8–78.

24. According to Kazemzadeh, Baku was a "Bolshevik island in an anti-Bolshevik sea" (the rest of Azerbaidzhan). Ibid., p. 128.

25. Ibid.

26. *ZV*, 15 November 1931; *BSE*, vol. 50, pp. 22–23.

27. Beria mentioned this meeting in a letter to bolshevik leader Sergo Ordzhonikidze, written several years later. See RTsKhIDNI, f. 85, op. 29, d. 414, l. 3.

28. On bolshevik spies among the Musavats, see A. G. Karaev, *Iz nedavnogo proshlogo* (Baku: Bakiinskii rabochii, 1926), p. 123.

29. Popov and Oppokov, "Berievshchina," pt. 3, pp. 73–75.

30. Kazemzadeh, *Struggle for Trancaucasia*, pp. 307–309.

31. Ibid., 308. *Bor'ba za pobedu Sovetskoi vlasti v Gruzii. dokumenty i materialy (1917–1921 gg.)* (Tbilisi: "Sabchota Sakartvelo," 1958), pp. 586–606; G. V. Khachapuridze, *Bolsheviki gruzii v boiakh za pobedy sovetskoi vlasti* (Moscow: Gosizdat, 1947), pp. 256–257.

32. See *Bor'ba za pobedu*, pp. 602–605. Beria's detractors later claimed that he behaved in a cowardly manner when he was arrested, revealing his true identity and refusing to take part in the hunger strike. See Popov and Oppokov, "Berievshchina," pt. 3, pp. 74–76.

33. *BSE*, vol. 5; *ZV*, 15 November 1931; Popov and Oppokov, "Berievshchina," pt. 3, p. 72.

34. Popov and Oppokov, "Berievshchina," pt. 3, p. 72.

35. See M. G. Iskenderov, *Iz istorii bor'by kommunisticheskoi partii Azerbaidzhana za pobedu sovetskii vlasti* (Baku: Azerbaidzhanskoe Gosudarstvennoe Izdatel'stvo, 1958), pp. 449–527.

36. Kaminskii reportedly stood up at a 1937 Central Committee plenum in Moscow and said that he learned while he was working in Baku that Beria had been a secret agent of the Musavat government before 1920. (See chapter 4.)

37. See Iskenderov, *Iz istorii*, pp. 527–528.

38. See Stephen Blank, "Bolshevik Organizational Development in Early Soviet Transcaucasia: Autonomy vs. Centralization, 1918–1924," in Ronald Grigor Suny, ed., *Transcaucasia. Nationalism and Social Change. Essays in the History of Armenia, Azerbaijan and Georgia* (Ann Arbor: Michigan Slavic Publications, 1983), pp. 305–338.

39. For the history and organization of the Vecheka, see George Leggett, *The Cheka: Lenin's Political Police* (Oxford: Clarendon Press, 1981).

40. Popov and Oppokov, "Berievshchina," pt. 3, pp. 77–78. His arrest may have had something to do with his undercover work within the Musavat government which, as we have noted, cast an ambiguous shadow on Beria.

41. See his memoirs: Evgenii Dumbadze, *Na sluzhbe cheka i kominterna. Lichnye vospominaniia* (Paris: "Mishen'", 1930), p. 30.

42. See Bagirov's biography in *BSE*, vol. 4, pp. 24–25; and L. Polonskii, in *Bakiinskii rabochii*, 15 June 1988.

43. According to a recently published report, dating back to the 1950s, Bagirov was actually deprived of party membership in 1921 for cruel and inhuman treatment of prisoners. See *Izvestiia TsK KPSS*, no. 11 (1989): 47. If this were the case, he managed to reinstate himself quickly.

44. See Leggett, *The Cheka*, pp. 220–221; and Z.M. Iusif-Zade, ed., *Chekisty Azerbaidzhana. Dokumenty, ocherki, rasskazy* (Baku: Azerneshr, 1981), p. 46.

45. Dekanozov went with Beria to serve in Georgia the next year, 1922. His name was probably a Russianized version of the Georgian name Dekanozishvili. See *ZV*, 16 November 1937 and the report of Dekanozov's testimony at Beria's trial in Popov and Oppokov, "Berievshchina," pt. 1, p. 40.

46. This report was reprinted in Iusif-Zade, *Chekisty*, pp. 31–57.

47. Ibid., p. 26.

48. Ivan Vasil'evich Viktorov, *Podpol'shchik, voin, chekist* (Moscow: Politizdat, 1963), p. 72.

49. Ibid., pp. 78–80. Also see chapter 5.

50. See Leggett, *The Cheka*, pp. 270–271.

51. See Bertram Wolfe, *Khrushchev and Stalin's Ghost* (New York: Praeger, 1957), pp. 201–203; and Alexander Orlov, *The Secret History of Stalin's Secret Crimes* (New York: Random House, 1953), pp. 77–81, 196–199.

52. See a brief biography of Kaminskii in *Voprosy istorii KPSS*, no. 11 (1965): 124–128.

53. Popov and Oppokov, "Berievshchina," pt. 3, p. 68.

54. Ibid., pt. 4, p. 89.

55. *ZV*, 15 November 1931.

56. Popov and Oppokov, "Berievshchina," pt. 4, p. 89.

57. Ibid., pp. 87–88. Nino's father had been a nobleman. Another uncle was Evgenii Gegechkori, Minister of Foreign Affairs for the menshevik government. See Vitalii Bezhnin, "Sergo Beriia o svoem ottse," *Kievskie Novosti*, pt. 4, 27 November 1992, p. 12. This series of interviews with Beria's son Sergo, although

fascinating, cannot be considered totally reliable from a factual point of view, especially since Sergo Beria goes out of his way to defend his father. Also see Levan Golidze, "Beriia sebe zhal?" *Literaturnaia gazeta*, 22 May 1922.

58. The interview with Nino Beria first appeared in Georgian in the paper "7 Dge," and was later translated into Russian. See T. Koridze, "Ia nikogda ne vme-shivalas' v dela Lavrentiia," *Komsomol'skoe znamia*, 30 September 1990.

59. Ibid.

60. Ibid.

61. Ibid. One source of this rumor was Stalin's daughter, Svetlana Alliluyeva. See Svetlana Alliluyeva, *Only One Year*, trans. Paul Chavchavadze (New York: Harper & Row, 1969), p. 411.

62. Nino says in her interview: "Lavrentii was always busy with work. Almost no time was left for his family. He worked a great deal. Now it is easy to be critical but then a real struggle was being waged. The Soviet regime had to be victorious" (*Komsomol'skoe znamia*, 30 September 1990).

63. Beria's replacement in his Azerbaidzhan post was Anton I. Gaberkorn, who had previously headed the Organization-Instruction Department of the Azerbaidzhan Central Committee. See Iusif-Zade, *Chekisty*, pp. 80–81.

64. The Chekist Dumbadze claims that only 3 percent of Cheka employees in Georgia were Georgians, but this may have been an underestimate. See Dumbadze, *Na sluzhbe Cheka*, p. 37.

65. On the problems facing the new bolshevik regime in Georgia, see Suny, *Making of the Georgian Nation*, pp. 209–225; and Stephen Jones, "The Establishment of Soviet Power in Transcaucasia: The Case of Georgia 1921–1928," *Soviet Studies* 40, no. 4 (October 1988): 616–639.

66. As quoted in *Communist Takeover and Occupation of Georgia*. Special Report no. 6 of the Select Committee on Communist Aggression. U.S. House of Representatives (Washington, D.C.: Government Printing Office, 1954) p. 11.

67. Ibid.

68. For an account of the "Georgian affair," see Suny, *Making of the Georgian Nation*, pp. 215–218; and A. Ilin, "The Georgian Incident," *Pravda*, 12 August 1988, p. 3.

69. Robert H. McNeal, *Stalin: Man and Ruler* (New York: New York University Press, 1988), p. 14. Trotsky's reluctance to take on Stalin at this stage is seen by historians as a lost opportunity, which contributed to Trotsky's ultimate defeat by Stalin.

70. See McNeal, *Stalin*, p. 54.

71. This was A. N. Mikeladze. See his biography in ZV, 12 March 1966. Mikeladze worked closely with Beria for the next decade and a half. He served in various Cheka posts in Georgia until 1937, when he was purged.

CHAPTER TWO
SERVICE IN THE GEORGIAN POLITICAL POLICE

1. *Ocherki istorii Kommunisticheskoi Partii Gruzii, 1883–1970* (Tbilisi: Izdatel'stvo TsK KP Gruzii, 1971), pp. 430–435; Grigorii Uratadze, *Vospominaniia gruzinskogo sotsial-demokrata* (Stanford: Stanford University Press, 1968), p.

163; Suny, *Making of the Georgian Nation*, p. 234. Tsintsade was expelled from the Communist party in 1927 because of alleged participation in the Trotskyite opposition. He died in 1937 as a purge victim.

2. For a brief biography of Kvantaliani, who was born in 1889, see A. N. Inauri, ed., *Shchit-nadezhnyi mech-ostryi (chekisty gruzii na strazhe zavoevanii velikogo oktiabria)* (Tbilisi: "Sabchota Sakartvelo," 1985), p. 81.

3. E. A. Skripilev, ed., *Sovetskoe gosudarstvo i pravo v periode stroitel'stva sotsialisma (1921–1935 gg.)* (Moscow: Politizdat, 1968), p. 402. This illustrates that political opposition in Transcaucasia was seen by bolshevik leaders to be serious enough to warrant a continuation of tough police measures.

4. Anton Antonov-Ovseenko, "Kar'era palacha," pt. 1, p. 144.

5. See Kevin Windle, "Fiction as History: L. P. Beria in 'Thaw' Fiction," Collected papers of the 1988 Melbourne Meeting of the Twentieth Century Study Group (Berg: Oxford, 1989) for the various descriptions of Beria. Stalin's daughter, Svetlana Alliluyeva, described Beria's face as "repulsive at the best of times." See Svetlana Alliluyeva, *Twenty Letters to a Friend*, trans. Priscilla Johnson McMillan (New York: Harper & Row, 1967), p. 7.

6. *Komsomol'skoe znamia*, 30 September 1990. Even if Nino's recollections were accurate, their modest life-style did not last long. Soon Beria was to acquire the lavish taste that many other important bolshevik officials exhibited.

7. N. Kvantaliani (possibly the son of the Cheka chief), "Shtrikhi k portretu palacha," *Neva*, no. 11 (1989): 204–207; and personal interview with Vakhtang Chichinadze, former deputy minister of education in Georgia, October 1990.

8. Leggett, *The Cheka*, pp. 262–263.

9. Antonov-Ovseenko, "Kar'era palacha," pt. 1, p. 144.

10. As quoted in Leggett, *The Cheka*, p. 189.

11. Geronti Kikodze, "Notes of a Contemporary," *Mnatobi*, no. 1 (January 1989): 4. Translated from Georgian for this author by Glen Curtis.

12. Dumbadze, *Na sluzhbe Cheka*, p. 62. Shul'man, it seems, was notorious among those who had contact with the Georgian Cheka. The Menshevik David Sagirashvili, who was arrested in 1922, noted: "While in Metekhi Prison [a notorious Cheka prison on the outskirts of Tbilisi], I witnessed brutal executions and acts of despotism by the Chekisty, especially at the hands of a certain Schulmann, who was addicted to morphine and cocaine." See Roy De Lon, "Stalin and Social Democracy, 1905–1922: The Political Diaries of David A. Sagirashvili" (Ph.D. diss., Georgetown University, 1974), p. 127.

13. Popov and Oppokov, "Berievshchina," pt. 2, p. 85; TsKhSD, f. 5, op. 30, d. 4, ll. 88–90.

14. *ZV*, 13 September 1922.

15. An unpublished manuscript, apparently written by menshevik leaders, states that the Georgian Cheka carried out thirty thousand political arrests in 1921–22, but this estimate seems high. See "The Terror in Georgia," unpublished, undated manuscript, from the Nicolaevsky Collection, Hoover Archives, p. 18.

16. Dumbadze, *Na sluzhbe*, p. 58.

17. For a detailed personal account of the terror and persecution inflicted by the Bolsheviks and the Cheka in Georgia, see Mzia Bakradze and Bela Tsveradze,

"Several Episodes of a Bloody Time," *Literaturuli Sakartvelo* (Tbilisi), no. 46 (11 November 1988). Translated from Georgian for this author by Vladimir Babishvili.

18. This is not to say that Mensheviks were not arrested before 1923. David Sagirashvili, a menshevik resistance leader, was imprisoned by the Cheka in Metekhi Prison and then deported to Germany in October 1922 along with sixty-two other Mensheviks. See DeLon, "Stalin," pp. 126–130.

19. A Georgian Central Committee report on the struggle against the Mensheviks sets forth this change in strategy. See *Materialy k politicheskomu otchetu TsK KPG* (Tbilisi, 1924). Also see Suny, *Making of the Georgian Nation*, pp. 220–223; In March 1923 the Cheka discovered an underground menshevik printshop and arrested numerous oppositionists. See I. Ia. Trifonov, "Razgrom men'shevistsko-kulatskogo miatezha v Gruzii v 1924 godu," *Voprosy istorii*, no. 7 (1976): 44. This was followed by mass arrests in the spring and summer of 1924.

20. Jones, "The Establishment of Soviet Power," pp. 632–633; and Trifonov, "Razgrom," pp. 49–50.

21. Copies of Dzhugeli's letters to Kvantaliani are reproduced in "The Terror in Georgia."

22. D. Charachidze, *H. Barbusse, Les Soviets et la Georgie*, (Paris: Editions Pascal, 1930), p. 147.

23. Ibid., pp. 148–150.

24. *Communist Takeover and Occupation of Georgia*, p. 16.

25. Ibid. This estimate, from the testimony of a Mr. Alexander Tzomaia, was much higher than others, which were in the range of four thousand or less. See Charachidze, *H. Barbusse*, pp. 144, 149–151; also see Jones, "Establishment of Soviet Power," p. 633; and Suny, *Making of the Georgian Nation*, p. 224.

26. Lists of prominent rebel leaders who were executed were published regularly in *Zaria vostoka* at this time. Reports of the bloody repression caused an outcry among socialists abroad. Leaders of the Second International sent a resolution to the League of Nations condemning the Soviet government. In an effort to counteract the negative publicity, a prominent German Social Democrat, Klara Zetkin, visited Georgia and then wrote a booklet on the Caucasus, in which she claimed that only 320 persons had been shot. See *Na osvobozhennom kavkaze*, 2d rev. ed. (Moscow: Izdat. "Staryi Bol'shevik," 1935), p. 38.

27. Bakradze and Tsveradze, "Several Episodes."

28. As quoted in Suny, *Making of the Georgian Nation*, p. 224. Also see M. Kakhiani, *Itogi i uroki vystuplenii v gruzii* (Tbilisi: Izdatel'stvo Sov-Kavkaz, 1925).

29. Dumbadze, *Na sluzhbe*, p. 60.

30. See *Dni* (Paris), 24 September 1924; *Ocherki istorii Kommunisticheskoi Partii Gruzii. Chast' 2, (1921–1963 gody)*. (Tbilisi: Izdatel'stvo TsK KP Gruzii, 1963), pp. 50–51. According to the official indictment against the rebel leaders, they had a spy within the Cheka, who acted as an interpreter and thus was one of those "unreliable elements." See *Delo o paritetnom komitete antisovpartii gruzii* (Tiflis, 1925), p. 75.

31. On the relationship between Beria and Ordzhonikidze, see Kvantaliani, "Shtrikhi"; Georgii Bezirgani, "Sud nad L.P.," *Vechernii Tbilisi*, 21 August 1990; and Bezhnin, Sergo Beriia," pt. 2, p. 13.

32. *Slovo* (Berlin), no. 371, 28 December 1926. Also see *Dni*, 26 February 1926.

33. Interview with Devi Sturua, Tbilisi, October 1990. His father, Georgii Sturua, was a party colleague of Beria and a family friend. Beria's son says that Kirov introduced his father to Stalin. See Bezhnin, "Sergo Beriia," pt. 2, p. 13.

34. Antonov-Ovseenko, "Kar'era palacha," pt. 1, pp. 145–146. Also see Anatolii Sul'ianov, *Arestovat' v Kremle. O zhizni i smerti marshala Beriia: Povest'* (Minsk: Mast. lit., 1991), pp. 12–13.

35. Suren Gazarian, "O Berii i sude nad berievtsami v gruzii," *SSSR. Vnutrennie protivorechii*, no. 6 (1982): 114. Mogilevskii, who was Jewish, had been in the Cheka since 1918. See Leggett, *The Cheka*, p. 455.

36. L. Trotskii, "Za stenami kremlina," *Biulletin oppozitsii*, no. 73 (January 1939): 2–15.

37. *ZV*, 25 March 1925, as quoted in Antonov-Ovseenko, "Kar'era palacha," pt. 1, p. 146. For a biographical sketch of Mogilevskii, see Inauri, *Shchit-nadezhnyi*, pp. 74–76.

38. See his biography in *Sibirskie ogni*, no. 10 (1969): 141–144. Pavlunovskii had previously been the VeCheka/OGPU plenipotentiary in Siberia. He apparently grew close to Ordzhonikidze, who remained head of the Zakkraikom until September 1926, because he became Ordzhonikidze's deputy at the Workers' and Peasants' Inspectorate in Moscow in 1928 and served under him for the next nine years.

39. *Politicheskii dnevnik* (Amsterdam), no. 55 (April 1969): 539–540.

40. Beria was promoted at the end of 1926, at which time Kvantaliani was transferred to "leading work in Soviet organs." He died in the purges in 1937. See Inauri, *Shchit-nadezhnyi*, p. 81.

41. Popov and Oppokov, "Berievshchina," pt. 2, p. 85; TsKhSD, f. 5, op. 30, d. 4, l. 88.

42. Eager to demonstrate to his mentor that he was a good fellow, Beria immediately sent a copy of the letter to Ordzhonikidze, who was in Moscow. RTsKhIDNI, f. 85, op. 27, d. 72, l. 8.

43. See Antonov-Ovseenko, "Kar'era palacha," pt. 1, p. 147. Bagirov, who was chief of the GPU in Azerbaidzhan, was the victim of a similar car attack. See *Za svoboda*, 6 April 1930. Apparently terrorist attacks on GPU officials were common.

44. RTsKhIDNI, f. 85, op. 29, d. 370.

45. Suny, *Making of the Georgian Nation*, pp. 234–235; *Ocherki ist. Kompart. Gruzii, 1883–1970*, pp. 478–479. *Ocherki ist. Kompart. Gruzii, 2*, pp. 67–68.

46. *TsGIA*, Tbilisi, f. 600, op. 2, d. 144.

47. RTsKhIDNI, f. 85, op. 27., d. 71, ll. 1–2.

48. Ibid.

49. See *Izvestiia TsK KPSS*, no. 11 (1989): 74; Polonskii in *Bakiinskii rabochii*; and *ZV*, 5 October 1929.

50. See Bagirov's brief biography in *ZV*, 15 December 1933.

51. RTsKhIDNI, f. 85, op. 27, d. 71, l. 2.

52. RTsKhIDNI, f. 85, op. 27, d. 72, ll. 1–6.

53. Ibid.

54. Suny, *Making of the Georgian Nation*, pp. 237–245; P. N. Lomashvili, *Velikii perevorot* (Tbilisi: "Sabchota Sakartvelo," 1972), pp. 225–229.

55. Suny, *Making of the Georgian Nation*, p. 245.

56. Lomashvili, *Velikii perevorot*, p. 276.

57. Ibid., pp. 277–278.

58. As cited in Antonov-Ovseenko, "Kar'era palacha," pt. 1, p. 147.

59. Lomashvili, *Velikii perevorot*, pp. 312–313.

60. Ibid.

61. *Segodnia*, no. 314, 13 November 1930.

62. Ibid.

63. Lomashvili, *Velikii perevorot*, pp. 328–334.

64. Antonov-Ovseenko, "Kar'era palacha," pt. 1, p. 144. Redens was married to Stalin's sister-in-law, Anna Alliluyeva.

65. RTsKhIDNI, f. 85, op. 27, d. 72, l. 2.

66. RTsKhIDNI, f. 85, op. 27, d. 74, l. 4.

67. See *VI S'ezd kommunisticheskoi partii (b) Gruzii. Stenograficheskii otchet* (Tiflis, 1929), p. 59. This was a charge that Stalin would later level at Beria.

68. Agabekov, *OGPU*, p. 155.

69. Antonov-Ovseenko, "Kar'era palacha," pt. 1, p. 144. This story was also related by the former GPU/NKVD official Alexander Orlov, who defected to the West in 1938 and who claimed to have known Beria well. See Alexander Orlov, "The Beria I Knew," *Life Magazine*, 6 July 1953, pp. 42–44. But Orlov's version is somewhat different. Svetlana Alliluyeva was another who mentioned Beria's connivances against Redens. See Alliluyeva, *Twenty Letters*, pp. 57–58.

70. TsKhSD, f. 5, op. 30, d. 4, l. 86.

71. Dumbadze, *Na sluzhbe cheka*, p. 93.

72. Agabekov, *OGPU*, pp. 155–156.

73. Antonov-Ovseenko, "Kar'era palacha," pt. 1, p. 152.

74. See McNeal, *Stalin*, p. 178; and Gazarian, "O Berii," pp. 113–114.

75. Once when he could not make it to Gagra right away, Beria wrote to Ordzhonikidze: "Redens, who was in Gagra, sent me a telegram saying that Comrade Koba [Stalin] would be there either on 16 or 17 August [1929]. If you see him please tell him all that I told you." See RTsKhIDNI, f. 85, op. 27, d. 70.

76. Svetlana Alliluyeva, *Twenty Letters*, pp. 19–20.

77. See Gazarian, "O Berii," pp. 113–114; and Antonov-Ovseenko, "Kar'era palacha," pt. 1, p. 148.

78. On Lominadze and his clash with Stalin, see R. W. Davies, "The Syrtsov-Lominadze Affair," *Soviet Studies* 33, no. 1 (January 1981): 29–50.

79. A fuller version of the meeting is presented in Roy Medvedev, *Let History Judge. The Origins and Consequences of Stalinism*, rev. and exp. ed., trans. and ed. George Shriver (New York: Columbia University Press, 1989), pp. 462–463. Also see *Izvestiia TsK KPSS*, no. 3 (1989): 155–156. According to Medvedev, Ordzhonikidze told the Georgian group that he had been trying to make Stalin realize for a long time that "Beria is a crook." But Medvedev's story is doubtful, since Ordzhonikidze was still on close terms with Beria at the time.

80. Beria's wife mentioned a scandal involving Kartvelishvili and another official's wife, which she implies was the pretext for his removal. See *Komsomol'skoe*

znamia, 30 September 1990. In any case, Beria later took out his revenge against Kartvelishvili by having him arrested in 1937 and charged with trying to kill him.

81. *Ocherki ist. Kompart. Gruzii 2*, pp. 115–116. The announcement of Beria's appointment appeared in *ZV*, 15 November 1931. His replacement as GPU chief was Konstantin (Tite) Lordkipanidze. A Georgian, he had been in the Cheka since 1921, serving as Beria's subordinate. See Inauri, *Shchit-nadezhnyi*, pp. 85–96.

CHAPTER THREE
LEADER OF GEORGIA AND TRANSCAUCASIA: 1931–1936

1. RTsKhIDNI, f. 17, op. 18, d. 29 (protocol of the Georgian CC bureau for 11 November 1931); Suny, *Making of the Georgian Nation*, p. 255.

2. Suren Gazarian, "Eto ne dolzhno povtorit'sia," *Zvezda*, no. 1 (January 1988): 37–38, 75.

3. Antonov-Ovseenko, "Kar'era palacha," pt. 1, p. 150.

4. RTsKhIDNI, f. 17, op. 18, d. 29 (protocol of the 7 December 1931 Georgian party bureau session).

5. *ZV*, 9 January 1932.

6. The speech was printed in three consecutive issues of *ZV*, 27, 28, and 29 January 1932.

7. Medvedev (*Let History Judge*, p. 463) claims that Beria replaced thirty-two raikom secretaries with chiefs of raion police administrations. Although this may be an overestimate, several examples of moves from police to party were documented in the press. See *ZV*, 29 November 1934; 24 and 27 November 1937.

8. *ZV*, 1 March 1932.

9. RTsKhIDNI, f. 85, op. 29, d. 412, ll. 1–14.

10. Ibid., d. 414, l. 3.

11. See, for example, Boris Nicolaevsky, *Power and the Soviet Elite* (New York: Praeger, 1965), pp. 183–184; *Politicheskii dnevnik*, pp. 539–541.

12. Gazarian, "O Berii," p. 115.

13. See *ZV*, 18 October 1932, where Orakhelashvili's departure from the Transcaucasian party bureau is mentioned, along with Agniashvili's promotion to full bureau membership. When Beria assumed the Georgian party leadership in early 1934 Agniashvili moved to the post of second secretary of the Georgian party (see *ZV*, 15 January 1934) where he stayed until late 1935. He perished in the 1936–37 purges.

14. See *ZV*, 15 December 1933, for the announcement of Bagirov's promotion and an account of his career.

15. See, for example, *ZV*, 4 February 1933; 17 July 1936.

16. RTsKhIDNI, f. 85, op. 29, d. 413. The person who told Beria about the incident was Bagirov, who had been in Moscow at the time.

17. *ZV*, 4 November, 8 November, and 27 November 1934. (Also see chapter 4, where this trip is discussed further.)

18. RTsKhIDNI, f. 85, op. 29, d. 370.

19. RTsKhIDNI, f. 85, op. 29, d. 414.

20. See *ZV*, 6 and 14 March; 14 April 1933.

21. *Ocherki ist. Kompart. Gruzii*, 2, pp. 122–123; *Ocherki istorii kommunisticheskikh organizatsii Zakavkaz'ia. chast' vtoraia. 1921–1936 gg.* (Baku: Azerbaidzhanskoe Gosudarstvennoe Izdatel'stvo, 1971), pp. 231–232.

22. *Pravda*, 28 May 1933.

23. The April 1933 plenum of the Zakkraikom was devoted to the problem of making progress in drilling, extraction, and refining oil, which called for improvements in technology. See *Ocherki ist. kom. organ. Zakav.*, pp. 228–229; ZV, 17 April 1933.

24. *ZV*, 12 August 1933.

25. *Ocherki ist. kom. organ. Zakav.*, pp. 232, 256.

26. Ibid., pp. 232, 214–215; Lang, *History of Georgia*, p. 253.

27. Beria's speech to the Seventeenth Party Congress in Moscow in January 1934 was reprinted in *XVII S'ezd vsesoiuznoi kommunisticheskoi partii(b). Stenograficheskii otchet.* (Moscow: Partizdat, 1934), pp. 129–132.

28. See McNeal, *Stalin*, p. 179. Stalin's daughter noted that Beria's renovations made the poor cobbler's hut where her father was born look like a Moscow subway station. See Alliluyeva, *Twenty Letters*, p. 203.

29. Ibid.

30. Alliluyeva, *Twenty Letters*, pp. 203–204. Svetlana Alliluyeva adds that they probably detested one another, thus implying that Nino viewed the task of attending to Stalin's mother, an uneducated peasant, with displeasure.

31. *ZV*, 28 October 1935.

32. Beria's sexual practices with adolescent schoolgirls are described in lurid detail in Thaddeus Wittlin's biography, *Commissar. The Life and Death of Lavrenty Pavlovich Beria* (New York: Macmillan, 1972), but much of it seems to have been invented by the author.

33. Robert C. Tucker, "The Rise of Stalin's Personality Cult," *American Historical Review* 84 (April 1979): 347–366.

34. John Barber argues that Stalin wrote the letter with the limited aim of tightening up ideological orthodoxy and that the letter was not intended to have the effect it had. See John Barber, "Stalin's Letter to the Editors of Proletarskaya Revolyutsiya," *Soviet Studies* 28, no. 1 (January 1976): 21–41. Whatever Stalin's motives, however, the outcome was the same and the letter marked a milestone in the development of the cult of Stalin.

35. *ZV*, 23 March 1932. The article appeared in *Pravda* on 21 March.

36. The editors referred to comments Beria made in his concluding remarks at the Congress. He did not make any reference to Zhgenti in his lengthy report, which was published in ZV, 27–29 January 1932.

37. *ZV*, 9 April 1932. Zhgenti was not in total disgrace. He later managed to publish an article praising Stalin's revolutionary accomplishments. (See "Zheleznaia nepreklonnaia volia," ZV, 5 October 1935.) But this did not put him back in the party's good graces and he was purged in 1937.

38. *ZV*, 12 April 1932.

39. *ZV*, 14 April 1932. Further resolutions on Stalin's letter were issued by various local Georgian party organizations and there was continued discussion in the press. See, for example, ZV, 17 April 1932.

40. *ZV*, 9 March 1933.

41. *ZV*, 10 April 1933.

42. *ZV*, 12 January 1934.

43. See, for example, F. E. Makharadze, *Ocherki revoliutsionnogo dvizheniia v Zakavkazii* (Tiflis: Gosizdat Gruzii, 1927).

44. Orakhelashvili was the author of *Zakavkazskie organizatsii v 1917 godu* (Tiflis: Zakkniga, 1927).

45. *ZV*, 14 January 1934.

46. A. Enukidze, *Bol'shevistskie nelegal'nye tipografii*, 3d ed. (Moscow: Molodaia gvardiia, 1934). The first edition appeared in 1923.

47. *Pravda*, 16 January 1935.

48. Bertram D. Wolfe, *Three Who Made a Revolution. A Biographical History* (Boston: Beacon Press, 1948), p. 443.

49. RTsKhIDNI, f. 17, op. 2, d. 547, ll. 56–57.

50. *ZV*, 24 June 1935.

51. Anatoli Rybakov, *Children of the Arbat*, trans. Harold Shukman (Boston: Little, Brown, 1988). Roy Medvedev says there is no doubt that the book was Stalin's idea. See *Let History Judge*, p. 464. If this were the case, Beria, as a good opportunist, no doubt accepted the project eagerly.

52. Ibid., p. 505. Whether this account bears any truth, Kirov's murder in December 1934 conveniently eliminated a prominent Bolshevik who had considerable knowledge about events in Transcaucasia and who might not have remained silent when these events were deliberately falsified to glorify Stalin's role.

53. L. Beriia, "Bol'sheviki zakavkaz'ia v bor'be za sotsializm," *Bol'shevik*, no. 11 (1934). The article was reprinted in *ZV*, 20 July 1934.

54. Beria may have been inspired by a pamphlet published in Georgia in 1934 by the Abkhaz leader Nestor Lakoba, who glorified Stalin's revolutionary role in 1901–1902. See *Stalin i Khashim (1901–1902 gody)* (Sukhumi, 1934).

55. Popov and Oppokov, "Berievshchina," pt. 2, p. 85. Beria admitted that he subsequently had Bediia shot, but claimed that it was because Bediia had ties with the oppositionist Lominadze.

56. Ibid. Also see Georgii Bezirgani, "Rukopis', sgorevshaia: k voprosu ob istorii sozdaniia i ischeznoveniia odnoi knigi," *Vechernii Tbilisi*, 9 August 1990. That the book was the work of several persons is clear from the inconsistencies and discrepancies that appear throughout.

57. TsKhSD, f. 5, op. 30, d. 4, l. 73.

58. Ibid.

59. *ZV*, 24, 25 July 1935.

60. *ZV*, 15 August 1935.

61. E. Iaroslavskii, "Zapolnen bol'shoi probel v izuchenii istorii bol'shevizma," *ZV*, 16 November 1935.

62. M. Shchnev, "Krupneishii vklad v sokrovishchinitsu bol'shevizma," *Proletarskaia revoliutsiia*, no. 6 (1935).

63. RTsKhIDNI, f. 17, op. 3, d. 370, l. 50.

64. L. Beria, *On the History of Bolshevik Organizations in Transcaucasia*, translated from the Russian seventh edition (Moscow: Foreign Languages Publishing House, 1949).

65. L. Beriia, *K voprosu ob istorii bol'shevistskikh organizatsii v zakavkaz'e. Doklad na sobranii tifliskogo partaktiva 21–22 July 1935* (Moscow: Partizdat, 1935), p. 13.

66. *K voprosu* (1935), pp. 15–16.

67. See, for example, the memoirs of V. E. Bibineishvili, *Za chetvert veka* (Moscow: Molodaia gvardiia, 1931). Bibineishvili was exposed as "an enemy of the people" in 1937.

68. R. Arsenidze, "Iz vospominanii o Staline," *Novyi zhurnal*, no. 72 (1963): 225. Also see Wolfe, *Three Who Made a Revolution*, pp. 432–433; and a review of Beria's book by R. Arsenidze in *The Caucasian Review*, no. 1 (1955): 163–165. Wolfe, who points out numerous distortions in Beria's book, notes that even the authoritative *Great Soviet Encyclopedia* in a volume published in 1930 presents the entire Georgian Social Democratic organization as solidly behind Lenin's platform until 1905.

69. Wolfe, *Three Who Made a Revolution*, p. 416. As Wolfe puts it: "More than mere precocity of genius, this begins to suggest [of Stalin] an astonishing ability to get around, the more astonishing when we consider that he himself has recorded that he and his fellow-students lived in a barracks atmosphere, spied on in all their movements."

70. Beria, "Bol'sheviki zakavkaz'ia."

71. L. Beria, *On the History*, p. 30.

72. Arsenidze, "Iz vospominanii," p. 228. Wolfe, on the other hand, cites a menshevik paper as claiming that Stalin was actually expelled from the Tbilisi organization by a party tribunal for spreading slander against one of the members. See Wolfe, *Three Who Made a Revolution*, p. 420.

73. Beria, *K voprosy* (1935), p. 21. By the seventh edition, Stalin's role has become much larger: he "delivered four or five brilliant speeches" at a 31 December 1901 Social Democratic conference in Batumi (Beria, *On the History*, p. 37). The initial edition of the book documented claims about Stalin in Batumi by citing the reminiscences of Arakel Okuashvili and G. Chkheidze. Apparently these men later fell into disfavor and were purged, because subsequent editions dropped them as sources and dredged up alleged tsarist police reports instead.

74. Enukidze, *Bol'shevistskie tipografii*, pp. 12–28. Nor is Stalin mentioned in the memoirs of others connected with the press. See Wolfe, *Three Who Made a Revolution*, p. 440.

75. As Wolfe points out, the account was still the same, despite Enukidze's apologies (Wolfe, *Three Who Made a Revolution*, p. 443).

76. Beria, *K voprosu* p. 25.

77. Beria, *On the History*, p. 51.

78. Beria, *K voprosu* p. 26.

79. Beria, *On the History* p. 53.

80. Beria, *K voprosu* p. 28.

81. Ibid., p. 40.

82. Beria, *On the History* pp. 82–87.

83. Beria, *K voprosu* pp. 36–38.

84. Arsenidze, "Iz vospominanii," p. 229. As Wolfe notes, at the two united congresses of Bolsheviks and Mensheviks in 1906 and 1907, the Caucasian Bol-

sheviks were not even able to get enough votes for a single uncontested delegate. Even within the bolshevik organization Stalin was not the leading figure at this time. Thus, for example, Beria tells us that Stalin was running the Bolshevik Committee for Transcaucasia, when in fact he had only a secondary role. See Wolfe, *Three Who Made a Revolution*, pp. 430–435.

85. RTsKhIDNI, f. 298, op. 1, d. 29.

86. Dmitri Volkogonov, *Triumph and Tragedy*, trans. and ed. Harold Shukman (New York: Grove Weidenfeld, 1991), p. 213.

87. As quoted in Beria, *K voprosu* p. 67.

88. F. Makharadze, "V poriadke samokritiki," *ZV*, 4 February 1936.

89. See Gazarian, "O Berii," p. 119.

90. See *Bor'ba za pobedu*, p. 728.

91. See Antonov-Ovseenko, "Kar'era palacha," pt. 1, pp. 152–153.

92. See, for example, *ZV*, 5 June 1936, where workers in the oil industry claimed that all their successes were due to Beria's leadership. Also see Gazarian, "O Berii," p. 122.

93. M. D. Bagirov, *Iz istorii bol'shevistskoi organizatsii Baku i Azerbaidzhana* (Moscow: Gosizdat, 1946). Somewhat surprisingly, Bagirov mentions Beria's role in the revolutionary movement in Baku only once, perhaps because he did not want to detract from Stalin's glory.

94. See *ZV*, 22 February 1936; Antonov-Ovseenko, "Kar'era palacha," pt. 1, p. 152.

95. Nato Vachnadze, *Vstrechi i vpechatleniia* (Moscow: Goskinoizdat, 1953), p. 86.

96. *Priem delegatsii sovetskoi gruzii rukovoditaliami partii i pravitel'stva v Kremle* (Moscow: Partizdat TsK VKP(B), 1936). The reception lasted ten hours.

97. "Pobeda Leninsko-Stalinskoi natsional'noi politiki," *Pravda*, 25 February 1936. This article later was translated into English (and possibly other languages) and issued as a booklet.

98. For a further discussion of Georgia's economic development at this time, see *Ocherki ist. kompart. Gruzii*. 2, pp. 147–150.

99. After Beria's fall in 1953 the mansion became headquarters for the Georgian Komsomol (Communist Youth League) and later housed the offices of Georgian President Zviad Gamsakhurdia.

100. Averell Harriman stayed there on a visit to Stalin in October 1945. See Averell W. Harriman and Elie Abel, *Special Envoy to Churchill and Stalin* (New York: Random House, 1975), pp. 511–512.

CHAPTER FOUR
THE PURGES IN GEORGIA

1. See Robert C. Tucker, *Stalin in Power: The Revolution from Above, 1928–1941* (New York: W. W. Norton, 1990), pp. 288–298; Robert Conquest, *Stalin and the Kirov Murder* (New York: Oxford University Press, 1989); and "Zapiska P. N. Pospelova ob ubiistve Kirova," *Svobodnaia mysl'*, no. 8 (1992): 64–71.

2. Popov and Oppokov, "Berievshchina," pt. 4, p. 90.

3. This account is based on archival materials, including copies of the telegrams sent by Stalin to Ordzhonikidze, reprinted in "Ordzhonikidze-Kirov-

Stalin," *Svobodnaia mysl'*, no. 13 (1991): 53–63. According to the son of T. I. Lordkipanidze, who was chief of the Georgian NKVD, the latter knew about the danger facing Kirov and tried unsuccessfully to get a transfer to Leningrad in the autumn of 1934. In November 1934 Lordkipanidze was replaced by a Beria protégé. See V. Lordkipanidze, "Ubiistvo Kirova. nekotorye podrobnosti," *Argumenty i fakty*, no. 6 (February 1989): 4.

4. ZV, 24 June 1935.

5. *Ocherki ist. kom. organ. Zakavkaz'ia*, p. 251. In Georgia, the proportion of expulsions was lower—approximately 14.3 percent from May 1935 to May 1936. See *Kommunisticheskaia partiia gruzii v tsifakh (1921–1970 gg.)* (Tbilisi: TsK KP Gruzii, 1971), p. 71.

6. McNeal, *Stalin*, pp. 174–175. Also see Nicolaevsky, *Power and the Soviet Elite*, pp. 218–225. Nicolaevsky states that Enukidze was a strong supporter of Kirov.

7. See Amy Knight, *The KGB: Police and Politics in the Soviet Union* (Boston: Unwin/Hyman, 1990), pp. 24–25.

8. ZV, 15 and 16 January 1936.

9. Merkulov became a full member of the Georgian party bureau in November 1937 and Mil'shtein became third secretary of the Tbilisi party committee in August 1938. See ZV, 24 November 1937 and 20 May 1938.

10. See *Ocherki ist. kompart. Gruzii, 1883–1970*, pp. 576–577.

11. *Pravda*, 12 June 1936.

12. Ashot Artsuni, "Smert' A. Khandzhiana i Sobytiia v Sov. Armenii," *Kavkaz, no. 9/33* (September 1936): 26–28.

13. ZV, 11 July 1936.

14. Ibid.

15. See Artsuni, "Smert'"; and Ashot Artsuni, "Samoubiistvo A. G. Khandzhiana," *Kavkaz*, no 8/32 (August 1936): 29–31.

16. *Izvestiia*, 28 October 1961.

17. Antonov-Ovseenko, "Kar'era palacha," pt. 1, p. 155. Suren Gazarian presents a similar account (Gazarian, "Eto ne dolzhno povtorit'sia, p. 65). Also see Medvedev, *Let History Judge*, pp. 413, 624–625.

18. TsGIA, Tbilisi, f. 8, op. 2, d. 735, ll. 1–17.

19. See ZV, 23 September 1936. Khandzhian's successor, Amatuni, was himself arrested less than a year later.

20. Fazil' Iskander, *Sandro iz chegema: Roman* (Moscow: Moskovskii rabochii, 1989). Lakoba had joined the ranks of Stalin's glorifiers in 1934, a year before Beria's book appeared, with his pamphlet *Stalin i Khashim*.

21. See Darrell Slider, "Crisis and Response in Soviet Nationality Policy: The Case of Abkhazia," *Central Asian Survey* 4, no. 4 (1985): 51–68.

22. See Khrushchev, "Memuary," pt. 1, p. 86; Danilov "K biografii"; Gazarian, "O Berii," p. 117; and Medvedev, *Let History Judge*, p. 495. In the novel *Sandro iz chegema*, Stalin predicts that Beria will "devour Lakoba."

23. See ZV, 20 January 1936.

24. Khrushchev says that Beria later ordered Lakoba's body to be dug up and burned on the pretext that an "enemy of the people" did not deserve to be buried in Abkhazia, but suggests that Beria may have done this to hide evidence that Lakoba had been poisoned. See Khrushchev, "Memuary," pt. 1, p. 86.

25. Razveiat' vprakh vragov sotsializma," *Pravda*, 19 August 1936.

26. Ibid.

27. As Ronald Suny points out, however, only one name was specifically mentioned, that of M. Okudzhava. See Suny, *Making of the Georgian Nation*, pp. 273–274.

28. At this time Stalin sent his famous telegram to Moscow, charging that the NKVD was "four years behind" in unmasking the Trotsky-Zinoviev bloc. It is not clear why he saw fit to dispose of Iagoda, who was later shot, but one reason may have been that Stalin needed a scapegoat on which to pin the Kirov murder.

29. See "Materialy fevral'sko-martovskogo plenuma TsK BKP(B) 1937 goda," *Voprosy istorii*, nos. 2–3 (1992): 3–4.

30. RTsKhIDNI, f. 17. op. 2, d. 576.

31. O. V. Khlevniuk, *1937-i: Stalin, NKVD i sovetskoe obshchestvo* (Moscow: Respublika, 1992), p. 129.

32. *Pravda*, 29 October 1936; and RTsKhIDNI, f. 85, op. 29. d. 418.

33. "Ordzhonikidze-Kirov-Stalin," pp. 62–63.

34. This point was made by Walter Kolarz in an unpublished manuscript for a news broadcast "Ordzhonikidze and Beriya," 6 January 1954. From the Bertram Wolfe collection, Hoover Archives.

35. "Ordzhonikidze-Kirov-Stalin," pp. 59–60.

36. *Politicheskii Dnevnik*, no. 55 (April 1969): 541.

37. See Kikodze, "Notes of a Contemporary."

38. See Khlevniuk, *1937-i*, pp. 76–80; Tucker, *Stalin in Power*, pp. 424–429.

39. Khlevniuk, *1937-i*, p. 77. This particular passage actually was from his original plenum report and was toned down considerably before publication.

40. See *Izvestiia TsK KPSS*, no. 12 (1989): 106; no. 1 (1991): 152; and no. 2 (1991): 149. Also see Sul'ianov, *Arestovat' v Kremle*, pp. 58–59. At one of the CC plenums, either in February–March or June 1937, Kaminskii is said to have stood up and accused Beria of being a spy.

41. *ZV*, 22 May 1937. Also see Suny, *Making of the Georgian Nation*, p. 275.

42. See J. Arch Getty, *The Origins of the Great Purges. The Soviet Communist Party Reconsidered, 1933–38* (Cambridge: Cambridge University Press, 1985), pp. 155–163.

43. Figures on party expulsions in Georgia rather than on elections show a different picture. The *proverka*, or checking of party documents, in 1935–36 and the accompanying exchange of party cards had resulted in the expulsion of about 9,600 full and candidate members from the Georgian Communist Party. By May 1937 around 3,100 additional members had been purged from the party's ranks, a total of around 12,700 (about 23 percent) in three years. See *Kommunisticheskaia partiia v tsifrakh*, pp. 71–79; *Ocherki ist. kompart. Gruzii 2*, p. 160. But these persons were not necessarily arrested.

44. *ZV*, 22 May 1937.

45. *Pravda*, 22 May 1937. Significantly, this article was not reprinted in *Zaria vostoka*, as it normally would have been.

46. See Getty, *Origins of the Great Purges*, pp. 165–171. An earlier sign of trouble for Beria was the fact that his opening report to the congress on 15 May was not published in *Zaria vostoka* until 21 May, and on the second page!

47. RTsKhIDNI, f. 17, op. 18, d. 66, ll. 83–101.

48. *Pravda*, 5 June 1937.

49. RTsKhIDNI, f. 17, op. 18, d. 66 (protocol of the Georgian party bureau meeting, 8 July 1937). This resolution has been reproduced from the archives in Volkogonov, *Triumph and Tragedy*, p. 300.

50. Popov and Oppokov, "Berievshchina," pt. 2, p. 86.

51. See Medvedev, *Let History Judge*, p. 386. Apparently having heard about the joke, Stalin asked Mdivani: "When are you going to stop wagging your tongue?" Mdivani replied, "When Beria stops spying." See Bek Bulat, "Lavrentii Beriia." Nicolaevsky Collection, Hoover Archives.

52. Gazarian, "Eto ne dolzhno povtorit'sia," p. 71.

53. Curiously, although Beria had mentioned the name of Sergo Kavtaradze as being a member of Mdivani's terrorist group in his 5 June congress report, he was not listed as a defendant in the trial. Kavtaradze was a former revolutionary comrade of Stalin's who had at one time been allied with Trotsky. Apparently Stalin undercut Beria and gave Kavtaradze a last-minute reprieve, for he was released from prison and subsequently became deputy people's commissar for foreign affairs. See Medvedev, *Let History Judge*, pp. 548–549. Also see N. Markin, "Delo Mdivani-Okudzhava, 1922–1937," *Biulleten' Oppozitsii*, nos. 56–57 (July–August 1937): 7–9.

54. ZV, 12 July 1937; Gazarian, "Eto ne dolzhno povtorit'sia," p. 16.

55. Gazarian, "Eto ne dolzhno povtorit'sia, pp. 4–35.

56. Beria evidently had no qualms about attacking those who had worked closely with him in the past, but the case of Argba may have been an exception. As noted above, Argba had been involved in Beria's efforts to undermine Lakoba, and subsequently became party chief in Abkhazia. As late as May 1937 he was elected a member of the Georgian party bureau. But then he was singled out for criticism by Moscow, which gave Beria little choice but to purge him.

57. See ZV, 23 July 1937. Iu. D. Sumbatov-Topuridze, a longtime Beria ally who was chief of the Azerbaidzhan NKVD, also received an award.

58. Popov and Oppokov, "Berievshchina," pt. 2, p. 86.

59. These remarkable documents, which include top secret Politburo resolutions on the purges and correspondence between party officials and the NKVD, were reprinted in: Nataliia Gevorkian, "Vstrechnye plany po unichtozheniiu sobstvennogo naroda," *Moskovskie novosti*, no. 25 (21 June 1992): 18–19.

60. See a report on the trial in ZV, 26–28 August 1937. For the next several days *Zaria vostoka* was filled with demands from the public for the death sentence to be meted out to the traitors.

61. ZV, 26 September 1937. Also see D. Hadjibeyli, "The Trials of Adzharian Leaders," *The Caucasian Review*, no. 8 (1959): 21–26.

62. ZV, 29 October 1937.

63. Boris Souvarine, *Stalin. A Critical Survey of Bolshevism*, trans. C. L. R. James (New York: Longmans, Green: 1939), p. 638.

64. Roy Medvedev, "O Staline i Stalinizme," *Istoriia SSSR*, no. 4 (July–August 1989); Antonov-Ovseenko, "Kar'era palacha," pt. 1, pp. 156–157: and Gazarian, "O Sude Berii," pp. 141–142.

65. On 27 April 1937 Bediia published an article in *Izvestiia*, glorifying Stalin's role in the 1 May 1901 demonstrations in Tbilisi.

66. Popov and Oppokov, "Berievshchina," pt. 2, p. 84.

67. See Gevorkian, "Vstrechnye plany."

68. Popov and Oppokov, "Berievshchina," pt. 2, p. 86. Tsereteli later became head of the NKVD Guards Directorate in Moscow. Firsthand accounts by victims of NKVD torture in Georgia appear in Gazarian, "Eto ne dolzhno povtorit'sia," pp. 29–39; and V. Zagidze, "V zastenkakh NKVD v Gruzii," *Ob'edinennyi Kavkaz*, nos. 1–2 (1953): 45–49.

69. Popov and Oppokov, "Berievshchina," pt. 2, p. 87.

70. Donald Rayfield, "The Killing of Paolo Iashvili," *Index on Censorship*, no. 6 (1990), p. 10.

71. *ZV*, 21 May 1937.

72. Rayfield, "The Killing," p. 10.

73. Ibid., p. 14.

74. Kikodze, "Notes of a Contemporary."

75. See a report on the case, taken from recently released archival records, in *7 Dge* (Tbilisi), 28 October 1990.

76. Kikodze, "Notes of a Contemporary."

77. Ibid. This story is retold in fictional form in the Georgian movie *Repentance*, an allegorical story of the purges in Georgia.

78. Ibid.

79. *Ocherki ist. kompart. Gruzii*, 2, p. 160.

80. *KP Gruzii v tsifrakh*, pp. 70–83. For a discussion of recent estimates of purge victims in the Soviet Union as a whole, see Alec Nove, "How Many Victims in the 1930s?-II," *Soviet Studies* 42, no. 4 (1990), pp. 811–814. Also see Volkogonov, *Triumph and Tragedy*, p. 307. Volkogonov estimates that between 4.5 and 5.5 million people were arrested in 1937–38 and, of these, that 800,000 to 900,000 were sentenced to death.

81. Popov and Oppokov, "Berievshchina," pt. 2, p. 87.

82. Kikodze, "Notes of a Contemporary."

83. *ZV*, 3 December 1937.

84. *Pravda*, 20 December 1937. In fact, both were killed before this. Soviet sources now give Enukidze's execution date as 30 October 1937. See *Izvestiia TsK KPSS*, no. 12 (1989): 90. Orakhelashvili was shot on 11 December 1937. See Robert Conquest, *Inside Stalin's Secret Police. NKVD Politics 1936–39* (Stanford, Calif.: Hoover Institution Press, 1985), p. 53.

85. See *Izvestiia TsK KPSS*, no. 11 (1989): 55. This source makes it clear that Orakhelashvili was tried in Georgia, rather than in Moscow, as the 20 December announcement indicated. Also see *Pravda*, 10 June 1963; and Lado Arveladze, "V sviazi s rasstrelom enkavedistov v Sovetskoi Gruzii," unpublished manuscript, the Nicolaevsky Collection, Hoover Archives.

86. *Pravda*, 19 January 1938; "Konets kar'ery Ezhova," *Istoricheskii arkhiv*, no. 1 (1992): 124.

87. *ZV*, 14 February 1938. The text of his report was not published.

88. Gevorkian, "Vstrechnye plany."

89. The NKVD continued to persecute artists and writers, however. Documents from the Georgian state archives show that the NKVD was still collecting evidence and preparing cases against members of the intelligentsia as late as 1940. Central State Historical Archives of Georgian SSR, Tbilisi, f. 8, op. 426, d. 1600.

90. D. Hadjibeyli, "Some Echoes of the 1937 Purge in Azerbaidzhan," *The Caucasian Review*, no. 1 (1955): 36–46.

91. *ZV*, 27 and 28 September 1937; Suny, *Making of the Georgian Nation*, pp. 276; 373, n. 51. He remained leader of the Armenian Communist Party until 1953, when Beria fell.

92. *ZV*, 25 November 1937.

93. *ZV*, 20–22 December 1937.

94. *ZV*, 27 January 1938.

CHAPTER FIVE
MASTER OF THE LUBIANKA

1. *Pravda*, 23 April 1938.

2. See, for example, the text of his report to the Tbilisi party apparatus, *ZV*, 3 June 1938.

3. See *ZV*, 11 April 1938; 21 May 1938.

4. Conquest, *Inside Stalin's Secret Police*, p. 70. His replacement was M. G. Raev, who remained in this job for less than six months and was succeeded by S. F. Emelianov.

5. Gazarian, "O Berii," pp. 119–120; Pavel Gol'dshein, *Tochka opory* (Jerusalem, n.d), book 2, pp. 34–35; Geronti Kikodze, "Notes of a Contemporary"; Bulat, "Lavrentii Beriia."

6. According to an NKVD employee who wound up in the hands of the Germans in 1941, Ezhov had already arrested Kaganovich's brother. See Testimony of NKVD Official Zhigunov, 1941, from a translated German intelligence document, file number EAP 3-a-11/2, GMDS, March 1951, National Archives, pp. 67–68. None of this is mentioned in the rather bland biography of Kaganovich, written by his grand nephew, an American. See Stuart Kahan, *The Wolf of the Kremlin* (New York: William Morrow, 1987).

7. Medvedev, *Let History Judge*, pp. 456–457. Some sources say that the commission was not set up until October 1938, thus after Beria had become deputy NKVD chairman. See Conquest, *Inside Stalin's Secret Police*, p. 78.

8. Khrushchev, "Memuary," pt. 1, p. 77.

9. TsKhSD, f. 5, op. 30, d. 4, ll. 94–95.

10. Khrushchev, "Memuary," pt. 1, p. 74–78.

11. For the announcement see unpublished Sovnarkom Resolution, no. 926, 22 August 1938, at TsGA.

12. Beria was identified publicly as Georgian party first secretary as late as 21 August 1938, when he delivered a speech to the USSR Supreme Soviet. See *ZV*, 23 August 1938.

13. Sandro Anageli, "K politicheskim sobytiiam v Gruzii," *Ob'edinennyi kavkaz*, no. 5 (May 1953): 20; TsKhSD, f. 5, op. 15, d. 448, ll. 82–90; 193–202.

14. *XIII S'ezd Kompartii Gruzii (b), 15–19 marta 1940 g. stenotchet* (Tbilisi: Zaria Vostoka, 1940).

15. Khrushchev, "Memuary," pt. 1, pp. 77–78. Conquest, *Inside Stalin's Secret Police*, chronicles the downfall of Ezhov. Medvedev claims that at the end of September a close associate of Ezhov named Ilyitsky foresaw such doom that he

rowed a boat into the Moscow River and shot himself. *Let History Judge*, p. 457. Dismissals of two NKVD deputy ministers, M. P. Frinovskii and S. B. Zhukovskii were reported in unpublished resolutions of the Sovnarkom, dated 8 September and 3 October 1938 (available at TsGA).

16. RTsKhIDNI, f. 17. op. 3, d. 1003, ll. 85–86, reprinted in *Istoricheskii arkhiv*, no. 1 (1992), pp. 126–128.

17. RTsKhIDNI, f. 17, op. 3, d. 1003, ll. 82–84, reprinted in *Istoricheskii arkhiv*, no. 1 (1992), pp. 129–131. The announcement of the change at the helm in the NKVD did not appear in *Pravda* until 8 December 1938.

18. Ezhov remained in the post of commissar for water transport, to which he had been assigned in April 1938, until after the Eighteenth Party Congress in March 1939. He was arrested after the Congress and shot in early 1940. Khrushchev says that Stalin and Beria were planning first to arrest Ezhov's wife, who was in the hospital, in order to force her to compromise her husband. But Ezhov warned her and she poisoned herself. See Khrushchev, "Memuary," pt. 1, p. 79.

19. See his recent biography by Arkady Vaksberg, *Stalin's Prosecutor. The Life of Andrei Vyshinsky* (New York: Grove Weidenfeld, 1991).

20. In his letter to Stalin Ezhov apologized for not recognizing the suspicious behavior of several of his colleagues, including Litvin and Uspenskii. See "Konets kar'ery Ezhova," pp. 129–30.

21. Conquest, *Inside Stalin's Secret Police*, pp. 80–81. Anna Alliluyeva then appealed to Stalin, but he refused to have anything to do with the matter.

22. Medvedev, *Let History Judge*, pp. 469–470; Anton Antonov-Ovseenko, "Beriia," *Iunost'*, no. 12 (1988): 73–74. At the Twentieth Party Congress Khrushchev read aloud Mikhail Kedrov's letter from Lefortovo Prison, protesting his innocence.

23. TsKhSD, f. 5, op. 30, d. 4, l. 94.

24. Gvishiani's son, D. M. Gvishiani, married the daughter of Aleksei Kosygin and became a leading official during the Khrushchev era.

25. See an unpublished manuscript by Robert M. Slusser, "Stalinism and the Secret Police," April 1979.

26. Ibid.

27. TsKhSD, f. 5, op. 30, d. 4, ll. 76–77.

28. Bek Bulat, "Lavrentii Beriia."

29. As quoted in Medevedev, *Let History Judge*, p. 486.

30. Zhigunov Testimony, p. 69.

31. Robert Conquest, *The Great Terror. A Reassessment* (New York: Oxford University Press, 1990), p. 627.

32. Zhigunov Testimony, pp. 68–70; Conquest, *Inside Stalin's Secret Police*, pp. 106–107.

33. Vladimir and Evdokia Petrov, *Empire of Fear* (New York: Praeger, 1956), p. 86. Petrov later joined the foreign intelligence section of the security police, defecting with his wife to the West in 1953.

34. RTsKhIDNI, f. 77, op. 1, d. 194a, ll. 4.

35. Another indication of Beria's prestige was the publication in 1939 of a collection of his articles and speeches, covering the years 1936–38, entitled *Under the Glorious Banner of Lenin-Stalin*. See the announcement in *ZV*, 20 May 1939.

36. See U.S. Department of State, *Foreign Relations of the United States*, vol. 1, 1941 (Washington: GPO, 1958), pp. 601–602.

37. *Pravda*, 16 March 1939.

38. See A. I. Romanov, *Nights Are Longest There. Smersh from the Inside*, trans. Gerald Brooke (London: Hutchinson, 1972), p. 178.

39. Edward Crankshaw, "Beria, Russia's Mystery of Mysteries," *New York Times Magazine*, 2 April 1950.

40. Craig Thompson, "Russia's Best-Known Secret," *Colliers*, 13 March 1948. Beria was described in *Time* magazine's cover story on him, dated 22 March 1948, as "a steady, quiet type who has a wife, two [*sic*] children and a suburban villa to which he commutes in a Packard—with the shades always drawn."

41. Djilas, *Conversations with Stalin*, p. 108. Apparently Beria put on quite a bit of weight right after the war. See Romanov, *Nights Are Longest*, p. 178.

42. See Khrushchev, "Memuary," pt. 1, p. 80; Andrei Sakharov, *Vospominaniia* (New York: Izdatel'stvo Imeni Chekhova, 1990), p. 211. Romanov, on the other hand, claims that "Beria spoke Russian well, with far less of a Caucasian accent than, for example, Stalin had" (Romanov, *Nights Are Longest*, p. 178).

43. Antonov-Ovseenko, "Beriia," p. 72.

44. Ibid.

45. Alliluyeva, *Twenty Letters*, p. 136.

46. Ibid., p. 8.

47. Ibid., p. 137.

48. Gustav Hilger and Alfred G. Meyer, *The Incompatible Allies. A Memoir-History of German-Soviet Relations, 1918–1941.* (New York: Macmillan, 1953), pp. 313–314.

49. *Izvestiia TsK KPSS*, no. 2 (1991), pp. 156–157; V. F. Nekrasov, ed., *Beriia: Konets Kar'ery* (Moscow: Politizdat, 1991), p. 387.

50. Gazarian, "O Berii," pp. 142–143.

51. "Duel," *Sovershenno sekretno*, no. 8 (1991): 27–28.

52. Nikolai Zhusenin, "Beriia. Neskol'ko epizodov odnoi prestupnoi zhizni," *Nedelia*, no. 8 (22–28 February 1988), p. 12.

53. Volkogonov, *Triumph and Tragedy*, p. 333. Volkogonov doubts that Stalin was ignorant of Beria's perversions: "Even though he professed to value asceticism and puritanism, the General Secretary must have known that Beria was a notorious profligate."

54. Romanov, *Nights Are Longest*, p. 179.

55. *Komsomol'skoe znamia*, 30 September 1990. A Soviet article based on testimony from the Beria case in 1953 claims that Nino Beria told investigators that she had stopped having sexual relations with her husband after 1941 because of his womanizing. See V. F. Nekrasov, "Lavrentii Beriia," pt. 1, *Sovetskaia militsiia*, no. 3 (1990): 21.

56. Bezhnin, "Sergo Beria," pt. 4, p. 12.

57. Edward Ellis Smith, "The Alliluyevs," *Per Se* (Spring 1968): 20–21.

58. See Natal'ia Kraminova, "O zhenshchine c plakata 'Rodina-mat' zovet,'" *Moskovskie novosti*, 9 October 1988. This is an article about Tamara Toidze, the wife of the artist Irakliia Toidze, who painted portraits of Soviet leaders, including Beria. Tamara Toidze came to know Nino Beria through her husband. She

quotes Nino as saying: "I need a husband and a son, but no one needs me." Also see "The Beria Dossier," *Sputnik*, no. 12 (December 1988): 85–92.

59. Alliluyeva, *Only One Year*, pp. 411–413.

60. Kraminova, "O zhenshchine"; Nekrasov, "Lavrentii Beriia," pt. 1; Bezhnin, "Sergo Beriia," pt. 1, pp. 12–13.

61. Alliluyeva, *Only One Year*, p. 413.

62. Ibid.; "The Beria Dossier"; Bezhnin, "Sergo Beriia," pt. 2, pp. 12–13.

63. Bertram Wolfe, *Khrushchev and Stalin's Ghost* (New York: Praeger, 1957), p. 162 (from Khrushchev's secret speech).

64. Anatolii Golovkov, "Ne otrekaias' ot sebia," *Ogonek*, no. 7 (February 1988): 28. Kosarev's wife, Maria Naneishvili, survived her arrest and years in labor camps to recount this experience.

65. V. F. Pitkina, a former Komsomol secretary, was questioned extensively by Beria and endured endless torture at the hands of Shvartsman, but never confessed. She was released from the camps in 1954. See ibid., pp. 28–29; and I. Rashkovets, "Ne sklonivshie golovy," *KVS*, no. 4 (February 1991): 59–62. The notorious Shvartsman rose in the ranks of the NKID to become a colonel and deputy chief of the investigation department by the late 1940s. See Anatolii Golovkov, "Vechnyi isk," *Ogonek*, no. 18 (April 1988): 30.

66. Conquest, *Inside Stalin's Secret Police*, p. 90.

67. An exception was the former candidate member of the Politburo, R. I. Eikhe, who for some reason was not shot until 1940. According to Khrushchev, Eikhe was tortured brutally under Beria's auspices. See Wolfe, *Khrushchev and Stalin's Ghost*, p. 146.

68. See Walter Laqueur, *Stalin. The Glasnost Revelations* (New York: Charles Scribner's Sons, 1990), pp. 91–92.

69. Zhusenin, "Beriia"; Vaksberg, *Stalin's Prosecutor*, pp. 118–119.

70. See "The Beria Dossier," pp. 89–90; Konstantin Rudnitskii, "Krushenie teatra," *Ogonek*, no. 22 (May 1988): 10–14.

71. "The Beria Dossier," pp. 90–91; Conquest, *The Great Terror*, pp. 435–436.

72. Alexander Gershkovich, *The Theater of Yuri Lyubimov. Art and Politics at the Taganka in Moscow*, trans. Michael Yurieff (New York: Paragon House, 1989), pp. 41–42. One of the female members of the group, Nina Alekseeva, claimed much later that she had had an affair with Beria. See Bezhnin, "Sergo Beriia," pt. 4, p. 12.

73. For a discussion of the various interpretations of the NKID purge, see Teddy J. Uldricks, "The Impact of the Great Purges on the People's Commissariat of Foreign Affairs," *Slavic Review*, vol. 36, no. 2 (June 1977): 187–204.

74. Evgenii Gnedin, "Sebia ne poteriat' . . ." *Novyi Mir*, no. 7 (1988): 175.

75. Z. Sheinis, *Maxim Maksimovich Litvinov. Revoliutsioner, Diplomat, Chelovek* (Moscow: Politizdat, 1989), p. 363.

76. Ibid., pp. 363–364.

77. Gnedin, "Sebia ne poteriat' ", pp. 181–183. Gnedin spent the next sixteen years in labor camps and exile. He was released and rehabilitated in 1955. On Kobulov, see Zhigunov Testimony, p. 70. Referred to affectionately as "Bakhsho," Kobulov was, according to one source, "very industrious and slavishly devoted to Beria. Instead of a mind, he had diligence and servility; in-

stead of his own opinion—whatever pleased you" (Sul'ianov, *Arestovat' v Kremle*, p. 354).

78. *Khrushchev Remembers*, vol. 1, ed. and trans. Strobe Talbott (Boston: Little, Brown, 1970), p. 262.

79. Uldricks, "Impact of the Great Purges," p. 192. All of Litvinov's subordinates, with the exception of Gnedin, perished in NKVD camps. See Sheinis, *Litvinov*, p. 364.

80. Uldricks, "Impact of the Great Purges," p. 198.

81. See M. Loginov, "Kul't lichnosti chuzhd nashemy stroiu," *Molodoi kommunist*, no. 1 (1962): 53–54.

82. *Soviet Diplomacy and Negotiating Behavior: Emerging New Context for U.S. Diplomacy*, vol. 1 (Washington: GPO, 1979), p. 88.

83. Hilger and Meyer, *Incompatible Allies*, p. 282.

84. Ibid., p. 322.

85. See *Nazii-Soviet Relations, 1939–41. Documents from the Archives of the German Foreign Office* (Washington: GPO, 1948). It is probably an exaggeration, however, to say, as Boris Nicolaevsky does, that "Beria's ministry in general was instrumental in bringing about this pact" (Nicolaevsky, *Power and the Soviet Elite*, p. 124). Molotov, in a series of interviews before his death in 1986, noted that the appointment of Dekanozov was Stalin's idea and that Dekanozov "was not a bad worker" (Chuev, *Sto sorok besed s Molotovym*, pp. 28–29).

86. Conquest, *Inside Stalin's Secret Police*, p. 96.

87. *Khrushchev Remembers*, vol. 1, p. 131.

88. Aleksandr Akulichev and Aleksei Pamiatnykh, "Katyn': Podtverdit' ili oprovergnyt,'" *Moskovskie novosti*, 21 May 1989.

89. Gennadii Zhavoronkov, "Taina chernoi dorogi," *Moskovskie novosti*, 17 June 1990. One document reproduced in the Soviet press is purportedly a message, dated 10 May 1940, from the Minsk NKVD chief, informing NKVD officers L. F. Raikhman and L. M. Zarubin that the three camps holding Polish officers had been liquidated, apparently on their orders. See Akulichev and Pamiatnykh, "Katyn." Raikhman, who was still alive in 1989, denied any involvement in the Katyn massacre, but his name has repeatedly been linked with the crime. See Vladimir Abarimov, "Vokrug Katyny," *Literaturnaia gazeta*, 6 September 1989, p. 9.

90. *New York Times*, 15 October 1992.

91. Natal'ia Lebedeva, "I eshche raz o Katyn," *Moskovskie novosti*, 6 May 1990 and "Tainy katynskogo lesa," *Moskovskie novosti*, 6 August 1989. As head of the NKVD Beria would have given the order to NKVD troops guarding the camps. Also see Lev Yelin, "The Man Who Knows the Truth about Katyn," *New Times*, no. 17 (1991): 28–31, which gives details of correspondence between Beria and the chief of the NKVD Department for POWs, P. K. Soprunenko.

92. See a review of a book on Katyn in *Voprosy istorii*, no. 7 (July 1990): 173–176.

93. Von Niemann, "From the Diary of a Chekist," 27 March 1944. Hoover Archives, Breglieb Collection, folder 14. Von Niemann's first name is not given.

94. Ibid., pp. 10–11.

95. S. Swianiewicz, *Forced Labour and Economic Development. An Enquiry into the Experience of Soviet Industrialization* (London: Oxford University Press,

1965), pp. 41–42; and Jan T. Gross, *Revolution from Abroad. The Soviet Conquest of Poland's Western Ukraine and Western Belorussia* (Princeton, N.J., Princeton University Press, 1988). Bessarabia, which was returned to Soviet control in June 1940, underwent similar deportations.

96. See M. M. Gorinov, "Sovetskaia strana v kontse 20-x—nachale 30-x godov," *Voprosy istorii*, no. 11 (November 1990): 39. This estimate is lower than most Western estimates, which have been in the range of four to five million, or higher. See, for example, S. G. Wheatcroft, "On Assessing the Size of Forced Concentration Camp Labour in the Soviet Union, 1929–56," *Soviet Studies* 32, no. 2 (April 1981): 265–295.

97. See Nove, "How Many Victims?"

98. V. N. Zemskov, "GULAG," *Sotsiologicheskie issledovanie*, no. 7 (July 1991): 3–16.

99. Swianiewicz, *Forced Labour*, pp. 209–303.

100. Ibid., p. 36.

101. See Lev Razgon, "Captive in One's Own Country," *New Times*, no. 33 (1991): 32. Also see Sul'ianov, *Arestovat' v Kremle*, pp. 73–74.

102. Iaroslav Golovanov, "Zolotaia kleta," *Literaturnaia gazeta*, 9 November 1988 pp. 12–13.

103. See Anna Livanova, "Tak bylo. Iz istorii sovremennosti," *Ogonek*, no. 3 (January 1988): 14.

104. See Knight, *The KGB*, pp. 35, 254–256. Also see a report from U.S. Ambassador Laurence Steinhardt to the Secretary of State on this reorganization when it was first announced in February 1941 in *Foreign Relations of the United States*, vol. 1, pp. 601–602. Steinhardt interpreted it as a setback for Beria. In April 1943 the state security administration was again separated from the NKVD. See chapter 6.

105. See archival documents reproduced in the *Vestnik* of the Soviet Ministry of Foreign Affairs, no. 5 (May 1990).

106. *Nazi-Soviet Relations, 1939–41*, p. 337; O. V. Vishlev, "Pochemu medlil I. V. Stalin v 1941 g. (iz germanskikh arkhivov)," *Novaia i noveishaia istoriia*, no. 1 (January–February 1992): 86–100.

107. *Nazi-Soviet Relations, 1939–41*, p. 337; *Foreign Relations of the United States*, vol. 1, pp. 606, 656.

108. Hilger and Meyer, *Incompatible Allies*, pp. 331–332.

109. Tucker, *Stalin in Power*, p. 623, citing *Ogonek*, no. 33 (15–21 August 1989).

110. Nekrasov, "Lavrentii Beriia," pt. 2, p. 40. If this was true, Dekanozov cannot have stayed in Beria's bad graces for long.

111. *Rossiia*, 6 March 1964. This general, Ianushaitis, claimed that Beria quietly listened to him for many hours, never reproaching him or raising his voice. He was convinced enough that he even had Ianushaitis give a report of his views on the imminence of a German attack to 150 NKVD officers. Beria seems to have made a favorable impression on Ianushiatis, who noted that he had a good memory and was reasonably well informed about the outside world, considering that he had never been abroad and that his only information came from NKVD intelligence.

112. Many of these documents have been reproduced from the archives and have appeared in recent Soviet and Russian publications. See, for example, *Pravda*, 8 May 1989, p. 4; *Izvestiia TsK KPSS*, no. 4 (1990): 198–223; *Gudok*, 20 July 1991, p. 3; and I. Z. Evgen'ev, "Voennye razvedchiki dokladyvali . . ." *VIZ*, no. 2 (1992): 36–41.

113. See, for example, Vishlev, "Pochemu medlil Stalin?"

114. *Izvestiia TsK KPSS*, no 4 (1990), p. 221.

115. *Pravda*, 8 May 1989, p. 4.

116. Ibid.

117. *Znamia*, no. 6 (1990), p. 165. Another Soviet source says Beria's statement to Stalin was made in response to Dekanozov's report rather than Golikov's. See Nekrasov, "Beriia," pt. 2, p. 40.

CHAPTER SIX
THE WAR YEARS

1. *Istoriia velikoi otechestvennoi voiny Sovetskogo Soiuza 1941–1945*, vol. 1 (Moscow: Voenizdat, 1960), pp. 477–478; Tucker, *Stalin in Power*, p. 625; and John Erickson, *The Road to Stalingrad. Stalin's War with Germany*, vol. 1 (New York: Harper & Row, 1975), pp. 69–70.

2. *Istoriia velikoi otech. voiny*, vol. 1, pp. 476–477.

3. Ibid., p. 479.

4. As one of his own generals later wrote: Stalin "failed to authorize all urgent or decisive defence measures along the frontier for fear that this would serve the Hitlerites as a pretext for attacking our country." As cited in Robert Paul Carell, *Hitler's War on Russia. The Story of the German Defeat in the East*, trans. Ewald Osers (London: George G. Harrap, 1964), pp. 62–63.

5. Erickson, *Road to Stalingrad*, p. 91. On an earlier occasion, in March 1941, Navy Commander Admiral Kuznetsov had prepared orders for Soviet naval anti-aircraft guns to open fire on German photoreconnaissance planes in the Baltic. But Stalin "with Beria at his side" countermanded the orders and chastized Kuznetsov (Erickson, p. 95).

6. See L. M. Spirin, "Stalin i voina," *Voprosy istorii KPSS*, no. 5 (May 1990): 90–105; *Izvestiia TsK KPSS*, no. 6 (June 1990): 216–222.

7. As Robert Tucker observes of Stalin, "he, who had all along been a hero of history in his own eyes, was for once, and inescapably, confronted with the reality of himself as a colossal bungler of high policy and, as such, an enemy of the people" (Tucker, *Stalin in Power*, p. 625).

8. *Khrushchev Remembers*, vol. II, p. 7. Perhaps this was Beria's crude paraphrasing of what Stalin said.

9. Khrushchev, "Memuary," pt. 4, p. 86. Robert McNeal also mentions this incident but questions Khrushchev's reliability as a source. See McNeal, *Stalin*, p. 239.

10. Interview with Sudoplatov in *New Times*, no. 15 (1992): 42; Khrushchev, "Memuary," pt. 6, p. 68.

11. *Izvestiia TsK KPSS*, no. 6 (1990): 196–197.

12. Ibid., no. 8 (1990): 208.

13. Erickson, *The Road to Stalingrad*, pp. 138–139. As Erickson points out, Beria and Malenkov were promoted over the heads of men who were already full members of the Politburo—Kaganovich, Mikoian, Andreev, Kalinin, Khrushchev, and Zhdanov. John Erickson, *The Soviet High Command. A Military-Political History, 1918–1941* (Boulder: Westview Press, 1984), p. 598.

14. See the excerpts from a draft letter written by George Kennan while serving in the American Embassy in 1945, reprinted in the *Slavic Review* 27 (1968): 481–484.

15. Petrov, *Empire of Fear*, pp. 83–86. Also see Romanov, *Nights Are Longest*, pp. 177–178; and Alexander Werth, *Russia at War, 1941–45* (New York: E. P. Dutton, 1960), pp. xxiii, 217. For a general description of the wartime functions of the NKVD and its troops see V. V. Korovin, "Uchastie organov gosudarstvennoi bezopasnosti v osushchestvlenii funktsii oborony strany," *Sovetskoe gosudarstvo i pravo*, no. 5 (May 1975): 53–60.

16. Erickson, *The Road to Stalingrad*, pp. 175–176.

17. On the functions of the OOs during the war, see Amy Knight, "The KGB's Special Departments in the Soviet Armed Forces," *ORBIS* 28, no. 2 (Summer 1984): 262–267; and Robert Stephan, "Smersh: Soviet Military Counter-intelligence during the Second World War," *Journal of Contemporary History* 22 (1987): 585–613.

18. Erickson, *The Road to Stalingrad*, p. 176.

19. Ibid., p. 142.

20. Ibid., p. 160.

21. Aleksandr I. Solzhenitsyn, *The Gulag Archipelago, 1918–1956*, trans. Thomas P. Whitney (New York: Harper & Row, 1973), p. 79.

22. As cited in Werth, *Russia at War*, pp. 227–228, who refers to Simonov's novel *The Living and the Dead*.

23. Solzhenitsyn, *The Gulag*, p. 126. The defector "A. I. Romanov," who worked under Abakumov strongly disagreed with Solzhenitsyn's description of Abakumov, asserting that he was not a bad person at all. Romanov had similar positive things to say about Beria. See Romanov, *Nights Are Longest*, pp. 177–189.

24. Solzhenitsyn, *The Gulag*, pp. 126–127. Once Riumin beat a prisoner so heavily on the stomach that he broke through the intestinal wall.

25. Solzhenitsyn, *The Gulag*, p. 297.

26. K. F. Telegin, *Ne otdali Moskvy*, 2d ed. (Moscow: "Sovetskaia rossiia," 1975), pp. 114–121. Telegin was arrested on orders from Abakumov in 1948 and remained in prison until after Beria's arrest in 1953. See Sul'ianov, *Arestovat' v Kremle*, pp. 212–221.

27. Ibid., pp. 129–132; *Za Moskvu, za rodinu* (Moscow: Moskovskii Rabochii, 1964), pp. 178–184.

28. Seweryn Bialer, ed., *Stalin and His Generals. Soviet Military Memoirs of World War II* (New York: Pegasus, 1969), pp. 457–459.

29. Leonid Gurunts, "Iz zapisnykh knizhek," *Zvezda*, no. 3 (1988), p. 185.

30. As cited in Bialer, *Stalin and His Generals*, pp. 453–54.

31. N. G. Pavlenko, "Razmyshleniia o sud'be polkovodtsa (zapiski voennogo istorika)," *VIZ*, no. 12 (1988): 29.

32. Werth, *Russia at War*, p. 228.

33. *Foreign Relations of the U.S.*, vol. 1, p. 653.

34. *Pravda*, 8 November 1941. In Stalin's days, and indeed until recently, newspaper photographs of leaders on these occasions were often done by montage to ensure conformity and, for example, to prevent Stalin from appearing shorter than the others. Thus something usual, like Beria not saluting, could have been changed in the picture.

35. Some of these communications have been reproduced from Soviet party archives. See *Izvestiia TsK KPSS*, no. 8 (1990): 217–220; no. 2 (1991): 210–211; and *Pravda*, 8 May 1989.

36. See a resolution of the GKO, dated 15 October 1941, and reprinted in *Izvestiia TsK KPSS*, no. 12 (December 1990): 217.

37. Werth, *Russia at War*, pp. 235, 269, 620.

38. See David Holloway, "Innovation in the Defense Sector," in Ronald Amann and Julian Cooper, eds., *Industrial Innovation in the Soviet Union* (New Haven: Yale University Press, 1982), p. 304. Malenkov was responsible for aircraft and aeroengines, Molotov for tanks, Mikoian for fuel and stores, and Kaganovich for rail transport. The latter two joined the GKO in September 1943.

39. Victor Kravchenko, *I Chose Freedom. The Personal and Political Life of a Soviet Official* (Garden City, N.Y.: Garden City Publications, 1946), p. 404.

40. See L. Ivashov and A. Emelin, "Arkhipelag GULAG: 1941–1945," *Krasnaia zvezda*, 4 August 1990. According to this article, approximately 1.8 million new prisoners reached the GULAG between 22 June 1941 and 1 July 1944. The term *GULAG* is used here in the broader sense, apparently encompassing all persons deprived of freedom, not just those in labor camps.

41. Ibid.; and Holloway, "Innovation in the Defense Sector," p. 335. According to Victor Kravchenko, the war industries depended primarily on forced labor. See Kravchenko, *I Chose Freedom*, p. 404.

42. Nekrasov, "Beriia," pt. 2, p. 24.

43. Ivashov and Emelin, "Arkhipelag GULAG."

44. See Knight, *The KGB*, pp. 229–231; and *Sovetskaia voennaia entsiklopediia*, vol. 2 (Moscow: Voenizdat, 1976), pp. 164–165.

45. Erickson, *The Road to Stalingrad*, p. 378; Werth, *Russia at War*, pp. 578–581.

46. *BSE*, 2d ed., vol. 13 (1952), p. 53.

47. Simonov, "Glazami cheloveka moego pokaleniia," pt. 2, p. 94; TsKhSD, f. 5, op. 30, d. 4, ll. 39–41 (letter to Khrushchev from Shtemenko, 1953); and Bezhnin, "Sergo Beriia," pt. 1, p. 13. Unfortunately, Shtemenko makes no mention whatsoever of Beria in his memoirs on the war years, though he discusses the trip to the Causcasus. See S. M. Shtemenko, *General'nyi shtab v gody voiny* (Moscow: Voenizdat, 1968).

48. I. V. Tiulenev, *Cherez tri voiny* (Moscow: Voenizdat, 1960), pp. 196–197; Erickson, *The Road to Stalingrad*, pp. 378–379; and Volkogonov, *Triumph and Tragedy*, p. 334.

49. Volkogonov, *Triumph and Tragedy*, pp. 481–482.

50. Tiulenev, *Cherez tri voiny*, pp. 196–197.

51. TsKhSD, f. 5, op. 30, d. 4, l. 41.

52. See John A. Armstrong, ed., *Soviet Partisans in World War II* (Madison: The University of Wisconsin Press, 1964), pp. 74–88. Also see Zhigunov's testimony, pp. 119–122.

53. *Izvestiia TsK KPSS*, no. 9 (1990): 197–198.

54. Armstrong, *Soviet Partisans*, pp. 130–132.

55. Ibid., pp. 50–51, 68; John Erickson, *The Road to Berlin. Continuing the History of Stalin's War with Germany* (Boulder, Colo.: Westview Press, 1983), pp. 123–124. In 1953 Strokach provided Beria's opponents with damaging testimony against him.

56. Lavrentii Tsanava, *Vsenarodnaia partizanskaia voina v belorussii protiv fashistskikh zakhvatchikov*, vol. 1 (Minsk: Gosizdat BSSR, 1949), p. 23; also see Sul'ianov, *Arestovat' v Kremle*, p. 103.

57. See an interview with Mazurov published, shortly before he died, in *Sovetskaia Rossiia*, 19 February 1989, pp. 3–4.

58. Armstrong, *Soviet Partisans*, pp. 338, 352–353. On Fitin, see Conquest, *Inside Stalin's Secret Police*, pp, 102; 204. Fitin apparently took over this post when Dekanozov departed in 1939.

59. See George Hill, "Reminiscences of Four Years with the NKVD," unpublished manuscript, Hoover Archives, pp. 153–161.

60. Ibid., pp. 155–157.

61. See John R. Deane, *The Strange Alliance* (New York: Viking, 1947), pp. 50–65; and Anthony Cave Brown, *Wild Bill Donovan. The Last Hero* (New York: Times Books, 1982), pp. 423–425, 647–677. The NKVD was obviously prepared to take advantage of the spirit of openness on the part of their Western counterparts. Brigadier Hill was said to have leaked secret information to the Soviets after becoming involved with a woman who was an NKVD plant. See Nikolai Tolstoy, *Stalin's Secret War* (London: Jonathan Cape, 1981), p. 334.

62. See *New York Times*, 8 June 1991, where these documents are reproduced.

63. John Dziak makes this point in his book *Chekisty. A History of the KGB* (Lexington, Mass.: Lexington Books, 1988), p. 106.

64. Knight, "The KGB's Special Departments," pp. 264–265.

65. See Erickson, *The Road to Stalingrad*, pp. 343–344; E. H. Cookridge, *Gehlen. Spy of the Century* (London: Hodder and Stoughton, 1971), pp. 74–78.

66. In fact, although SMERSH did prove more effective than its predecessor organization, it continued to be hampered by serious weaknesses and, because it was composed mainly of police personnel, was no less ruthless and repressive with the Red Army than it had been when under the NKVD. See Knight, "The KGB's Special Departments," pp. 265–66.

67. TsKhSD, f. 5., op. 30, d. 4, ll. 94–95.

68. On Serov and Kruglov, see *BSE*, vol. 51 (Moscow, 1958), p. 268; Medvedev, *Khrushchev*, pp. 63–164, 68; *Khrushchev Remembers*, vol. 1, p. 338; and *Izvestiia TsK KPSS*, no. 6 (1990): 221.

69. See James T. Reitz, "The Soviet Security Troops—the Kremlin's Other Armies," in David Jones, ed., *Soviet Armed Forces Annual* (Gulf Breeze, Fla.: Academic International Press, 1982), p. 307; and Zhigunov testimony.

70. See *Izvestiia TsK KPSS*, no. 9 (1990): 195. The document reproduced here was a request, dated 3 August 1941, from the military command of the Southern Front for deportation of Germans from the Ukraine. Stalin then forwarded the document to Beria with an order to deport them.

71. Beria's communiques are reproduced in the journal *Kommunist*, no. 3 (1991): 101–112. Also see Nikolai Bugai, "V bessrochnuiu ssylku," *Moskovskie novosti* 14 October 1990; and Vera Tolz, "New Information about the Deportation of Ethnic Groups under Stalin," *Report on the USSR*, 16 April 1991, pp. 16–20.

72. *Kommunist*, no. 3 (1991): 104.

73. Ibid., pp. 103–104.

74. Ibid., pp. 108–110. RTsKhIDNI, f. 644, op. 1: d. 252, ll. 137–142; d. 26, ll. 64–66. The last of the major deportations occurred in November 1944, when more than ninety-one thousand Turks, Kurds, and Khemshils were deported from the border regions of Beria's native Georgia.

75. Bugai, "V bessrochnuiu ssylku."

76. Nikolai Bugai, "Pravda o deportatsii chechenskogo i ingushskogo narodov," *Voprosy istorii*, no. 7 (July 1990): 40–41.

77. By 1948, for example, 144,704 of the 608,749 deported Chechens, Ingushi, Karachi, and Balkars had perished. Ibid., p. 111. Another recent Soviet source gives the official numbers of different national categories of deportees under Stalin, estimating that 2,753,356 persons were deported altogether. See *Argumenty i fakty*, 30 September–6 October 1989, p. 6.

78. *Kommunist*, no. 3 (1991): 101.

79. Ibid., p. 112.

80. Nekrasov, "Beriia," pt. 1, p. 23.

81. See Reitz, "The Soviet Security Troops," pp. 312–314; Erickson, *The Road to Berlin*, p. 403. According to V. Zemskov, already by July 1944 there were more than five million prisoners in the GULAG. See *Argumenty i fakty*, 1–7 September 1990.

82. Erickson, *The Road to Stalingrad*, p. 403. In Averell Harriman's memoirs, it is noted that of all the Russians present at Yalta, Beria was to be the one most directly concerned with the carrying out of the repatriation agreement. See Harriman and Abel, *Special Envoy*, p. 416.

83. See Pavlenko, "Razmyshleniia," pp. 29–31; Anatoli Granovsky, *All Pity Choked. The Memoirs of a Soviet Secret Agent* (London: William Kimber, 1955), pp. 209–210.

84. Elena Rzhevskaia, "V tot den' pozdnei osen'iu," *Znamia*, no. 12 (1986): 163–165. According to this article, based on interviews with Zhukov, he was bothered by this for many years afterward. In his memoirs, Zhukov does not mention this but merely says that he doubted for sometime that Hitler had committed suicide because the body had not been found. See G. Zhukov, *Reminiscences and Reflections*, vol. 2 (Moscow: Progress Publishers, 1985), pp. 394–395. Ironically, it was OSS chief Donovan who furnished the NKVD, in a message to Fitin, with information on Hitler's dentition, coming from Hitler's dentist, so that pathologists could more easily identify the corpse. See Brown, *Wild Bill Donovan*, p. 755.

85. See Pavlenko, "Razmyshleniia," pp. 30–31. According to the memoirs of navy commander N. G. Kuznetsov, Stalin was not hostile to Zhukov, saying to him: "I don't believe all that nonsense. But it still would be better for you to go somewhere away from Moscow for a while." See N. G. Kuznetsov, *Nakanune* (Moscow, 1966), p. 212.

86. Medvedev, *Let History Judge*, p. 783.

87. *Pravda*, 11 July 1945.

88. For detailed accounts of Soviet behavior at wartime conferences among the allies, see *Soviet Diplomacy and Negotiating Behavior*.

89. George F. Kennan, *Memoirs*, vol. 1, 1925–1950 (Boston: Little, Brown, 1967), p. 524.

90. Ibid., p. 526.

91. Nicholas Merab Kviatashvili, unpublished memoirs (Washington, D.C., n.d,) pp. 13–33.

92. Mikhail Kaniuka and Vitalii Bezhnin, "Tegeran-43. Trudnye mesiatsy," *Kievskie Novosti*, no. 14, 2 April 1993 (excerpts from a book on Sergo Beria).

93. Ibid., p. 19.

94. Winston S. Churchill, *The Second World War: Closing the Ring* (Boston: Houghton Mifflin, 1951), p. 374.

95. Charles E. Bohlen, *Witness to History, 1929–1969* (New York: W. W. Norton, 1973), pp. 354–355. Bohlen noted that Beria "was quiet and spoke little. He looked like a school master, a characteristic of chiefs of secret police."

96. Harriman and Abel, *Special Envoy*, pp. 415–416. Kathleen Harriman described Beria as "little and fat with thick lenses, which give him a sinister look, but quite genial."

CHAPTER SEVEN
KREMLIN POLITICS AFTER THE WAR

1. Arnold Kramish, *Atomic Energy in the Soviet Union* (Stanford: Stanford University Press, 1959), pp. 15–47; Leonard Nikishin, "Razbudivshie dzhinna," *Moskovskie novosti*, 8 October 1989.

2. See a recently published account of Soviet intelligence gathering on the bomb, based on some archival sources: Vladimir Skomoroklov, "Vokrug atomnoi bomby," *Kur'er Sovetskoi Razvedki*, no. 1 (1991), pp. 11–15.

3. Vladimir Chikov, "How the Soviet Intelligence Service 'Split' the American Bomb," Parts 1–2, *New Times*, nos. 16–17 (April–May 1991): 37–40, 36–37. The author bases his information on secret KGB archives. Also see *Pravda*, 16 July 1992.

4. Nikishin, "Razbudivshie dzhinna." Also see Chikov, "Soviet Intelligence Service," which gives the impression that this meeting took place in the late spring of 1942; and Chikov, "Kak raskryvali," pts. 1–3 *Armiia*, nos. 18–19 (1991) and no. 2 (1992): 66–71, 69–73, 70–77.

5. Chikov, "Soviet Intelligence Service," pt. 1. Fitin remained head of foreign intelligence until 1944, when he was succeeded by P. V. Fedotov. In 1946 Fedotov was replaced by S. R. Savchenko, who had headed the security organs in the Ukraine during the war.

6. See the memoirs of Feklisov, "Podvig Klausa Fuksa," pts. 1–2, *VIZ*, no. 12 (1990) and no. 1 (1991): 22–29, 34–43. A U.S. intelligence report confirmed that Fuchs disclosed complete details of the atomic weapon tested at Almagordo and employed at Nagasaki. See "Atomic Energy Program, Status," Office of Scientific Intelligence Report, CIA/SI 118–51, 6 March 1952, *DDQ* 6, no. 2 (April–June 1980): 135C.

7. Chikov, "Soviet Intelligence Service," pt. 1. According to one source, Zarubin had collected military and political intelligence from the Polish officers captured by the Soviets and later killed at Katyn. See Romanov, *Nights Are Longest*, pp. 137–138.

8. See *Report on Soviet Espionage Activities in Connection with the Atomic Bomb*, U.S. Congress, House Committee on Un-American Activities, Eightieth Congress, 1948; Oliver Pilat, *The Atom Spies* (New York: G. P. Putnams & Sons, 1952).

9. Chikov, "Soviet Intelligence Service," pt. 2.

10. Feklisov, "Podvig Klausa Fuksa," pt. 2, p. 43.

11. Nikishin, "Razbudivshie dzhinna."

12. Stalin is reported to have said: "A single demand of you, comrades, provide atomic weapons in the shortest possible time. You know that Hiroshima has shaken the whole world. The equilibrium has been destroyed. Provide the bomb—it will remove a great danger from us." As cited in David Holloway, "Innovation in the Defense Sector," p. 389.

13. Ibid., pp. 390–391.

14. See "Uchenyi i vlast'," *Ogonek*, no. 25 (June 1989): 19.

15. See Nikishin, "Razbudivshie dzhinna"; Holloway, "Innovation in the Defense Sector," pp. 336–341.

16. Decisions relating to the project were kept secret from all but a few highly placed members of the leadership. The Central Committee, for example, was not privy to information on the project. See *Izvestiia TsK KPSS*, no. 1 (1991): 144.

17. "Uchenyi i vlast'," p. 19.

18. Ibid.

19. Ibid.; "Risk-2," Soviet television, 1 August 1988, BBC Summary of World Broadcasts, SU/0227/C/1, 11 August 1990.

20. "Izmeniat', chot i izmenit eshche vozmozhno," *Ogonek*, no. 35 (August 1990), pp. 6–7.

21. Ibid.

22. Nikishin, "Razbudivshie dzhinna." Golovin reaffirmed his impressions of Beria in a talk at the Kennan Institute, Washington D.C., 7 October 1992.

23. Yuli Khariton and Yuri Smirnov, "The Khariton Version," *The Bulletin of the Atomic Scientists*, May 1993, p. 26.

24. Sakharov, *Vospominaniia*, pp. 195–196.

25. Vladimir Rudolph, "The Administrative Organization of Soviet Control, 1945–48," in Robert Slusser, ed., *Soviet Economic Policy in Postwar Germany* (New York: Research Program on the USSR, 1953), pp. 42–49.

26. See "Soviet Atomic Energy Program, Status," Office of Scientific Intelligence Report, CIA/SI 113–51, 28 July 1951, *DDQ* 6, no. 2 (April–June 1980): b

135; "Soviet Atomic Energy Program, Status," Office of Scientific Intelligence Report, CIA/SI 118–151, 6 March 1952 *DDQ* 6, no. 2 (April–June 1980): 135C.

27. See the memoirs of a German scientist who worked in the Hertz group at Sukhumi: Heinz und Elfi Barwich, *Das rote Atom* (Munich: Scherz Verlag, 1967), pp. 31–46; Also see Office of Scientific Intelligence Special Report, OSI/SR-2/49, 31 October 1949, "German Scientists at Sukhumi, USSR," *DDQ* 6, no. 1 (1979): 19b; and *Literaturnaia gazeta*, no. 14 (10 April 1991), p. 5.

28. Barwich, *Das rote Atom*, pp. 103–120. Sometime in 1950 Gustav Hertz was apparently killed in an accident while testing one of his nuclear devices. See Department of State Message, F790010–1449, dated 5 July 1951, National Archives, no. 761.5611/7–551, RG 59, Box 694.

29. Kramish, *Atomic Energy*, pp. 115–120.

30. Nikishin, "Razbudivshie dzhinna."

31. According to a top secret CIA memorandum, the "highest Soviet authority" (presumably Stalin) was seriously disturbed over the lack of progress on the bomb in the summer of 1947. See memorandum no. 22729, R. H. Hillenkoetter, Director of Central Intelligence, 6 July 1948, *DDQ* 5, no. 1 (1979): 17c.

32. See Memorandum no. 22729, R. H. Hillenkoetter, Director of Central Intelligence, 6 July 1948. Truman Library, Papers of Harry Truman, *DDQ* 5, no. 1 (1979): 17C; and "Status of the USSR Atomic Energy Project," Office of Scientific Intelligence, Nuclear Energy Branch, OSI/SR-10/49. 1 July 1949, *DDQ* 5, no. 1 (1979).

33. *Moskovskii Bol'shevik*, 15 January 1946.

34. *Pravda*, 20 March 1946.

35. State Department telegram, no. 145, 15 January 1946. National Archives, doc. no. 961.00/1–1546, RG 59, Box 6642.

36. Other Politburo members in early 1946 were Stalin, Andreev, Zhdanov, Malenkov, Molotov, Mikoian, Kalinin, Kaganovich, Voroshilov, and Khrushchev.

37. TsKhSD, f. 5, op. 30, d. 4, ll. 96–102 (Letter from Merkulov to Khrushchev, July 1953).

38. From April to July 1946 the following deputy ministers were identified: *MGB*: S. I. Ogol'tsev, N. N. Selivanovskii, A. S. Blinov, N. K. Kovalchuk, M. G. Svinelupov, and P. V. Fedotov; *MVD*: V. S. Riasnoi, E. V. Chernyshev, A. V. Appollonov, I. A. Serov, A. 20P. Zaveniagin, S. S. Mamulov, and B. P. Obruchnikov. See a U.S. State Department Report, dated 26 July 1946, National Archives, doc. no. 861/002/7–2646, RG 59. This source reports rumors of Merkulov's removal, although it was not officially announced until October 1946.

39. See the following U.S. State Department telegrams: no. 145, doc. no. 861.001/1–1546, 15 January 1946; no. A-18, 15 June 1946, doc. no. 861.00/6–1546; no. 1764, 5 June 1946, doc. no. 861.00/6–546, National Archives, RG 59, Box 6642; and no. 3387, 4 September 1946, doc. no. 861.00/9–446; no. 4079, 5 November 1946, doc. no. 861.00/11–546, National Archives, RG 59, Box 6640.

40. *Khrushchev Remembers*, vol. 2, p. 295. Beria's influence over foreign policy was furthered by the appointment of a close protégé, former editor of *Zaria vostoka* V. G. Grigorian, to head the Central Committee foreign policy commis-

sion sometime in 1948. See Werner Hahn, *Postwar Soviet Politics. The Fall of Zhdanov and the Defeat of Moderation: 1946–50* (Ithaca: Cornell University Press, 1982), p. 107.

41. *Khrushchev Remembers*, vol. 2, pp. 295–296.

42. Walter Bedell Smith, *My Three Years in Moscow* (New York: Lippincott, 1949) p. 52.

43. ZV, 27 January 1946.

44. Ibid.

45. See L. P. Beriia, *Rech' na sobranii izburatelei Tbilisskogo-Stalinskogo izburatel'nogo okruga* (Moscow: Gosizdat, 1946).

46. See Rudolph, "The Administrative Organization of Soviet Control."

47. Ibid.

48. Nikolai Grishin, "The Saxony Mining Operation ('Vismut')," in Slusser, *Soviet Economic Policy*, pp. 127–153.

49. On the earlier stages of the Zhdanov-Malenkov rivalry, see Sheila Fitzpatrick, "Culture and Politics under Stalin: A Reappraisal," *Slavic Review* 35, no. 2 (June 1976): 211–231.

50. Gavriel Ra'anan says Zhdanov and Beria began to dislike each other in the late thirties, when Zhdanov was a supporter of Ezhov. He claims that during the war Beria undermined paramilitary activities in the Leningrad area, which Zhdanov was in charge of, and also instigated a reprimand of Zhdanov by Stalin in August 1941. See Gavriel D. Ra'anan, *International Policy Formation in the USSR* (Hamden, Conn.: Archon Books, 1983), pp. 19–22, 171–172.

51. See Hahn, *Post-War Soviet Politics*, pp. 51–52.

52. See Rudolph, "Administrative Organization of Soviet Control," pp. 41–43; *Foreign Relations of the United States*, vol. 6 (1946), pp. 809–811; and State Department message, no. A1390, 22 December 1947, doc. no. 861.00/12-2247, National Archives, R. G. 59, Box 6640.

53. Rudolph, "Administrative Organization of Soviet Control," pp. 42–44.

54. U.S. Department of State, *Foreign Relations of the United States*, vol. 4 (1948), pp. 821–822; vol. 5 (1949), pp. 651–654; and McNeal, *Stalin*, pp. 272–273.

55. Gavriel D. Ra'anan, *International Policy Formation*, pp. 25–50; also see Hahn, *Postwar Soviet Politics*, pp. 9–25.

56. *Izvestiia TsK KPSS*, no. 3 (1989): 152; Hahn, *Postwar Soviet Politics*, p. 106; and A. Afanasiev, "Pobeditel'," *Komsomol'skaia pravda*, 15 January 1988.

57. See the memoirs of Gusarov's son, Vladimir Gusarov, *Moi papa ubil Mikhoelsa* (Frankfurt am Main: Posev, 1978), pp. 93–100; R. Platonov and V. Velichko, "Zloveshchaia ten' Tsanavy," *Kommunist Belorussii*, pts. 1–2 (February–March 1991): 62–69, 64–73; and Sul'ianov, *Arestovat' v Kremle*, pp. 260–263. Tsanava came close to losing his job in 1946–47, because of several negative reports from Belorussia, but Abakumov protected him.

58. See Benjamin Pinkus, *The Soviet Government and the Jews, 1948–1967. A Documented Study* (Cambridge: Cambridge University Press, 1984), pp. 147–155; and Louis Rapoport, *Stalin's War against the Jews. The Doctor's Plot and the Soviet Solution* (New York: Free Press, 1990), pp. 80–91.

59. "Protokol No. 7," *Izvestiia TsK KPSS*, no. 12 (1989): 35–40. For a translation and commentary on this document, see Shimon Redlich, "Rehabilitation of the Jewish Anti-Fascist Committee: Report No. 7," *Soviet Jewish Affairs* 20, nos. 2–3 (1990): 85–98.

60. Documents from the Archives of the Jewish Antifascist Committee, exhibited at RTsKhIDNI, August 1992; and RTsKhIDNI, f. 17, op. 128, d. 1058, ll. 132–133. Another important figure in the campaign was Mikhail Suslov, who took over the CC Agitation and Propaganda Department and became a CC Secretary in mid-1947.

61. Report of Deputy MVD Chief Serov on the deaths of Mikhoels and Golubev-Potapov, 11 February 1948, KGB Archives, f. 6, op. 150 (exhibited at RTsKhIDNI, August 1992).

62. The letter, dated 2 April 1953, from the KGB Archives, was published in *Argumenty i Fakty*, no. 19 (May 1992), p. 5.

63. Pinkus, *Soviet Government and the Jews*, p. 90; Shimon Redlich, *Propaganda and Nationalism in Wartime Russia. The Jewish Antifascist Committee in the USSR, 1941–1948* (Boulder: East European Monographs, 1982), pp. 11, 84; and exhibit at RTsKhIDNI, August 1992 (letter to Beria from Mikhoels and Sh. Epshtein, dated 26 May 1944).

64. RTsKhIDNI, f. 17, op. 127, d. 478, ll. 44–45; Arkhiv Tsk KPU, f. 1, op. 23, d. 3851, ll. 3–5. I am grateful to Professor Shimon Redlich for sending me copies of these documents. Also see Shimon Redlich, "Discovering Soviet Archives. The Papers of the Jewish Anti-Fascist Committee," *The Jewish Quarterly* 39, no. 4 (Winter 1992–93): pp. 15–19.

65. Harrison Salisbury, *American in Russia* (New York: Harper & Brothers, 1955), pp. 89–91; TsKhSD, f. 5, op. 15, d. 407, ll. 113–119.

66. Chuev, *Sto sorok besed*, p. 318.

67. Nekrasov, *Beriia*, p. 340. For further details, see chapter 9.

68. Hahn, *Postwar Soviet Politics*, pp. 55–56, 141.

69. KGB archives, f. 6, op. 150, d. 5 (Exhibit at RTsKhIDSI, August 1992); *Izvestiia TsK KPSS*, no. 12 (1989): 37.

70. RTsKhIDNI, f. 17, op. 118, d. 305, ll. 21–22.

71. *Izvestiia TsK KPSS*, no. 12 (1989): 37–38 (Report of the Politburo Rehabilitation Commission). The authors of this report say that "direct responsibility for the illegal repressions of persons accused in connection with the Case of the Jewish Antifascist Committee lies with G. M. Malenkov, who was directly connected with the investigation and the court examination." But they ignore the fact that Malenkov was not even in the Secretariat when the campaign was launched. In fact, Khrushchev, who later denounced both Beria and Malenkov for a whole range of evil deeds, never accused them of involvement in the anti-Semitic campaign.

72. See U.S. State Department Airgram, 8 December 1947, No. A-1323, National Archive doc. no. 861.00/12–847, RG 59; and Smith, *My Three Years*, p. 71.

73. ZV, 18 April 1948; *Vedomosti verkhovnogo soveta GSSR*, nos.1–2 (14–15), November 1948. Rapava's replacement, Rukhadze, also had a long association with Beria, but was not a Mingrelian.

74. TsKhSD, f. 5, op. 15, d. 448, ll. 190–192 (letter from V. Budzhiashvili to Malenkov, 30 July 1953).

75. After the war Shavdiia was imprisoned as a German collaborator. In 1946 he admitted his crimes, but was not punished and was instead placed under Beria's guardianship. See Nekrasov, *Beriia*, pp. 340–341.

76. *Izvestiia TsK KPSS*, no. 1 (1991): 184; Volkogonov, *Triumph and Tragedy*, pp. 507–508.

77. *Izvestiia TsK KPSS*, no. 1 (1991): 168–169.

78. *Time*, 22 March 1948, pp. 30–31.

79. See Jonathan R. Adelman, ed., *Terror and Communist Politics: The Role of the Secret Police in Communist States* (Boulder: Westview Press, 1984), pp. 155–174, 175–194; and Zbigniew K. Brzezinski, *The Soviet Bloc: Unity and Conflict* (New York: Praeger, 1961).

80. Khrushchev later claimed that Beria and Abakumov engineered the split, but no other sources corroborate this. See Hahn, *Postwar Soviet Politics*, p. 98, citing a Khrushchev speech in *Pravda*, 26 May 1955.

81. *Izvestiia TsK KPSS*, no. 2 (1989): 126–135.

82. See Hahn, *Postwar Soviet Politics*, pp. 163–170; Ra'anan, *International Policy Formation*, pp. 158–159; 177–178.

83. *Sovetskaia Belorussiia*, 19 April 1989.

84. V. Kolotov, "Predsedatel' Gosplana," *Literaturnaia gazeta*, 30 November 1963, p. 2.

85. Chuev, *Sto sorok besed*, p. 324.

86. *Izvestiia TsK KPSS*, pp. 126–135.

87. Like his predecessor, Vyshinskii was apparently not an assertive foreign minister, but was merely there to do Stalin's bidding. U.S. Ambassador Walter Kirk observed after a meeting with Stalin in August 1949: "He [Stalin] certainly dominates the situation here—and Vyshinskii was hopping around like a pea on a hot griddle to do his slightest wish." See U.S. Department of State, *Foreign Relations of the United States*, vol. 5, p. 654.

88. Chuev, *Sto sorok besed*, p. 256; *Khrushchev Remembers*, vol. 2, p. 300. Khrushchev recalled: "Those dinners were frightful. We would get home from them early in the morning, just in time for breakfast, and then we'd have to go to work."

89. *Khrushchev Remembers*, vol. 2, p. 300.

90. Khrushchev, "Memuary," pt. 3, pp. 72–73. Also see Chuev, *Sto sorok besed*, p. 255.

91. Alliluyeva, *Only One Year*, p. 386. She recalls that Mikoian and Stalin's private secretary Poskrebyshev were usually the victims, since they were the most "patient and submissive."

92. Djilas, *Conversations with Stalin*, pp. 158–159. Djilas observed strong signs of senility in Stalin by this time and felt that his intellect was declining.

93. State Department telegram, no. 813, 1 April 1949. National Archives, no. NND760050, RG 59, Box 6641.

94. Smith, *My Three Years*, p. 78.

95. Ibid., p. 83.

96. In lengthy interviews given toward the end of his life, Molotov never showed animosity toward either Beria or Malenkov.

97. Alliluyeva, *Only One Year*, p. 420.

98. *Khrushchev Remembers*, vol. 1, p. 250.

99. For an enlightening discussion of Mao's approach to his subordinates and to the question of his succession, see Frederick C. Teiwes, "Mao and His Lieutenants," *The Australian Journal of Chinese Affairs*, no. 19/20 (1988): 1–80.

100. For the text of Beria's speech, see *Pravda*, 21 December 1949.

CHAPTER EIGHT
BERIA UNDER FIRE: 1950–1953

1. *Khrushchev Remembers*, vol. 1, p. 250.

2. See U.S. Deptartment of State report, no. 2570, 8 February 1951, National Archives, RG 59, Box 3804.

3. See Robert Conquest, *Power and Policy in the U.S.S.R. The Struggle for Stalin's Succession, 1945–1960* (New York: Harper & Row, 1967), pp. 112–128; Hahn, *Postwar Soviet Politics* pp. 136–140.

4. *ZV*, 10 March 1950.

5. As quoted in Hahn, *Postwar Soviet Politics*, p. 139.

6. *Khrushchev Remembers*, vol. 1, p. 250.

7. This article was cited in *ZV*, 19 September 1952, in a speech by Sh. D. Getiia, the successor to Mgeladze as first secretary in Abkhaziia. Also see Conquest, *Power and Policy*, p. 137.

8. *Bakiinskii rabochii*, 16 June 1988; Anatolii Golovkov, "Vechnyi isk," *Ogonek*, no. 18 (April 1988): 28–30.

9. See Nekrasov, *Beriia*, p. 361. Her name was Aleksandra Nakashidze.

10. *Khrushchev Remembers*, vol. 1, pp. 311–312.

11. *BSE*, 2d ed., vol 5, pp. 22–23.

12. Ibid., vol. 2, pp. 428–429.

13. See *Khrushchev Remembers*, vol. 1, pp. 309–313.

14. V. Kutuzov, "'Chernaia kukhnia' Abakumova," *Krasnaia zvezda*, 30 September 1989.

15. See *Izvestiia TsK KPSS*, no. 1 (1991): 154. TsKhSD, f. 5, op. 30, d. 4, ll. 101–102.

16. Kutuzov, "'Chernaia kukhnia.'" Abakumov remained in prison until his trial and execution in December 1954.

17. Instead of appealing to Stalin, as Abakumov requested, Beria passed the letters on to the USSR Procurator, Safronov. See Sul'ianov, *Arestovat' v Kremle*, pp. 255–258.

18. TsKhSD, f. 5, op. 30, d. 4, l. 101.

19. For biographical information on these men see TsGA, f. 5446, op. 87, d. 2348, l. 48; and *Krasnaia zvezda*, 24 October 1964; 3 September 1975; and 17 September 1985. Mironov rose to become head of the powerful Administrative Organs Department of the Central Committee under Khrushchev. Epishev subsequently, from 1962 to 1985, served as head of the MPA; and Makarev served as his deputy until his death in 1975.

20. Two such men were N. I. Savinkin, who eventually became chief of the AO Department; and V. V. Zolotukhin, a former Moscow party offical and an associate of Khrushchev.

21. A. I. Skryl'nik, *General armii A. A. Epishev* (Moscow: Voennoe Izdatel'stvo, 1989), p. 208.

22. Kutuzov, " 'Chernaia kukhnia' "; *Izvestiia TsK KPSS*, no. 8 (1991): 221. Likhachev had been an emissary for the MGB in Czechoslovakia in 1949 (see below). It is not clear who was Tsanava's immediate replacement in Belorussia, but M. I. Baskakov, who was associated with Ignat'ev, took over as MGB chief in September 1952. From 1947 to 1950 he had been minister of state security in Uzbekistan, while Ignat'ev was there. See Arnold Beichman and Mikhail Bernstam, *Andropov: New Challenge to the West* (New York: Stein and Day, 1983), pp. 121–123.

23. See Nekrasov, "Beriia," pt. 2, p. 41; and TsGA, f. 5446, op. 87, d. 2348. Another party official brought into the MGB at this time was S. N. Lialin, formerly secretary of the Tula Obkom. By 1952 he was a deputy minister of state security. He survived the Beria purges and served as a leading KGB official under Khrushchev.

24. See Charles H. Fairbanks, Jr., "Clientelism and Higher Politics in Georgia, 1949–1953," in Suny, *Transcaucasia.*, pp. 339–368. Fairbanks cites as a case in point the Historical and Ethnographical Museum of Georgian Jews, which remained open until 1952, despite the campaign against "cosmopolitanism."

25. See Iurii Krotkov, "Rasskazy o marshale Beriia," *Novyi Zhurnal*, no. 95 (June 1969): 86–117. This article is based on personal accounts by two Georgian officials.

26. Ibid. The name of the official in question, who related the story to Krotkov, is not revealed.

27. Ibid.; and TsKhSD, f. 5, op. 15, d. 448, ll. 63–69 (report on a July 1953 plenum in Georgia, at which the secretary of the Gagra *Raikom* (district committee) made similar accusations against Beria).

28. *Izvestiia TsK KPSS*, no. 1 (1991): 150.

29. *ZV*, 18 November 1951.

30. For Baramiia's speech, see *XIV s'ezd Kompartii (Bol'shevikov) Gruzii, 25–29 Ianvaria 1949 goda* (Tbilisi: Zaria Vostoka, 1949). It should be noted that, Baramiia barely mentioned First Secretary Charkviani in his speech.

31. *ZV*, 25 January 1952.

32. *ZV*, 16 January 1952.

33. See Fairbanks, "Clientelism and Higher Politics"; Conquest, *Power and Policy*, p. 139; *ZV*, 14 January 1952.

34. *ZV*, 27 January 1952.

35. *Izvestiia TsK KPSS*, no. 1 (1991), p. 151.

36. See his biography in *ZV*, 25 January 1946.

37. *ZV*, 3 April 1952.

38. The recent purges of Mingrelians were instigated by Stalin rather than by Charkviani, but Charkviani may have tried to gain from these purges by promoting his allies. Furthermore, some believe he was cultivating his own patronage network by the late forties. (This is the interpretation of Conquest, *Power and*

Policy, pp. 137–140.) It is significant that at the Fourteenth Congress of the Georgian Communist Party in early 1949, Charkviani was referred to for the first time as a leader, along with Stalin and Beria. See *XIV s'ezd Kompartii (Bolshevikov) Gruzii.*

39. *Vtoraia sessiia verkhovnogo soveta gruzinskoi SSR. stenograficheskii otchet* (Tbilisi, 1952).

40. Gogua's post was assumed by Z. N. Chkhubianishvili, formerly chairman of the Georgian Council of Ministers. For the latter, this was a demotion. Karanadze was replaced by V. A. Loladze, deputy minister in the Georgian MGB. Karanadze's biography appeared in *ZV*, 20 January 1946, p. 3, when he ran as a deputy to the Georgian Supreme Soviet. In April 1953 after Stalin's death, he resurfaced as a deputy minister in the MVD.

41. Not surprisingly, the delegate was a Mingrelian, A. I. Kandaria, a member of the Central Committee.

42. *ZV*, 16 and 17 April 1952.

43. *ZV*, 17 April 1952.

44. *ZV*, 16 April 1952.

45. *ZV*, 30 April 1952, 20 May 1952.

46. *ZV*, 19 and 24 April 1952.

47. R. A. Kvirkveliia, appointed a Georgian CC Secretary in late 1951, lost his job at the end of May 1952. See *ZV*, 28 May 1952. The two officials who remained from the "old leadership" were CC Secretary V. G. Tskhovrebashvili and Tbilisi *Gorkom* Secretary G. N. Dzhibladze.

48. His dismissal was revealed in *ZV*, 1 July 1952.

49. Kochlavashvili was not dismissed by Beria after Stalin's death (he was made a deputy of the MVD), but was ousted along with Beria later in 1953.

50. The speech was published in *ZV*, 16,17, and 18 September 1952.

51. Ibid.

52. Ibid.

53. See U.S. Department of State report, no. 761.006–1650, 16 June 1950, National Archives, RG 59, Box 3799.

54. See, for example, *Pravda*, 21 December 1949; and *Izvestiia*, 10 March 1950.

55. See Khrushchev's secret speech, where he ridicules the idea, apparently held by Stalin, of Georgia leaving the Soviet Union and joining Turkey. Bertram Wolfe, *Khrushchev and Stalin's Ghost*, p. 196.

56. See Conquest, *Power and Policy*, p. 144; *Pravda*, 30 January 1953.

57. On Mgeladze's speech see Lazar M. Pistrak, "The Purges in Georgia," 17 April 1953, Hoover Institution, Nicolaevsky Collection.

58. For an analysis of the nationality issue at the congress see Charles Fairbanks, Jr., "National Cadres as a Force in the Soviet System: The Evidence of Beria's Career, 1949–53," in Jeremy Azrael, ed., *Soviet Nationality Policies and Practices* (New York: Praeger, 1978), pp. 144–186.

59. Ibid.

60. *Khrushchev Remembers*, vol. 1, pp. 277–278. Khrushchev indicates that they disagreed over the reports: "I knew that when I submitted a draft of the

report, I could expect the others to attack it—especially Beria, who would pull Malenkov along with him." In fact, Malenkov, who gave the keynote address to the congress, ridiculed Khrushchev's agricultural proposals, in particular the concept of agro-towns.

61. *Khrushchev Remembers*, vol. 1, p. 281.

62. Molotov also seems to have been a victim. In a collection of interviews given late in his life, he expressed his disappointment that Stalin had become suspicious of him and excluded him from his inner circle. He intimates that Khrushchev was behind this: "Stalin was overworked. And someone took advantage of this. They put things over on him, tried to please him. Therefore [Stalin] trusted Khrushchev and didn't trust me." See Chuev, *Sto sorok besed*, p. 271. Also see p. 465.

63. See Hahn, *Postwar Soviet Politics*, p. 145–146; Conquest, *Power and Policy*, pp. 40, 70, 208.

64. Skryl'nik, *Epishev*, p. 209.

65. TsKhSD, f. 5, op. 15, d. 397, l. 124.

66. That these men were allied with Beria can be deduced from the timing of their initial appointments to the police and from the fact that all were arrested after Beria fell.

67. TsGA, f. 5446, op. 87, d. 2348, resolution no. 752. This resolution was in fact one of the few not signed by Stalin.

68. Eitingon had worked with Sudoplatov, carrying out "special assignments," such as the murder of Trotsky. See *Moscow News*, no. 32 (August 1992): 9.

69. Simonov, "Glazami cheloveka moego pokaleniia," pt. 2, p. 93.

70. TsKhSD, f. 5, op. 30, d. 4, ll. 39–50.

71. TsKhSD, f. 50, op. 30, d. 4, ll. 41–50.

72. Beria also released several military officials who had been arrested on the basis of materials fabricated by Abakumov in April 1946. They included A. I. Shakhurin and A. A. Novikov.

73. See Ra'anan, *International Policy Formation*, p. 59; and Nicolaevsky, *Power and the Soviet Elite*, pp. 170–171.

74. See Jiri Pelikan, ed., *The Czechoslovak Political Trials, 1950–1954* (Stanford: Stanford University Press, 1971), pp. 80–114; TsKhSD, f. 4, op. 8, d. 838. On Boiarskii, who is still alive and living in Moscow, see Evgeniia Al'bats, *Mina zamedlennogo deistviia* (Moscow: Russlit, 1992), pp. 97–150. Beschastnov's biography appears in *Deputy verkhovnogo soveta SSSR* (Moscow: Politizdat, 1974).

75. Pelikan, ibid., pp. 101–113, 161, 164, 171, 216, 230.

76. See Pinkus, *Soviet Government and the Jews*, pp. 198–199; and Yehoshua A. Gilboa, *The Black Years of Soviet Jewry* (New York: Little, Brown, 1971), pp. 260–282.

77. *Izvestiia TsK KPSS*, no. 12 (1989): 34–40.

78. Fairbanks, "National Cadres," p. 161,

79. *Kommunist*, no. 1 (January 1953), as cited in Pinkus, *Soviet Government and the Jews*, pp. 218–219.

80. *Pravda*, 13 January 1953.

81. For two recent studies of this episode, see Rapoport, *Stalin's War against the Jews*; and the memoirs of one of those arrested for the plot: Yakov Rapoport, *The Doctor's Plot. Stalin's Last Crime* (London: Fourth Estate, 1991).

82. *Pravda*, 13 January 1953.

83. *Izvestiia TsK KPSS*, no. 1 (1991): 142.

84. See A. N. Kolesnik, "Glavnyi telokhranitel' vozhdia," *VIZ*, no. 12 (1989): 85-92.

85. *Izvestiia TsK KPSS*, no. 1 (1991): 151. Kuz'michev was rearrested after Beria's fall.

86. See "Kak byl arestovan Beriia," *Moskovskie novosti*, 10 June 1990, p. 8; TsKhSD, f. 5, op. 30, d. 4, l. 67. If this is so, Vlasik was soon back in prison. In January 1955 he was sentenced to ten years. The sentence was later commuted to five years. See Kolesnik, "Glavnyi telokhranitel.'" Volkogonov (*Triumph and Tragedy*, pp. 569-570) claims that Beria instigated the case against Vlasik but this is unlikely, especially since Vlasik was sentenced *after* Beria's fall. Beria's son Sergo insists that Volkogonov is wrong, stressing that only Stalin could make a decision to move against Vlasik. See Bezhnin, "Sergo Beriia," pt. 5, p. 13.

87. See Department of State telegrams, nos. 3982 and 4008, dated 16 January 1953. National Archives, RG 59, Box 3805.

88. Conquest, *Power and Policy*, p. 171. Conquest does go on to say, however, that "when all is said we cannot exclude the possibility that in his last years the old dictator may have become especially capricious, and that in the last months of the Doctors' Plot he had lost control in some quite unpredictable way" (p. 172).

89. Excerpts from the unpublished memoirs of Dr. A. L. Miasnikov, *Literaturnaia gazeta*, 1 March 1989, p. 13.

90. David Gai, "The Doctors Case," *Moscow News* (February 1988): 16; Rapoport, *Stalin's War*, pp. 134-135.

91. Ibid., pp. 131-132.

92. Wolfe, *Khrushchev and Stalin's Ghost*, pp. 202-204; *Khrushchev Remembers*, vol. 1, pp. 282-286. Khrushchev observes: "If Stalin had been a normal person, he wouldn't have given Timashuk's letter a second thought" (p. 282).

93. Nicolaevsky, *Power and the Soviet Elite*, p. 110.

94. Poskrebyshev was transferred to the post of secretary to the Presidium of the Central Committee, where he remained until he was quietly retired in 1954. He died in 1965. See *Izvestiia TsK KPSS*, no. 3 (1989): 169.

95. *Khrushchev Remembers*, vol. 1, p. 283 (quote from the editor and translator, Strobe Talbott).

96. Ibid., p. 314.

97. Ibid., pp. 313-314.

98. Pinkus, *Soviet Government and the Jews*, pp. 91-94, 401.

99. This point is discussed in Conquest, *Power and Policy*, pp. 167-170.

100. *Khrushchev Remembers*, vol. 1, p. 286; *Sovetskaia voennaia entsiklopediia*, vol. 3 (Moscow: Voenizdat, 1977), pp. 303-304; Sul'ianov, *Arestovat' v Kremle*, pp. 265-266.

101. TsKhSD, f. 5, op. 15, d. 407, ll. 1-107.

102. Ibid.

CHAPTER NINE
THE DOWNFALL OF BERIA

1. *Khrushchev Remembers*, vol. 1, pp. 316–318.
2. A. T. Rybin, "Riadom s I. V. Stalinym," *Sotsiologicheskie issledovanie*, no. 3 (1988): 84–94.
3. *Literaturnaya gazeta*, 1 March 1989, p. 13 (citing L. Miasnikov).
4. Svetlana Alliluyeva, "Dva poslednikh razgovora," *Moskovskie novosti*, 21 October 1990. She says she first learned about this new evidence in 1966.
5. Ibid.
6. *Pravda*, 4 March 1953.
7. *Khrushchev Remembers*, vol. 1, p. 318.
8. Alliluyeva, *Twenty Letters to a Friend*, pp. 7–8.
9. *Khrushchev Remembers*, vol. 1, pp. 322–323.
10. Ibid., pp. 319–323; *Izvestiia TsK KPSS*, no. 1 (1991): 149–150.
11. *Izvestiia TsK KPSS*, no. 1 (1991): 150.
12. Ibid., p. 160.
13. Khrushchev recalled: "If Bulganin and I had objected to the way Beria and Malenkov were running the meeting, we would have been accused of being quarrelsome and disorderly and of starting a fight in the party before the corpse was cold" (*Khrushchev Remembers*, vol. 1, p. 324).
14. As Robert Conquest points out, the "junior" men eventually returned to the center when Khrushchev became dominant and survived after the antiparty group (Malenkov, Molotov, and Kaganovich) was expelled from the leadership in 1957. See Conquest, *Power and Policy*, p. 200.
15. The composition of the Secretariat, as announced on 7 March, was as follows: Ignat'ev, Pospelov, Shatalin, Khrushchev, Malenkov, Suslov, Mikhailov, and Aristov.
16. *Pravda*, 10 March 1953.
17. TsKhSD, f. 5, op. 30., d. 4, l. 68.
18. Simonov, "Glazami cheloveka," pt. 1, p. 111.
19. This was pointed out by Fairbanks, "National Cadres," pp. 165–167. Also see a report from a U.S. State Department observer: Department of State telegram, no. 1277, 9 March 1953, National Archives, Record Group 59, Box 3806.
20. *Komsomol'skoe znamia*, 30 September 1990. As Bertram Wolfe observed, "It is impossible for a man laboring under the double handicap of Police Chief and Georgian immediately to lay open claim to the apostolic succession. More than any other of the aspirants, Beria needs for a time the protective shield of 'collective leadership.'" See Bertram D. Wolfe, "The Struggle for the Soviet Succession," *Foreign Affairs* 31, no. 4 (July 1953): 563.
21. According to a U.S. intelligence report, Beria and Malenkov gave the impression publicly of close collaboration right up to the time of Beria's arrest in June. See Office of Intelligence Research, no. 6242, "Career and Views of G. M. Malenkov," 6 August 1953, *DDQ* 5, no. 1 (January–March 1979): 85B.
22. *Pravda*, 21 March 1953. The press referred to this meeting as a CC plenum but, as Bertram Wolfe pointed out, it was inconceivable that a full plenum (216

persons) could have taken place, especially given that editors of provincial papers remained uninformed of what happened and continued to refer to Malenkov as leader of party and state until 21 or 22 March. See Wolfe, "Struggle for the Soviet Succession," pp. 549–550.

23. *Izvestiia TsK KPSS*, no. 1 (1991): 160–161. Khrushchev was not designated "first secretary" until several months later.

24. These changes were reported in various sources, including *Izvestiia TsK KPSS*, no. 1 (1991): 208.

25. *Izvestiia TsK KPSS*, no. 1 (1991): 213–214. Savchenko, who had been in his post since 1949, was replaced by V. S. Riasnoi, a deputy chief of the MVD since 1946.

26. Nekrasov, "Beriia," pt. 2, p. 41.

27. Ibid., pp. 41–42.

28. Ibid., p. 41; Davith Mchedluri, "Beria's Criminal Act," *Literaturuli Sakartvelo*, nos. 38–40 (September 1991), translated from Georgian by Vladimir Babishvili.

29. U.S. Department of State, foreign service despatch no. 63, 3 August 1953, p. 2. National Archives, RG 59, Box 3808; *Izvestiia TsK KPSS*, no. 1 (1991): 143.

30. Nekrasov, "Beriia," pt. 3, p. 42. The decree was published in *Pravda*, 28 March 1953.

31. "Beria's End," unpublished, unattributed manuscript, 1953, Nicolaevsky Collection, Hoover Archives, pp. 2–3.

32. *Pravda*, 4, 6 and 7 April, 1953.

33. *Izvestiia TsK KPSS*, no. 2 (1991): 185.

34. Simonov, "Glazami Chekoveka," pt. 1, pp. 114–115. Simonov, who read the documents, adds that they showed that Stalin was very ill mentally by this time.

35. "Beria's End," p. 4. A similar impression was conveyed by the Indian Ambassador to Moscow, K. P. S. Menon, who wrote at the time that "the diplomatic corps is enjoying a feeling of unalloyed relief" (K. P. S. Menon, *The Flying Troika* [London: Oxford University Press, 1963], p. 51).

36. *Izvestiia TsK KPSS*, no. 1 (1991): 143.

37. Ibid., p. 161.

38. As cited in Wolfgang Leonhard, *The Kremlin Since Stalin*, trans. Elizabeth Wiskemann and Marian Jackson (London: Oxford University Press, 1962), p. 66.

39. See ZV, 15 April 1952. Two of the three candidate members were dismissed and one was promoted to full membership.

40. TsKhSD, f. 5, op. 15, d. 448, l. 165.

41. ZV, 16 April 1953.

42. Indeed, Bagirov gave up his party post at this time to become chairman of the Council of Ministers in Azerbaidzhan. See *Bakiinskii rabochii*, 19 April 1953.

43. ZV, 16 April 1953. He went on to state that Rukhadze and his accomplices had been arrested.

44. TsKhSD, f. 5, op. 15, d. 448, l. 121.

45. *Izvestiia TsK KPSS*, no. 1 (1991): 184–186.

46. Mchedluri, "Beria's Criminal Act," p. 6; Fairbanks, "National Cadres,"

pp. 168–170; "Dokumenty General-Leitenanta T. A. Strokacha o Podgotovke Beriei Zagovora v 1953 g.," *Novaia i noveishaia istoriia*, no. 3 (1989): 166–176 (documents from the party archives).

47. *Izvestiia TsK KPSS*, no. 1 (1991): 180; "Dokumenty General-Leitenanta T. A. Strokacha."

48. He wrote to Khrushchev in June requesting a transfer from the prison in Lvov to another prison. Khrushchev forwarded the note to Beria. TsKhSD, f. 5, op. 30, d. 43.

49. No copy of the report was available, but it was discussed at the July 1953 plenum. See *Izvestiia TsK KPSS*, no. 1 (1991): 146, 180. Also see *Khrushchev Remembers*, vol. 1, pp. 329–330.

50. *Pravda*, 13 June 1953. An indication of how controversial this plenum was is the fact that it was not reported in *Pravda* until nine days after it took place. See *Izvestiia TsK KPSS*, no. 1 (1991), p. 180, where the date of the plenum is given as 2–4 June.

51. TsKhSD, f. 5, op. 30, d. 3, ll. 56–63.

52. Bohdan R. Bociurkiw, "The Ukrainian Catholic Church in the USSR under Gorbachev," *Problems of Communism* (November–December 1990): 3.

53. RTsKhIDNI, f. 17, op. 132, d. 7, ll. 1, 10, 11 (letter from Khrushchev to Stalin, 1945).

54. For a copy of the decree regarding Latvia, see Radio Liberty, *Sobranie dokumentov samizdata* (New York: Radio Liberty Committee, 1972), vol. 21, no. 1042: 3. Also see *Pravda*, 18 and 28 June 1953.

55. *Izvestiia TsK KPSS*, no. 1 (1991): 208.

56. On the second day of the plenum Beria was arrested in Moscow. Khrushchev and Malenkov called Minsk and told the party leaders to retain Patolichev as first secretary. See Aleksandr Lukashuk, "Zharkoe leto 53-go," *Kommunist Belorussii*, no. 7–8 (1990): 69–82. Zimianin, in a letter to Khrushchev after Beria's arrest, recounted Beria's efforts to recruit him. TsKhSD, f. 5, op. 30, d. 4, ll. 31–34. Also see Platonov and Belichko, "Zloveshchaia ten' Tsanavy," pt. 1, p. 63.

57. *Khrushchev Remembers*, vol. 1, p. 330.

58. Ibid.

59. Ibid., pp. 327–328. Also see Mchedluri, "Beria's Criminal Act," pp. 26–27.

60. For an excellent English-language study of relations between the Soviet Union and East Germany at this time, see Victor Baras, "Beria's Fall and Ulbricht's Survival," *Soviet Studies* 27, no. 3 (July 1975): 381–395.

61. *Izvestiia TsK KPSS*, no. 1 (1991): 143–144; Iurii Shpakov, "Komanda brat'iam po lageriu," *Moskovskie novosti*, 15 July 1990, p. 8; Georgii Bezirgani, "Bzlet i padenie Lavrentiia Beriia," *Kommunist Gruzii*, no. 11 (November 1990), pp. 84–85.

62. Andrei Gromyko, *Memories*, trans. Harold Shukman (London: Hutchinson, 1989), p. 316.

63. *Izvestiia TsK KPSS*, no. 1 (1991), pp. 157, 162–164. In his reminiscences Molotov says that the intitial program for the GDR was drafted in the foreign

ministry by him and Gromyko and that Beria then countered their proposal with a more radical plan. See Chuev, *Sto sorok besed*, pp. 333–334.

64. Myron Rush, *How Communist States Change Their Rulers* (Ithaca and London: Cornell University Press, 1974), p. 58.

65. Shpakov, "Komanda brat'iam po lageriw." *Izvestiia TsK KPSS*, no. 1 (1991): 157–158. Also see James Richter, "Reexamining Soviet Policy Towards Germany During the Beria Interregnum," Working paper No. 3, Cold War International History Project, Woodrow Wilson Center, June 1992.

66. Abe Stein, "The Downfall of Beria," *The New International* 19 (May–June 1953): 122–123.

67. See Shpakov, "Komanda brat'iam po lageriu"; Leonhard, *The Kremlin since Stalin*, pp. 70–71; Rush, *How Communist States Change Their Rulers*, pp. 54–60.

68. Baras, "Beria's Fall," pp. 384–385.

69. See Heinz Brandt, *The Search for a Third Way* , trans. Salvator Attanasio (New York: Doubleday, 1970), p. 195; and Stein, "The Downfall of Beria," pp. 121–122.

70. Stein, "Downfall of Beria," p. 121. Also see Brandt, *Search for a Third Way*, pp. 202–220; and Baras, "Beria's Fall," pp. 385–387.

71. Leonhard, *Kremlin since Stalin*, p. 72. Russian historian Roy Medvedev claims that Beria flew to Berlin after the uprising began to consult with communist leaders (Medvedev, *Khrushchev*, trans. Brian Pearce [Garden City, N. Y.: Anchor Press/Doubleday, 1983], p. 60). Molotov recalls: "He may have flown there [to Berlin]. I cannot remember" (Chuev, *Sto sorok besed*, p. 345).

72. *Khrushchev Remembers*, vol. 1, pp. 393–394.

73. Ibid., pp. 330–331.

74. "An Interview with V. M. Molotov" *Literaturuli Sakartvelo*, 27 October 1989, translated by Vladimir Babishvili.

75. Ibid.

76. As Andrei Gromyko expressed it: "Beria's dismissive judgment of the GDR was enough to get him kicked out of the leadership." Gromyko, *Memories*, p. 317.

77. *Khrushchev Remembers*, vol. 1, pp. 330–335. Other accounts, however, suggest that Khrushchev was not being truthful here and that Saburov and Pervukhin were not consulted beforehand. See below.

78. *Khrushchev Remembers*, vol. 1, p. 332.

79. *Izvestiia TsK KPSS*, no. 1 (1991): 187–188.

80. The commandant of the Kremlin was Lieutenant General N. K. Spiridonov, an NKVD officer loyal to Beria. He had been fired from this post in December 1952 (*Postanovleniia Soveta Ministrov SSSR*, no. 5183, 16 December 1952, TsGA), but Beria had apparently reinstated him after Stalin died.

81. See his biography in *SVE*, vol. 1 (Moscow, 1976), p. 264; and S. Bystrov, "Special Mission," *Krasnaia zvezda*, 18, 19, and 20 March 1988 (based on the recollections of I. Zub).

82. On Moskalenko's career, see *SVE*, vol. 5 (1978), p. 408; and *Khrushchev Remembers*, vol. 2, p. 4.

83. Bystrov, "Special Mission." Moskalenko replaced Artemev as commander

of the Moscow Military District immediately after Beria's arrest, but this was not announced until July 1953. He was promoted to full Central Committee membership in 1956, while Batitskii took over Moskalenko's air defense post in 1954 and later became a candidate member of the Central Committee.

84. See Fost, "Kak byl arestovan Beriia" (based on Moskalenko's recollections). These officers also were rewarded after the coup. Zhukov replaced Bulganin as minister of defense in 1955 (although he later fell out with Khrushchev); Brezhnev rose in the party apparatus (eventually to replace Khrushchev as party leader); Getman became commander of the Precarpathian Military District; Pronin and Shatilov were later identified as leading officers in DOSAFF (civil defense).

85. Ibid.; and Bystrov, "Special Mission." Also see a brief account by Zhukov in *Beriia: Konets Kar'ery*, pp. 281–283.

86. The accounts are taken from Fost, "Kak byl arestovan Beriia"; Bystrov, "Special Mission."

87. *Khrushchev Remembers*, vol. 1, pp. 335–339. On the missing record, see *Izvestiia TsK KPSS*, no. 1 (1991): 143.

88. Bezhnin, "Sergo Beriia," pt. 1, pp. 12–13.

89. Bystrov, "Special Mission."

90. Fost, "Kak byl arestovan Beriia."

91. Ibid. See also Mchedluri, "Beria's Criminal Act."

92. Fost, "Kak byl arestovan Beriia." Maslennikov shot himself to death not long after Beria's trial. It is noteworthy that Moskalenko's account is reprinted in the book *Beriia: Konets Kar'ery* but parts of it, including the mention of Maslennikov and Vlasik, have been left out, apparently because they were considered too politically sensitive, even today.

93. Fost, "Kak byl arestovan Beriia." This account mentions only the "garrison guardhouse of the city of Moscow," but Zub recalled that it was at Lefortovo. See Bystrov, "Special Mission."

94. Fost, "Kak byl arestovan Beriia."

95. Foreign Service Dispatch, no. 368, 6 April 1954, National Archives, RG 59, Box 3810.

96. Fost, "Kak byl arestovan Beriia"; Bystrov, "Special Mission."

CHAPTER TEN
THE AFTERMATH

1. Bystrov, "Special Mission"; Fost, "Kak byl arestovan Beriia."

2. Bezhnin, "Sergo Beriia," pt. 1, p. 13.

3. *Komsomol'skoe znamia*, 30 September 1990.

4. *Izvestiia TsK KPSS*, no. 1 (1991): 143.

5. The military procuracy, which investigated crimes committed by servicemen and members (or former members) of the security organs, was under the USSR Procuracy.

6. Anatolii Golovkov, "Vechnyi isk," *Ogonek*, no. 18 (April 1988): 28–30.

7. *Khrushchev Remembers*, vol. 1, p. 339.

8. These letters, mentioned above, are in the party archives: TsKhSD, f. 5, op. 30, d. 4, ll. 64–104.

9. *Khrushchev Remembers*, vol. 1, p. 340. Khrushchev refers to only one report by Merkulov, but in fact there were two.

10. The fate of some Beria men in the USSR MVD—such as Ordyntsev and Obruchnikov—was never made clear, but since they disappeared from public view they were presumably arrested as well. Obruchnikov's testimony (probably given in prison) was cited in the Beria trial documents. See Popov and Oppokov, "Berievshchina," pt. 7, p. 61. Pavel Artemev, whose association with Beria was less close, was not arrested but was transferred to the Urals Military District.

11. Iu. Krotkov, "Konets Marshala Beriia," *Novyi zhurnal*, no. 133 (December 1978): 222–226. This was reprinted in abridged form in Nekrasov, *Beria*, pp. 254–261.

12. See *Khrushchev Remembers*, vol. 1, p. 338; *BSE*, vol. 51, p. 268. Kruglov was later investigated for his role in deporting the Chechen-Ingush people during the war and committed suicide. See Medvedev, *Khrushchev*, pp. 113–114.

13. Krotkov, "Konets Marshala Beriia," p. 218.

14. Ibid., p. 230. Conquest speculates that Gvishiani may have been spared because his son was married to the daughter of Kosygin, who may have intervened to save him. See Conquest, *Inside Stalin's Secret Police*, p. 156.

15. The report, cited numerous times above, appeared in *Izvestiia TsK KPSS*, nos. 1 and 2 (1991). Also see an article with excerpts and analysis of the plenum: Nikolai Mikhailov, "Neizvestnye podrobnosti 'dela Berii,' v iiule 53-go . . ." *Izvestiia*, 3, 4 January 1991.

16. *Izvestiia TsK KPSS*, no. 1 (1991): 141–147.

17. Ibid.

18. Ibid., p. 158.

19. Ibid.

20. Ibid., p. 159.

21. Ibid., p. 164.

22. Ibid., pp. 164–165.

23. Ibid., p. 177.

24. Ibid., p. 188.

25. Ibid., no. 2 (1991), p. 156.

26. Ibid., pp. 158–159.

27. Ibid., pp. 182–183. Bakradze said that the Shariia was released from prison in mid-March 1953, well before the official rehabilitation was decided on by the CC on 10 April, so Beria was making decisions on his own in regard to Georgia.

28. Ibid., no. 1 (1991), p. 200.

29. Ibid., pp. 202–203.

30. Ibid., p. 203.

31. Ibid., no. 2 (1991), p. 181.

32. Maslennikov apparently did suffer repercussions because of his ties with Beria. He reportedly committed suicide in 1954.

33. *Izvestiia TsK KPSS*, no. 1 (1991): 212.

34. Simonov, "Glazami cheloveka," pt. 1, p. 117.

35. *Izvestiia TsK KPSS*, no. 2 (1991), pp. 200–206.

36. *Pravda*, 10 July 1992.

37. Simonov, "Glazami cheloveka," pt. 1, p. 116.

38. TsKhSD, f. 5, op. 15, d. 407, ll. 113–130; TsKhSD f. 5, op. 30, d. 4, l. 23.

39. See Department of State telegram, no. 797, 16 November 1953, National Archives, RG 59, Box 3808.

40. Ibid. and Department of State telegram, no. 42, 28 July 1953, National Archives, RG 59, Box 3808.

41. D. Burg, "Konets Beriia," *Sotsialisticheskii Vestnik*, no. 12 (December 1961): 224–225.

42. Ibid.

43. The Indian Ambassador, K. P. S. Menon was in Tbilisi at this time, but had little success in divining public reaction to Beria's fall. See *The Flying Troika. Extracts from a Diary by K. P. S. Menon* (London: Oxford University Press, 1963), pp. 48–9, 54–4, 68. Also see Foreign Service Dispatch, no. 71, 18 August 1953, National Archives, RG 59, Box 3808.

44. See Burg, "Konets Beriia," p. 226; John Ducoli, "The Georgian Purges (1951–53)," *Caucasian Review*, no. 6 (1959): 54–61.

45. Krotkov, "Konets Marshala Beriia," p. 226.

46. ZV, 15 July 1953; TsKhSD, f. 5, op. 15, d. 448, ll. 63–69 (letter to Khrushchev from Mirtskhulava, 16 July 1953).

47. The plenum also accused former first secretaries Charkviani and Mgeladze of having "permitted crude perversions of the policy of the party in the national question" and having taken "advantage of the patronage of Beria." See Foreign Service Dispatch, no. 28, 24 July 1953, National Archives, RG 59, Box 3808.

48. See Conquest, *Power and Policy*, p. 147.

49. Ducoli, "The Georgian Purges," pp. 58–59. Also see *Deputaty verkhovnogo soveta SSSR*, p. 169. Inauri later became head of the Georgian KGB, remaining in that post until the late 1980s. Antonov had been in line for the job of chief of staff of the Ministry of Defense in 1948, but Beria managed to get his protégé Shtemenko appointed instead. See Simonov, "Glazami cheloveka," pt. 1, pp. 93–94.

50. TsKhSD, f. 5, op. 15, d. 448, ll. 82–92.

51. TsKhSD, f. 5, op. 15, d. 448, ll. 150–165, 190.

52. Ducoli, "The Georgian Purges," p. 59.

53. Kandida Charkviani, for example, was still alive and living in Tbilisi in the autumn of 1990.

54. *Bakiinskii rabochii*, 19 July 1953.

55. Ibid., 15 June 1988.

56. *Kommunist* (Erevan), 4 December 1953.

57. U.S. Foreign Service Dispatch, no. 240, 7 December 1954, National Archives, RG 59, Box 3811.

58. TsKhSD, f. 5, op. 15, d. 446, ll. 2–20, 30–50; d. 447 ll. 1–20.

59. See Nikolai Khokhlov, *In the Name of Conscience* (New York: David McKay, 1959), pp. 205–207; and Paniushkin's obituary in *Pravda*, 14 November 1974.

60. Foreign Service Dispatch, no. 113, 20 July 1953, National Archives, RG 59, Box 3808.

61. Petrov, *Empire of Fear*, p. 88.

62. Ibid., pp. 88–89.

NOTES TO PAGES 216-220

63. U.S. State Department, item no. 6750/54, 6 August 1954, National Archives, RG 59, Box 3111.

64. Brandt, *Search for a Third Way*, p. 230.

65. Ibid., p. 241.

66. See Conquest, *Power and Policy*, p. 221; Rush, *How Communist States Change Their Rulers*, pp. 63–66.

67. Leonhard, *The Kremlin since Stalin*, p. 75.

68. See Pelikan, *Czechoslovak Political Trials*, pp. 116–122.

69. Bohlen, *Witness to History*, pp. 355–356.

70. Thus, one American analyst in the Moscow Embassy wrote: "Malenkov could have achieved it [Beria's removal] only through complete control of the party and, while the necessity for purging Beriya shows a weakness in the regime, nevertheless it strengthens Malenkov's position by removing the only serious rival for power." Department of State telegram, no. 54, 11 July 1953, National Archives, RG 59, Box 3808.

71. See *Pravda*, 9 August 1953.

72. Foreign Service Dispatch, no. 138, 20 October 1953, National Archives, RG 59, Box 3808.

73. TsKhSD, f. 5, op. 15, d. 448, ll. 82–100.

74. This infamous law was introduced after the murder of Kirov and was used to expedite countless political cases during the purges.

75. *Pravda*, 17 December 1953.

76. TsKhSD, f. 4, op. 30, d. 4, l. 149.

77. Isaac Deutscher, "Beria's Trial—The Old Show?" *The Reporter*, 2 February 1954, p. 22.

78. Fost, "Kak byl arestovan Beriia." Here Moskalenko says that he and Rudenko began the investigation on 29 July and continued for the next six months. Yet the trial occurred after five months. This creates the impression that a great deal of editing was done on these reminiscences.

79. *Khrushchev Remembers*, vol. 1, p. 324.

80. Knight, *The KGB*, pp. 51–52. Lunev was first deputy chairman of the KGB by 1959.

81. See Hahn, *Postwar Soviet Politics*, p. 146.

82. Excerpts from Kuchava's memoirs on the trial were published in Nekrasov, *Beriia*, pp. 296–300.

83. See a series of translations from the Italian paper *Corriere Della Sera* in *Atlas* 3, no. 3 (March 1962): 175–181. One of the Italians in the group that talked to Khrushchev, Giancarlo Pajetta, later denied the story. Also see Burg, "Konets Beriia," p. 223.

84. Alliluyeva, *Only One Year*, pp. 375–376.

85. See Vladimir Tolz, "The Death and 'Second Life' of Lavrentii Beria," *Radio Liberty Research*, 23 December 1983. A curious comment made by Kaganovich at the July 1953 plenum may have contributed to the rumors if it was repeated outside higher party circles. Speaking of Beria's capture he said: "We restrained ourselves until the end and then with one blow finished off this scoundrel." *Izvestiia TsK KPSS*, no. 1 (1991): 190.

86. Georgii Bezirgani, "Sud nad L. L.," *Vechernii Tbilisi*, 21 August 1990, and "Vzlet i padeniie Beriia." According to the official record, Beria was shot at 7:50 P.M. on the twenty-third; the others were shot at 9:20 P.M. See Popov and Oppokov, "Berievshchina," pt. 7, p. 62.

87. Bezirgani, "Vzlet i padenie Beriia," p. 89.

88. Bezhnin, "Sergo Beriia," pt. 1, pp. 12–13.

89. See Bystrov, "Special Mission."

90. Nekrasov, *Beriia*, pp. 296–297 It might be added that Molotov claims to have listened to the trial via some sort of radio. See Chuev, *Sto sorok besed*, p. 340. But he could hardly be expected not to support the official version.

91. Foreign Service Dispatch, no. 368, 6 April 1954, National Archives, RG 59, Box 3810.

92. Krotkov, "Konets Marshala Beriia," pp. 230–231. One such report from Kruglov, dated 24 August 1953, was made available to this author at the TsKhSD, although it was unnumbered, so it is not clear to which fund it belonged.

93. *Pravda*, 23 July 1954.

94. Ibid., 24 December 1954; Conquest, *Power and Policy*, pp. 100–101.

95. See Conquest, *Power and Policy*, pp. 450–451.

96. Ibid., pp. 451–453; and *Bakiinskii rabochii*, 27 May 1956.

97. Tatu, *Power in the Kremlin*, p. 144.

98. Krotkov, "Konets Marshala Beriia," pp. 229–230.

99. *Komsomol'skoe Znamia*, 30 September 1990; Bezhnin, "Sergo Beriia," pt. 1, p. 13.

100. *Komsomol'skoe Znamia*, 30 September 1990; also see Mchedluri, "Beria's Criminal Act."

CHAPTER ELEVEN
BERIA RECONSIDERED

1. G.M. Gilbert, *The Psychology of Dictatorship* (New York: The Ronald Press, 1950), p. 117.

2. Gilboa, *The Black Years of Soviet Jewry*, pp. 320–321.

3. Graeme Gill, *The Origins of the Stalinist Political System* (Cambridge: Cambridge University Press, 1990), p. 325.

BIBLIOGRAPHY

BOOKS AND MONOGRAPHS

Adelman, Jonathan R., ed. *Terror and Communist Politics: The Role of the Secret Police in Communist States*. Boulder: Westview Press, 1984.

Afanasyan, Serge. *L'Armenie, L'Azerbaidjan et La Georgie de l'independance a l'instauration du pouvoir sovietique 1917–1923*. Paris: L'Harmattan, 1981.

Agabekov, Georges. *OGPU: The Russian Secret Terror*. New York: Harper & Row, 1975.

Al'bats, Evgeniia. *Mina zamedlennogo deistviia (Politicheskogo portreta KGB)*. Moscow: Russlit, 1992.

Alliluyeva, Svetlana. *Twenty Letters to a Friend*. Translated by Priscilla Johnson McMillan. New York: Harper & Row, 1967.

———. *Only One Year*. Translated by Paul Chavchavadze. New York: Harper & Row, 1969.

Armstrong, John A., ed. *Soviet Partisans in World War II*. Madison: The University of Wisconsin Press, 1964.

Bagirov, M. D. *Iz istorii bol'shevistskoi organizatsii Baku i Azerbaidzhana*. Moscow: Gosizdat, 1946.

Barwich, Heinz, and Elfi Barwich. *Das rote Atom*. Munich: Scherz Verlag, 1967.

Beichman, Arnold, and Mikhail Bernstam. *Andropov: New Challenge to the West*. New York: Stein and Day, 1983.

Beriia, L. P. *K voprosu o Prazhskoi konferentsii*. Baku: Azpartizdat, 1935.

———, ed. *Sergei Mironovich Kirov v borbe za neft'*. Baku, 1935.

———. *K voprosu ob istorii bol'shevistskikh organizatsii v zakavkaz'e. Doklad na sobranii tifliskogo partaktiva 21–22 July 1935*. Moscow: Partizdat, 1935.

———. *Fifteen Years of Soviet Georgia*. Moscow: Cooperative Publishing Society, 1936.

———. *Rech' na sobranii izburatelei Tbilisskogo-Stalinskogo izburatel'nogo okruga*. Moscow: Gosizdat, 1946.

———. *On the History of Bolshevik Organizations in Transcaucasia*. Translated from the Russian seventh edition. Moscow: Foreign Languages Publishing House, 1949.

Beriia, L. P., and G. Broido, eds. *Lado Ketskhoveli; spornik*. Moscow: Partizdat, 1938.

Bialer, Seweryn, ed. *Stalin and his Generals. Soviet Military Memoirs of World War II*. New York: Pegasus, 1969.

Bibineishvili, V. E. *Za chetvert veka*. Moscow: Molodaia Gvardiia, 1931.

Bohlen, Charles. *Witness to History, 1929–1969*. New York: W. W. Norton, 1973.

Bol'shaia sovetskaia entsiklopediia. 2d ed. Moscow: Gosudarstvennoe nauchnoe izdatel'stvo, 1950–58.

Bor'ba za pobedy Sovetskoi vlasti v Azerbaidzhane, 1918–1920. Dokumenty i materialy. Baku: Izdatel'stvo akademii Nauk Azerbaidzhanskoi SSR, 1967.

Bor'ba za pobedy Sovetskoi vlasti v Gruzii. Dokumenty i materialy (1917–1921 gg.). Tbilisi: Sabchota Sakartvelo, 1958.

Brandt, Heinz. *The Search for a Third Way.* Translated by Salvator Attanasio. New York: Doubleday, 1970.

Brown, Anthony Cave. *Wild Bill Donovan. The Last Hero.* New York: Times Books, 1982.

Brzezinski, Zbigniew K. *The Soviet Bloc: Unity and Conflict.* New York: Praeger, 1961.

Carell, Robert Paul. *Hitler's War on Russia. The Story of the German Defeat in the East.* Translated by Ewald Osers. London: George G. Harrap 1964.

Carr, E. H. *What Is History?* London: Pelican Books, 1964.

Charachidze, D. *H. Barbusse, Les Soviets et la Georgie.* Paris: Editions Pascal, 1930.

Chuev, Feliks. *Sto sorok besed s Molotovym; iz dnevnika F. Chueva.* Moscow: Terra, 1991.

Churchill, Winston S. *The Second World War: Closing the Ring.* Boston: Houghton Mifflin, 1951.

Conquest, Robert. *Power and Policy in the USSR. The Struggle for Stalin's Succession, 1945–1960.* New York: Harper & Row, 1967.

———. *Inside Stalin's Secret Police: NKVD Politics: 1936–39.* Stanford, Calif: Hoover Institution Press, 1985.

———. *Stalin and the Kirov Murder.* New York: Oxford University Press, 1989.

———. *The Great Terror. A Reassessment.* New York: Oxford University Press, 1990.

Cookridge, E. H. *Gehlen. Spy of the Century.* London: Hodder and Stoughton, 1971.

Deane, John R. *The Strange Alliance.* New York: Viking, 1947.

Delo o paritetnom komitete antisovpartii gruzii. Tiflis, 1925.

Djilas, Milovan. *Conversations with Stalin.* New York: Harcourt, Brace and World, 1962.

Dumbadze, Evgenii V. *Na sluzhbe Cheka i Kominterna. lichnye vospominaniia.* Paris: Mishen', 1930.

Dunmore, Timothy. *Soviet Politics, 1945–53.* New York: St. Martin's Press, 1984.

Dziak, John. *Chekisty. A History of the KGB.* Lexington, Mass.: Lexington Books, 1988.

Enukidze, A. S. *Nashi podpolnye tipografii na Kavkazye.* Moscow: "Novaia Moskva," 1925.

———. *Bol'shevistskie nelegal'nye tipografii.* 3d edition. Moscow: Molodaia Gvardiia, 1934.

Erickson, John. *The Road to Stalingrad. Stalin's War with Germany.* Vol. 1. New York: Harper & Row, 1975.

———. *The Road to Berlin. Continuing the History of Stalin's War with Germany.* Boulder: Westview Press, 1983.

———. *The Soviet High Command. A Military-Political History, 1918–1941.* Boulder: Westview Press, 1984.

Gershkovich, Alexander. *The Theater of Yuri Lyubimov. Art and Politics at the*

Taganka in Moscow. Translated by Michael Yurieff. New York: Paragon House, 1989.

Getty, J. Arch. *The Origins of the Great Purges. The Soviet Communist Party Reconsidered, 1933–38*. Cambridge: Cambridge University Press, 1985.

Gilboa, Yehoshua A. *The Black Years of Soviet Jewry*. New York: Little, Brown, 1971.

Gilbert, G. M. *The Psychology of Dictatorship*. New York: The Ronald Press, 1950.

Gill, Graeme. *The Origins of the Stalinist Political System*. Cambridge: Cambridge University Press, 1990.

Gol'dshein, Pavel. *Tochka opory*. Book 2. Jerusalem: n.d.

Granovsky, Anatoli. *All Pity Choked. The Memoirs of a Soviet Secret Agent*. London: William Kimber, 1955.

Gromyko, Andrei. *Memories*. Translated by Harold Shukman. London: Hutchinson, 1989.

Gross, Jan T. *Revolution from Abroad. The Soviet Conquest of Poland's Western Ukraine and Western Belorussia*. Princeton, N.J.: Princeton University Press, 1988.

Gusarov, Vladimir. *Moi papa ubil Mikhoelsa*. Paris: Frankfurt am Main: Posev, 1978.

Hahn, Werner. *Post-War Soviet Politics. The Fall of Zhdanov and the Defeat of Moderation: 1946–50*. Ithaca: Cornell University Press, 1982.

Harriman, Averell W., and Elie Abel. *Special Envoy to Churchill and Stalin, 1941–46*. New York: Random House, 1975.

Hilger, Gustav, and Alfred G. Meyer. *The Incompatible Allies. A Memoir-History of German-Soviet Relations, 1918–1941*. New York: Macmillan, 1953.

Inauri, A. N., ed. *Shchit-nadezhnyi mech-ostryi (chekisty gruzii na strazhe zavoevanii velikogo oktiabria)*. Tbilisi: "Sabchota Sakartvelo," 1985.

Iskander, Fazil'. *Sandro iz chegema: Roman*. Moscow: Moskovskii Rabochii, 1989.

Iskenderov, M. G. *Iz istorii bor'by Kommunisticheskoi partii Azerbaidzhana za pobedu Sovetskoi vlasti*. Baku: Azerbaidzhanskoe Gosudarstvennoe Izdatel'stvo, 1958.

Istoriia velikoi otechestvennoi voiny Sovetskogo Soiuza 1941–1945. Vol. 1. Moscow: Voenizdat, 1960.

Iusif-Zade, Z. M., ed. *Chekisty Azerbaidzhana. Dokumenty, ocherki, rasskazy*. Baku: Azerneshr, 1981.

Kahan, Stuart. *The Wolf of the Kremlin*. New York: William Morrow, 1987.

Kakhiani, M. *Itogi i uroki vystuplenii v gruzii*. Tbilisi: Izdatel'stvo Sov-Kavkaz, 1925.

Karaev, A. G. *Iz nedavnogo proshlogo*. Baku: Bakiinskii rabochii, 1926.

Kautsky, Karl. *Georgia. A Social-Democratic Peasant Republic. Impressions and Observations*. Translated by H. J. Stenning. London: International Bookshops, 1921.

Kazemzadeh, Firuz. *The Struggle for Transcaucasia, 1917–21*. New York: Philosophical Library, 1951.

Kennan, George F. *Memoirs*. Vol. 1, 1925–1950. Boston: Little, Brown, 1967.

Khachapuridze, G. V. *Bol'sheviki gruzii v boiakh za pobedy Sovetskoi vlasti*. Moscow: Gosizdat, 1947.

Khachapuridze, G. V., and F. E. Makharadze. *Ocherki po istorii rabochego i krestianskogo dvizheniia v Gruzii*. Moscow: Zhurnal'no-gazetnoe Obedinenie, 1932.

Khlevniuk, Oleg. *1937-i: Stalin, NKVD i Sovetskoe obshchestvo*. Moscow: "Respublika," 1992.

Khokhlov. Nikolai. *In the Name of Conscience*. New York: David McKay, 1959.

Khrushchev, Nikita. *Khrushchev Remembers*. Vol. 1. Translated and edited by Strobe Talbott. Boston: Little, Brown, 1970. Vol. 2. *The Last Testament*. Translated and edited by Strobe Talbott. Boston: Little, Brown, 1974.

Knight, Amy. *The KGB: Police and Politics in the Soviet Union*. Boston: Unwin/Hyman, 1990.

Kommunisticheskaia partiia gruzii v rezoliutsiiakh i resheniiakh s'ezdov, konferentsii i plenumov TsK. Vol. 1, 1920–1976. Tbilisi: Tsk KP Gruzii, 1976.

Kommunisticheskaia partiia gruzii v tsifrakh (1921–1970 gg.) (Sbornik statisticheskikh materialov). Tbilisi: TsK KP Gruzii, 1971.

Kramish, Arnold. *Atomic Energy in the Soviet Union*. Stanford: Stanford University Press, 1959.

Kravchenko, Victor. *I Chose Freedom. The Personal and Political Life of a Soviet Official*. Garden City, N.Y.: Garden City Publications, 1946.

Kuznetsov, N. G. *Nakanune*. Moscow, 1966.

Lakoba, Nestor. *Stalin i Khashim (1901–1902 gody): Nekotorye epizody iz batumskogo podpol'ia*. Sukhumi, 1934.

Lang, David. *A Modern History of Soviet Georgia*. New York: Groove Press, 1962.

Laqueur, Walter. *Stalin. The Glasnost Revelations*. New York: Charles Scribner's Sons, 1990.

Lomashvili, P. N. *Velikii perevorot*. Tbilisi: "Sabchota Sakartvelo," 1972.

Leonhard, Wolfgang. *The Kremlin since Stalin*. Translated by Elizabeth Wiskemann and Marian Jackson. London: Oxford University Press, 1962.

Leggett, George. *The Cheka: Lenin's Political Police*. Oxford: Clarendon Press, 1981.

Levytsky, Boris. *The Uses of Terror. The Soviet Secret Police, 1917–1970*. Translated by H. A. Piehler. New York: Coward, McCann & Geoghegan, 1972.

Makharadze, F. E. *Ocherki revoliutsionnogo dvizheniia v Zakavkazii*. Tiflis: Gosizdat Gruzii, 1927.

Malaia sovetskaia entsiklopediia. Moscow: Politizdat, 1937.

Materialy k politicheskomu otchetu TsK KPG. Tbilisi, 1924.

McCagg, W. O. *Stalin Embattled, 1943–48*. Detroit: Wayne State University Press, 1978.

McNeal, Robert H. *Stalin. Man and Ruler*. New York: New York University Press, 1988.

Medvedev, Roy. *Khrushchev*. Translated by Brian Pearce. Garden City, N.Y.: Anchor Press/Doubleday, 1983.

———. *Let History Judge. The Origins and Consequences of Stalinism*. Translated and edited by George Shriver. New York: Columbia University Press, 1989.

Mel'gunov, S. P. *"Krasnyi Terror" v Rossii, 1918–1923*. 2d expanded edition. Berlin, 1923.

Menon, K. P. S. *The Flying Troika. Extracts from a Diary by K. P. S. Menon*. London: Oxford University Press, 1963.

Merkviladze, V. N. *Sozdanie i ukreplenie Sovetskoi gosudarstvennosti v Gruzii 1921–36*. Tbilisi: Izdatel'stvo Sabchota Sakartvelo, 1969.

Nekrasov, V. F., ed. *Beria: Konets kar'ery*. Moscow: Politizdat, 1991.

Nicolaevsky, Boris. *Power and the Soviet Elite*. New York: Praeger, 1965.

Ocherki istorii kommunisticheskikh organizatsii Zakavkaz'ia. Chast' 2. 1921–1936 gg. Baku: Azerbaidzhanskoe Gosudarstvennoe Izdatel'stvo, 1971.

Ocherki istorii kommunisticheskoi partii Gruzii, 1883–1970. Tbilisi: Izdatel'stvo TsK KP Gruzii, 1971.

Ocherki istorii kommunisticheskoi partii Gruzii. Chast' 2. (1921–1963 gody). Tbilisi: Izdatel'stvo TsK KP Gruzii, 1963.

Orakhelashvili, Mamia. *Zakavkazskie organizatsii v 1917 godu*. Tbilisi: Zakkniga, 1927.

Orlov, Alexander. *The Secret History of Stalin's Secret Crimes*. New York: Random House, 1953.

Ordzhonikidze, Z. *Put' bol'shevika*. Moscow: Gospolitizdat, 1945.

Pelikan, Jiri, ed. *The Czechoslovak Political Trials, 1950–1954*. Stanford: Stanford University Press, 1971.

Petrov, Vladimir and Evdokia. *Empire of Fear*. New York: Praeger, 1956.

Pilat, Oliver. *The Atom Spies*. New York: G. P. Putnams & Sons, 1952.

Pinkus, Benjamin. *The Soviet Government and the Jews, 1948–1967. A Documented Study*. Cambridge: Cambridge University Press, 1984.

Rana'an, Gavriel D. *International Policy Formation in The USSR*. Hamden, Conn.: Archon Books, 1983.

Rancour-Laferriere, Daniel. *The Mind of Stalin. A Psychoanalytic Study*. Ann Arbor: Ardis, 1988.

Rapoport, Louis. *Stalin's War against the Jews. The Doctor's Plot and the Soviet Solution*. New York: Free Press, 1990.

Rapoport, Yakov. *The Doctor's Plot. Stalin's Last Crime*. London: Fourth Estate, 1991.

Redlich, Shimon. *Propaganda and Nationalism in Wartime Russia. The Jewish Antifascist Committee in the USSR, 1941–1948*. Boulder: East European Monographs, 1982.

Romanov, A. I. *Nights Are Longest There. Smersh from the Inside*. Translated by Gerald Brooke. London: Hutchinson, 1972.

Rush, Myron. *How Communist States Change Their Rulers*. Ithaca and London: Cornell Univerity Press, 1974.

Rybakov, Anatolii. *Children of the Arbat*. Translated by Harold Shukman. Boston: Little, Brown, 1988.

Sakharov, Andrei. *Vospominaniia*. New York: Izdatel'stvo Imeni Chekhova, 1990.

Salisbury, Harrison. *American in Russia*. New York: Harper & Brothers, 1955.

Sheinis, Z. *Maxim Maksimovich Litvinov. Revoliutsioner, Diplomat, Chelovek*. Moscow: Politizdat, 1989.

Shtemenko, S. M. *General'nyi shtab v gody voiny* Moscow: Voienizdat, 1968.

Skripilev, E. A., ed. *Sovetskoe gosudarstvo i pravo v periode stroitel'stva sotsialisma (1921–1935 gg.).* Moscow, 1968.

Skryl'nik, A. I. *General armii A. A. Epishev.* Moscow: Voennoe Izdatel'stvo, 1989.

Smith, Walter Bedell. *My Three Years in Moscow.* New York: Lippincott, 1949.

Solzhenitsyn, Alexander I. *The Gulag Archipelago, 1918–1956.* Translated by Thomas P. Whitney. New York: Harper & Row, 1973.

Souvarine, Boris, *Stalin. A Critical Survey of Bolshevism.* Translated by C. L. R. James. New York: Longmans, Green, 1939.

Sovetskaia voennaia entsiklopediia. Vols. 2,3. Moscow: Voenizdat, 1976–1977.

Soviet Diplomacy and Negotiating Behavior: Emerging New Context for U.S. Diplomacy. Vol 1. Washington: GPO, 1979.

Sul'ianov, Anatolii. *Arestovat' v Kremle. O zhizni i smerti marshala Beriia: Povest'.* Minsk: Mast. lit., 1991.

Suny, Ronald Grigor. *The Making of the Georgian Nation.* Stanford, Calif.: Hoover Institution Press, 1988.

Swianiewicz, S. *Forced Labour and Economic Development. An Enquiry into the Experience of Soviet Industrialization.* London: Oxford University Press, 1965.

Telegin, F. *Ne otdali Moskvy.* 2d ed. Moscow: "Sovetskaia Rossiia," 1975.

Tatu, Michel. *Power in the Kremlin from Khrushchev to Kosygin.* New York: Viking Press, 1967.

Tiulenev, I. V. *Cherez tri voiny.* Moscow: Voenizdat, 1960.

Tolstoy, Nikolai. *Stalin's Secret War.* London: Jonathan Cape, 1981.

Tsanava, Lavrentii. *Vsenarodnaia partizanskaia voina v belorussii protiv fashistskikh zakhvatchikov.* Vol. 1. Minsk: Gosizdat BSSR, 1949.

Tucker, Robert C. *Stalin as Revolutionary. 1879–1929: A Study in History and Personality.* New York: W. W. Norton, 1973.

———. *Stalin in Power: The Revolution from Above, 1928–1941.* New York: W. W. Norton, 1990.

Uratadze, Grigorii. *Vospominaniia gruzinskogo sotsial-demokrata.* Stanford: Stanford University Press, 1968.

Vachnadze, Nato. *Vstrechi i vpechatleniia.* Moscow: Goskinoizdat, 1953.

Vaksberg, Arkady. *Stalin's Prosecutor. The Life of Andrei Vyshinsky.* New York: Grove Weidenfeld, 1991.

Viktorov, Ivan Vasil'evich. *Podpol'shchik, voin, chekist.* Moscow: Politizdat, 1963.

Volkogonov, Dmitri. *Triumph and Tragedy.* Translated and edited by Harold Shukman. New York: Grove Weidenfeld, 1991.

Werth, Alexander. *Russia at War, 1941–45.* New York: E. P. Dutton, 1960.

Wolfe, Bertram D. *Khrushchev and Stalin's Ghost.* New York: Praeger, 1957.

———. *Three Who Made a Revolution. A Biographical History.* Boston: Beacon Press, 1948.

Wittlin, Thaddeus. *Commissar. The Life and Death of Lavrenty Pavlovich Beria.* New York: Macmillan, 1972.

Za Moskvu, za rodinu. Moscow: Moskovskii Rabochii, 1964.

Zetkin, Klara. *Na osvobozhennom kavkaze*. 2d revised edition. Moscow: Iz-datel'stvo "Staryi Bol'shevik," 1935.

Zhukov, G. K. *Reminiscences and Reflections*. Vol. 2. Moscow: Progress Publishers, 1985.

ARTICLES

Abarimov, Vladimir. "Vokrug Katyny." *Literaturnaia gazeta*, 6 September 1989.

Akulichev, Aleksandr, and Aleksei Pamiatnykh. "Katyn': Podtverdit' ili opro-vergnut.'" *Moskovskie novosti*, 21 May 1989.

Alliluyeva, Svetlana. "Dva poslednikh razgovora," *Moskovskie novosti*, 21 October 1990.

Anageli, Sandro. "K politicheskim sobytiiam v Gruzii." *Ob'edinennyi kavkaz*, no 5 (May 1953): 19–22.

Antonov-Ovseenko, Anton. "Kar'era palacha." Parts 1–2. *Zvezda*, no. 9 (1988): 141–164; no. 5 (1989): 72–109.

———. "Beriia." *Iunost'*, no. 12 (1988): 66–84.

Arsenidze, R. "Iz vospominanii o Staline." *Novyi zhurnal*, no. 72 (1963): 222–233.

Artsuni, Ashot. "Samoubiistvo A. G. Khandzhiana." *Kavkaz*, no. 8/32 (August 1936): 29–31.

———. "Smert' A. Khandzhiana i Sobytiia v Sovetskoi Armenii." *Kavkaz*, no. 9/33 (September 1936): 26–28.

Bakradze, Mzia, and Bela Tsveradze. "Several Episodes of a Bloody Time." *Lite-raturuli Sakartvelo* (Tbilisi), 11 November 1988. Translated from Georgian by Vladimir Babishvili.

Baras, Victor. "Beria's Fall and Ulbricht's Survival." *Soviet Studies* 27, no. 3 (July 1975): 381–395.

Barber, John. "Stalin's Letter to the Editors of Proletarskaya Revolyutsiya." *Soviet Studies* 28, no. 1 (January 1976): 21–41.

"The Beria Dossier." *Sputnik*, no. 12 (December 1988): 85–92.

Beriia, L. "Bol'sheviki zakavkaz'ia v bor'be za sotsializm." *Bol'shevik*, no. 11 (1934).

———. "Razveiat' vprakh vragov sotsializma. " *Pravda*, 19 August 1936.

Bezhnin, Vitalii. "Sergo Beriia o svoem ottse." Parts 1–5, *Kievskie novosti*, 23 October; 13, 20, and 27 November; 4 December 1992.

Bezirgani, Georgii. "Bzlet i padenie Lavrentiia Beriia." *Kommunist Gruzii*, no. 11 (November 1990): 75–90.

Blank, Stephen. "Bolshevik Organizational Development in Early Soviet Trans-caucasia: Autonomy vs. Centralization, 1918–24." In *Transcaucasia. Nationalism and Social Change. Essays in the History of Armenia, Azerbaijan and Georgia*, edited by Ronald Grigor Suny (Ann Arbor: Michigan Slavic Publications, 1983).

Bociurkiw, Bohdan. "The Ukrainian Catholic Church in the USSR under Gorbachev." *Problems of Communism* (November–December 1990): 1–11.

Bugai, Nikolai. "Pravda o deportatsii chechenskogo i ingushskogo narodov." *Voprosy istorii*, no. 7 (July 1990): 40–41.

———. "V bessrochnuiu ssylku." *Moskovskie novosti*, 14 October 1990.

Burg, D. "Konets Beriia." *Sotsialisticheskii Vestnik*, no. 12 (December 1961): 224–225.

Bychowski, Gustav. "Joseph V. Stalin: Paranoia and the Dictatorship of the Proletariat." In *The Psychoanalytic Interpretation of History*, edited by Benjamin B. Wolman (New York: Basic Books, 1971).

Chikov, Vladimir. "How the Soviet Intelligence Service 'Split' the American Bomb." Parts 1–2. *New Times*, nos. 16–17 (April–May 1991): 37–40; 36–37.
———. "Kak raskryvali." Parts 1–3. *Armiia*, nos. 18–19 (1991): 66–71; 69–73; no. 2 (1992): 70–77.

Christensen, Julie. "Tengiz Abuladze's 'Repentance' and the Georgian Nationalist Cause." *Slavic Review* 50, no. 1 (Spring 1991): 163–175.

Crankshaw, Edward. "Beria, Russia's Mystery of Mysteries." *New York Times Magazine*. 2 April 1950.

Danilov, S. "K biografii L. Beria." *Na rubezhe* (Paris), nos. 3–4 (1952): 31–32.

R. W. Davies. "The Syrtsov-Lominadze Affair." *Soviet Studies* 33, no. 1 (January 1981): 29–50.

Deutscher, Isaac. "Beria's Trial—The Old Show?" *The Reporter*, 2 February 1954, p. 22.

"Dokumenty General-Leitenanta T. A. Strokacha o podgotovke Beriei zagovora v 1953 g." *Novaia i noveishaia istoriia*, no. 3 (1989): 166–176.

Ducoli, John. "The Georgian Purges (1951–53)." *Caucasian Review*, no. 6 (1959): 54–61.

"Duel." *Sovershenno sekretno*, no. 8 (1991): 27–28.

Evgen'ev, I. Z. "Voennye razvedchiki dokladyvali . . ." *VIZ*, no. 2 (1992): 36–41.

Fairbanks, Charles H., Jr. "National Cadres as a Force in the Soviet System: The Evidence of Beria's Career: 1949–53." In *Soviet Nationality Policies and Practices*, ed. Jeremy Azreal (New York: Praeger, 1978).
———. "Clientelism and Higher Politics in Georgia, 1949–1953." See Suny, 1983.

Feklisov, A. S. "Podvig Klausa Fuksa." Parts 1–2. *VIZ*, no. 12 (1990): 22–29; no. 1 (1991): 34–43.

Fitzpatrick, Sheila. "Culture and Politics under Stalin: A Reappraisal." *Slavic Review* 35, no. 2 (June 1976): 211–231.

Fost, Ivan. "Kak byl arestovan Beriia." *Moskovskie novosti*, 10 June 1990. Based on Moskalenko's recollections.

Gai, David. "The Doctors Case." *Moscow News*, no. 6 (1988): 16.

Gazarian, Suren. "O Berii i sude nad berievtsami v gruzii." *SSSR. Vnutrennie protivorechia*, no. 6 (1982): 109–146.
———. "Eto ne dolzhno povtorit'sia." *Zvezda*, no. 1 (January 1988): 33–79.

Gevorkian, Nataliia. "Vstrechnye plany po unichtozheniiu sobstvennogo naroda." *Moskovskie novosti*, no. 25 (21 June 1992).

Gnedin, Evgenii. "Sebia ne poteriat' . . ." *Novyi Mir*, no. 7 (1988): 173–209.

Golovanov, Iaroslav. "Zolotaia kletka." *Literaturnaia gazeta*, 9 November 1988.

Golovkov, Anatolii. "Vechnyi isk." *Ogonek*, no. 18 (April 1988): 29–31.
———. "Ne otrekaias' ot sebia." *Ogonek*, no. 7 (February 1988): 28.

Gorinov, M. M. "Sovetskaia strana v kontse 20-x—nachale 30-x godov." *Voprosy istorii*, no. 11 (November 1990): 31–47.

Grishin, Nikolai. "The Saxony Mining Operation ('Vismut')." In *Soviet Economic Policy in Postwar Germany*, ed. Robert Slusser (New York: Research Program on the USSR, 1953).

Gurunts, Leonid. "Iz zapisnykh knizhek." *Zvezda*, no. 3 (1988): 184–188.

Hadjibeyli, D. "The Trials of Adzharian Leaders." *The Caucasian Review*, no. 8 (1959): 21–26.

———. "Some Echoes of the 1937 Purge in Azerbaidzhan." *The Caucasian Review*, no. 1 (1955): 36–46.

Holloway, David. "Innovation in the Defense Sector." In *Industrial Innovation in the Soviet Union*, ed. Ronald Amann and Julian Cooper (New Haven: Yale University Press, 1982).

"An Interview with V. M. Molotov." *Literaturuli Sakartvelo*, 27 October 1989. Translated from Georgian by Vladimir Babishvili.

Jones, Stephen. "The Establishment of Soviet Power in Transcaucasia: The Case of Georgia 1921–1928." *Soviet Studies* 40, no. 4 (October 1988): 616–639.

———. "The Mingrelians." *Encyclopedia of World Cultures*. New York: G. K. Hall: 1993.

Kaniuka, Mikhail, and Vitalii Bezhnin. "Tegeran-43. Trudnye mesiatsy." *Kievskie Novosti*, no. 14 (2 April 1993).

"Kar'era politicheskogo avantiurista." *Argumenty i fakty*, no. 43 (1987): 5.

Khariton, Yuli, and Yuri Smirnov. "The Khariton Version." *The Bulletin of the Atomic Scientists*, no. 5 (May 1993): 20–31.

Khrushchev, Nikita. "Memuary Nikity Sergeevicha Khrushcheva." *Voprosy istorii*, pts. 1–7, nos. 6–12 (June–December 1990).

Kikodze, Geronti. "Notes of a Contemporary." *Mnatobi*, no. 1 (January 1989), p. 4. Translated from Georgian by Glen Curtis.

Knight, Amy. "The KGB's Special Departments in the Soviet Armed Forces." *ORBIS* 28, no. 2 (Summer 1984): 257–280.

Kolesnik, A. N. "Glavnyi telokhranitel' vozhdia." *VIZ*, no. 12 (1989): 85–92.

Kolotov, V. "Predsedatel' Gosplana." *Literaturnaia gazeta*, 30 November 1963, p. 2.

"Konets kar'ery Ezhova." *Istoricheskii arkhiv*, no. 1 (1992): 123–143.

Korovin, V. V. "Uchastie organov gosudarstvennoi bezopasnosti v osushchestvlenii funktsii oborony strany." *Sovetskoe gosudarstvo i pravo*, no. 5 (May 1975): 53–60.

Kraminova, Natal'ia. "O zhenshchine s plakata 'Rodina-mat' zovet.'" *Moskovskie novosti*, 9 October 1988.

Krotkov, Iurii. "Rasskazy o marshale Beriia." *Novyi Zhurnal* 95 (June 1969): 86–117.

———. "Konets Marshala Beriia." *Novyi zhurnal* 133 (December 1978): 212–232.

Kvantaliani, N. "Shtrikhi k portretu palacha." *Neva*, no. 11 (1989): 204–207.

Lebedeva, Nataliia. "Tainy katynskogo lesa." *Moskovskie novosti*, 6 August 1989.

———. "I eshche raz o Katyn." *Moskovskie novosti*, 6 May 1990.

Livanova, Anna. "Tak bylo. Iz istorii sovremennosti." *Ogonek*, no. 3 (January 1988): 14.

Loginov, M. "Kul't lichnosti chuzhd nashemy stroiu." *Molodoi kommunist*, no. 1 (1962): 53–54.

Lolidze, Levan. "Beriia sebe zhal?" *Literaturnaia gazeta*, 22 May 1992.

Lordkipanidze, V. "Ubiistvo Kirova. nekotorye podrobnosti," *Argumenty i fakty*, no. 6 (February 1989).

Lukashuk, Aleksandr. "Zharkoe leto 53-go: zametki na poliakh stenogrammy iiuin'skogo (1953 g) plenuma TsK KP Belorussii." *Kommunist Belorussii*, no. 7–8 (1990): 69–82.

Markin, N. "Delo Mdivani-Okudzhava, 1922–1937." *Biulleten' Oppozitsii*, nos. 56–57 (July–August 1937): 7–9.

"Materialy fevral'sko-martovskogo plenuma TsK BKP(B) 1937 goda." *Voprosy istorii*, nos. 2–3 (1992): 3–4.

Mchedluri, Davith. "Beria's Criminal Act." *Literaturuli Sakartvelo*, nos. 38–40 (September 1991). Translated from Georgian by Vladimir Babishvili.

Medvedev, Roy. "O Staline i Stalinizme." *Istoriia SSSR*, no. 4 (July–August 1989).

Moroz, Oleg. "Polslednii diagnoz." *Literaturnaia gazeta*, 28 September 1988, p. 12.

Nekrasov, V. F. "Lavrentii Beriia." Parts 1–2. *Sovetskaia militsiia*, nos. 3–4, (1990): 18–24, 40–46.

Nikishin, Leonard. "Razbudivshie dzhinna." *Moskovskie novosti*, 8 October 1989.

Nove, Alec. "How Many Victims in the 1930s?-II." *Soviet Studies* 42, no. 4 (1990): 811–814.

"Ordzhonikidze-Kirov-Stalin." *Svobodnaia mysl'*, no. 13 (1991): 53–63.

Orlov, Alexander. "The Beria I Knew." *Life Magazine*, 6 July 1953, pp. 42–44.

Pavlenko, N. G. "Razmyshleniia o sud'be polkovodtsa (zapiski voennogo istorika)." Parts 1–3. *VIZ*, nos. 10–12 (1988): 14–27, 20–27, 29–37.

Platonov, R., and V. Velichko. "Zloveshchaia ten' Tsanavy." Parts 1–2. *Kommunist Belorussii*, nos. 2–3 (February–March 1991): 62–69, 64–73.

Popov, B. S., and V. G. Oppokov. "Berievshchina." Parts 1–7. *VIZ* nos. 5 and 7 (1989): 38–41, 82–87; nos. 1, 3, and 5 (1990): 68–78, 81–90, 85–90; nos. 1 and 10 (1991): 44–56, 56–62.

Rashkovets, I. "Ne sklonivshie golovy." *KVS*, no. 4 (February 1991): 59–62.

Rayfield, Donald. "The Killing of Paolo Iashvili." *Index on Censorship*, no. 6 (1990): 9–12.

Razgon, Lev. "Captive in One's Own Country." *New Times*, no. 33 (1991): 32–33.

Redlich, Shimon. "Rehabilitation of the Jewish Anti-Fascist Committee: Report No. 7." *Soviet Jewish Affairs* 20, nos. 2–3, (1990): 85–98.

———. "Discovering Soviet Archives, The Papers of the Jewish Anti-Fascist Committee." *The Jewish Quarterly* 39, no. 4 (Winter 1992–93): 15–19.

Reitz, James T. "The Soviet Security Troops—the Kremlin's Other Armies." In *Soviet Armed Forces Annual*, ed. David Jones (Gulf Breeze, Fla: Academic International Press, 1982).

Rigby, T. H. "Was Stalin a Disloyal Patron?" *Soviet Studies* 38, no. 3 (July 1986): 311–324.

Rudnitskii, Konstantin. "Krushenie teatra." *Ogonek*, no. 22 (May 1988): 10–14.

Rudolph, Vladimir. "The Administrative Organization of Soviet Control, 1945–48." See Slusser, 1953, pp. 42–49.

Rybin, A. T. "Riadom s I. V. Stalinym." *Sotsiologicheskie issledovanie*, no. 3 (1988): 84–94.

Rzhevskaia, Elena. "V tot den' pozdnei osen'iu." *Znamia*, no. 12 (1986): 157–177.

Schapiro, Leonard. "What Is Fascism?" *The New York Review of Books* 14, no. 3 (February 1970).

Shchnev, M. "Krupneishii vklad v sokrovishchinitsu bol'shevizma." *Proletarskaia revoliutsiia*, no. 6 (1935).

Shpakov, Iurii. "Komanda brat'iam po lageriu." *Moskovskie novosti*, 15 July 1990.

Simonov, Konstantin. "Glazami cheloveka moego pokoleniia." Parts 1–2. *Znamia*, nos. 4–5 (April–May 1988): 49–121, 69–96.

Skomorokhov, Vladimir. "Vokrug atomnoi bomby." Kur'er sovetskoi razvedki, no. 1 (1991): 11–15.

Skorokhodov, A. "Kak nas gotovili na voiny s Beriei." *Literaturnaia gazeta*, 27 July 1988, p. 13.

Slider, Darrell. "Crisis and Response in Soviet Nationality Policy: The Case of Abkhazia." *Central Asian Survey* 4, no. 4 (1985): 51–68.

Smith, Edward Ellis. "The Alliluyevs." *Per Se* (Spring 1968): 20–21.

"Soldat zhelezhoi gvardii dzerzhinskogo." *Sibirskie ogni*, no. 10 (1969), pp. 141–144.

Spirin, L. M. "Stalin i voina." *Voprosy istorii KPSS*, no. 5 (May 1990): 90–105.

Stein, Abe. "The Downfall of Beria." *The New International* 19, no. 3 (May–June 1953): 111–129.

Stephan, Robert. "Smersh: Soviet Military Counterintelligence during the Second World War." *Journal of Contemporary History* 22 (1987): 585–613.

Suny, Ronald Grigor. "Beyond Psychohistory: The Young Stalin in Georgia." *Slavic Review* 50, no. 1 (Spring 1991): 48–58.

Suvenirov, O. F. "Vsearmeiskaia tragediia." *VIZ*, no. 3 (March 1989): 39–47.

Teiwes, Frederick C. "Mao and His Lieutenants." *The Australian Journal of Chinese Affairs*, no. 19/20 (1988): 1–80.

Tolz, Vera. "New Information about the Deportation of Ethnic Groups under Stalin." *Report on the USSR*, 16 April 1991.

Tolz, Vladimir. "The Death and 'Second Life' of Lavrentii Beria." *Radio Liberty Research*, 23 December 1983.

Thompson, Craig. "Russia's Best-Known Secret." *Colliers*, 13 March 1948.

Trifonov, I. Ia. "Razgrom men'shevistsko-kulatskogo miatezha v Gruzii v 1924 godu." *Voprosy istorii*, no. 7 (1976): 41–55.

Trotskii, L. "Za stenami kremlina." *Biulleten oppozitsii*, no. 73 (January 1939): 2–15.

Tucker, Robert C. "Svetlana Alliluyeva as Witness of Stalin." *Slavic Review* 27, no. 2 (June 1968): 296–312.

———. "The Rise of Stalin's Personality Cult." *American Historical Review* 84 (April 1979): 347–366.

"Uchenyi i vlast'." *Ogonek*, no. 25 (June 1989): 19.

"Izmeniat', chot i izmenit eshche vozmozhno." *Ogonek*, no. 35 (August 1990): 6–7.

Uldricks, Teddy J. "The Impact of the Great Purges on the People's Commissariat of Foreign Affairs." *Slavic Review* 36, no. 2 (June 1977): 187–204.

Vishlev, O. V. "Pochemu medil I. V. Stalin v 1941 g. (iz germanskikh arkhivov)." *Novaia i noveishaia istoriia*, no. 1 (January–February 1992): 86–100.

Walters, Elizabeth. "The Politics of Repentance: History, Nationalism and Tengiz Abuladze." *Australian Slavonic and East European Studies* 2, no. 1 (1988): 113–142.

Wheatcroft, S. G. "On Assessing the Size of Forced Concentration Camp Labour in the Soviet Union, 1929–56." *Soviet Studies* 32, no. 2 (April 1981): 265–295.

Windle, Kevin. "From Ogre to 'Uncle Lawrence': The Evolution of the Myth of Beria in Russian Fiction from 1953 to the Present." *Australian Slavic & East European Studies* 3, no. 1 (1989): 1–16.

Wolfe, Bertram. "The Struggle for the Soviet Succession." *Foreign Affairs* 31, no.4 (July 1953): 548–565.

Yelin, Lev. "The Man Who Knows the Truth about Katyn." *New Times*, no. 17 (1991): 28–31.

Zagidze, V. "V zastenkakh NKVD v Gruzii." *Ob'edinennyi Kavkaz*, nos. 1–2 (1953).

"Zapiska P. N. Pospelova ob ubiistve Kirova." *Svobodnaia mysl'*, no. 8 (1992): 64–71.

Zemskov, V. N. "GULAG." *Sotsiologicheskie issledovanie*, no. 7 (July 1991): 3–16.

Zhavoronkov, Gennadii. "Taina chernoi dorogi." *Moskovskie novosti*, 17 June 1990.

Zhusenin, Nikolai. "Beriia. neskol'ko epizodov odnoi prestupnoi zhizni." *Nedelia*, no. 8 (22–28 February 1988).

NEWSPAPERS AND JOURNALS IN RUSSIAN

Bakiinskii rabochii
Bor'ba
Dni
Istoricheskii zhurnal
Izvestiia TsK KPSS
Kavkazskii rabochii
Komsomol'skoe znamia
Komunisti (Tbilisi)
Leningradskaia pravda
Literaturnaia gazeta
Politicheskii dnevnik (Amsterdam)
Pravda
Pravda gruzii
Proletarskaia revoliutsiia
Rossiia

Segodnia
7 Dge
Slovo (Berlin)
Svobodnaia mysl'
Vedomosti verkhovnogo soveta GSSR
Voprosy istorii KPSS
Zaria vostoka
Za svoboda

ARCHIVAL SOURCES AND GOVERNMENT DOCUMENTS

Communist Takeover and Occupation of Georgia. Special Report no. 6 of the
Select Committee on Communist Aggression. U.S. House of Representatives.
31 December 1954. Washington, D.C.: U.S. GPO, 1954.
Declassified Documents Quarterly.
Hoover Institution Archives, Stanford, California. Boris Nicolaevsky Fund, Bertram Wolfe Collection, Breglieb Collection.
*Nazii-Soviet Relations, 1939–41. Documents from the Archives of the German
Foreign Office.* Washington: GPO, 1948.
RTsKhIDNI (Russian Center for the Storage and Study of Documents of Recent
History). Moscow.
TsGA (Central State Archives). Moscow.
TsGIA (Central State Historical Archives). Tbilisi.
TsKhSD (Center for the Storage of Contemporary Documentation). Moscow.
U.S. Congress. House Committee on Un-American Activities, Eightieth Congress.
Report on Soviet Espionage Activities in Connection with the Atomic Bomb.
Washington: GPO, 1948.
U.S. Department of State. *Foreign Relations of the United States.* Vol. 1 (1941),
Vol. 4 (1948), Vol. 5 (1949). Washington: GPO, 1958.
United States National Archives, Washington, D.C., Record Group 59.

CONFERENCES AND PROCEEDINGS

Deputy verkhovnogo soveta SSSR. Moscow: Politizdat, 1974, 1984.
Priem delegatsii sovetskoi gruzii rukovoditaliami partii i pravitel'stva v Kremle.
Moscow: Partizdat TsK VKP(B), 1936.
XVII S'ezd vsesoiuznoi kommunisticheskoi partii(b). Stenograficheskii otchet.
Moscow: Partizdat, 1934.
VI S'ezd kommunisticheskoi partii (b) Gruzii. Stenograficheskii otchet. Tbilisi,
1929.
XIII S'ezd Kompartii Gruzii (b), 15–19 marta 1940 g. stenotchet. Tbilisi: Zaria
Vostoka, 1940.
XIV s'ezd Kompartii (Bol'shevikov) Gruzii, 25–29 ianvaria 1949 goda. Tbilisi:
Zaria Vostoka, 1949.
Vtoraia sessiia verkhovnogo soveta gruzinskoi SSR. Stenograficheskii otchet.
Tbilisi, 1952.

UNPUBLISHED MANUSCRIPTS

Arveladze, Lado. "V sviazi s rasstrelom enkavedistov v Sovetskoi Gruzii." Boris Nicolaevsky Collection, Hoover Archives.

"Beria's End." 1953. Boris Nicolaevsky Collection, Hoover Archives.

Bulat, Bek. "Lavrentii Beriia." Boris Nicolaevsky Collection, Hoover Archives.

De Lon, Roy. Stalin and Social Democracy, 1905–1922: The Political Diaries of David A. Sagirashvili. Ph.D. diss. (Georgetown University, 1974).

Hill, George. "Reminiscences of Four Years with the NKVD." Hoover Archives.

Kolarz, Walter. "Ordzhonikidze and Beriya," 6 January 1954. The Bertram Wolfe collection, Hoover Archives.

Kviatashvili, Nicholas Merab. Unpublished memoirs. Washington D.C., n.d.

Peoples and Languages of the Caucasus. Language and Communication Research Center, Columbia University, 1955.

Pistrak, Lazar M. "The Purges in Georgia," 17 April 1953. Boris Nicolaevsky Collection, Hoover Archives.

Richter, James. "Reexamining Soviet Policy Towards Germany During the Beria Interregnum." Working paper No. 3, Cold War International History Project, Woodrow Wilson Center, June 1992.

Salia, Nina, ed. "Georgia. An Introduction." Paris: Centre National de la Recherche Scientifique, 1975.

Slusser, Robert M. "Stalinism and the Secret Police." April 1979.

"Testimony of NKVD official Zhigunov, 1941," file number EAP 3-a-11/2, GmDS, National Archives.

"The Terror in Georgia." n.d. The Boris Nicolaevsky Collection, Hoover Archives.

Von Niemann. "From the Diary of a Chekist," 27 March 1944. Breglieb Collection, folder 14. Hoover Archives.

Windle, Kevin. "Fiction as History: L. P. Beria in 'Thaw' Fiction." Collected papers of the 1988 Melbourne Meeting of the Twentieth-Century Study Group. Berg: Oxford, 1989.

INDEX

buro, 94, 134, 141; Supreme Soviet Presidium, 86; Transcaucasian Central Committee, 45, 50; Transcaucasian GPU, 44; Zakkraikom, 46
—publications: in 1925, 35–36; in 1928 ("What Have the Mensheviks Come To"), 41; in 1934, 58, 60; in 1935 (*On the History of Bolshevik Organizations in Transcaucasia*), 7, 57–64, 70, 71, 81–82, 149, 242n.51; in 1936, 65, 70, 72–73 ("Scatter the Ashes of the Enemies of Socialism"); in 1937, 77; in 1938, 87; in 1939 (*Under the Glorious Banner of Lenin-Stalin*), 250n.35; in 1953 ("Measures to Improve the Political Situation in the GDR"), 191–92
—reform initiatives, 9, 183–86, 194, 226–27
—residences: Baku, 16, 17; Gagra, 65, 159, 244n.100; Moscow, 97, 98; Tbilisi, 30, 65, 159, 244n.99
—sexual activity, 54, 97, 160, 207, 241n.32, 251n.53, 252n.72
—tried, 174, 217–24
—war years, 110–31
Beria, Marfa Peshkova (daughter-in-law), 98, 224, 279n.99
Beria, Marta Ivanovna (mother), 15, 16
Beria, Nino (wife): Bakradze and, 89; on husband's work life, 235n.62; imprisoned, 201, 223–24; interviewed, 10, 224, 235n.62, 236n.6; on Kartvelishvili, 239n.80; on living standards, 30; on Malenkov, 182; marital unhappiness of, 9, 97, 251n.55, 252n.58; Prianishnikov and, 99; relatives of, 149, 157, 234n.57; Sergo born to, 35; Stalin's mother and, 53, 241n.30; T. Toidze and, 251n.58
Beria, Pavel Khukhaevich (father), 15
Beria, Sergo (son): birth of, 35; education of, 97–98; on father's arrest, 197; on father's death, 221; father's fondness for, 9; on father's sexual activities, 97; Iagoda and, 67; imprisoned, 201, 223; interviewed, 10, 235n.57; on Kirov, 238n.33; on Vlasik, 270n.86; in wartime, 120, 130–31
"Beria Document," 191–92
Beschastnov, Aleksei, 169
Bessarabian deportations, 254n.95
Bezirgani, Georgii, 220–21
Bibineishvili, V. E., 243n.67
Bikini atomic explosions, 139

Bliukher, Marshal V. K. and Glafira, 99
Bohlen, Charles, 131, 201, 217, 260n.95
Boiarskii, V. A., 169, 269n.74
Bolkvadze, Vano, 61–62
Bolshevik Revolution anniversary celebrations, 117, 141
Bolsheviks: Armenia invaded by, 20, Azerbaidzhani, 22; in Baku, 17; N. Gegechkori and, 24–25; Georgia invaded by, 14, 20, Georgian, 18–19, 26–28, 69, 77–78, 85; Musavat and, 206; Social Democrats and, 13; terrorist ideology of, 34, Transcaucasian, 48–49, 60, 64, 243–44n.84. *See also* Azerbaidzhan Communist Party; Georgian Communist Party; RSDRP(B); Transcaucasian Communist Party
border defense construction, 110
border guards, 122
"bourgeois nationalism," 165, 172, 188
Brandt, Heinz, 216
Brezhnev, Leonid, 122, 158, 169, 181, 197, 199, 275n.84
Britain: atomic research in, 133, 134; intelligence service of, 123; military commanders of, 128; Secret Operations Executive, 122, 123; Teheran Embassy, 130, 131; in World War I, 17
Budzhiasvili, V. D., 214
Bug River, 111
Bukharin, Nikolai, 73, 75, 85
Bulganin, Nikolai: in anti-Beria coup, 195, 197, 198, 199; in CC plenum (1953), 206; as Council of Ministers deputy, 181; in joint CC–Council of Ministers–Presidium meeting (1953), 271n.13; Stalin's death and, 176, 180; Voroshilov and, 128; Zhukov and, 275n.84
Bulgarian deportees, 127
Bulgarian uranium mining, 138
"By Way of Self-Criticism" (Makharadze), 63
Byzantium, 12, 14

Canberra Embassy, 216
Carr, E. H., 3
Caspian Company, 17
Catholic Church, 189
Central Committees. *See under* All-Union Communist Party; Azerbaidzhan Communist Party; CPSU; Georgian Communist Party; RSDRP

Beria's arrest and, 194, 195, 197–200, 201–2; dachas proposed for, 190–91; de-Stalinization and, 184, 185; Doctor's Plot and, 171; foreign policy and, 205; formed, 166; Poskrebyshev as secretary of, 270n.94; protocols of, 183; at Stalin's death, 180, 181
—Secretariat: Beria's trial and, 218; Council of Ministers and, 168; Doctors' Plot and, 174, 175; foreign policy and, 186, 191; after Stalin's death, 181, 183, 271n.15; Transcaucasian purges and, 215
Crankshaw, Edward, 95, 155
Crimean Jewish republic (proposed), 170
Crimean NKVD, 69
Czechoslovakia, 138, 169, 207, 217, 267n.22

Danilov, S., 15, 16
Day of Physical Culture, 160
de-Stalinization, 184–86, 189–90, 226
death penalty, 156
Death to Spies (Soviet Military Counter-intelligence). See SMERSH
defense industries. See military industries
Dekanozov, Vladimir: in AzCheka, 22; Beria's fall and, 202–3, 218; CPSU Central Committee and, 167; education of, 31; family of, 223; Fitin and, 258n.58; Georgian posts of, 69, 187, 234n.45; as GUGB Foreign Department head, 91; in Lithuania, 104; Merkulov and, 144; Molotov and, 125, 253n.85; Nazi invasion plans and, 107–8, 109, 254n.110, 255n.117; Nazi-Soviet Treaty and, 102–3; NKID and, 100, 101, 102; purged, 214; mentioned, 30
Dekanozova, Nora Tigranovna, 202–3
democracy, intra-party, 75–76, 162
deportations, 126–29, 228, 259n.77, 276n.12; to Abkhazia, 72; of Baltic populations, 104–5; from Bessarabia, 254n.95; of Georgian Mensheviks, 237n.18; of Georgian minorities, 259n.74; of Germans, 259n.70; of Jews, 147–48, 174; from Transcaucasia, 164
destruction battalions, 121
Deutscher, Isaac, 219
"Dizzy with Success" (Stalin), 41
Djilas, Milovan, 8, 95, 132, 152–53, 265n.92

Doctors' Plot, 148, 169–75, 210; Conquest on, 270n.88; Eitingon and, 167; Konev and, 174, 219; repudiated, 185–86; Stalin's death and, 175, 176
Don River hydroelectric system, 185
Donovan, William, 123, 259n.84
Dulles, Allen, 217
Dumbadze, Evgenii, 21, 31, 32, 34, 235n.64
Dzerzhinskii, Feliks, 20, 22, 23, 27, 91
Dzhavakhishvili, Mikheil, 83
Dzhibladze, G. N., 268n.47
Dzhugashvili, Beso, 6
Dzhugashvili, Ekaterina, 7–8, 53–54, 241n.30
Dzhugeli, Valiko, 32

East German crisis, 191–94, 195, 196, 207, 273n.63, 274n.71, 274n.76
East German purge, 216–17
Eastern European satellites, 150, 216–17
economic crimes, 156, 161
economic planning, 51–53
economic productivity, 65, 94, 105. See also industrial production
economic reforms, 184–85, 192–93
Efimov, P. I., 214
Eikhe, R. I., 252n.67
Eisenhower, Dwight D., 186
Eitingon, N. I., 167, 184, 269n.68
Elektrosyla, 138
Emelianov, S. F., 223, 249n.4
Enukidze, Avel: on Baku printing press, 61, 62, 69, 243n.75; historical writings of, 57, 63; Kirov and, 245n.6; purged, 68–69, 85, 248n.84
Epishev, A. A., 158, 167, 173, 184, 266n.19
Erickson, John, 112, 114, 128, 255–56n.13
Erkomoshvili (textile merchant), 16
espionage, 124–25, 133–34, 237n.30. See also military intelligence operations; Musavat espionage
Estonia, 104
Etingon, N. I., 147
Extraordinary Commission for Combating Counterrevolution and Sabotage. See AzCheka; Georgian Cheka; VeCheka
Extraordinary Commission for Expropriating the Bourgeoisie and Improving the Lot of the Workers, 19

Obkom secretary, 155–59; MVD and, 184; on nationalities policy, 190; on Nineteenth Party Congress, 165–66, 268–69n.60; Pervukhin and, 274n.77; Rybin on, 178; Saburov and, 274n.77; on Safronov, 202; Serdiuk and, 273n.48; Serov and, 125, 203; Shtemenko and, 168; on Soviet-Nazi peace proposal, 112; on Stalin's death, 176, 177, 179, 180; on Stalin's dinners, 152, 265n.88; on Stalin's paranoia, 166; on Timashuk, 270n.92; Transcaucasian purges and, 215; Twentieth Party Congress address, 45, 215, 223, 225, 250n.22, 268n.55; Ukrainian Jews and, 147, 148; Western perceptions of, 217; Zimianian and, 273n.56; Zolotukhin and, 267n.20; mentioned, 4, 111
Khrustalev, I., 177
KI (Committee of Information), 150
Kikodze, Geronti, 31, 67, 84
Kirichenko, A. I., 188, 189
Kirk, Walter, 265n.87
Kirov, Sergei Mironovich: assassinated, 67–68, 242n.52; on AzCheka, 23, 24; Azerbaidzhan Communist Party and, 19; S. Beria on, 238n.33; as *Children of the Arbat* character, 57–58; Enukidze and, 245n.6; Georgian Bolsheviks and, 18–19; Iagoda and, 246n.28; Lordkipanidze and, 245n.3; procedural law (1934) and, 278n.74
Kirponos, Lt. Gen. M. P., 111
Kobulov, Amaiak, 91, 103, 125, 167
Kobulov, Bogdan Z.: as commissar of state security, 125; in CPSU CC, 167, 210; GULAG and, 105; honored, 80; Kozarev and, 99; E. Mikeladze and, 83; as MVD first secretary, 184; NKID and, 101; in NKVD, 69; North Caucasus deportations and, 126, 127; purged, 214; Soviet Military Administration in Germany and, 144; at Transcaucasian Front, 120; tried, 218; mentioned, 30, 91, 103, 252n.77
Kochlavashvili, A. I., 138, 139, 163, 268n.49
Kolarz, Walter, 246n.34
kolkhoz construction. *See* collectivization
Komarov, V. I., 169
Komsomol, 30, 99, 161, 163, 244n.99
Konev, I. S., 174, 219
Korean armistice negotiations, 186
korenizatsiia, 25

Kosarev, Aleksandr, 98–99
Kossior, S. V., 98
Kosygin, Aleksei, 250n.24, 276n.14
Kozlov, Frol, 170
Kravchenko, Victor, 118
Krinitskii, A. I., 40, 41, 42, 43
Krotkov, Iurii, 202, 213
Kruglov, Sergei, 125; anti-Beria coup and, 200, 203, 222; in CC plenum (1953), 209; death of, 276n.12; Khrushchev and, 228; as MVD first deputy, 184; as NKVD chief, 140; mentioned, 141
Kuchava, M. I., 219, 220, 221–22
Kudriavstev (MVD officer), 216
kulak suppression campaign, 40–42, 49, 52, 80
Kurchatov, A. I., 132, 133, 134, 135, 137, 139
Kutaisi city party committee, 163
Kutaisi *Oblast*, 161
Kuz'michev, S. F., 167, 171, 184, 270n.85
Kuznetsov, A. A., 141, 145, 148, 151
Kuznetsov, N. G., 174, 255n.5, 260n.85
Kvantaliani, E. A., 29, 30, 32, 35, 80, 238n.40
Kviatashvili, Nicholas, 130–31
Kvirkveliia, R. A., 268n.47

labor camps. *See* GULAG
Lakerbaia (pseudonym). *See* Beria, Lavrentii Pavlovich
Lakoba, Mikhail, 72, 81
Lakoba, Nestor: Argba and, 247n.56; death of, 72; disinterred, 245n.24; Orakhelashvili and, 50–51; *Stalin i Khashim*, 242n.54, 245n.20; mentioned, 39, 81
Lakoba, Rauf, 81
Landai, L. D., 106
Lang, David, 11
Latvia, 104
League of Nations, 237n.26
Leffland, Ella, 47
legal Marxism, 59, 60
Lenin, Vladimir: Baku printing press and, 61; death of, 153; Georgian/Armenian Sovietization and, 20; Georgian Bolsheviks and, 27; German Social Democrats and, 54, 243n.68; Mdivani and, 79; Stalin and, 55, 56; terrorism and, 34; *What Is to Be Done?* 61; mentioned, 13, 111
Leningrad Case, 151, 222–23